JAMES BOND

THE LEGACY

JAMES BOND
THE LEGACY

JOHN CORK & BRUCE SCIVALLY

BXTREE

First published 2002 by Boxtree
an imprint of Pan Macmillan Ltd
Pan Macmillan, 20 New Wharf Road, London N1 9RR
Basingstoke and Oxford
Associated companies throughout the world
www.panmacmillan.com

ISBN 0 7522 6498 2

Editorial
Editorial consultant - Philip Dodd
Senior commissioning editor - Emma Marriott, Boxtree
Eon consultant - David Wilson, Eon Productions

Design and picture research
Wherefore Art?, London.
Art Direction by David Costa. Design by Sian Rance, assisted by Elina Arapoglou and Helena Lekka
Picture research for Eon Productions - Meg Simmonds and Jenni McMurrie

The Publishers would like to thank all at Eon Productions for their invaluable support and involvement with the book,
particularly Michael Wilson, Barbara Broccoli, Keith Snelgrove, David Wilson, Anne Bennett, David Pope, Michael Tavares, Meg Simmonds and Jenni McMurrie.
Additional thanks to John English and Charlotte Parry-Crooke for editorial advice and support.

3 5 7 9 8 6 4 2

A CIP catalogue record for this book is
available from the British Library.

Printed by the Bath Press, Bath

Foreword by Michael G. Wilson

For the past 40 years James Bond has been a major part of my life. I was in my third year at an engineering college when my mother called to tell me Cubby, my stepfather, had just made a deal for the Fleming books. I have to confess, at the time I had no idea who Fleming and James Bond were. Well, it was only a matter of months before I, like most of my contemporaries around the world, was caught up in Bond mania. Two years later I had the chance to work on the Fort Knox location of *Goldfinger* as a third Assistant Director while on summer break from law school. Within ten years I was working full time for Eon Productions; James Bond has been a major part of my life ever since. Working with Cubby on a daily basis for over 20 years, being Dick Maibaum's writing partner, and working with the Bond directors, actors and crews is an experience beyond price.

During the 1960s and 70s James Bond became a household word. Indeed, "Bond, James Bond" is considered the best loved and most recognizable line in cinema history. This book examines the Bond films and their impact on popular culture throughout the world. The films, in turn, have been influenced by contemporary society. The five actors who have portrayed Bond have managed to reinvent him, it seems, each decade. Yet there is at the core of the character something immutable. He is a hero, not without faults, but fundamentally good, incorruptible and totally dedicated to his quest.

James Bond has been a remarkable adventure in my life, that has left an equally remarkable wake across the globe. When my stepfather Cubby Broccoli and his partner Harry Saltzman launched the Bond films, they made a decision to make movies for a wide audience. The audiences responded beyond anyone's wildest expectations. Cubby felt obligated to give those dedicated and loyal fans first-class entertainment. Barbara Broccoli and I feel the same, as do the hundreds of talented technicians and artists who make these films. None of us would be here without the audience.

If you ever went with a friend or a date to a Bond film, if you ever cheered when a Bond trailer played in a cinema, if you ever fantasized that your car was a gadget-laden Aston Martin, or if you ever ordered a martini, shaken, not stirred, well, this book is dedicated to you. Welcome to the world of James Bond, the real world as you've never seen it before. Enjoy.

We created the films. You created the legacy.

Introduction

James Bond changed my life. My earliest memory of seeing any film in any cinema is watching secret agent 007 stand on the back of a boat, firing a flare into the water and witnessing the oil-covered Adriatic Sea erupt in flames. The film was *From Russia With Love*, and I was three and a half years old.

At the age of eleven, a friend and I decided to see *Live And Let Die*. Unable to corral our families into driving us to the showing, we rode our bicycles. We went as boys but came out as secret agents on a dangerous mission. Within 18 months I had read all the James Bond novels, John Pearson's biography of Ian Fleming, and numerous literary analyses of 007. Friends and I would count down the hours until the Bond films were shown on ABC. At the age of 17, through various complicated machinations, United Artists invited me to the US premiere of *Moonraker*. The publicity department flew my mother and I first class to New York and booked us a suite at the Warwick Hotel. As I stepped out of the limo in front of the Rivoli Theater in my tuxedo, a New York radio station was actually playing 'The James Bond Theme'. A gentleman from UA presented me to Roger Moore with the introduction, "This is the world's biggest Bond fan." While the statement was the usual publicity department hyperbole, it did cross my mind that this James Bond thing seemed to have its perks. All this wasn't bad for a kid from Alabama whose family had absolutely no connection to the film business.

Where would I be without James Bond? I wouldn't have moved to Los Angeles, pursued a career in film and thus met my wife or had my son. I certainly would not have been invited to honeymoon at a lovely house in Jamaica called Goldeneye (where Fleming wrote his Bond novels), nor would I have met the remarkable family of producer Albert R. 'Cubby' Broccoli, the guiding force behind the cinematic success and longevity of 007.

In early 2001, I was asked if I would write a book on James Bond's impact on popular culture and culture's impact on the world of Bond. I said I would if I could bring in a co-author -

Bruce Scivally - one of the most talented and knowledgeable writers I know. Bruce also has a talent for getting things done with a quiet, unassuming flair. In 1983 Bruce attended a pre-premiere screening of the non-Eon James Bond film, *Never Say Never Again*, even though his name was not on the list of invited guests. Bruce, as usual, had a trump card - Sean Connery. The actor got on the phone to the publicity people from Warner Brothers and told them he would appreciate it if they allowed Mr. Scivally to see the film.

Our devoted interest in 007 is not unusual. The impact of James Bond on teenage boys should be documented by a team of well-funded sociologists. 007 is everything an adolescent male dreams of becoming: a sexually irresistible, socially astute, witty, dangerous, heroic enigma - the dedicated individualist the rest of the world can't live without. Neither Bruce nor I own a gun, and no one will mistake my Volvo station wagon for an Aston Martin, nor Bruce's ubiquitous glass of iced tea for a martini, shaken not stirred, but we don't need to surround ourselves with Bond's props to admire the Bond persona. It is what lies within the character that intrigues us so, the certainty of purpose, the inner calm when faced with danger, the unquestioning sense of self.

This book asks the question, 'How has James Bond changed the world?' It may seem like a stretch to say that a fictional character has had any real impact on the tide of global affairs, yet Bond has been lurking as a cultural force for 50 years. He represented a new type of idol for the post-war era and changed the way we think about spies, gadgets and cinematic heroes. While James Bond neither started the Cold War nor ended it, he played a role in how both the West and the East perceived it. 007 gave us a context for understanding the shifting

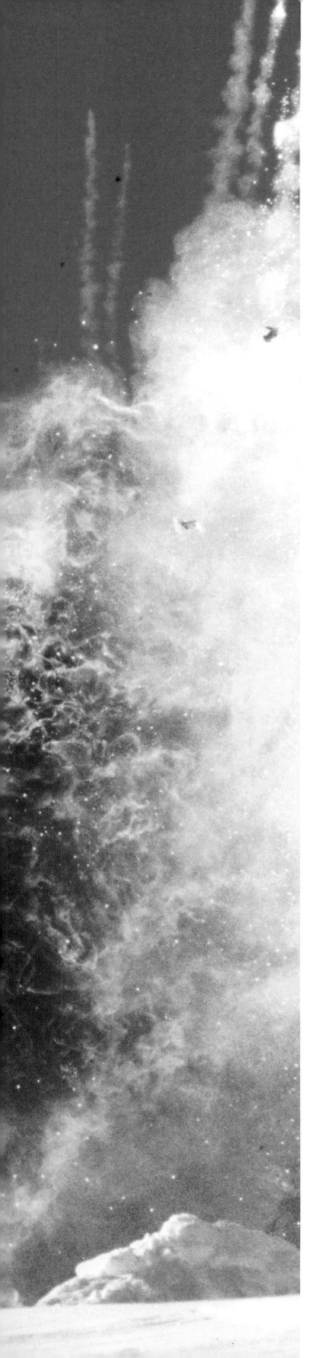

paradigms of global politics and undeclared wars. Bond has survived long enough to subtly shape the way the CIA, MI6 and other global intelligence services operate.

Bond helped redefine our understanding of villainy. He did not fight the street thugs or the spies of old who, when exposed, skittered like roaches looking for cover. Instead, Bond battled the giant figures of malevolence, the larger-than-life self-proclaimed geniuses and prophets who happily embrace their beliefs and obsessions. Whether they were well-funded delusional idealists or coldly calculating corporate puppetmasters, 007 gave us reason to distrust unbridled capitalism just as much as soulless Communism.

While our paranoia was stoked by the lurking evil within Bond's world, we have taken our comfort from his indulgences. James Bond did not ignite the sexual revolution, but he offered a primer in the art of seduction that was enticing for both sexes. Bond was the first popular hero who embraced uncomplicated sex as a natural dividend of his life of danger. Within the novels and films, there is a universe of elegance, style and taste that is deeply engrained in our cultural aesthetic.

The unique nature of James Bond and the mythology that surrounds him has inspired an entire legacy that reaches far beyond the character. Bond's unmatched success has changed the way films are made and marketed, helping to usher in the big blockbuster and the action-hero franchise. The creativity behind the Bond novels has inspired countless authors. The movies have launched hundreds of films and television shows. Fashion designers and architects have used Bond's world as inspiration. In short, Bond's influence has propagated across the globe in strange and unforeseeable ways.

James Bond has placed an indelible stamp on our culture. There is a particular mix of ingredients which had never been sampled by cinemagoers until 007 hit movie screens. The recipe is like the secret mixture of ingredients in Coca-Cola - very hard to duplicate yet very easy to distribute. Viewers know what they are getting every time they see the white dots move across the screen, opening to reveal the inside of a gun barrel. They like the taste, and they almost always return for more.

James Bond, however, is not a soft drink. He is closer to Bollinger '61 served with Royal Beluga, soft toast and sour cream. He is the cinematic equivalent of the Aston Martin, the hand-built, high-performance British sports car so deeply associated with 007. He is simply and consistently the best. Each Bond film is crafted with care, refined through a relentlessly collaborative process. Like Aston Martin, the Bond filmmakers do many things the old-fashioned way while also pushing for innovations. The key is always quality and value, extravagance without being profligacy.

Having had the chance to meet and get to know many of the talented men and women on the Bond team, they are uncompromising problem solvers, singularly ego-less in an industry filled with egos. Few could be described as 'like James Bond' in either attitude or style, which is just as well. Real-life James Bonds do not make great movies. The Bond team does. They are, as many have described them, a family, a large extended family of dedicated individuals. It is largely through the efforts and creativity of this cinematic family that Bond's longevity and success has exceeded even the most ambitious predictions.

With this book, we have tried to take the reader on a journey back through the world surrounding Bond, through the Cold War, the explosion of spymania, and the real-life espionage adventures and global changes that have occurred during the 40 years since James Bond first became a cinematic hero. This is a history of the modern world seen through a spyglass focused on the realm of a fictional character. We have tried to explain the appeal, define the impact and map the odyssey of a pop culture phenomenon. Most of all, we have tried to enjoy ourselves and not take it all too seriously.

When we began this book, I asked myself if I could define James Bond's impact in just a simple sentence. The answer was 'No'. That impact has dissipated through our society in so many ways that defied simple definition. Then I asked myself the converse - 'What would the world be like without James Bond?' That answer was simpler. Had Ian Fleming not created secret agent 007, the world would be more ordinary, filled with less intrigue, more pasteurized, safer, inelegant, sexless, and a helluva lot less enjoyable.

So fix yourself a vodka martini, medium-dry, shaken not stirred, with a twist of lemon, find yourself a comfortable chair where no one can sneak up behind you, hum a few bars of 'The James Bond Theme', then turn the page and enter the real world of 007. You will find amazing adventures, beautiful women, incredible enemies, and the remarkable story of the most successful fictional secret agent ever created.

John Cork
Los Angeles, May 2002

1. The Birth Of Bond

At the age of 17, Ian Fleming was poised to win Eton's coveted athletics prize, the *Victor Ludorum*, for the second year in a row, a feat accomplished only once before in the school's history. But there was a problem. At exactly the same time he was to take part in an important race, he was also due to be thrashed with a birch switch as punishment for some misdemeanour. The young Fleming did not waste his time pleading his case. He merely asked to be beaten 15 minutes early, then ran the race, with his running shorts still bloodied from the beating, and won the school prize. The story captures just one aspect of James Bond's creator, albeit an important one - Ian Fleming flouted conventions, endured the consequences, but still accomplished the remarkable. He withdrew from the military academy at Sandhurst under a cloud, but became a vital resource during the Second World War, serving in Naval Intelligence and creating his own group of daring commandos. A long affair with Lady Rothermere, wife of press baron Esmond Harmsworth, would seem to preclude a career in the close-knit world of London newspapers, but soon after the war Fleming was managing the foreign correspondents for the *Sunday Times* group. In almost every aspect of his life Fleming defied the odds and achieved success on his own terms. This included his ability to escape the natural strictures of his career by leaving behind "the cold and grimy winters of England" for his own personal paradise.

Czechoslovakia, Hungary and Poland. China had fallen under Communist rule. Communists controlled North Vietnam, had won elections in France, and fomented bitter revolution in Greece. Thousands of Americans were dying in brutal fighting in war-torn Korea. The US had tested unimaginably powerful hydrogen bombs, sentenced Soviet spies to death, and blacklisted Hollywood writers and directors who had once been members of the US Communist Party.

This global tension set the stage for Ian Fleming, but the direct impetus for the creation of James Bond, as the espionage historian David Stafford has observed, occurred on 25th May 1951. On that date, two British diplomats went missing. Donald Maclean and Guy Burgess, it soon became apparent, were Soviet spies who had worked in a variety of sensitive positions, including the British Embassy in Washington. The West had unearthed large numbers of spies during the post-war years, including those who had passed atomic secrets to the Soviets, but none had been as damaging as Maclean and Burgess. For the British, the injury was particularly insidious since Maclean and Burgess were considered "the right sort", educated in the elite surroundings of Trinity College, Cambridge, and very much part of the revered "old boy" network that controlled so much power in the UK. There was a greater concern, too. Only a handful of individuals knew that Maclean and Burgess were under suspicion for espionage, but the pair's disappearance made it clear they had been tipped off. Obviously, there was another spy in MI6.

Six months after the Cambridge spy case hit the press, Fleming began typing the first James Bond novel, CASINO ROYALE.

Ian Fleming had long wanted to write an espionage novel; the case of the Cambridge spies, as they became known, may have provided the framework. As Fleming's biographer Andrew Lycett has noted, "What raised CASINO ROYALE out of the usual run of thrillers was Ian's attempt to reflect on the disturbing moral ambiguities of a post-war world that could produce traitors like Burgess and Maclean." Fleming wrote a story of the other side of the "old boy" network, the story of a dashing, heterosexual spy, who, upon doubting the importance of the Cold War battles, learns the bitter difference between good and evil. Fleming's hero falls in love with Vesper Lynd, a beautiful agent high up in MI6 who is being tragically manipulated by the Soviets. Secret agent 007 is unable to prevent the devastating consequences, including Vesper's suicide. 007 does not save the world. He does not get the girl. He does, though, vow to fight. "He would attack the arm that held the whip and the gun. The business of espionage could be left to the white-collar boys. They could spy and catch the spies. He would go after the threat behind the spies, the threat that made them spy."

Ian Fleming appropriated the name James Bond from an ornithologist who had authored a volume entitled *Birds Of The West Indies*. Fleming had a copy at Goldeneye and was struck by how colourless and flat the author's name sounded. "Nothing like Peregrine Carruthers or 'Standfast' Maltravers," Fleming noted. James Bond's namesake was not a daring spy, but a tall, good-looking man who had done much of his research on Caribbean birds very near Fleming's Jamaican home.

Many have said the fictional James Bond was Ian Fleming. This is certainly true up to a point. The two shared similar backgrounds, features, tastes, wardrobes and weaknesses. Both men enjoyed high-stakes gambling, sea-island cotton shirts, a well-made cocktail and custom-made cigarettes adorned with three gold bands.

For Fleming, this paradise existed in Jamaica, then a British colony. Fleming fell in love with the island on a brief visit during the Second World War. He described Jamaica as a "tropical luxury", and the social mores as the sort that would "raise in you that moral eyebrow which the heat might otherwise have drugged". Fleming later told an interviewer he thought Jamaica was wonderful, "as I suppose any Scotsman would".

After the war, Fleming purchased a large plot of land on the unspoiled North Shore. There, on a coral bluff next to the banana port of Oracabessa, Fleming built a low, modern house facing the Caribbean. He called it 'Goldeneye', and it was here that James Bond was born.

By 1952, the year Fleming created 007, the world was huddling against the gale of the Cold War. There existed a daily struggle for global leadership; the balance of power teetered ominously from month to month. Berlin and Germany stood divided. The Iron Curtain was draped over Bulgaria, Romania, Albania, Yugoslavia,

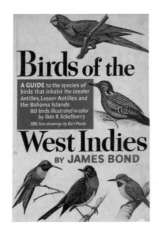

Previous pages: Ian Fleming throwing a machete on a beach near his home in Jamaica, his favourite place in the world. Fleming once described James Bond as "an efficient and not very attractive blunt instrument... a highly romanticized version of a true spy."

Above: Goldeneye, Fleming's house in Jamaica. Fleming was reading Carson McCullers' novel, *Reflections In A Golden Eye*, around the time he built the house. He had also been involved with planning the defence of Gibraltar in the Second World War - the plan was named Operation Goldeneye. Finally, the area around the property is called Oracabessa, Spanish for 'golden head'.

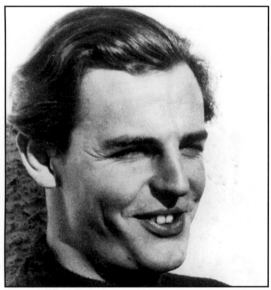

The Cambridge spies, Guy Burgess (**top**) and Donald Maclean (**bottom**), had close connections to Ian Fleming. Burgess and Maclean both knew Fleming's long-time friend Cyril Connolly, who was so stunned by the defections that he immediately penned a book, *The Missing Diplomats*, where he seemed to be unable to fathom that this pair of well-bred, public school-educated men could be traitors. The Cambridge spies came to represent the dangers of blind trust in the "old boy" network of the upper classes. Ian Fleming's brother, Peter, perfectly captured the attitude prevalent before the defection of Maclean and Burgess, when he noted in his first book (written years before), "an Old Boy is worth two young men". It was just this view that allowed the Cambridge spies to flourish.

On 7th July 1957, the first James Bond comic strip drawn by John McLusky appeared in the London *Daily Express* (**below**). The strip, a serialization of *Casino Royale*, ran only during the week for 139 days. McLusky eventually adapted thirteen Fleming novels, creating an image of a handsome, debonair 007 that is said to have influenced the casting of Sean Connery in the role.

Fleming found a publisher in London, Jonathan Cape, who agreed to publish CASINO ROYALE. But the author had larger plans for secret agent 007 than a one-off novel. Fleming began to envision James Bond as a unique hero for the Cold War, as a symbol of a new England with a brand-new Queen, as a modern-day St. George battling the global dragons who threatened Britain. When Fleming started his second 007 adventure, LIVE AND LET DIE, all of the self-doubt and innocence in the character of James Bond disappeared. In its place, Fleming developed Bond as "a healthy, violent, non-cerebral man in his middle thirties, and a creature of his era. I wouldn't say he is typical of our times, but he is certainly of the times." The opening sentence of LIVE AND LET DIE defines Bond's world: "There are moments of great luxury in the life of a secret agent." Fleming seemed determined to create a lavish world, far from the deprivations of the post-War years. He indulged his readers' senses and challenged their expectations. The *Sunday Times Literary Supplement* proclaimed, "Mr. Ian Fleming is without a doubt the most interesting recent recruit among thriller-writers."

Indeed, Fleming re-invented the popular image of the spy. His Bond novels remained free of trenchcoats, fedoras and, after *Casino Royale*, the theme of betrayal. Fleming saw Bond as a mythic figure who stood above the law. Bond used a gun rather than a sword, and he rode in Bentleys and Aston Martins rather than on a white horse.

While the Soviets berated the "materialistic, capitalistic, decadent West", Fleming made his readers feel good about their desires. He wrote in detail about clothes, cars, alcohol, perfume, food and, of course, carnal desire. The Bond novels were fables, with Bond as an icon who represented Fleming's values, vanquishing villains who represented the evils of the world. They were ceaselessly original stories - energetic, imaginative and ingenious.

Fleming's novels quickly became bestsellers in Great Britain, and a fast-growing cadre of readers began to anticipate the publication of a new Bond adventure each spring.

007 took off more slowly in the US, where CASINO ROYALE was released to an indifferent reception in 1954, even though CBS broadcast a live teleplay based on the book that autumn. When Bond appeared in paperback, the first book to hit the stands was MOONRAKER, retitled TOO HOT TO HANDLE. Next, CASINO ROYALE was re-christened YOU ASKED FOR IT. Although two of the first four books had major sequences set in the US, this failed to spur sales.

Fleming, though, was hard at work on the novel which would establish Bond as a literary phenomenon rather than a mere bestseller. This story was based on Fleming's experience of travelling to Istanbul for an Interpol conference, as well as the true story of the assassination of an American spy.

In February 1950, Eugene Karp, a naval attaché to the American Embassy in Bucharest, Romania, tried to flee the country, fearing imminent arrest on charges of espionage. Karp apparently gathered papers relating to a US spy network in Eastern Europe, then travelled across the border to Budapest, the Hungarian capital. There, he nervously booked a single passage on the Orient Express to Paris. The Soviet counter-espionage machine was already on his tail. Authorities later found the drugged sleeping car conductor unconscious in Karp's compartment, but no sign of Karp. The next day, Karp's mangled, lifeless body was discovered in a railway tunnel south of Salzburg. He had been beaten and thrown beneath the train by agents of the Hungarian secret police.

Fleming used the real-life incident as a point of departure for FROM RUSSIA WITH LOVE. In Fleming's nail-biting plot, the murder of Bond would appear to be a suicide after an affair with a Soviet cipher clerk on board Europe's most famous train. The outcome for the Soviets would be the humiliation of the West and the death of a key British agent.

After completing the book, Fleming hired his first literary agent in October 1956 to handle his foreign language rights. Peter Janson-Smith immediately sold rights in Fleming's previous four books to a Dutch publisher. It would not be long before the Bond novels were translated into dozens of languages, marking the start of James Bond's prodigious international success.

Fleming's name soon hit the press in association with global events not related to Bond. On 31st October 1956, Britain, France and Israel launched a massive attack against Egypt in order to seize control of the Suez Canal. It was a political disaster for Prime Minister Sir Anthony Eden, who found himself near nervous exhaustion from the international

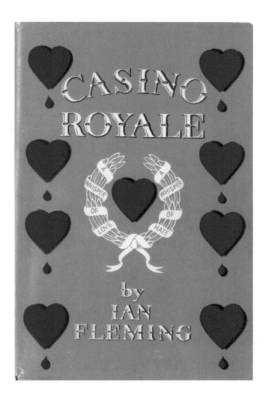

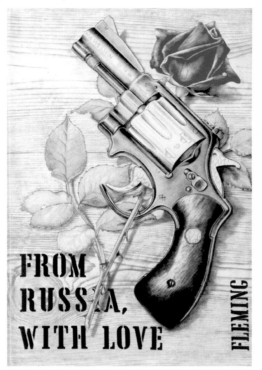

reprimands. Doctors prescribed undisturbed rest to prevent a breakdown. On 24th November that year, Eden flew to Jamaica to stay at Fleming's home, Goldeneye. Suddenly, Fleming, who had always mingled with impressive figures, became a name of note in his own right.

Shortly after the UK publication of FROM RUSSIA WITH LOVE in 1957, the *Daily Express* contacted Fleming with an offer to turn James Bond into a comic strip. Consequently Fleming was not only on the forefront of the news pages but also the comic page. Bond's fame in England and Europe reached across all class barriers. Even Prince Philip let it be known he was a fan of the Bond novels.

Fleming now earned his first rave reviews in America. The *New York Herald-Tribune* critic James Sandoe declared, "It is quite apparent that Mr. Fleming is intensely observant, acutely literate and can turn a cliché into a silk purse with astute alchemy. No question."

A few months later, a young US senator laid up at home with a cold called a friend to ask if she had anything he could read. She replied that she had a thriller written by someone she knew. The friend was Marion 'Oatsie' Leiter, whose husband had provided the surname for Bond's CIA ally, Felix Leiter. The senator was John F. Kennedy.

In March 1960, Fleming arrived in Washington on business. During the course of the trip, thanks to Oatsie Leiter, Fleming met Senator Kennedy. JFK, who was running for President at the time, appreciated Fleming's wit and style as much as he enjoyed the Bond novels. Ian Fleming had just secured his most influential fan.

In New York, Truman Tally, a book editor at the New American Library, suggested that Signet, the NAL paperback imprint, purchase the existing Bond novels and publish them in a uniform set, much the way they were being sold in England. Tally wanted to create an easily identifiable, quality thriller series for his readers, and in the Bond novels he saw well-written adventures and the potential for sales far above existing levels. Tally's plan was put into action, and the Bond books began appearing on paperback racks across the US.

In November 1960, America elected JFK president. The young and vibrant Chief Executive moved into the White House amid a ground swell of optimism throughout the Western world. Fleming could not help but enjoy the fact that the most important man on the planet also happened to be a James Bond fan. As he remarked to

writer Jack Fishman, "It is very nice to know that a President, Prince Philip, and former CIA Chief Allen Dulles enjoy my books. It's also very good for sales."

1961 was shaping up to be both a very interesting year for 007, and a turning point in the history of spy films.

Above: The golden typewriter was used by Ian Fleming to write *Live And Let Die* in 1953 at Goldeneye, but it remained in London during his subsequent trips. When he was in Jamaica, Fleming often followed a routine he had established when he began writing *Casino Royale*. After a morning swim on the reef, he had a breakfast of scrambled eggs and Blue Mountain coffee with Ann (who became his wife when the first 007 novel was completed). At nine, he then went to one of his carefully selected locations to write. Fleming had two desks at Goldeneye that have survived to this day: a large flat-topped desk, and a corner desk in his bedroom. In the early years, Fleming often wrote in the main living room, but later, when he had a more difficult time exiling houseguests, he would take his typewriter into the bedroom. Eventually, he had his living room desk installed in a small building on the edge of his property so he could escape all household distractions. Fleming generally spent his afternoons and nights with friends and guests, but would take an hour in the early evening to review his daily work.

Before James Bond arrived on the big screen, espionage thrillers had come in many flavours and colours. Spy films often sought to de-mythologize secret agents, to reduce them to human scale. The image of 007 could not be further removed from the first spy of the cinema.

In 1898, a man turned the crank of a cinema camera, photographing a real-life secret agent. The short movie was a documentary recording the execution of a man convicted of espionage during the Spanish-American War. By 1909, just a year after Ian Fleming's birth, the first spy film series appeared, with silent screen legend Gene Gauntier writing and starring in the Civil War-based *Girl Spy* adventures. By 1917, the cinematic spy was well established in England. He was a darkly handsome, wholly villainous German, bent on sabotage, and he found himself defeated by a daring group of young paramilitaries - the Boy Scouts. The film industry had a long way to go before it was ready for 007.

Early spy thrillers tended to reflect the moral tone of nations during the First World War and the interwar years. Spies were mostly enemies: devious, destructive, and in the case of a whole sub-genre inspired by the legendary Mata Hari, tremendously tragic and sexual. These characters, though, were not created in a vacuum. James Bond and the fictional spies who preceded him were all shaped by centuries of history.

Mata Hari - a real-life Dutch-born dancer who was executed in Paris in 1917 on charges of spying for Germany during the First World War - herself had precursors in myths and Biblical stories, such as Samson and Delilah. Homer's *Iliad* and *Odyssey*, while not spy stories, are filled with heroic deceits, double-crosses and disguises - tricks much enjoyed by the Greeks in plays and stories.

The way in which the public thought of spies was, for centuries, coloured by the infamy of history's most famous turncoats. Brutus lured Caesar to his death in the Senate. Judas betrayed Jesus for silver. Benedict Arnold betrayed the American Revolution for which he fought. Each of these historical figures was a classic secret agent. Throughout the ages, these men have been portrayed as the vilest of villains.

During the Spanish Civil War in the 1930s, as four Nationalist army columns moved towards a besieged Madrid, General Emilio Mola Vidal declared that the key to his victory would not be his troops in the field, but his 'fifth column': agents who spread deception and dissent, engaged in espionage and committed acts of sabotage. Vidal's acknowledgement of a 'fifth column' gave a name to the often invisible force of espionage in shaping history.

Usually fifth column agents have short lives and wretched deaths. Historically, though, there have been a few agents whose daring and success in such endeavours have seemed virtually limitless. These secret agents became the prototype for the spies of literature and film.

Ian Fleming designed Goldeneye himself; it includes 15-inch thick coral walls that act as a natural heating and cooling system, helping to keep the house at a moderate temperature. Fleming also designed a small corner desk in the master bedroom, where he wrote many of his Bond thrillers. Among others who have also worked at that desk, Sting composed many of the songs for the Police album, *Synchronicity*, at Goldeneye.

The spy films directed by Alfred Hitchcock (including *Notorious* with Ingrid Bergman and Cary Grant, **right**) were often fast-paced and laced with deadpan humour. David Picker of United Artists thought that Hitchcock would make a good director for a James Bond film.

"Here, sire, is a man, all brains and no heart."
Introduction of Karl Schulmeister to Napoleon in 1805

If Karl Schulmeister was not the first master-spy, he was certainly one of the most successful. On behalf of Napoleon, he infiltrated the Austrian military organization and deceived its leadership. He had fake newspapers printed and filled them with stories of rebellions in Paris. Schulmeister bribed others to report similar news to Austrian leaders. In October 1805, the Austrian commander, Baron Von Leiberich, marched his entire army onto the battlefield, confident he could defeat Napoleon's obviously weakened troops. The crack French forces, who were massive in number, immediately overwhelmed Von Leiberich's army. Schulmeister eventually became head of the French Secret Service before political intrigue stripped him of power. Later, when the Austrian Army again fought Napoleon, they made a point of surrounding Schulmeister's estate with cannons and blowing his home to pieces.

The British equivalent of Schulmeister went by the name Sidney Reilly, although he was born in the Russian Ukraine under the name Sigmund Rosenblum.

Before his arrest and execution in Russia in the 1920s, Reilly managed to serve as a key agent in British intelligence operations for almost three decades. His primary accomplishments involved gaining Persian Gulf oil rights for Britain and countering German sabotage efforts in America in the early years of the First World War. Reilly had the ability to search out secrets in virtually any place on the planet.

When Britain wanted to know about Russian fortifications in Manchuria or assessments of the Trans-Siberian railroad, Reilly delivered. When they needed information from behind enemy lines during the Great War, Reilly went into Germany. He improbably claimed to have personally attended Kaiser Wilhelm II's military planning sessions.

Master spies like Schulmeister and Reilly were vastly different from James Bond. They were not killers. They did not blow up buildings or factories. They fought silent wars extracting information rather than thrusting with swords or firing a gun.

While real spies were helping to topple governments, British authors like John Buchan and E. Phillips Oppenheim were writing tales of daring secret agents.

These authors directly inspired the filmmakers who launched the spy adventure as a genre - a genre which probably would not exist if not for the contribution of Alfred Hitchcock. When Hitchcock made *The Man Who Knew Too Much* in 1934, he broke new ground and became the first filmmaker to capture the suspense and excitement of the popular spies of literature. A few years later, Hitchcock took the spy adventure to further heights with *The 39 Steps* and *The Lady Vanishe*s. Hitchcock's spy adventures involved innocents caught up in espionage plots, but delivered spectacular action and devious villains.

In America, serials and double-bill 'programmers' in the 1930s offered action-filled spy thrillers such as the Brass Bancroft films starring Ronald Reagan. Bancroft fought spies and counterfeiters for the Secret Service, going undercover near the Mexican border.

With the outbreak of the Second World War, Hitchcock re-visited the spy genre with *Foreign Correspondent*. In the film, reporter Joel McCrea finds himself trapped in Europe during the events leading up to a fictional war, jumping from one adventure to the next. The film's jaw-dropping action, which included a cockpit view of a plane crash, left audiences gasping.

Hunting Nazi and Japanese spies became an obsession for Hollywood screen heroes during the war years, yet two of the most notable and influential of the Nazi-hunting films came out just after the war. From Hitchcock again, *Notorious* set a unique tone, telling the very personal story of a woman who must debase herself (by marrying and loving a man she despises) in order to redeem herself for her country. The film beautifully portrays the emotional cost of living a lie while still delivering all the suspense and tension of classic Hitchcock.

In 1945, Henry Hathaway directed the influential American drama *The House On 92nd Street*, which combined traditional documentary techniques and Hollywood style to tell the true story of a young German American who infiltrates a Nazi spy cell in New York. The film uses a narrator and was shot in many of the locations where actual events occurred. Authentic spy-camera footage gathered in the case was utilized in the finished film, which had been made with the extensive co-operation of the FBI. *The House On 92nd Street* spawned a host of similar reality-based spy films, such as *O.S.S.*, starring Alan Ladd. All these films used documentary techniques, narrators, and claimed to be based on true events.

The Second World War itself brought about a tremendous change in the public perception of spying in the US and Britain. During the previous World War, saboteurs had been perceived as wretched men and women responsible for tragedies like the massive 'Black Tom' explosion on a New Jersey pier in 1916. Films like Hitchcock's *The Secret Agent* and *Saboteur* accurately reflected the public mood toward such figures.

During the war, the adventures and successes of the French Resistance, Tito's partisans, the Dutch Orange underground and organized groups of Allied commandos often included acts of sabotage and assassination. Quickly, governments, films and newspapers celebrated the gains made by these groups, and so popularized the notion of fifth column warfare in a heroic light.

One of the most stylish spy films of the 1950s was Joseph L. Mankiewicz's *Five Fingers*, starring James Mason as the lovesick butler at the British Embassy in Turkey who sells out his country to the Nazis in order to win the heart of his love. Although the film still uses narration, and proclaims its story's authenticity, the character interplay is much more like the Garbo and Dietrich spy films of the 30s. The movie also captured a wonderfully British attitude of imperturbability, and became so popular it inspired an American television series a few years later.

Action-filled B-films such as the Dick Barton movies - which were based on wartime radio plays on the BBC - offered a different view of spies. Barton faced mastermind villains and hairbreadth adventures, but they were looked on as children's comics made for the cinema. Fleming's James Bond novels did not seem to fit easily into either the genre of *The House On 92nd Street* nor the Dick Barton sagas, and it was probably this quality of the stories which prevented them from reaching cinemas for so long.

Bond's journey to the big screen seemed to start well. In 1954, Ian Fleming sold the television and film rights to CASINO ROYALE. The result was a live broadcast on CBS's show, *Climax!*, on 21st October 1954. Barry Nelson played an oddly Americanized 'card-sense' Jimmy Bond. With a script by one of Hitchcock's favourite writers, Charles Bennett, and a delightfully sinister performance by Peter Lorre as the villain, Le Chiffre, the project was an interesting first attempt to give dramatic form to James Bond.

Various attempts to launch a Bond film or television series came and went throughout the 50s, culminating in 1959

with a partnership which would have lingering reverberations in the world of 007. It seemed like a good idea at the time: Fleming's life-long friend Ivar Bryce, lawyer Ernest Cuneo, and Fleming himself would form a partnership to make a James Bond film. Bryce, who was independently wealthy, could finance the project, which would be directed by an energetic Irishman - Kevin McClory - who had worked closely with noted filmmakers John Huston and Michael Todd. The whole business was destined to end up in a mess.

In 1960, Fleming went to Jamaica to write a new novel, THUNDERBALL, which was largely based on the treatments prepared earlier in the year. Noted writer Jack Whittingham produced two drafts of the script, but by late 1960, Fleming considered the film project dead. Kevin McClory, apparently, did not.

At the end of 1960, the film producer Harry Saltzman approached Ian Fleming to option the Bond novels. The two men shared the same lawyer, but Fleming's negotiating strategy in these situations was usually to demand an absurd amount of money to see if the offer was legitimate. In this case, Fleming asked for $50,000 for a six-month option, and $100,000 per title if and when any films were made. Much to Fleming's surprise, Saltzman agreed.

Almost simultaneously, Kevin McClory read a proof copy of THUNDERBALL, and decided that it infringed upon work he had done on the film story with Fleming, Cuneo, Bryce and Whittingham.

These two events occurred just as *Life* magazine was preparing to publish a list of President Kennedy's ten favourite books. On the list (topped by David Cecil's *Melbourne*), Kennedy paid tribute to his dinner with Ian Fleming a year earlier and included FROM RUSSIA WITH LOVE. The list was published in the issue of *Life* dated 17th March 1961, the very same day that Kevin McClory sued Fleming and Bryce in the London High Court.

Within weeks, three events - Harry Saltzman's option, Kennedy's list and McClory's lawsuit - had suddenly and starkly laid out very different courses for the fate of James Bond. Over the next 40 years, as the success of the Bond phenomenon grew, those differing courses ultimately collided and frequently erupted into a pitched battle, with the prize worth hundreds of millions of dollars.

The undisputed winner of that war proved to be a man whose name has yet to be mentioned, the man who had the single greatest influence over the cinematic legacy of James Bond - producer Albert R. 'Cubby' Broccoli.

Harry Saltzman and Cubby Broccoli took decidedly different paths to the world of James Bond. Harry's journey was like that of a bumble-bee, zipping from a youth in New Brunswick, Canada to New York City and thence France and London. Harry was a showman, and he was constantly looking for the grandest show, the new challenge, the big one that would top them all.

Saltzman's career began in the 1920s when he travelled around selling soap from the back of a wagon. When entering a village, the wheel of his wagon fell off and before a gathered crowd, Saltzman changed the wheel, getting himself covered in black axle grease in the process. Saltzman then washed the

"Cubby was always a hands-on producer. Long before Bond, he made a film called *Hell Below Zero* and they had to go out to the Antarctic. Most producers like to stay at home at Les Ambassadeurs, put their feet up, and get some other individual to go out and take the flak. Cubby was up there on these whaling boats where the guys, for their average diversion, would go at each other with knives." Donald Zec

"When you look at the Warwick films, most of them are big exciting action-adventure films with all the elements that later on worked so incredibly well within the James Bond franchise."

Barbara Broccoli

thick grease off with his soap, proving its strength and resulting in many sales. There was a catch - the 'grease' was actually just black soap and the whole event was just for show.

After Saltzman's mother passed away, the future producer moved to New York under a fake name and began booking vaudeville acts, becoming so successful that East Coast booking agencies began making very real threats against his health. Saltzman was still a teenager when he fled to France and began to manage a touring circus.

The circus led to the theatre, which somehow led to selling black market horsemeat during the Second World War. A few years after the war, Saltzman was producing television shows in Europe for the American market. A dispassionate examination of Harry Saltzman's credits reveals an inner struggle between high and low art. Saltzman loved the circus, but he equally loved great acting and compelling drama. He produced *The Iron Petticoat* with Katharine Hepburn and Bob Hope and then helped create Woodfall Productions, the influential company that made *Look Back In Anger*, *Saturday Night And Sunday Morning*, and *The Entertainer*. By late 1960, Saltzman was out of Woodfall, declaring himself sick of "kitchen sink dramas". He was ready to move on, and James Bond was a bold first step.

By the time Ian Fleming published CASINO ROYALE, 'Cubby' Broccoli had pursued a range of careers: as a farmer, a casket company bookkeeper, a jewellery and cosmetics salesman, an assistant director, a racing promoter and a talent agent. One might think Broccoli was just as erratic as Saltzman, but once Broccoli became a film producer, he quickly established himself as a solid, trustworthy force in the movie industry, a position he never relinquished. Broccoli's success began when he joined forces with the Academy Award-winning director Irving Allen to form Warwick Films. They made films with American stars, British crews, international locations and solid production values. The movies reflected Cubby's tastes. He loved travel and adventure, once joining the crew of a yacht to sail from California to Hawaii. He also loved the glamour of Hollywood, having Cary Grant as the best man at his wedding. The first three Warwick films - *The Red Beret* (*Paratrooper* in the US), *The Black Knight* and *Hell Below Zero* - were all tremendous international successes.

Broccoli and Allen's partnership did not last. In 1960, the pair broke from the Warwick mould, producing *The Trials Of Oscar Wilde*, which they financed with their own money. The lavishly produced film garnered solid reviews, but failed to find an audience. After Broccoli split from Allen, he spent months trying to find the right project. He knew the basics. He knew the formula for his past successes: exotic locations, high adventure, handsome men and beautiful women.

Broccoli had seen two films that he felt captured the spirit of the movies he wanted to be making. The first was *North By*

Previous pages: Cubby Broccoli had reason to be content on location in Trinidad during the shooting of *Fire Down Below* in 1956. He was happily married, with seemingly limitless opportunities. Within a few years, Cubby's then wife, Nedra Broccoli, died of cancer, his partnership with Irving Allen dissolved, and he found himself in serious financial trouble. It is a measure of the man that he was able to re-build both his personal life and career.

Top right: Peter Finch in the title role of *The Trials Of Oscar Wilde*, Broccoli's last film in partnership with Irving Allen.

Right: One day in 1965, Albert R. Broccoli (**left in photo**) walked into the Audley Street offices of Eon Productions and saw his producing partner, Harry Saltzman (**right in photo**), who said he wanted to start filming a movie called *Fings Ain't Wot They Used T'Be* that June. "Where are you going to get the money?" asked Cubby. "Details, Cubby," replied Harry. "Details."

Northwest, Alfred Hitchcock's 1959 masterpiece starring Broccoli's friend Cary Grant. Like *Foreign Correspondent*, the film raced along on an amazing journey. The well-dressed and well-mannered players engaged in espionage, sexual duplicity, murder and daring acts of violence. The film was a throwback to the Hitchcock classics of the 1930s, and as such eschewed the docu-drama tone of other spy films of the times.

The second film which struck Broccoli was a grand Second World War sabotage adventure, *The Guns Of Navarone*. The film used its Greek setting as a chance to extol the mythic nature of its heroic band of commandos. Broccoli wanted to make myths. He started working on a version of the *Arabian Nights* tales, but he could not get himself excited about the project. He wanted something that was more immediate, something that felt fresh and new.

"Cubby and Harry were a marvellous team for many reasons. They were both creative, they were both innovative, they were both very good businessmen, and they really, truly worked well together." Charles 'Jerry' Juroe

2. The Phenomenon Begins

On 31st December 1959, the creator of James Bond welcomed in the 60s by going to see a spy film. The movie was *Our Man In Havana*, and Ian Fleming gave a New Year's Day interview on BBC radio in which he discussed the film. Just two and a half years later, Ian Fleming's secret agent had transformed the entire spy genre, creating the longest-running series in film history and redefining global notions of espionage. Why did 007 become an icon of the decade? In short, the Western world needed a new hero for a new generation. In 1960, the ideology of the West was in trouble. After a decade and a half of fighting the Cold War against the Soviets, it appeared to many that Communism was expanding to become the dominant form of government around the globe. Newspaper headlines heralded Russian victories in the space race while documenting human rights tragedies in South Africa, Algeria and the American South. The sorting of the good guys from the bad became more complicated on a daily basis. What the West needed was an icon of its own values, as complex and confusing as they might be. Was there someone, somewhere who could sort out the mess in the world, untie the Gordian knot of global politics with a swift, decisive stroke? Cubby Broccoli thought he knew the answer. The world needed James Bond.

Many observers might have thought Ian Fleming's literary spy was an unlikely choice to become the single most successful cinematic figure of the era. After all, Bond was a product of Great Britain, a nation whose star seemed to be on the wane. While in 1960 it was true that the sun still never set on the British Empire, twilight was clearly closing in. James Bond's popularity was not, however, tied to a colonial England. Bond was a product of a newly burgeoning empire.

Whatever Great Britain might have lost in the way of global political import during the late 1950s and early 60s, the nation gained it back in terms of cultural impact during the first half of the new decade. The cutting edges of fashion, music, film, architecture, design, literature and art could all be found in England. It was as if the world, realizing that the British Empire was disappearing, recognized the importance of the nation's culture and embraced it wholeheartedly.

James Bond came to represent all aspects of this cultural rebirth. He would dress in the best clothes, be accompanied by a sophisticated musical score and walk through some of the most brilliantly designed sets ever created for film. His literary adventures would outsell the Bible during the early to mid-1960s, and his cinematic exploits would change the way films were made, watched, and marketed. James Bond was everything that made modern Britain so attractive to the outside world. He was elegance, tradition, sexual liberation and stability all rolled into one.

While Ian Fleming laid out the ingredients, it is through the character's interpretation by others that the cinematic phenomenon of James Bond exists. Bond's success and longevity remain because the character can be translated from printed page to silver screen to comic strips to popular art, and onwards to toys, music, fashion and technology. The essential core of James Bond resonates strongly enough that it has become part of our cultural lexicon.

The problem for Cubby Broccoli was that he did not have the rights to the Bond novels. He had tried to secure them in 1958, when his then business partner, Irving Allen, undertook the negotiations with Fleming. But Allen was not enthusiastic, declaring that the books were not even good enough for television.

In the spring of 1961, Cubby learned from the writer Wolf Mankowitz that Harry Saltzman had been unable to set up his expensive James Bond option, and time was quickly running out. With Mankowitz's help a meeting between Saltzman and Broccoli was convened within 24 hours. Harry wanted a partner. Cubby wanted to buy the Bond rights free and clear. They agreed to become equal partners, and suddenly, Cubby Broccoli was in the Bond business.

In 1961, newly-elected US President John F. Kennedy met Soviet leader Nikita Khruschev for the first time in Vienna (**top**). Kennedy, noticing a medal on Khruschev's chest, asked what it was. Khruschev said it symbolized the Lenin Peace Prize. Kennedy replied, "I hope you keep it." On 12th April 1961, the Soviets launched Yuri Gagarin into orbit, winning the race to safely send the first man into space. On 5th May, Navy Commander Alan B. Shepherd Jr. became the first American in space. He was followed by Virgil I. Grissom on 21st July and, on 20th February 1962, John Glenn (**middle**) became the first American to orbit the earth. The space race became part of the backdrop of the 007 films *Dr. No* and *You Only Live Twice*. Four months after Yuri Gagarin's space flight, Cold War tensions increased when East Germany erected the Berlin Wall (**bottom**) to stop the flood of refugees.

Centre right: When Albert R. Broccoli and Harry Saltzman became partners, they named their company Danjaq, a combination of the first names of their wives, Dana Broccoli and Jacqueline Saltzman. From left - Cubby, Dana, Sean Connery, Jacqueline and Harry.

UNITED ARTISTS CORP., 729 SEVENTH AVE., NEW YORK 19, N. Y. • TEL. CIRCLE 5-6000
from Mort Nathanson, National Publicity Director

Bond has been described as "The Thinking Man's Mickey Spillane." The novels, which include "Diamonds are Forever," "From Russia With Love," "Live and Let Die," "Goldfinger" and "Moonraker," combine hair-raising action and plenty of sex.

"Dr. No" and the other Fleming novels to be filmed by Eon Productions will be made with the cooperation of the British secret service. This is the first time that such cooperation has been officially offered.

Carib Ocho Rios
SEA & COUNTRY CLUB
"A Most Unusual Resort" OCHO RIOS JAMAICA

MEMO.		DATE	EXPLANATION	CHARGES	CREDITS	BAL. DUE
	1					144.56
	2	FEB15-62	BEV' ••••	7.05		
	3	FEB15-62	RES' ••••	1.25		119.41
LAUNDRY	4	FEB15-62	— P'OUT	4.07		123.48
	5	FEB15-62	PHONE —	0.10		123.58
	6	FEB15-62	SERV. —	0.50		124.08
	7	FEB15-62	RES'R —	2.50		
	8	FEB15-62	RES'R —	5.00		131.58
	9	FEB15-62	BEV'G	3.55		135.13
	10	FEB17-62	NEWS	0.50		135.63
	11	FEB17-62	SERV	0.50		136.13
	12	FEB17-62	RES'R	2.50		
	13	FEB17-62	SERV	3.20		141.83
LAUNDRY	14	FEB18-62	SERV. —	0.50		142.33
	15	FEB19-62	— P'OUT	3.75		
	16	FEB19-62	— P'OUT	9.00		
	17	FEB19-62	— P'OUT	3.00		158.08
	18	FEB20-62	— TR.CR.	158.08		0.00
	19					
	20					
	21					
	22					
	23					
	24					

PRINTED IN U.S.A. B-98—G1955—PRESS OF THE NATIONAL CASH REGISTER CO., DAYTON, OHIO

LAST BALANCE IS AMOUNT DUE UNLESS OTHERWISE INDICATED

PRINTERS 661-662

Cubby Broccoli and Harry Saltzman were not the only two people in the film industry pursuing James Bond. David Picker, an executive at United Artists, had made enquiries to Lew Wasserman at Universal/MCA. He thought James Bond might be a good idea for Alfred Hitchcock to consider. Picker recalled Wasserman's reply, "'Oh, well, we represent Mr. Bond through our London office.' He said, 'You can't get the rights.'"

In late June 1961, Cubby flew to New York with Harry Saltzman. There, Cubby set up a meeting at United Artists to pitch the project directly to UA chiefs Arthur Krim, Robert Benjamin and David Picker. Picker nearly fell out of his chair when Cubby announced that they wanted to do a Bond film at UA. It was the deal he had been hoping for. In less than an hour, they hammered out the terms. The first James Bond film would be produced for just under a million dollars. They all shook hands and agreed to start work on the initial 007 adventure. On 29th June 1961, UA sent out a press release, which carried the headline 'UA SETS PRODUCTION DEAL WITH BROCCOLI, SALTZMAN FOR FILMING AND DISTRIBUTION OF FLEMING THRILLERS' and went on to announce plans for "a series of motion pictures", the first, it stated, to be filmed "with the cooperation of the British secret service."

UA wanted to make a film based on THUNDERBALL, the most recent of the Fleming books. Richard Maibaum, writer of *O.S.S.* and an uncredited contributing writer on Hitchcock's *Foreign Correspondent*, took the assignment to write the film script, completing his first draft in August 1961.

Maibaum certainly did his best to adapt the novel for the silver screen. Bond's second line of dialogue simply reads: "Bond. James Bond." These words would go on to become 007's ultimate signature introduction, and in 1999 the phrase was deemed the most famous line uttered in movie history.

The *Thunderball* script, however, was written under a cloud. Kevin McClory's lawsuit against Ian Fleming and Ivar Bryce had tried to stop the presses on the novel before it hit bookstores. The initial motion for an injunction proved unsuccessful, and Saltzman and Broccoli felt the McClory suit would soon be settled. It was not. When it became clear that no quick resolution was forthcoming, the film version of THUNDERBALL was shelved.

In August, Richard Maibaum and Wolf Mankowitz hammered out a treatment for *Dr. No.* They decided the villain was too preposterous, so they created a new villain who had a pet monkey. The monkey, a sort of living talisman for the mastermind, became the title character, Dr. No. Cubby Broccoli hit the roof. All the money and effort spent on these novels, and the writers toss out Ian Fleming's brilliant villain and make Dr. No a monkey? It was outrageous. Broccoli told the pair to simply adapt the book. "I'm a great believer in not tampering with an original winner," Cubby remarked in his autobiography.

The writers did still tamper, but within the Fleming mould. They introduced additional characters, such as Sylvia Trench, whom Bond seduces even as he defeats her at the *chemin de fer* table. They brought in the sultry but evil secretary, Miss Taro, to whom Bond makes love as he waits for the assassin coming to kill him.

In short, the writers wisely increased the sex quotient. They reasoned that Bond needed to be an irresistible image of masculinity, an idealized male sex symbol, who, unlike clean-cut American heroes, never flinched when faced with the prospect of a sexual liaison.

The scriptwriters had to make some quick decisions about how to deal with current events around the world. Mankowitz and Maibaum decided to move beyond the Cold War. Dr. No would work for SPECTRE, the villainous organization which featured in the novel THUNDERBALL.

The Special Executive for Counterintelligence, Terrorism, Revenge and Extortion became the perfect vehicle to respond to the shifting quicksands of temporal politics. This month the global villains might be right-wing French secret police bombing leftist groups. Next month the bad guy might be North Vietnamese leader Ho Chi-Minh. As Dr. No proclaims in the script, "East - West... points of the compass... each as stupid as the other." The choice was clear - James Bond would stand apart from politics. He would simply fight evil.

Even before the script for *Dr. No* was completed, Cubby Broccoli and Harry Saltzman began to undertake the most important job facing a producer - pulling together the right team for the project.

Ultimately, they decided they needed an English director, one who could understand and portray James Bond's world. Although many directors were approached, Cubby Broccoli did not have to look far.

He chose the first director he had ever worked with in England; when Broccoli and Irving Allen came to London in 1953 to produce their initial Warwick Pictures production, *The Red Beret* (which was released as *Paratrooper* in the US), they chose Terence Young to direct it.

The Cambridge-educated Young had a sense of personal style which was evident in his wardrobe: tailored suits and hand-made shirts, which he would change three times a day if he could. Young reasoned that "any fool can be uncomfortable". Even in remote locations, Young would dine at a table graced with a white tablecloth, and the crew would be served Dom Perignon - often paid for out of the director's own pocket.

Young certainly enjoyed travelling to far-flung locations. It was once said of him that if he had a choice of two scripts, he would take the one with the most distant location. His film work carried him from Lapland (*Valley Of The Eagles*) to Sudan (*Storm Over The Nile*) and Kenya (*Safari*). The Bond films took him to Jamaica, Venice, Istanbul and the Bahamas. At the height of his success, Young had a home in Switzerland and apartments in London, Rome and Paris.

Terence Young's love of adventure and travel, plus his sense of charm, elegance and wit, put a stamp of style on the series that continues to the present day.

Before Terence Young signed on to direct *Dr. No*, and long before Richard Maibaum typed his first Bond script, the producers were looking hard for an actor to play 007. In fact, even before Broccoli and Saltzman had their deal in place with United Artists, the search for James Bond hit the press. In June 1961, the columnist Pat Lewis mentioned that actor Patrick Allen was up for the part. Harry Saltzman had told her, "It's the acting plum of the decade". Saltzman went on to mention Michael Craig and Patrick McGoohan for Bond, but concluded by saying, "I'd prefer to use an unknown."

A month later, Lewis announced, "Harry Saltzman and Albert 'Cubby' Broccoli are having trouble casting James Bond for their upcoming series of feature films." Lewis announced a 'find James Bond' contest. Ian Fleming offered a description of the role: "He likes gambling, golf, and fast motor-cars. He smokes a great deal, but without affectation. All his movements are relaxed and economical."

Lewis put out her own criteria: "Competitors must be aged between 28 and 35; measure between 6ft. and 6ft. 1in. in height; weigh about 12st.; have blue eyes, dark hair, rugged features - particularly a determined chin - and an English accent."

Hopefuls were told to dash off their vital statistics on the back of a photo and send it to Harry Saltzman's office, where six finalists would be chosen for screen-testing with judges including Saltzman and Broccoli, Ian Fleming and Pat Lewis herself. It has been reported that Sean Connery won the contest. He did not. The winner was announced in late September: 28-year-old Peter Anthony, a professional model, was selected as "the man who came closest to" James Bond. Cubby Broccoli noted a "Greg Peck quality about him... but unfortunately he lacks the technique to cope with such a demanding part as Bond at first try." Pat Lewis ended her column by leaking what was already known in the film industry. She stated, "Who will get the part? My hunch is that it will go to Sean Connery."

In fact, by this date, Cubby Broccoli and Harry Saltzman were already in heavy negotiations with Connery, having prodded a reluctant United Artists into backing an offer for a three-year, six-film deal. Connery, burned from a contract with 20th Century-Fox, was wary of long-term commitments and demanded freedom to do other films. The producers agreed, scaling back plans for two Bond films a year to one, but extending the term for five films to be made in five years. Connery's wife, Diane Cilento, pushed him to sign. Eventually, Connery did, changing movie history, and launching a career which can be described as nothing short of amazing.

Left and opposite: The son of the Police Commissioner of the International Sector of Shanghai, Terence Young was sent to school in England and educated at Cambridge, where he excelled at sports. He studied to become a priest, but his interest in cinema led him to write film reviews for the campus paper. He landed a summer job at B.I.P. Studios and developed an interest in writing screenplays. Young soon became known as one of Britain's best screenwriters.

He had a natural gift for languages, and when French director René Clair was filming *The Ghost Goes West*, Young was employed as Clair's assistant. From then on, Young frequently assisted foreign directors working in England, including Jacques Feyder and Josef von Sternberg. During the Second World War, Young served with the Welsh Guards' Armoured Tank Division. He would later comment that he learned more about tank warfare in two weeks than he had absorbed about moviemaking in five years. Young was twice wounded in action.

In 1948, Young directed his first feature, *One Night With You*. The film failed to make much of an impression, but his next, *Corridor Of Mirrors*, featuring a new actress, Lois Maxwell, was awarded the 'Best Film Of The Year' award in France and earned him the sobriquet 'The Boy Director'. Drawing upon his experiences in the Welsh Guards, Young directed *They Were Not Divided*, a war drama whose cast featured Desmond Llewelyn.

Four years later Young directed *Action Of The Tiger*. Among the cast was a young Scottish actor named Sean Connery. During the production, Connery read the script of Young's next film and asked if he could be in it; Young demurred, saying there was no part for him, but not to worry - he'd remember him for future roles.

Following pages: The men who brought James Bond to life, from left to right - producer Albert R. 'Cubby' Broccoli, actor Sean Connery, novelist Ian Fleming and producer Harry Saltzman.

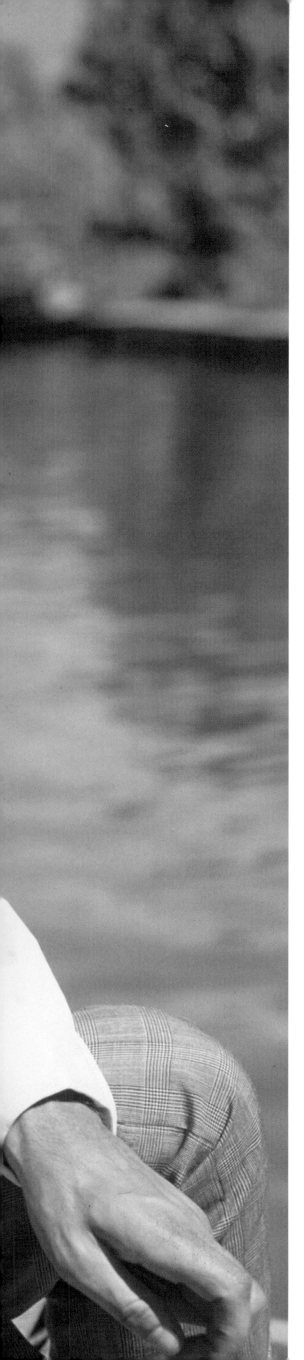

The very mention of Sean Connery's name brings the image of James Bond to mind. For those who grew up watching the Bond films in the 1960s, Connery seems to define the ruthlessly elegant *bon vivant*.

Connery and Bond shared certain similarities - both had Scottish heritage, and both served in the Royal Navy. Connery, born on 25th August 1930, grew up in the impoverished Fountainbridge area of Edinburgh, sleeping in the bottom drawer of his parents' wardrobe, and he left the Navy due to ulcers. While James Bond enjoyed an expensive education at Fettes (Tony Blair's *alma mater*), Connery the youngster only delivered milk to the school.

In the winter of 1952, at the age of 22, Connery travelled down to London to compete in the Mr. Universe contest. There, a friend who was in the chorus of *South Pacific* suggested Connery should try out for a role. After a 48-hour crash course in dancing, he landed the part. During the road company's nine weeks in Manchester, Connery was spotted playing football and invited to join Manchester United as a paid professional footballer. Fellow actor Robert Henderson talked Connery out of it, and convinced him to read the classics of the theatre. Connery dedicated himself to the task, particularly after the show's run ended and he returned to London. "I spent a lot of time alone," he told an interviewer. "I was living in a basement eating minestrone, which would last me three days. In the winter I'd cycle up to the library in Chelsea because it was warm there, and read and read."

In 1956, Connery's hard work began to pay off. He landed the leading role in a live television production of *Requiem For A Heavyweight*. His success in the part led to other TV offers, including *Anna Karenina* and the BBC series *Ace Of Kings*, and he also secured his first featured role in a movie, *No Road Back*. The following year, Connery signed a contract with 20th Century-Fox, who loaned him out to star in *Another Time, Another Place*; other films followed, including *Darby O'Gill And The Little People*, *Tarzan's Greatest Adventure* and *On The Fiddle*. After making an appearance in the star-laden war drama *The Longest Day*, he obtained a release from his Fox contract.

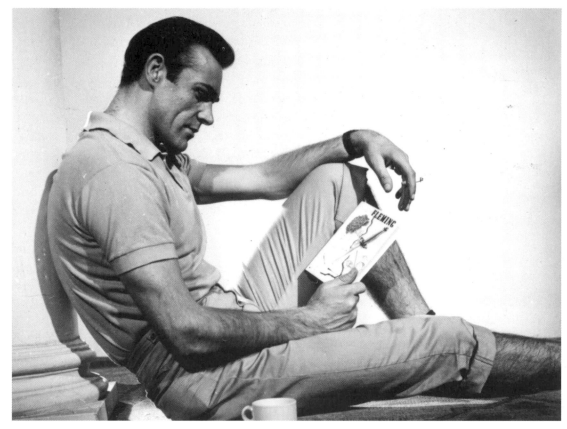

In the summer of 1961, Connery's name kept coming up for the part of Bond. Certainly, there were reasons to avoid the choice - his accent, the lack of polish. But Cubby Broccoli had met Connery during *Another Time, Another Place*, and remembered him. Peter Hunt, the editor of *On The Fiddle*, recommended the actor to the producers. It helped that the director of *Dr. No*, Terence Young, had previously worked with Connery on *Action Of The Tiger*. While in Los Angeles, Broccoli screened *Darby O'Gill* to get a better look at Connery. He thought he saw something worthwhile, and called his wife, Dana. Cubby wanted to know if Connery had sex appeal. Dana Broccoli confirmed the obvious. Connery would go on to be named 'Sexiest Man Alive' by *People* magazine in 1990, and later 'Sexiest Man Of The Century'.

That appeal comes not just from good looks, it comes from a particular confidence, a certainty within himself. Connery always seemed to know what he wanted, and how to demand it. He had studied movement with Yat Malmgren, where he developed a natural, authoritative grace, which was at once seductive and intimidating. When he met Cubby Broccoli, Harry Saltzman and UA

The ingredients of Bond. First, introduce him in an elegant setting appropriate for a man who takes chances - in this instance, the Le Cercle casino, where 007 utters the immortal introduction, "Bond. James Bond".

Second, dress him in a tuxedo - invented by Pierre Lorillard IV of Tuxedo Park, New York in 1886. Less formal than a white tie and tails, the black dinner jacket (or white in the tropics) and bow tie has become indelibly linked with 007's image.

Third, give Bond tailored shirts with turnback cuffs from Turnbull & Asser for a look of class and distinction - accentuated by his Rolex watch. Though a civil servant, agent 007 lives a life of enviable luxury.

And don't forget the libations. The martini, invented near the end of the American Civil War, was the fuel for the Jazz Age of the 1920s. The Dom Perignon bottle (**right**) is one of only two props known to survive from the filming of *Dr. No*.

executive Bud Ornstein, Connery arrived dressed in casual clothes, refused to do a traditional screen test, and told the producers exactly how he saw James Bond. When Connery left, Saltzman, Broccoli and Ornstein watched him out of the window as he crossed the street. The trio were struck by his walk - Connery moved "like a big jungle cat," Saltzman observed.

Cubby Broccoli and Harry Saltzman knew they needed a particular set of ingredients to make a Bond film successful. Harry Saltzman told the press in the summer of 1961 that the films would have a "formula of blood, sex and thunder", which seemed to miss a certain key element. Ian Fleming's reviewers noted the Bond recipe for anyone who needed it in shorthand. "Many critics like Mr. Fleming's combination of ingenuity, snobbery and sex," wrote James Sandoe in 1955. In 1958, *The New Statesman* published the most famous disapproving review of a Bond novel, which came under the headline 'Sex, Snobbery, and Sadism'. The pattern was obvious, though the Bond films would choose to emphasize ingenuity rather than sadism or blood.

Snobbery came in the form of Bond's elite tastes. The filmmakers knew Bond needed to represent the ultimate in urbane sophistication. 007's stylistic choices had to be impeccable. In short, Bond had to know more about the finer things in life than the audience, than anyone.

Production buyer Ron Quelch recalled the day in 1961 when the filmmaking team decided to accessorize 007.

"They were looking for everything that Bond might or might not have been wearing. Whether he would have cuff links or whether he wouldn't. Whether he would have a tie pin, whether he'd have an identity chain, what watch he was wearing, what sort of wallet he would carry, whether it would be an inside pocket job or a hip wallet. Everything that went to create the character of Bond was discussed at that meeting, and it took a long time, believe you me."

The tone was taken from Ian Fleming himself. Bond needed to be stylish, but not fussy. He needed to be suave, but never outlandish. He had to have a clean, unobtrusive look about him.

Terence Young provided the essentials for Bond's wardrobe. He took Sean Connery to famed shirt-maker Turnbull & Asser for custom-designed shirts with turnback cuffs (ones with buttons so that Bond could undress more quickly). Young had his tailor Anthony Sinclair cut Connery's suits. Sinclair's suits, which look traditional by today's standards, were considered somewhat rakish and fancy at the time. Bond needed to be "well turned-out", a fashion plate for the modern British man.

Style was key to quickly communicating the character of Bond. If he was to represent the best the Western powers had to offer, he had to be surrounded by the best. 007 could not just drink vodka, it needed to be Smirnoff's; he could not just wear a watch, it needed to be a Rolex. The champagne would be Dom Perignon.

When Rolex declined to provide a timepiece for the filmmakers and the budget precluded the producers from purchasing one, Cubby Broccoli pulled the one off his wrist and tossed it to a member of the art department.

While Connery knew how to move, Young needed to help him feel comfortable in the world of James Bond. Young asked Connery to sleep in one of his new suits to get the feel for it. He took Connery to fine restaurants in Mayfair, taught him how to order wine, judge champagne and conduct himself in such settings. Connery also spent time with Fleming, with whom he discussed Bond's character, his accent and the business of espionage.

Connery visited gaming clubs and learned the basics of *chemin de fer* and casino etiquette. The young Scotsman absorbed it all, and he adapted the information into an acting style which would define Bond.

There were grumblings in the British press about Connery's rough edges, but the casting proved to be a perfect mixture. Connery's working-class exterior made Bond a hero who was harder to label as a snob. He played Bond as a man who had earned his right to strong opinions, not as one who was born to them. Connery's Bond was elegant, but never effete. He was rugged, but always refined.

With 007 in place, the filmmakers had to define Bond's world. There were innumerable decisions to make. One could make the films in black and white, or as widescreen travelogues. Since much of *Dr. No* took place in the Caribbean, the filmmakers could offer an island feel (which Monty Norman did with the score) or reproduce Jamaica in the studio. As it was the first James Bond film, they could linger over the details of 007, maybe even include stories of how he had become a spy.

They chose, however, to make the film feel like Bond. He would be defined by his tastes and his actions, not by backstory. Like Bond himself, the films would have a unique stamp. The textures would be well-defined, with high-quality colour cinematography. The films would be sleek, and

"When I first met Fleming, there was certainly no dissension between us on how to see Bond. I saw him as a complete sensualist - senses highly tuned, awake to everything, quite amoral. I particularly like him because he thrives on conflict."

Sean Connery, in a 1965 interview with Sheldon Lane

virtually unadorned with pretence, in the same way that Bond dresses. The camera would not intrude like a voyeur (or spy), as in a Hitchcock film, but rather would move with and around James Bond, creating a sense of intimacy with the character.

The man in charge of executing the cinematography was a 47-year-old South African-born cameraman named Ted Moore. Director Terence Young felt that Moore provided an enormous contribution to the early James Bond films because he made them look dramatic, and photographed them in an American style. "It was really the first conscious American picture made in England," said the director. "The mixture with him was perfect."

Everyone understood that James Bond's cinematic universe would include plenty of exotic locales. This element has always been a part of the British adventure story, from Robert Louis Stevenson and C.S. Forester to Rudyard Kipling and Joseph Conrad. The British adventure hero is a man who journeys to distant lands; Fleming's Bond was no different. Bond, though, did not take the standard tourist route through his travels.

Cinematically, Terence Young and Ted Moore knew they had to exploit Jamaica's natural beauty for *Dr. No*, but they also knew they needed to avoid any of the travelogue feel of many location films. Bond had to move through the local culture, not be distracted by it. Thus, the filmmakers chose not to dwell on the scenery or customs.

As a result, *Dr. No* was shot with the efficiency of a studio movie, but featured the rich authenticity which could only be found by filming on location. To help ensure that the locations in Jamaica looked right, Broccoli and Saltzman brought in an experienced art director, Syd Cain, who had worked as a draftsman before the Second World War and in the art department of Ealing Studios after the war ended. Cain had worked often with Cubby Broccoli during the Warwick years. Unfortunately, when Maurice Binder designed *Dr. No*'s titles, he accidentally left Cain's name off the credits. Broccoli told Cain it would cost too much to do the titles over; Cain replied by telling him not to worry. Cubby gave him a solid gold pen instead.

Much of *Dr. No* would be shot in London's Pinewood Studios, and for that, the filmmakers faced the choice: should Bond's world look like his locations, or should it be somehow different?

The man who answered that question was German-born designer Ken Adam. Cubby Broccoli had hired Adam for his Warwick Films production, *The Trials Of Oscar Wilde*, and was so impressed with Adam's work that he immediately thought of him when it was time to produce *Dr. No*. "Ken turned us down at first," Broccoli wrote in his autobiography, but Cubby cajoled him into doing the film.

As Adam recalls, *Dr. No* "gave me the opportunity to design the film for our electronic age, with a tongue in the cheek style".

Adam set to work, using new materials and creating bold, sleek designs, which - like the German UFA films of the 1920s - had an Expressionistic quality. Expressionism created a heightened reality which took the viewer into the experience and mind of the characters, and for Adam the set design was a way to create a window into the drama. This was crucial for *Dr. No*, since there would be so little backstory to the characters.

Adam was certainly familiar with movements in modern architecture, and many have speculated that he was consciously

influenced by flamboyant Americans like Frank Lloyd Wright and John Lautner - two designers whom critics claimed built structures on the scale of their own egos. Nonetheless, their elaborate but sleek designs captured the flourish which Adam put into his set for the megalomaniacal villain, Dr. No. That set, with its giant aquarium window, had to be expansive, for Fleming had written it that way. Adam, however, took out the library bookshelves and club chairs of the novel and replaced them with raw stone walls, a radial fireplace, and beautiful antiques. Adam said he did not see any reason why the villains should have bad taste.

By the end of 1961, Truman Tally of Signet, Ian Fleming's American paperback publisher, learned some good news. Ian Fleming was now the top-selling thriller writer in the United States. Yet to date, not one of his novels had appeared on the *New York Times* bestsellers list.

To translate that kind of success into a hit film, the makers of *Dr. No* knew they had to give the movie's viewers the same kind of thrill they experienced reading the books in a shorthand way that was swiftly and easily digestible. While Maibaum had recognized the blunt poetry of "My name's Bond, James Bond", Young selected Bond's drink: the medium dry vodka martini, with a twist of lemon peel - shaken, not stirred.

In 1956, when Ian Fleming's doctor advised against his vices, the author had switched from vodka martinis to bourbon. By that time, however, he had already established the martini as 007's drink of choice, and the films would make the words "shaken, not stirred" a recognizable catch-phrase.

1956 was also the year in which Fleming had received a letter from Geoffrey Boothroyd, a technical representative for the chemicals group ICI. A member of several gun clubs, Boothroyd was bothered by James Bond's "rather deplorable taste in firearms". He explained that the .25 Beretta pistol used by Bond was a "ladies' gun", and suggested that 007 should carry a Centennial Model .38 Smith & Wesson Airweight in a Berns Martin Triple Draw holster. Armed with this information, and after further correspondence with Boothroyd, Fleming changed Bond's weapon in the novel DR. NO, not to a Smith & Wesson, but to a 7.65mm Walther PPK.

The *Dr. No* filmmakers preserved the scene in the novel in which Bond relinquishes his Beretta for the Walther PPK, and the weapon, like Bond's choice of libation, became an identifiable trademark. The filmic 007 carried the Walther PPK until 1997's *Tomorrow Never Dies*, when Bond switched to the Walther P99; after the film's release, gun stores reportedly sold so many of the weapon that most put it on backorder.

The man sending Bond on his exotic missions would also become an icon. M, the authoritative head of Her Majesty's Secret Service, became the prototypical father-figure, perfectly realized by Bernard Lee. Another iconic figure was M's secretary, Miss Moneypenny. Each character was given enough attention to establish a relationship which could be repeated for each successive film.

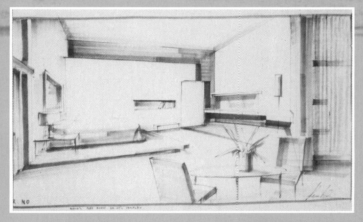

Above: Ken Adam's designs were in perfect sync with the cutting edge of architecture in Southern California, where Richard Neutra and other designers were creating simple, comfortable modern homes and buildings. Even the basic sets show an amazing sense of space, proportion, and modern style much like that which Neutra embraced. When Adam, who did not know Neutra's work, came to live in Los Angeles years later, he rented a Neutra house in Malibu.

"If you carry a double-O number, it means you're licensed to kill, not *get* killed... You'll carry the Walther." M to James Bond in *Dr. No*

The influence of Jamaican sounds led *Dr. No* composer Monty Norman to write the songs 'Three Blind Mice', 'Jump Up' and 'Underneath The Mango Tree'. "I asked several of my Jamaican friends what making love was in some kind of patois," said Norman, "and they suggested 'bool-loo-loop' and that was perfect for the song. Although I must admit now, I'm still not sure whether they were having me on or not." The song 'Jump Up', performed by Byron Lee and his orchestra (**opposite, top right**), became a hit single in Jamaica. "It was great working with people like Monty Norman," said Lee, "because I realized right away how brilliant he was in capturing the sound of our island music immediately."

Among the visitors to the *Dr. No* location was Noel Coward (**middle row, left,** with Sean Connery). Coward's Jamaican home, Firefly, was near Ian Fleming's Goldeneye.

Middle row, third from left: Director Terence Young confers with Jamaican location manager Chris Blackwell, who landed the job at the recommendation of Ian Fleming. With his earnings from *Dr. No*, Blackwell began Island Records, the recording label that introduced the world to reggae through artists such as Bob Marley. In the 1970s, when Ian Fleming's home, Goldeneye, was put up for sale, Blackwell tried to entice Marley into buying it. Marley ultimately decided the house was not his style, so Blackwell bought it himself. In 1989, Blackwell sold Island Records to Polygram for £200 million.

"I was really lucky that they liked it so much, because I stand there with a shell, and that's it. I was just standing there, doing nothing, by the sea."
URSULA ANDRESS

As the filmmakers began shooting *Dr. No* in January 1962, the Cold War continued to rage. A key moment in the struggle between East and West took place on Friday, 10th February 1962. The captured U2 pilot Francis Gary Powers walked across Glienicke Bridge from Potsdam to West Berlin. At the midpoint, he passed Soviet spymaster Rudolf Abel, who the Americans offered in exchange for Powers' freedom. While rising political tensions made real observers' blood run cold, halfway around the globe the temperature in the fictional world of 007 was getting hotter. The very next day, Terence Young called action on scene 146 of *Dr. No* at Laughing Waters beach in Jamaica. The moment marks the birth of The Bond Woman. The screenplay describes what cinematographer Ted Moore filmed as:

BOND'S EYELINE. DAY

WHAT HE SEES: HONEY, *standing at the water's edge, her back to him. She is naked except for a wisp of home-made bikini and a broad leather belt with an undersea knife in a sheath...*

What the script could not describe was the impact of Ursula Andress. Her introduction to the world of Bond had come via her husband, actor/photographer John Derek. A shot that Derek had taken in Greece of Andress playing in the surf in a wet black T-shirt eventually ended up in the London apartment of famed Hungarian-born agent John Shepridge (who had negotiated the sale of the film and television rights to CASINO ROYALE in 1954). Harry Saltzman noticed the photo on Shepridge's table and asked Shepridge, who was in another room, the name of the woman in the wet T-shirt. Shepridge called back, "Ursula Andress." Harry looked at the table again and saw several other photos of beauties in wet T-shirts. How did Shepridge know, sight unseen, which photo commanded Saltzman's attention? Obviously, the only one worth asking about was Andress.

The picture ultimately found its way to Cubby Broccoli's desk. Only when the *Dr. No* production crew was due to leave for Jamaica, and no one had been cast in the key role of Honey Ryder, did Cubby call casting director Max Arnow. Arnow tried to discourage Broccoli. "She has a voice like a Dutch comic." Nonetheless, the same looks which had driven two studios to sign unfulfilled contracts and an Italian actor to risk kidnapping charges persuaded Cubby Broccoli and Harry Saltzman to send Andress a script and an offer to play Honey Ryder.

Andress flew to Kingston, Jamaica, after a big send-off by her friends in Los Angeles. Soon, Tessa Prendergast Welborn, a Jamaican actress-turned-dressmaker whom Ursula knew from Welborn's boutique in Rome, began fitting costumes. Andress tried on various bikinis, but did not like any of them. So together one night, Ursula and Tessa sewed a white cotton bikini of their own, designed to fit Andress's athletic form.

Andress arrived at Laughing Waters around 8am on 11th February 1962. The first shots of the day were Bond and Honey running down the beach, looking for cover as Dr. No's gunboat approached. "Sean and I had to run as fast as we could, and, vroom! I slipped on this coral and opened my whole leg. And then, I'm supposed to be standing there, next shot, doing the song of 'Underneath The Mango Tree'." Andress's bloody leg was cleaned and patched with make-up. The crew set up for her entrance shot.

Marie Therese Prendergast, whose nickname was Tessa (**above**, with Ursula Andress), studied fashion design all over the world, including New York and Paris. In the 1950s, she became an actress, playing the Tahitian love interest opposite Burt Lancaster in *His Majesty O'Keefe* (1953). In the late 1950s, she married deep sea cameraman Scottie Welborn and set up a clothes design business with Liz de Lisserr in her native Jamaica. The marriage was short-lived, but Tessa found fame as a fashion designer when she created Ursula Andress's *Dr. No* bikini.

The result has become legendary. Andress was a new, more exotic type of sex symbol. Confident, comfortable with her sexuality, totally unpampered, self-reliant and dangerous, Andress's Honey Ryder defined what audiences - male and female - wanted in a Bond woman for the next 40 years.

The Bond Woman arrived at the birth of the sexual revolution. While promiscuity has existed since time immemorial, women always bore the brunt of the consequences - pregnancy and childbirth. In December 1960, the FDA in the United States changed that. With the approval of the birth control pill, women could take command of their sexuality if they so chose. In 1961, the pill became available in Great Britain, and suddenly the way filmmakers could portray sex changed.

Dr. No was one of the first films to fully embrace sex as a libidinous sport. Bond checks his watch as he calculates his time with Sylvia Trench. He callously pleasures himself with Miss Taro, knowing she has set him up to be killed, and knowing that she must keep him at her house at all costs. Bond does not take advantage of Honey Ryder, and obviously feels quite protective of her, but when they slide down into the boat together at the end of the movie, the implication cannot be clearer, and no one expects Honey to show up in the next film, either. Both will move on, and that, too, is OK.

Bond, who had notoriously enjoyed the company of one woman per novel (with a few notable exceptions), would now become a three-woman-per-film secret agent. 007 represented the "live for today, for tomorrow I might be gone" ethos of the nuclear age. The Bond Women, while easily seduced, were also happy seducers, taking full advantage of the new freedom of the sexual revolution.

In Chicago, Illinois, Hugh Hefner had been preaching the virtues of sexual freedom since the birth of James Bond - the first issue of *Playboy* was published in the same year as CASINO ROYALE. By 1962, the magazine was selling over a million copies a month, and Bond dovetailed precisely with Hefner's vision of the sexually liberated man. Bond was modern, stylish, well-read, well-mannered, but a rebel. He enjoyed himself in all circumstances. Hefner's monthly guidebook to sophisticated sexual indulgence, which included fiction by top authors, fashion spreads, and detailed features on cars, bachelor pad decor, food and drink, primed the audience for a character like 007 and a woman like Ursula Andress.

Make no mistake, the filmmakers knew what they had. United Artists and Eon Productions (the company formed by Broccoli and Saltzman to produce the Bond films) flew in influential journalists to watch filming in Jamaica, treating the likes of Halsey Raines of *The New York Times* to a pleasant day watching Ursula Andress dash around. They also brought in special photographers, including pin-up photographer Bunny Yeager, to shoot material on Andress. They predicted she would be big, and she was.

Following her appearance in *Dr. No*, fashion designers rushed white bikinis onto the market. Elvis wanted Andress for his next film (*Fun In Acapulco*). The white bikini became a ubiquitous symbol of self-assured sexiness. *Playboy* featured Cynthia Maddox in a white two-piece on its July 1964 cover, and knock-offs appeared in countless spy films of the era. The 1967 Bond film *You Only Live Twice* even featured a bevy of Japanese beauties in similar outfits. By the 1990s, Andress's look was considered classic, showing up in fashion spreads, and as a pop cultural reference in films like *Spice World* and *Austin Powers: The Spy Who Shagged Me*.

After *Dr No*. wrapped, Ursula Andress kept the famous white bikini. By 1999, she was fielding calls from Christie's in London, who wanted her to put it up for auction. On Valentine's Day 2001, she did. Amid a flurry of press, Ursula Andress's custom-made white bikini was sold for £41,125 to Planet Hollywood owner Robert Earl. James Bond's sexual magnetism was perfectly modulated for the early 60s. 007's appeal was part John F. Kennedy (**far right, middle**), and part Hugh Hefner (**far right, bottom**), so it is no surprise that both men were fans of Ian Fleming's fictional spy. Hefner's *Playboy* magazine began a long association with James Bond when Ian Fleming's 007 short story, 'The Hildebrand Rarity', appeared in the March 1960 issue.

"What my life was all about, in the Playboy mansion, was connected to James Bond. At one point I said, 'We both love the gadgets, we both love the girls. He's the only one that has the licence to kill. But I have a better licence.'" Hugh Hefner

While the filmmakers raised the level of sex, the grand scale of Fleming's supervillains caused the writers some consternation. Cinematically, as screenwriters Maibaum and Mankowitz discovered, it was hard to pull off an evil genius with a straight face, particularly one like Dr. No. Why does SPECTRE build his headquarters beneath the island Crab Key? So he can send American missile launches awry. And why does SPECTRE want to disturb those launches? Dr. No's simple reply: "Missiles are only the first step to prove our power". That sums up Dr. No's *raison d'être*. He does evil to prove he is capable of doing evil.

What makes Dr. No and all the Fleming villains so rich is their mythic stature. Dr. No is a real dragon (compared to the mechanical dragon he sends after Bond) with deadly claws (metal hands in the movie). Terence Young seemed to understand that the less real Dr. No seemed, the more evil he would appear to be. He barely turns his head, focuses his eyes beyond those to whom he speaks, and never blinks. Ultimately, he is so creepy and soulless that we don't care what Dr. No is trying to do or why. We understand the battle will be between Bond - and the hedonistic values he represents - and Dr. No's special brand of obedience and acquiescence through terror.

To play the half-German, half-Chinese Dr. No, filmmakers chose New York stage actor Joseph Wiseman, who had made something of a career out of playing villains. Wiseman was outfitted in a Mao Tse Tung-style jacket and pants set, which would become (after future Bond villain Ernst Stavro Blofeld was similarly turned out in three films) somewhat of a trademark costume, widely parodied over the years.

To balance the absurdity of Dr. No and the minion-assassins who do his bidding, the filmmakers wisely relied on humour or, more precisely, quips. Writers Johanna Harwood and Berkely Mather had both taken cracks at the script, and the final draft included many one-liners which would go on to define Bond and the entire action-hero genre he would inspire. The first *bon mot* delivered by 007 occurs after Mister Jones, an agent working for Dr. No, bites into a cyanide cigarette rather than subject himself to an interrogation by James Bond. Bond drives up to Government House in Jamaica and tells the guard, "Sergeant, make sure he doesn't get away".

This cool attitude in the face of death marked a key difference between the Bond of the printed page and the character on the silver screen. The literary Bond certainly

keeps his composure under pressure, but he never treats death or killing lightly. The cinematic Bond does. The humour of the films matched the panache of Fleming's effortless writing style, and it kept the audience from making moral judgments or asking too many questions about the action.

More importantly, it gave a voice to a new kind of masculine ideal, an unshakable sense of identity and purpose that regretted almost nothing. The Bond quips reflected a black humour and an irreverent arrogance which Connery wore well. While some of the *noir* films of the 1940s and 50s had similar cracks, none had the cavalier wit of the few choice lines in *Dr. No*. Terence Young and Sean Connery agreed early on that this element was vital, and at times they would challenge each other to come up with an appropriate line on the set.

One scene, however, which lacked humour was the death of Professor Dent. This single moment defined 007 as a very different kind of hero. The timbre of the scene - where Bond shoots Dent, who is armed only with an empty pistol, and then proceeds to pump more bullets into his back - made everyone nervous from the start. The shooting script contains three versions, but none include the extra bullets in the back.

Terence Young thought the scene, which does not appear in the novel, was necessary. Bond was a professional killer for the British Government. The double-O prefix, Bond's licence to kill, would be a key - if not the key - element of the character. Young felt it had to be seen on-screen. It proved to be a shocking moment, but it gave Bond's licence to kill real meaning, and it set 007 apart from every screen hero who had come before.

As the film neared completion, there were still many who doubted that the filmmakers had successfully translated Bond to the screen. They just didn't get it. The filmmakers had made every effort to define the tone and character for an audience, but with the film already shot and nearly completed, only one part of *Dr. No* remained to be finished: the titles.

When Harry Saltzman and Cubby Broccoli attended the premiere of Stanley Donen's 1960 comedy of manners, *The Grass Is Greener*, they noted how the audience was immediately put into the right mood of playful humour by the imaginative title sequence, which used babies on a lawn to represent the film's actors and creative talent. The pair quickly approached the title designer and asked if he would like to create the credits for the first James Bond adventure. Thus, Maurice Binder began an association that would endure for nearly three decades and have a lasting impact on cinema and pop art.

The opening gunbarrel became a signature device, instantly identifying each film as part of a series and drawing audiences, through the vortex of the barrel's rifling, into Bond's dangerous world. It employed a camera sighted down the barrel of a gun, which initially caused some problems. Unable to stop down the lens of a standard camera enough to bring the entire gunbarrel into focus, Binder created a pinhole camera to solve the problem. Suddenly, the barrel became crystal clear, as did one of the most arresting and graphically compelling images ever created for film.

The first cinematic 007 villain, Dr. No, was portrayed by Joseph Wiseman (**opposite, top**), a respected stage actor who had made his mark in films such as *Detective Story* and *Viva Zapata!* "I had no idea what I was letting myself in for," Wiseman said many years later. "I had no idea [Dr. No] would achieve the success it did... As far as I was concerned, I thought it might be just another Grade-B Charlie Chan mystery."

Left: Art director Syd Cain had the unenviable job of creating Dr. No's dragon in the swamps of Jamaica. The vehicle often sank and got stuck in the mud, forcing Cain to wallow in the mire. So much for the glamour of Bond.

"World domination. Same old dream."

James Bond to Dr. No

HARRY SALTZMAN & ALBERT R. BROCCOLI present

NOW meet the most extraordinary gentleman spy in all fiction!... JAMES BOND, Agent 007!*

Above, top: United Artists was eager to promote James Bond as a hero for the space age. On 15th May 1963, Major Gordon Cooper blasted off aboard Mercury 9, orbiting the earth 22 times. A clever publicist set up this shot during Cooper's parade in Manhattan, a few days before *Dr. No*'s Memorial Day opening in New York.

Above: The first piece of James Bond merchandise: the adaptation of *Dr. No* was originally drawn for the *Classics Illustrated* series before the company suspended publishing. DC Comics, publishers of *Superman* and *Batman*, printed the story in *Showcase Comics* #43, March/April 1963. The comic was also printed in England as part of the *British Classics Illustrated* series (#158A), as well as Greek and Swedish editions, and in *European Detective* (#6). The DC Comics version was censored; language that was thought to be racially demeaning was omitted, as was all racial skin colour. Bond would not appear in comic book form again in the US until 1981, with the Marvel Comics adaptation of *For Your Eyes Only*.

Binder's titles, like the films themselves, were marked by elegance, wit and sex. His use of rich colour and nude female silhouettes quickly became a celebrated design motif, imitated but never equalled. Philip Dodd, Director of the Institute of Contemporary Arts in London, believes Maurice Binder was an epic artist. "I once gave a lecture on Maurice to the most important set of craft and design people in Britain," Dodd said, "who are used to looking at William Morris chairs or beautiful Lucie Rie vases. I showed them Maurice's title sequences, and these people were absolutely bowled over by this material, because the title sequences were elegant, eloquent. They recognized he was one of the great designers, working on a scale that makes the small chair or the small vase simply look like an echo."

Britain first formally met the cinematic James Bond on 5th October 1962, at a lavish premiere staged at the London Pavilion Cinema. Ian Fleming attended, as did friends such as W. Somerset Maugham. J. Paul Getty, then the richest man in the world, came, and so did many luminaries in the British film industry. The audience loved the film, but the critics were mixed. Some did not even think Ursula Andress was particularly attractive. Others winced at the sardonic humour. While many praised the film as a wonderful thriller, there were a few notable voices of outrage. Richard Whitehall thought *Dr. No* was possibly paving the way for "a fascist cinema", but commenting on the bullet Bond puts into the back of Professor Dent, Whitehall rightly observed, "The British cinema will never be the same again."

Dr. No was an immediate hit in the UK, so much so that *Time* magazine in the US saw fit to review the film in mid-October 1962, months before any anticipated release in America. The review hit the stands just days before the Cuban Missile Crisis erupted. That the tensest moment in the Cold War occurred just as James Bond was having his first cinematic success was a coincidence which was not the subject of much written comment at the time. Here was a film featuring a Caribbean plot involving missiles, and in real life the world stood on the brink of nuclear war over missiles in the Caribbean. The similarities really ended there, but the atmosphere of fear over further Communist influence in the Caribbean was very real, and so was the worry about Western prestige, with failures happening in the US space programme.

Terence Young stated that he felt *Dr. No* was released on exactly the right week of the right month of the right year. It is true that James Bond appeared when the world needed him, but the relationship was and still is symbiotic.

Bond existed because it was the right time for him. It was an era when society was redefining itself, and Bond's character had grown into a personification of a certain part of that change. It may have been luck that the missile crisis brought attention to the Caribbean, and again focused the West on the need for spies to stop global threats. But it was not luck that Bond reflected the style and élan the West wanted to embody in the autumn of 1962.

There was a reason America had a young, vibrant and virile President who seemed to break the mould of stodgy, old leaders. There was a reason that Britain's Labour Party, in February 1963, selected the 46-year-old Harold Wilson - at the time the youngest party leader ever - to challenge the Conservatives. The public wanted youth, vigour, heroism, panache and sexual freedom. The signs - such as the growth of *Playboy* magazine, the election of Kennedy, and the introduction of the birth control pill - were all there. The political climate, with daily tales of espionage which had been mounting for over 16 years, could not have been clearer. The choice to make a Bond film and to portray Bond in this particular way was a blend of good judgement, vision and talent on the part of the filmmakers.

Dr. No went on to make back its entire negative cost through UK ticket sales alone. It became the second-highest grossing British film of 1962 in England. Shortly thereafter, the film began to play in Europe where the numbers were also huge. Some at UA were still sceptical. Would American audiences care for a hero in a Savile Row suit? Or would they be put off by a hero who is so elitist as to prefer the 1953 Dom Perignon to the '55 and who appears to be able to tell the difference between a shaken martini and one which is only stirred? Marketing could not be blamed for their scepticism. American audiences historically preferred heroes who lacked pretension - the John Wayne homespun types.

Broccoli and Saltzman wanted a quick release and were disturbed when it was not forthcoming. Those at UA had a different plan. They started limited screenings in the US in March 1963, trying to build word-of-mouth in influential circles. In Hollywood, UA hosted a screening, with a dinner at Chasen's in Sean Connery's honour. The idea was to promote him as a star, much the same way as David Lean and Columbia had done with Peter O'Toole. The event did not make much of an impact, other than generating uniformly good reviews in movie industry magazines.

Some at UA still thought the film would only play 'on the coasts' in New York, Boston, San Francisco and Los Angeles. Others thought the movie had too much hokum to play even those markets. For them, Bond was the wrong combination of ersatz sophistication and B-film thrills. The decision, announced in late March, was to dump the film in early May to movie theatres and drive-ins in the South and Southwest. UA offered the film on 'good terms', meaning the theatres got to keep a higher percentage of the ticket price. Theatre owners, spurred by the good reviews in the trades, snapped up the film, and 450 screens were quickly booked.

As the initial reaction from screenings trickled back to UA, and the rage from Broccoli and Saltzman mounted (they didn't want the film buried on the drive-in circuit), UA realized they had a potential US hit on their hands.

The immediate impact of *Dr. No* was to spur sales of Fleming's books (between 1961 and 1962 sales in the UK doubled from 670,000 paperbacks to 1.3 million), and to whet the audience's appetite for more. "There is every reason to suppose and expect... the producers have here the first of what very well could be the most successful series of films of its kind since the happy days of the Charlie Chan and Thin Man films," gushed *Product Digest*. *Cue* magazine called it "pure, unadulterated entertainment". Bosley Crowther of *The New York Times* cheerfully called *Dr. No* "escapist bunk", and *The New Yorker* called it a "trashy success".

The more respected critics obviously enjoyed themselves, but were a little embarrassed to admit they were proud of their reaction. No one seemed to foresee much in the way of cultural impact, or even to identify *Dr. No* as something new. Just as the British critics did, the Americans seemed to want to define Bond by what had come before: Mickey Spillane, Charlie Chan and Saturday serials.

All the aspects of the film which are so memorable were noted - Connery's performance ("On the strength of his triumph here... he could go on starring in Fleming decalcomanias until his legs give out"- *The New Yorker*); Ursula Andress's sex appeal (she "fills a wet bikini as if she were going downwind behind twin spinnakers" - *Time*); Bond's character ("hardhitting, imperturbable, girl-loving" - *Variety*); and the production values ("a thriller with style, freshness and imagination" - *The Film Daily*).

Critics could not be expected to see the future, but in the US they were made well aware that James Bond was here to stay. By the time that *Dr. No* was released, *From Russia With Love* was already shooting in England.

Left: United Artists hired graphic artist Mitchell Hooks to design the poster art for *Dr. No*. Hooks recalled, "Nobody knew what to do. I played around with Bond with various scenes in the movie, and I remember trying to incorporate the famous dry martini that James Bond was fond of, and we came up cold. I remember going back for a second effort. And I came up with the image of him with a gun. That came from that shot of Ian Fleming on his Bond books. He was posed holding a pistol in his hands. That was the inspiration for Bond holding a pistol in a kind of casual, debonair way; that went over good, along with the four voluptuous women standing next to him. And that was it." Every 007 movie poster since has shown Bond with gun in hand.

From Russia With Love should have been an easy film to make, but it was not. After finding one of the most beautiful women in the world to play Honey Ryder, Broccoli, Saltzman and Young searched the planet for the right combination of Slavic looks and international beauty to portray Tatiana Romanova, the Russian cipher clerk sent to seduce James Bond into a deadly trap. The filmmaking team interviewed over 200 actresses, even allowing reporter Donald Zec to sit in on casting sessions. Press releases hit hundreds of newsrooms in Europe and America at the end of February 1963, announcing the search for "a voluptuous, young Greta Garbo". The producers soon found Daniela Bianchi, a gloriously beautiful Italian model with the perfect delicate strength needed for the role.

It was still two months before *Dr. No* would open on the drive-in circuit in America, and the film was just opening in many international territories. Based on the grosses in England, France and Germany, UA agreed to double the budget for the second Bond film. Even if they never sold a ticket, the film would have been paid for out of the profits from *Dr. No* alone.

The troubled production faced numerous hurdles. Location work in Istanbul proved to be a nightmare. The boats for the big finale at sea did not run properly and the scene had to be re-shot in Scotland. On that location, a helicopter crashed with director Terence Young inside, and early one morning Daniela Bianchi's car veered off the road, crashing in a ditch and bruising her face. Although the script underwent numerous re-writes throughout the filming, the end result was nonetheless beautifully crafted. Early on, Harry Saltzman brought in Len Deighton, but the finished screenplay reflected the work of Richard Maibaum and Johanna Harwood (credited with the adaptation). While *Dr. No* had almost a science fiction element, *From Russia With Love* was much more a traditional spy film, where the motives of characters are not always obvious, and where Bond seems not to have a clear sense of what is really going on for much of the story.

Since *Russia* would not have a giant villain's lair or a grand nuclear reactor control room as in *Dr. No*, the writers looked for other elements to add a sense of ingenuity and spectacle. They chose two areas which would become part of the recipe for Bond's success: gadgets and action.

Bond's briefcase from Q Branch appears in the novel FROM RUSSIA WITH LOVE. Fleming included gold sovereigns, two throwing knives, a silencer hidden in a tube of shaving cream, a cyanide tablet concealed in the handle, and fifty rounds of .25 ammunition. In the movie, Q, played by actor Desmond Llewelyn for the first time, presents the briefcase to Bond with military precision. The ammunition has been reduced, the cyanide is gone, and now there is only one knife concealed, but the film version is still decidedly

deadlier. Bond has a folding sniper's rifle resting snugly inside and a tin of talc which will explode with tear gas if the case is not opened just the right way. Bond comments that it is "a nasty little Christmas present". In fact, it is the first James Bond film gadget.

From Russia With Love is filled with gadgets, from Red Grant's garrotte-wire watch to Rosa Klebb's poison-tipped spiked shoe, from Kerim Bey's periscope beneath the Russian Embassy to the bugging detection device Bond uses in Istanbul. The whole plot revolves around the British desire to steal the Lektor decoder, a gadget itself. The lethal nature of these ordinary-appearing items would become a hallmark of the Bond films, but 007's bag of tricks in *From Russia With Love* barely compares with the real world of espionage equipment.

The briefcase was an inspired invention, one which had its roots in the British Intelligence devices of the Second World War, when playing cards sent to prisoners in German stalags could be taken apart to disclose hidden maps, or blankets could be rubbed with a damp cloth to reveal patterns for civilian suits to aid in escape attempts. A vital element of these devices was their 'not just any' aspect. Bond's automobile in *Goldfinger* is not just any car, but a gadget-laden hand-built Aston Martin. His camera in *Thunderball* is not just any camera, but one that conceals a Geiger counter. His cigarettes in *You Only Live Twice* are not just any smokes, but ones that shoot out tiny jet-propelled missiles.

Such gadgetry was not simply the province of fiction. In the late 1950s, on two separate occasions, KGB agent Bodgan Stashinsky walked up to Ukrainian nationalists while holding a newspaper. Both men quickly dropped dead. Of course, Stashinsky was not holding just any newspaper. This one concealed a device which fired nerve gas into the face of its victims. In 1961, Stashinsky defected to the West and confessed his crimes.

The Soviets developed many gas and acid-firing devices, including canes, cigarette packs, even a wallet. Nerve gas, cyanide and acid were preferred methods of murder for intelligence services because the cause of death was often hard to pinpoint. Miniature guns have been even more popular, if not messier, since long before

"The Russians had seen the James Bond films. They were saying, 'Look at their technology...' I had lists and lists of the most sophisticated technological things the KGB was trying to steal." Oleg Gordievsky, former KGB agent

the Cold War. Pipes, mechanical pencils, lipstick applicators and decks of cards have all hidden single-shot weapons over the years.

Most real-life spy gadgetry has to do with concealment (hidden cameras) and eavesdropping (electronic bugging). A museum in Seoul, South Korea, at the headquarters of the country's National Intelligence Service, displays items used against them by the North Koreans, including a fountain pen that can shoot a needle at a victim with a twist of the cap and poison-coated lipstick that a female agent could apply to kill herself if captured.

While Bond's gadgets, and those used by his adversaries, were nothing new, the way the filmmakers chose to present them was groundbreaking. There was an immediate sexiness to the lethal aspect of these devices. Bond never takes the items too seriously, and, at its best, the gadgetry is employed in unexpected ways. The growth of the use of gadgets in the 007 films mirrored society's own enjoyment of miniaturization and technology. Ultimately, *From Russia With Love* is a film that somehow harks back to the past with the long train ride on the Orient Express and Bond's mechanical (as opposed to electronic) gadgets. This would soon change, but the connection between 007 and gadgets would not.

By the end of 1963, when the names James Bond and Ian Fleming seemed to be ubiquitous, Fleming's wife Ann nicknamed him 'Thunderbeatle', the fifth Beatle, as wealthy and famous as the four lads from Liverpool. That year he travelled to Istanbul to watch location filming of *From Russia With Love* **(above)**. In his autobiography, Cubby Broccoli wrote that when Fleming was in London, he revealed very little of himself, but in Istanbul, he was in his element. "He loved the sounds, the spicy smells, the bazaars, the street merchants and the belly dancers," wrote Broccoli. "Especially the belly dancers." One evening, when a gyrating dancer in a Turkish nightclub knocked the ash off the end of Fleming's cigarette, he remarked that after years of observation, he had determined that the buttocks, not the breasts, were the most appealing feature of a woman's anatomy.

"It was my ambition to always keep the whole thing moving as fast as I could. Everything in my mind was to make it interesting, to make it go. The character of James Bond had to be decisive. He couldn't be ponderous."

Peter Hunt

The car phone (**above**) was a seldom-seen gadget in 1963, although espionage author Len Deighton (who contributed to an early draft of *From Russia With Love*) had one installed in his VW Beetle. Bond's briefcase, which contained a sniper's rifle and exploding talc, set the stage for outlandish gadgets to come.

The fight on the Orient Express (**below**) between James Bond (Sean Connery) and Red Grant (Robert Shaw) became the standard against which future 007 fight scenes would be judged. None ever matched the raw brutality of the *From Russia With Love* fight, which was aided considerably by Peter Hunt's masterful editing.

While *Dr. No* offered a few brief fist fights and a car chase, *From Russia With Love* overflowed with action. The film featured a massive *mano a mano* battle between Bond and SPECTRE killer Red Grant, a daring raid on the Soviet Embassy in Istanbul, a blazing gun fight at a gypsy encampment, a violent death-match between two gypsy women, a truck-helicopter chase, and a boat chase which ends with massive explosions.

The finished product was exhilarating. No film outside of a war movie had tried to tie so much action together, and war movies lacked the sense of fun that *From Russia With Love* offered. Connery's physical size, sense of confidence and agility made him the perfect protagonist. The film launched a tradition of action and amazing stunts in the Bond movies that has resonated far beyond the 007 films to become its own cinematic genre.

After *From Russia With Love*, no Bond film would be complete without the spectacle and scope first seen here. The problem with action films in the early 1960s was that spectacle and scope generally slowed a film down. One man in particular was determined not to let that happen to 007: editor Peter Hunt.

Editing the 1956 film *A Hill In Korea*, Hunt first discovered the power of cutting a film to enhance the drama. "I had a trench with about six soldiers all drinking coffee and smoking cigarettes," he said, "and the continuity on that was impossible, because every close-up or every medium shot or wherever I wanted to cut on that, somebody was doing something different with their cigarette and drinking their coffee. It drove me mad... so I just abandoned that whole thing and said, 'This is nonsense. The scene has to be cut to the timing of the dialogue.' And I just cut it for that."

Working with Terence Young on *Dr. No*, Hunt developed a fast-paced, hard-charging style of editing that gave the Bond films a heightened, electric sense of urgency. When Bond tosses Mr. Jones out of the car, Hunt cuts across the action, making it look like Bond has hurled Jones down with tremendous force. When Bond flips Jones through the air, Hunt cuts back to reveal 007 already wiping his hands on his handkerchief. Moments later, Bond pulls back his right fist to deliver a blow, but connects with a hard left. The moment is cut so fast one has no time to notice, but the discontinuity makes the viewer feel the action. This early scene was just a precursor of things to come.

In *From Russia With Love*, during the gypsy camp fight, Hunt ellipses past all the mechanics of the battle, and focuses solely on the chaos of the action, bringing the viewer inside the experience. On the Orient Express, much of the fight was shot with multiple cameras, one of which was hand-held. Hunt cuts back and forth between the angles rapidly, emphasizing the violence. At the end, he uses a series of cuts to make it seem that Bond has rapidly twisted Red Grant's garrotte wire around Grant's own neck - an action never fully seen onscreen. During the helicopter chase - a scene clearly inspired by Hitchcock's *North By Northwest* - Hunt cuts out the lengthy time it takes the helicopter to turn around, creating a sense of relentless threat far different from Hitchcock's. Hitchcock combined fast cuts with the precision of a classical composer, creating each shot for a specific purpose. Hunt cut on internal rhythms, constructing a scene as if he were a jazz musician. The result changed the way we watch movies, and Hunt's editing style would forever alter the way editors cut action. Peter Hunt's style was new, bold, accessible (unlike the cutting seen in Godard films) and immensely entertaining. Quite simply, he brought the Bond films into the avant garde.

Peter Hunt's problem on *From Russia With Love* was not just continuity or pacing. It was plot. The script changes during shooting had made some earlier scenes somewhat obsolete and others almost nonsensical. Hunt worked closely with Terence Young to shape the film and give it a driving through-line. Hunt and Young re-ordered scenes, and even decided that by using Maurice Binder's gunbarrel graphic they could place one scene before the titles.

Dr. No also had a teaser sequence - the death of Strangways - which occurs just after the titles. *From Russia With Love,* though, had a more elaborate scene which Harry Saltzman dreamed up. Saltzman wanted the film to open with the death of James Bond. His concept was to startle the viewer, immediately destroying any sense of predictability. Sure, the public would come to the movie pretty much knowing Bond would defeat the villain, get the girl and stop the evil plot - the question was, how to best catch them off-guard? Saltzman's desire to twist expectations led to most of the early 'things are not what they seem' opening sequences. In four opening scenes produced while Saltzman was still Cubby Broccoli's partner, it is implied Bond is dead at the opening of the film. Apart from *From Russia With Love,* *Thunderball* opens with a shroud-draped casket which features the initials 'JB'. *You Only Live Twice* shows Bond shot in bed. *The Man With The Golden Gun* has Scaramanga shoot a James Bond mannequin.

While the opening scene in *From Russia With Love* was not the elaborate mini-movie which would come later, it was an immediate favourite with audiences, and it again refined the recipe for the Bond films.

When United Artists released *Dr. No* in the UK, they also released John Barry's recording of Monty Norman's 'The James Bond Theme'. The song quickly became a notable instrumental hit on the British charts (breaking into the Top Ten on one list, and charting for over two months). Barry's orchestration seemed to reflect perfectly the sexual energy, dark inner-nature and moral certainty of James Bond. Broccoli, Saltzman, Terence Young and UA decided Barry should score the next Bond film. While Barry did not write the title song (that being left to Lionel Bart, composer of the hit musical *Oliver!*), his sound permeates *From Russia With Love,* and came to define a key element of the James Bond phenomenon.

"Nobody ever cut films as we did the Bond pictures. *Dr. No* and *From Russia With Love* brought a breath of fresh air into the cutting rooms. Even David Lean, who is one of the greatest cutters of all time, has admitted it."

Terence Young

RUSSIA WITH LOVE"

MORZENY — "AHOY MR BOND!"

BOND FIRES

SHATTERS SEARCHLIGHT

MORZENY FIRES

BOND PULLS TATIANA DOWN AS
BULLETS SPRAY THE DECK

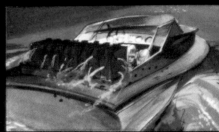

AND PIERCE PETROL CANS

MORE FIRING

C/U PETROL SPILLING

BOND — "TANIA! TAKE THE WHEEL"

BOND STARTS THROWING CANS

CUT TO SPECTRE BOATS

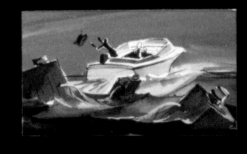

THE LAST OF THE PETROL CANS

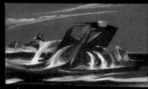

C/U FLOATING CANS

BOND LOOKS DOWN

KNEELS AND OPENS CHEST

FIRES OVER STERN

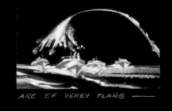

ARC OF VEREY FLARE

"The wardrobe was simple: a shirt, a jacket, very simple things. You can see now that the fashion is a bit dated. Most of all, my hairstyle in the final scene. It's like a cake on my head: it was horrible then and it's horrible now!"

DANIELA BIANCHI

In the summer of 1963, while Peter Hunt was editing, Terence Young was shooting and John Barry was composing, one might have been excused for thinking the Cold War was thawing. Certainly there was fallout from the Cuban Missile Crisis (MiGs firing near US shrimp boats), but there were also breakthroughs. In April, the US and USSR agreed to install a 'hotline' between the two leaders so they could directly communicate, and hopefully avoid any similar crisis in the future. On 11th May, the Soviets caused an uproar when they sentenced two spies - one a British citizen - but it was only the Soviet citizen who received the death penalty.

Then, in June, all hell broke loose in England. Secretary of War John Profumo resigned after it was revealed he was having an affair with a 21-year-old, Christine Keeler. Keeler, accused of being a call girl (which she has long denied), was also having an affair with a Soviet Naval Officer. Under the direction of Dr. Stephen Ward, Keeler had been asked to solicit and pass on information from Profumo to the Soviets. The British government had been compromised and humiliated at the highest levels by a pretty girl. By the end of July, a jury convicted Ward of running a prostitution ring, and espionage charges seemed likely to follow. Ward, coincidentally a fan of the Bond novels, committed suicide shortly thereafter.

At the beginning of July, Britain faced another global humiliation. Kim Philby, former SIS agent, had disappeared in January from his post as a Beirut correspondent for the London *Observer*. He had been booted out of MI6 in 1955, but only now, eight years later, could the government prove that Philby was the third man in the Cambridge spy ring.

Daniela Bianchi (**left**) was a Valentino model in Rome before representing Italy in the 1960 Miss Universe contest, where she won the title 'Miss Photogenic'. When Terence Young saw a picture of her, he invited her to London to screen test for *From Russia With Love*.

Above, top: Mandy Rice-Davies and Christine Keeler at the height of the Profumo scandal.

Above, bottom: The Camelot era came to a tragic end when Lee Harvey Oswald assassinated John F. Kennedy on 22nd November 1963.

To top it off, on the morning of 8th August, twelve bandits robbed a train of over £2.6 million in cash and loot. Sex, spies, trains, and master criminals - the headlines sounded like the ingredients for a hit film. They were.

Everyone anticipated that *From Russia With Love* would be a success. Even before the film's completion, the J. Arthur Rank organization booked it into its best cinemas with a guaranteed three-week run. The film premiered on 10th October 1963 at the Odeon Leicester Square, the largest and most luxurious cinema in the UK. By the end of the first week, *From Russia With Love* had broken the house record, clocking up £14,528 ($40,678) in ticket sales, virtually selling out every seat for every show.

The results were the same throughout Britain; *From Russia With Love* set record after record. It did not really matter what the critics said, the public had decided they wanted James Bond, and *From Russia With Love*'s first week was the biggest opening for any film in British history. This would prove only a harbinger of things to come, because the film kept making money at an astronomical rate. Soon, the film was heralded as "the most successful film ever released in Britain in any year", pulling in over £800,000 ($2.25 million) by late January 1964.

Sales of the novels in UK paperback editions more than tripled in 1963 to 4.4 million. In hardback, the latest novel, ON HER MAJESTY'S SECRET SERVICE, sold 75,000 copies before Christmas. Ian Fleming posed for Helmut Newton in the French magazine *Adam* for a feature detailing the look of Bond (Fleming acted as M). The *From Russia With Love* soundtrack sold in massive numbers and the title song became a hit in Britain.

On 20th November 1963, Ian Fleming was in court, and Harry Saltzman and Cubby Broccoli were watching very closely. Kevin McClory's lawsuit over the rights to *Thunderball* had finally come to trial. No longer was James Bond's cinematic success a theoretical concept. Bond was the most successful character in British films, ever. Within two weeks, Ivar Bryce - the man who was paying the bills - and Ian Fleming agreed to settle, granting Kevin McClory the screen rights to *Thunderball*. Just as James Bond was gaining unprecedented success, Broccoli and Saltzman were finding that they had no monopoly on secret agent 007.

Five days after *From Russia With Love*'s London premiere, an American James Bond fan applied for a job as a clerk filling book orders in Dallas, Texas. The fan was a bit of an odd fish. He had defected to Russia in 1959 and repatriated to the US in June of 1962. He had recently been arrested in New Orleans, handing out pamphlets for an organization called 'Fair Play For Cuba'. His name was Lee Harvey Oswald.

In America, a few advance prints of *From Russia With Love* were circulating. In November 1963, one of them was screened at the White House for John F. Kennedy. On 22nd November these two Bond aficionados would find their fates forever linked. As Kennedy's motorcade passed within a few hundred feet of Oswald's perch in Dealey Plaza in Dallas, Oswald fired three shots, two of which hit Kennedy, the second one fatally

wounding him. In the flurry of press speculation after the assassination, reports surfaced that both men had been reading Bond novels the night before the President was killed.

America went into shock, and then mourning, over the loss. For entertainment, they turned to the British. Less than two months after Kennedy's death, the Beatles appeared on the US charts with 'I Want To Hold Your Hand'. In February, the Fab Four appeared on *The Ed Sullivan Show*, and ignited a love affair for all things British among millions of American teenagers.

On 8th April 1964, *From Russia With Love* opened in thirty New York theatres, grossing $460,000 in its first week. By the end of the month, the film had already topped a million dollars in ticket sales at these theatres alone. UA held back the release for the rest of the country until the profitable Memorial Day weekend, but the reviews which poured in were largely ecstatic. The words "hokum" and "escapism" reappear over and over. There seemed to be a fine awareness that Bond, like the Beatles, was an enjoyable fact of life.

UA widely promoted the film, even flying an electric billboard over Los Angeles behind a helicopter, swooping across Dodger Stadium, the Hollywood Bowl and Hollywood Boulevard with a sign that read, 'James Bond Is Back'.

Americans were enjoying Bond. The film grossed $9.4 million in the US, a sizable hit during the summer. Bond was even more popular abroad. Again, France and Germany led the non-English-speaking world in their consumption of 007, but the global figures showed the film making nearly $17 million in international territories outside the US, Canada and Great Britain.

Everyone seemed to understand that this 'James Bond thing' would only get bigger. Ian Fleming could sense it. In Jamaica, the real James Bond (the ornithologist) had stopped by to meet the man who stole his identity, and told Fleming of the grief he had at customs when people thought he was joking about his name. Interview requests piled up.

In the UK, book sales continued to soar. Foreign translations skyrocketed. James Bond was an undeniable phenomenon.

All the cinematic ingredients had been put into place: the right actor, the portrayal of Bond, the sex, the humour, the gadgets, the exotic locations, the lavish sets, the look of the films, the music. Everything was lined up, including hordes of patrons eager to buy tickets. The bullet had been fired into the pond of popular culture. The filmmakers, however, busy making the third Bond adventure with a new director, could not have anticipated quite how far and how wide the ripples would spread.

3. Spymania

The world premiere of *Goldfinger* was held at the Odeon Leicester Square in London on 17th September 1964. Crowds began gathering early in the day. The show outside the cinema did not disappoint. United Artists arranged for the print of *Goldfinger* to be enclosed in golden cans and delivered to the Odeon by four models wearing golden pantsuits. As the 9pm premiere approached, Honor Blackman arrived in a gold and white outfit sporting a £10,000, 22-carat piece of jewellery which ran the length of the little finger on her left hand. It was called 'the goldfinger', and was adorned with a 6.5-carat diamond. The crowd screamed. A handful of police officers struggled to keep the thousands of fans back behind the barricades. A mêlée broke out and the crowd surged forward; one of the policemen lost his footing and crashed through the glass front of the cinema. Honor Blackman said later, "It was the first time I have seen photographers punched by the crowd." Quickly, the police hustled the actress inside. They shut off the lights outside the Odeon and rushed in 70 officers as reinforcements. Inside, the atmosphere was electric. Blackman got a rousing ovation from the packed house. "It was, I think, the most glamorous night of my life," she later recalled. All of this before anyone had seen the film. Welcome to Spymania, circa 1964.

In America and around the world, the dawning of 1964 uncorked a year primed for mania. It was as if all the shock, rage and fear that had consumed society in the weeks that followed John F. Kennedy's assassination needed to be released. Popular culture was changing so rapidly people could be forgiven for losing control. Indeed, Alistair Cooke wrote, "We may now be sliding down a slope into a period of moral anarchy." Yet at the same time there was a feeling, perhaps prompted by the impact of the Beatles' 'global folk music', or Tokyo's hosting of the 1964 Summer Olympics, that the world was moving towards a more universal culture.

James Bond came to represent all the elements of 1964. He was sexual, violent, modern, pushing boundaries at every turn. He was also a symbol of British panache, cultural superiority and Western influence on a global scale. Bond represented an optimistic future and a defeat of totalitarian values. He was an agent of the late President Kennedy's New Frontier, a cosmopolitan figure of the Space Age who maintained a healthy sense of tradition. He was stylish, efficient, good-looking - and most of all, he knew who he was, and was unapologetic about his values. He brought class and elegance to the sexual revolution. He brought moral certainty and a dark wit to the violence of the world, and the world could not get enough of him. In 1964, James Bond became an icon of the baby boomer generation.

With *Goldfinger*, the filmmakers made a conscious effort to produce a James Bond adventure which would be a huge hit in America. With the novels selling like hot cakes around the globe, no one thought about changing the plots: Fleming's formula worked. *Goldfinger*, with locations including Miami and Fort Knox, happened to offer an American canvas for Bond. The first London grosses of *From Russia With Love* were sufficient to convince the studio that *Goldfinger* deserved solid support. By the time *From Russia With Love* opened in the US, *Goldfinger* was well over halfway through shooting, with a budget that was nearly double that of its predecessor.

Why did *Goldfinger* succeed on such a grand scale? The *zeitgeist* was right, but the film has survived the test of time and become a classic, the prototypical 007 film, the model for what audiences expect and want from a James Bond thriller. How did *Goldfinger* strike such a chord, and why has it resonated so long?

The answer comes down to the addition of four new ingredients in the cinematic James Bond recipe: a new director; the establishing of a long-running character; the most famous car in the world; and the most sinister henchman ever created.

That new director brought a host of adjustments to the style of the Bond films, for with *Goldfinger*, James Bond became more sophisticated, more elegant and more refined than any person ever could be, or ever would be. It was the kind of worldly sophistication to be expected of an English director who was born in Paris.

After *From Russia With Love*, Terence Young had declared he wanted to be partners with Cubby Broccoli and Harry Saltzman on future Bond films. His overture was declined, and Young announced he was leaving Bond for good. Broccoli and Saltzman quickly approached Guy Hamilton to direct *Goldfinger*. Unlike Terence Young, Hamilton had not worked previously with Cubby Broccoli on the Warwick films, nor with Harry Saltzman.

Hamilton brought an outsider's view to the Bond phenomenon. He could recognize the ingredients that contributed to 007's success without having invested in their creation, and he had an innate understanding of the comic nature of the Bond adventures. As Hamilton noted, "Using the things that worked so wonderfully well in the two previous films, it was then not too difficult to have a target and know what you were trying to do."

Hamilton wanted to direct a film which celebrated everything audiences loved about Bond, and he did. His sensibilities were absolutely right for the James Bond of the era. He increased the sex quotient. He insisted that Bond be more elegant, the sets bigger, the action more elaborate and the gadgets more deadly. Most of all, he wanted the humour to be more self-aware and self-evident.

Taking a cue from the success of the pre-credits sequence in *From Russia With Love*, Hamilton created a mini-movie at the start of *Goldfinger*. In a few short minutes, Hamilton, the writers and the filmmaking team rolled every key element of the Bond phenomenon into three scenes.

The film opens with a shot of a seagull near a Mexican boat dock (international location). The gull, however, is Bond's elaborate headgear, a disguise for 007's snorkel (gadgets). Bond flings it away, fires a grappling hook over a wall, dispatches a guard (action), and breaks into an opium lab hidden in an oil storage tank (elaborate sets) to plant explosives. After unzipping his waterproof suit to reveal a white dinner jacket, which he complements with a red carnation (elegance), Bond enters a nightclub to watch a tarantella dancer (exotica) as the opium lab explodes. He proceeds to the dancer's dressing room and takes her into an embrace (sex), but as they kiss, he sees the reflection of a Mexican bandit in her eye. Bond whirls her around so that the bandit smashes her with the wooden cosh. Bond and the bandit fight (more action),

1964 was not all doom, gloom, and turpitude. The Beatles took the world by storm, first in Britain, then with shows in France, and in February with their arrival in the US (**top**); thousands swarmed into the Boston Post Office to get first day cancellations on a JFK commemorative stamp. Queen Elizabeth brought Prince Edward into the world, and British military forces leapt into action in a number of hotspots around the globe, such as Cyprus, Zanzibar and South Arabia. The UK forces tended to quash uprisings with speed and caution, which raised British pride. In the US, the Civil Rights Act, signed into law in July 1962, banned discrimination based on race in employment, public accommodation and facilities, union membership and federally funded programmes.

The New York World's Fair (**middle**) promised a brighter future, and President Lyndon B. Johnson promised a short war in Vietnam. There was a feeling that the world was moving toward a more global culture on many fronts. Japan played host to the 1964 Summer Olympics, where the nation impressed the world with clean cities, innovative architecture and bullet trains. *Goldfinger* tapped into this spirit of optimism by presenting a faster-paced, more humorous take on 007.

with 007 dispatching his attacker by tossing him into the bath followed by an electrical heater. "Shocking," says Bond as the bandit sizzles. He looks to the dancer who betrayed him, "Positively shocking" (humour).

Before the opening credits, Guy Hamilton established that he not only understood James Bond, he had mastered the delicate art of creating a pop culture myth. He also transformed Bond's character, blending his sense of elegance into a limitless knowledge of the arcane.

During a dinner, when M asks why Colonel Smithers objects to the brandy, Bond critiques, "I'd say it was a 30-year-old *fine* indifferently blended with an overdose of Bon Bois." Later, while imprisoned by Goldfinger, he mentally works out that it will take 60 men twelve days to load 10,500 tons of gold bullion onto 200 trucks. James Bond had suddenly become the most knowledgeable man on the planet.

This is no longer the detective thriller/Saturday afternoon serial world of *Dr. No*, or the darkly mysterious

one of *From Russia With Love*. It is a world of heightened absurdity, where a man can crush a golf ball with his bare hand, and a lesbian changes her sexual preferences after a (literal) roll in the hay with 007.

Hamilton also transformed one of the re-occurring MI6 characters into an audience favourite. Major Boothroyd, played by actor Peter Burton, first appeared in *Dr. No*. When Burton was unavailable for *From Russia With Love*, director Terence Young called on the Welsh actor Desmond Llewelyn. To cover the change, Llewelyn's character was referred to simply as 'Q', which was British Military Intelligence shorthand for Quartermaster. The introduction of the briefcase in *From Russia With Love* was played straight, but when Llewelyn began his scene with Connery for *Goldfinger*, Hamilton provided a key piece of direction. Llewelyn recalled, "I was working at a desk and Bond came in. I got up to greet him and Guy said, 'No, no, no, you don't take any notice of this man - you don't like him.' I thought, 'Well, but this is Bond, this is James Bond, and I'm just an ordinary civil servant, I must admire him like everybody else does'. And Guy says 'No, no, no, no - of course you don't. He doesn't treat your gadgets with any respect at all.'"

From that point on, the Bond/Q relationship was cemented, based on a conflict of interests. Bond took the role of the irrepressible schoolboy know-it-all, destroying Q's careful work with abandon. Llewelyn's Q was the committed British official who has lost sight of the big picture - a more humorous and affectionate take on Colonel Nicholson, who does not want his bridge blown up by commandos in *The Bridge On The River Kwai*. The reason Q worked so well was the addition of other aspects of his character. Q was the terse technocrat who contemplated imaginative ways to kill with a slightly unsettling, dispassionate glee. In mythical terms, he was The Magician, the figure who provides the hero with objects that possess special powers. As screenwriter Bruce Feirstein succinctly noted in the scene description for Llewelyn's last Bond film, Q is "Merlin to Bond's Arthur".

Even as critics sometimes complained that the technology was taking over the franchise, and even though the nature of the Bond/Q relationship would change over the years, the character of Q quickly permeated popular culture. One reason for this success was the inventive nature of the gadgets he provided to Bond. Key among them is the car which, when it first appears in the *Goldfinger* script, is not even afforded one line of description.

Above: Guy Hamilton was born in 1922, the son of the press attaché to the British Embassy in Paris, where he lived until he was sent to school in England aged nine. He fell in love with movies early on; he claims he was beaten at school when he was asked what he wanted to do and responded that he wanted to be a film director. "In those days... to want to be a film director was like wanting to run a brothel." Returning to France before the war, he spent six months in a Nice film studio learning his trade. Then, after going through the Second World War in the Royal Navy, he came under the tutelage of a prestigious mentor, Carol Reed. For Reed's *The Third Man*, Hamilton doubled Orson Welles (who played Harry Lime) in long shots and for shots of Harry Lime's shadow on walls as he fled the police. He also worked on a film directed by Otto Preminger, and travelled to Africa as part of the crew of John Huston's *The African Queen*. His tent-mate on that shoot was a young Irish crew member named Kevin McClory.

Right: Desmond Llewelyn went on to become a staple of the 007 films, appearing in every title after *Goldfinger* except *Live And Let Die* until his passing in 1999. For *Live And Let Die*, he was unavailable because he was on the road promoting *Diamonds Are Forever* in international territories. He was hopelessly typecast as Q, but relished the acclaim the role provided him, and in turn, audiences revelled in the scenes he had in each Bond adventure. His character was a vital part of Bond's heroic stature.

"I often said when I was director of Central Intelligence that I would be glad to hire several James Bonds."

Allen Dulles

In the novel GOLDFINGER, Ian Fleming had Bond drive a car from the motor pool - a 1957 battleship grey Aston Martin DB Mk III. The car sported "certain extras" such as "switches to alter the type and colour of Bond's front and rear lights if he was following or being followed at night, reinforced steel bumpers, fore and aft, in case he needed to ram, a long-barrelled Colt .45 in a trick compartment under the driver's seat, a radio pick-up tuned to receive an apparatus called the Homer, and plenty of concealed space that would fox most Customs men".

The car-maker was a perfect match for Bond. Aston Martin was the oldest producer of hand-built cars in the world. The cars were both exclusive and exotic: only 411 examples of the DB Mk III were constructed.

The filmmakers transformed Bond's company car in the same way they inflated every aspect of 007's world: it was sexier, more violent and new. Ken Adam chose the latest Aston Martin - the newly released DB5 which had been first exhibited at the Earl's Court Motor Show of 1963 - to replace the Mk III. Adam and special effects wizard John Stears collaborated with the rest of the creative team to build the ultimate wish-fulfilment vehicle. The new car retained the homing device, now complete with radar-style tracking screen, but, in the film, that is where the similarity ended. The DB5 sported rotating licence plates, an oil spray in the rear, a smoke screen, a bullet-proof shield, front-firing machine guns, a tyre scythe inspired by the chariot race from *Ben Hur*, and an ejector seat.

To grasp the cultural impact of the DB5, one needs to understand the omnipresent car culture in Europe and America during the 1950s and 60s. Cars were firmly established as status symbols, calling cards, reputation-makers. While the auto was the most visible external symbol of personality for the American and European middle-classes, it was also a symbol of the pasteurization of Western culture. 82 million autos clogged US roads in 1963 while 'Free World' manufacturers built over sixteen million cars in 1964. In 1963 in the States, one out of seven jobs was directly connected to the automobile industry.

Of all the Bond films, *Goldfinger* is the one most obsessed with the automobile. The film showcased the most popular mass-produced sportscar of 1964, Tilly Masterson's sleek Ford Mustang (**top**), which went on sale in April, selling over 300,000 by the end of the year, and also featured the crushing (along with the body that lay inside) of what was considered the most luxurious American car - a Lincoln Continental. The very act of destroying a car which was so valuable and so sought after in America seemed to mock establishment notions of status. Also notable was Goldfinger's Rolls Royce (**above**), a car that reeked of European old money, and whose peerless reputation is subverted by Goldfinger's use of it to smuggle gold out of England. Each car in the film enhanced and complemented the driver's on-screen image, and immediately telegraphed to the audience an inner knowledge of the character. The car would never be more of an essential part of the global *zeitgeist* than in the mid-1960s, and James Bond's Aston Martin defined the height of elegance, sophistication, humour, style and performance for the era.

The DB5 was able to tap into a love affair with technology, and the growing desire of the baby-boomer generation to exert its individuality and celebrate uniqueness. The Aston Martin both embraced the technological age and mocked it.

In contrast with these numbers, Aston Martin only built 1,023 DB5s from the summer of 1963 until 1965, when they introduced the DB6. At the time of the *Goldfinger* premiere, a factory-built car fetched £4,248, a figure higher than the average annual wage of the British worker, and more expensive than a Cadillac limousine.

Upon the film's release, the Aston Martin DB5 became the instantly tangible symbol of James Bond's personality, virility and values. For those Bond fans well-heeled enough, the car could be purchased (without gadgets). When Paul McCartney saw the film, he immediately bought himself one, telling a writer for *Disc*, "I'm quite a James Bond fan, you know." Rock'n'roll manager Spen Mason took Mick Jagger for a drive in his DB5 just after *Goldfinger* opened, and Graham Nash of the Hollies told Richard Green he was a fan of the film, adding that Bond had "got this car with machine guns and things all over it. Great!" In short, the filmmakers cultivated the image of a car which was so perfectly in tune with the times that it appealed to the trend-setters who, like Bond, would still be informing our notions of popular culture 40 years on.

The car is introduced in Q's lab, surrounded by an array of ordinary items rendered deadly - a tear gas-emitting parking meter, a hand grenade hidden in a thermos, and a bullet-proof rain slicker. The parody, though, had perfect pitch. The car's gadgets were a wink from the filmmakers toward the technology-obsessed times. The viewers could enjoy the joke and the fantasy of the Aston Martin simultaneously.

The DB5's lethal acccutrements made fun of the 'push-button conveniences' on some cars which rarely seemed to work. Classic examples include the Edsel's 'teletouch' steering wheel-mounted transmission, or the Ford Skyliner's hardtop which, at the touch of a button, folded back into the trunk, nearly eliminating any storage space.

As nations grappled with mounting highway accidents (1964 was the first year that front-seat safety-belts were required in American cars), the Aston Martin relished its dangerous image. While films like *Dr. Strangelove* - released just before *Goldfinger* went into production - and *Fail Safe* were openly fearful of the menace of deadly technology (in this case, nuclear weapons), the Aston Martin DB5, like Bond's throw-away lines, embraced the fear, and put the audience in control of it. In Bond's Aston Martin, we were in charge of the world's fate. We were invincible, unassailable.

"In the Fleming Bond novels there was a green label Bentley, and we all thought that was probably too antiquated," said production designer Ken Adam (**below**). "We all felt it would be nice to have the poshest English sports car, which at that time was the Aston Martin."

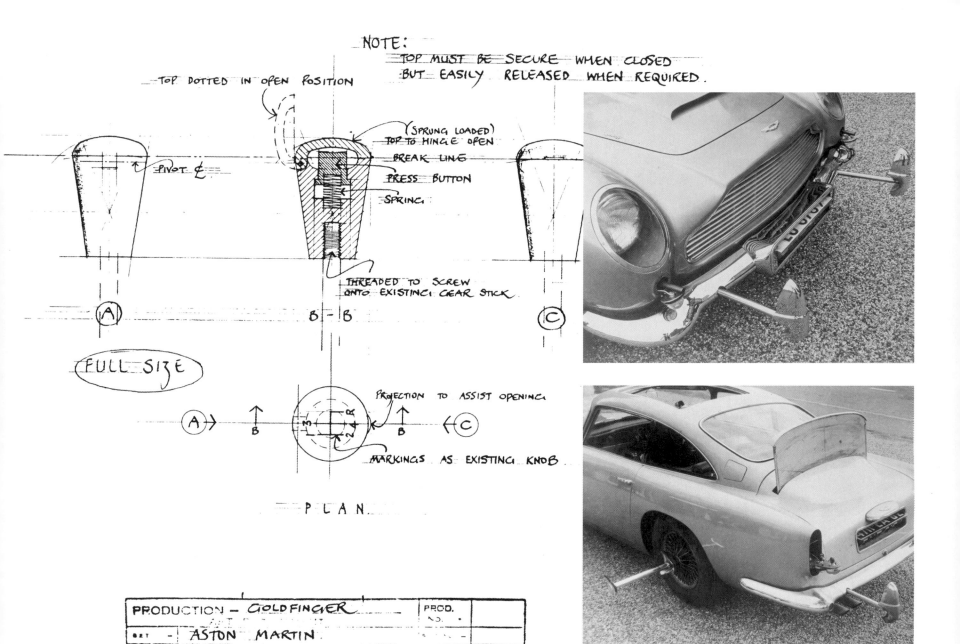
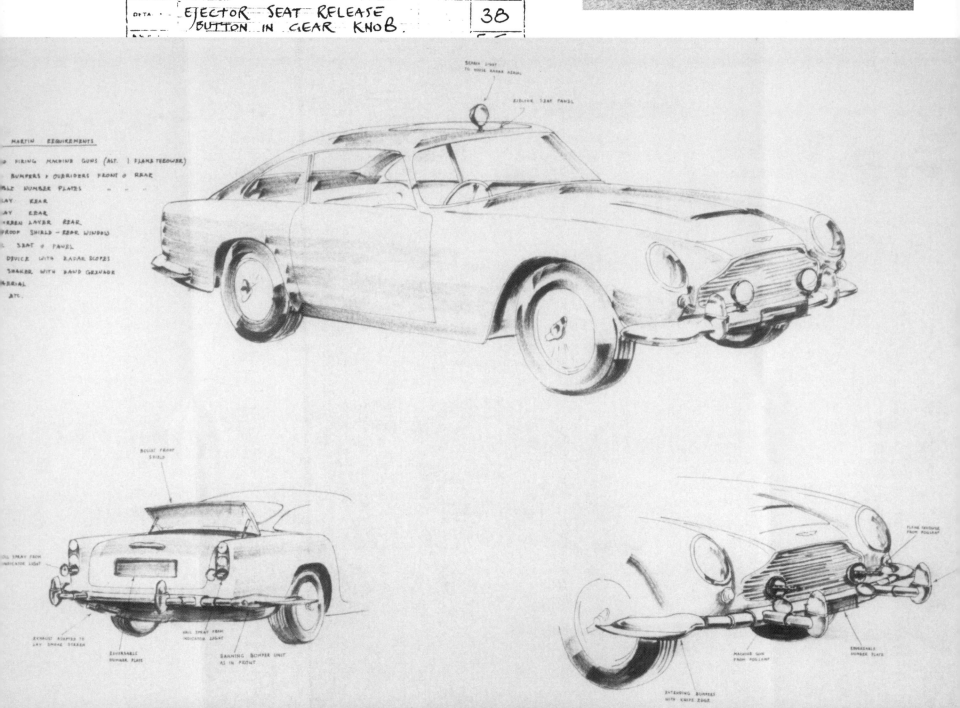

When Cubby Broccoli and Guy Hamilton saw a wrestling match on British television, they could not help but notice the size and brawn of a Hawaiian-born professional wrestler billed as Tosh Togo - real name Harold Toshiuki Sakata, the winner of a silver medal for weightlifting for the US team at the 1948 London Olympics. Broccoli and Hamilton immediately decided they had located Oddjob. However actor and wrestler Milton Reid (who had a minor part in *Dr. No*) wanted the role; he enlisted the support of British Equity, the actor's union. Sakata was not a member of Equity, so the union objected to him taking the part of Oddjob away from a British actor. For a while it looked as if Sakata would not get the part. Reid offered a solution. "I am perfectly willing to fight Togo anywhere, anytime - winner to get the part," he told the *Daily Mirror*. "I am no street brawler. I am a gent," Sakata replied. To complicate matters, Douglas Robinson declared he wanted the role. Equity eventually ruled that the producers could cast Sakata. All was not lost for Reid, though - he later appeared in *Casino Royale* and *The Spy Who Loved Me*. Sakata learned to hurl the metal-rimmed hat that became part of his trademark act. He once appeared on *The Tonight Show With Johnny Carson*, where he walked on-stage, karate-chopped Carson's desk to pieces, then departed.

The fourth and final new ingredient added to the Bond recipe in *Goldfinger* came in the form of Auric Goldfinger's henchman, Oddjob. Although there were secondary villains in both *Dr. No* and *From Russia With Love*, the appearance of Oddjob would forever leave a stamp on the public perception of the henchman.

Oddjob appears almost unaltered from Fleming's novel. "In his tight, almost bursting black suit and farcical bowler hat he looked rather like a Japanese wrestler on his day off." Oddjob was a karate expert who could shatter a fireplace mantle with a single kick and sever someone's neck with the flick of his metal-rimmed bowler. He grunted rather than talked (the result of a cleft palate in the novel), and leapt with the grace of a ballet dancer. Bond observed, "Faced with such a man... one could only go down on one's knees and wait for death".

The character came from a long lineage of killers in films and literature. He was invincible, like Goliath in the Bible or the Cyclops from Homer's *Odyssey*. He was Igor and the Frankenstein monster rolled together, dangerous and loyal, a more vicious incarnation of Steinbeck's Lennie in *Of Mice And Men*. Oddjob, though, heralded a new form of malevolence. His muteness and bizarre appearance separate him from the rest of the characters. He cannot blend into a crowd. He seems to enjoy his own menacing presence. He spends most of the movie overtly waiting to unleash his animal nature, and the audience spends the film both anticipating and dreading the inevitable moment.

The character of Oddjob - played by Harold Sakata - made the henchman *de rigueur* in popular entertainment. The Bond filmmakers themselves began to think in terms of 'the brain villain' and 'the brawn villain'. Oddjob's nearly silent offspring appear in almost every Bond film thereafter, and the character of the sadistic, mute, killing machine became a key part of the iconography of the genre.

Guy Hamilton had the good fortune to be working with a Fleming story that was ripe for cinematic exaggeration. The novel GOLDFINGER - which Anthony Burgess included on a list of his 99 best novels of the 20th century - is a story of excess which featured some of Fleming's grandest characters. The real question was whether the filmmakers could get away with some of Fleming's more explicit flourishes. Those included the implied nudity of Shirley Eaton as Goldfinger's paid companion. In the novel, Bond only hears the details of the character's death long after the fact. The filmmakers understood that audiences would be both shocked and attracted by the image of a nude, glittering corpse. To quieten critics who might object to showing Eaton's unclothed form, Broccoli and Saltzman opened the set and let the world's press lavishly photograph Eaton in full body make-up (the press also established that the actress was not completely naked). Hundreds of photos of the event appeared around the globe, and Eaton, gilded, ended up on the cover of *Life* magazine.

The filmmakers also had to decide how to deal with the risqué name of the key Bond woman in the film - Pussy Galore. The name had come from an infamous madam who operated in Sarasota, New York in the 1950s. Fleming lifted it for his novel, and it caused an immediate sensation among his readers. The character in the novel is the leader of a lesbian crime gang called The Cement Mixers; she falls for Bond at the end of the story.

The UK censor was concerned about the name, having received criticism for the sex and violence in the previous Bond films. The screenwriters toyed with calling the character Kitty Galore. The producers, though, wanted the sensationalism of the name to remain, so publicist Tom Carlile set to work. The clincher came on 24th February 1964, when Honor Blackman attended the premiere of the film *Move Over Darling* and was presented to Prince Philip, a Bond fan. The Prince, having read that Kevin McClory had approached actress Sylva Koscina to appear in his production of *Thunderball*, and finding both actresses in the reception line, queried each on the films in which they would appear. Tom Carlile had arranged for a photographer to get very good photos of the Prince and Blackman together, and one photo ran in three British dailies, including the front page of the *Daily Mail*. The headline over the picture cemented the acceptance of the character name. It simply read 'Pussy And The Prince'.

The name was one of many illustrative appellations Fleming concocted for the heightened world of Bond. For *Dr. No*, the filmmakers actually changed Fleming's Honeychile Rider to Honey Ryder because of the vaguely sexual connotation of Fleming's choice of spelling. With the arrival of Pussy Galore, the name as sex joke began a tradition. Comedians quickly seized on the concept. One men's magazine joke from the time ran, "Have you heard about the new frigid Bond girl? She's called 'Pussy No More'."

Audiences delighted in the device and soon writers were trying to outdo themselves dreaming up not-so-vaguely-sexual names for characters. Certainly for the Bond producers, the reaction to the name Pussy Galore inspired the same kind of response, with future Bond women including Plenty O'Toole, Holly Goodhead, Bibi Dahl, Octopussy, Jenny Flex and Xenia Onatopp.

"I had no paint on the front of me, and then I had two little cones - before Madonna, by the way - on my breasts, for my own modesty. And tiny mini panties, what we call thongs today. The way Guy Hamilton filmed it, in the foreground there's a cushion on the sofa, and the edge of the cushion just covers the g-string, the thong, so I look totally naked."

SHIRLEY EATON

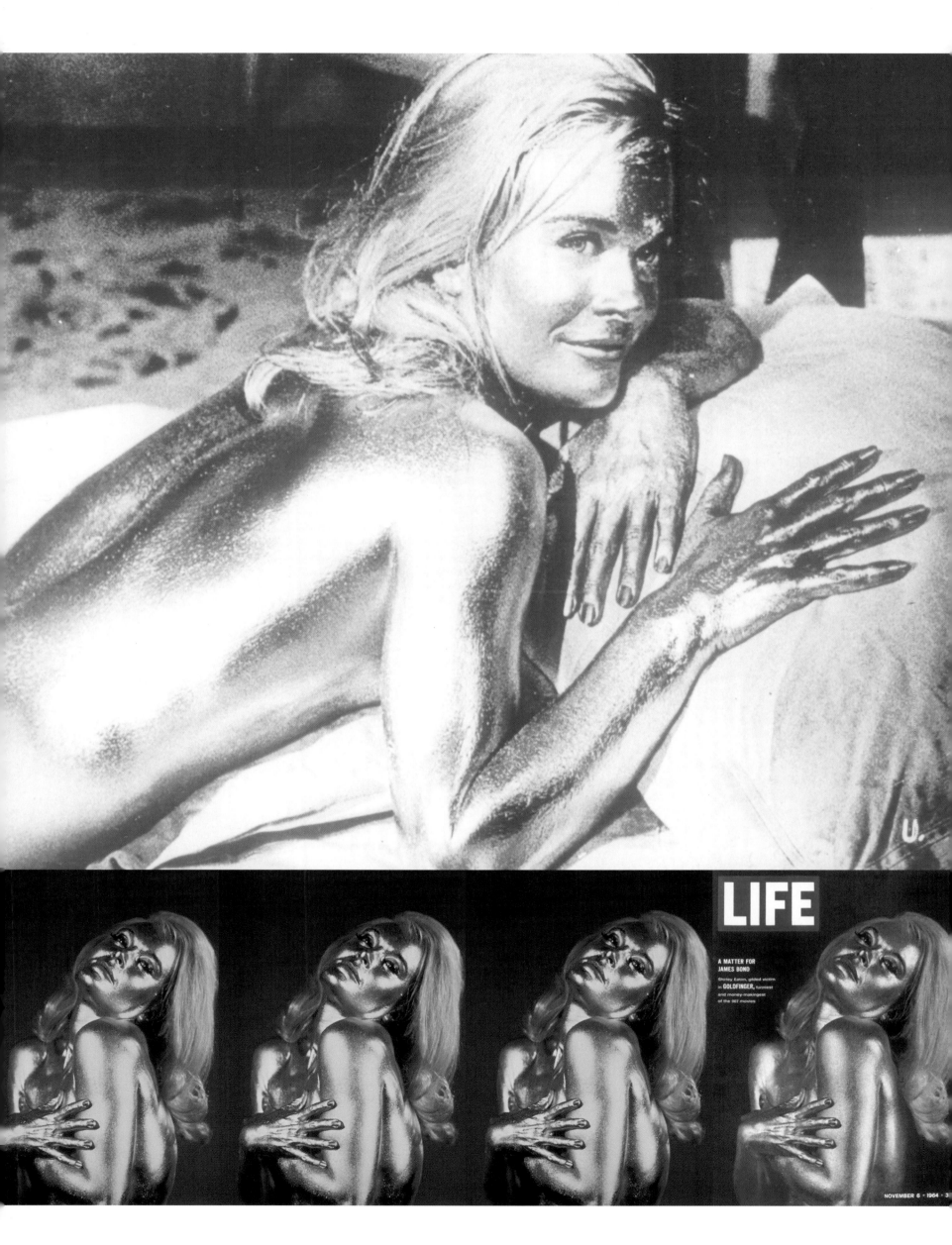

LIFE

A MATTER FOR
JAMES BOND
Shirley Eaton, gilded victim
in GOLDFINGER, funniest
and money-makingest
of the 007 movies

NOVEMBER 6 · 1964 · 3

With locations in Mexico, Florida, England, Switzerland and Kentucky, *Goldfinger* was the most globe-hopping Bond film to date. The filmmakers had taken care to gather all the ingredients of their previous successes. On 20th January 1964, the film began shooting in Miami. Already, Harry Saltzman and Cubby Broccoli knew the world would be waiting for this film - as long as they could get it out before Kevin McClory's production of *Thunderball*.

A month earlier, the entertainment press had been asking, "Who will be the new James Bond?" They were responding to Kevin McClory's announcement that, having won the screen rights to *Thunderball*, he would begin production in January in the Bahamas. *The Times* speculated, "But will McClory ever make his film? Will a script be ready in time? Will he find a good substitute Bond? Will Britain, or the world, accept a non-Connery Bond (I doubt it)."

McClory originally announced he wanted Connery for the role, but that was out of the question. By mid-January 1964, the British press was speculating wildly on the subject. McClory claimed he would not cast an American as Bond, but that the role needed to be filled by "a big animal-type actor". John Stratten wrote an article announcing 'The Battle Of The Bonds', which proclaimed Laurence Harvey as the front-runner in the role. Other papers stated Richard Burton was ready to take the part.

The film, however, did not start production in January, February or March. Soon, it became apparent that it was not going to be made any time too soon. Cubby knew, as did his partner Harry, that they had the trump card. They had Sean Connery.

Even before the US release of *From Russia With Love*, the success of Bond and the whole spy phenomenon was quickly percolating through Western society. Two new network series - *Jonny Quest* and *The Man From U.N.C.L.E* - were being planned in America, both of which contained central characters who were secret agents, and both were direct descendants of 007. One of the series was even dreamed up by Ian Fleming.

The modern era of television spies had began much earlier. Even as the cameras were beginning to roll on *Dr. No*, a weekly series hit UK TV screens presenting the adventures of an Irish-American NATO agent, John Drake. The show was called *Danger Man*, and 39 half-hour episodes were broadcast in the US and Britain in 1961. Patrick McGoohan starred as a spy with moral principles who, unlike James Bond, did not carry a gun and avoided violence wherever possible; "his main weapon against his adversaries is his intelligence," said McGoohan. The programme did well in Britain, and even led Cubby Broccoli and Harry Saltzman to consider McGoohan for 007. But *Danger Man* made little impact in the United States, for which it had been targeted, and production ceased.

The Avengers, like *Danger Man*, began in 1961 on British television, as a series about a doctor seeking revenge for the murder of his wife. The doctor was aided by a mysterious government agent, John Steed, played by Patrick Macnee. By season two, the doctor was gone, the tone was more whimsical, and Steed was now 'avenging' plots against the government along with Cathy Gale (Honor Blackman). The programme reached its greatest popularity when Diana Rigg joined the cast, replacing Blackman, who left the series to co-star in *Goldfinger*.

Despite some minor series such as *Secret File U.S.A.* (1955) and the British-produced anthology series *Espionage* (1963-64), American television had never been the right medium for spies. Now, on ABC, Hanna-Barbera pitched an animated adventure series which would hop around the globe with a government scientist and an American secret agent named 'Race' Bannon. The series focused on the scientist's ten-year-old son, Jonny Quest. Bond also invaded the biggest animated primetime hit, *The Flintstones*, with a famed episode entitled 'Dr. Sinister' in early November 1964, featuring the dashing spy Jay Bondrock.

The most popular of the American-produced spy shows was first born just as *Dr. No* was premiering in London. Television producer Norman Felton (the producer of *Dr. Kildare*) approached Ian Fleming about creating an international espionage series. Because of his deal with Broccoli and Saltzman, Fleming could only provide the character name Napoleon Solo. Writer Sam Rolfe fleshed out the figure, making him an agent for U.N.C.L.E. (called United Network Command for Law Enforcement after the United Nations objected to any implication of their involvement). Solo, who oddly enough had a Russian partner, agent Ilya Kuryakin, was sent on spy missions around the world by an M-like figure, Mr. Waverly.

Opposite: Stuntman Bob Simmons instructs Honor Blackman and Sean Connery in the fine art of judo flipping. As Cathy Gale on *The Avengers*, alongside Patrick Macnee as Steed (**top**), Blackman hurled men about with judo throws and often dressed in elaborate leather suits, which became something of a rage in Britain in 1963-64. Her influence was such that fashion writer Winefride Jackson foresaw a "battle between two types of womanhood" in 1964 - "the feminine grace of Audrey Hepburn and Honor Blackman". The casting of Blackman's *Goldfinger* role was announced on 8th January 1964 in London. Ten major UK papers carried the news within 72 hours. Six mentioned the name Pussy Galore. Four did not.

Above: When *The Man From U.N.C.L.E.* arrived in Great Britain, it launched its own fan movement. The BBC set up a special promotion whereby fans could send in for U.N.C.L.E. identity cards. By October 1966, the network had issued 100,000 cards, and by the end of November, that number had doubled. Fans could purchase U.N.C.L.E. toy guns, folding toy rifles, spy suitcases, books, an LP and two singles of music from the show.

Previous pages: Ian Fleming was wrong about paint suffocating someone by clogging pores but the notion was popularly believed. An urban myth even sprang up about Shirley Eaton dying during shooting - the producers had, nonetheless, taken the precaution of having a doctor on the set.

Chewing Gum. The cards were withdrawn because of the racy pictures of the Bond girls they contained, which were deemed inappropriate.

The one person who was not around to see this quantum leap in James Bond's cultural influence was his creator. Fleming spent much of the summer of 1964 recovering from a heart attack. As his health began to fail him in the early 1960s, Fleming became more ambivalent and sometimes depressive about Bond's success. He had visited the sets of all three films, and certainly enjoyed the films and the reaction of fans.

But Fleming also sensed he could not control the beast he had created. The phenomenon had become much bigger than the author. The money coming in was staggering.

Ann, Ian's wife, complained that James Bond destroyed Ian, but others doubt her conclusion. Fleming, quite simply, was Bond on so many levels. Like his fictional creation, Fleming could hardly change. His identity was tied to his certainty of style and his sense of exotic adventure. Fleming lived an uncompromising life in a world full of compromises. He was not suited to growing old. When his health collapsed, Ian Fleming refused to obey his doctors, and in August 1964 proceeded to smoke, drink and push himself physically. With his doctor as a house guest, Fleming took a cold leap in his private pool in Sevenhampton, near Swindon. When challenged that he had been told not to swim, he responded, "You didn't say I couldn't *dive*."

Within a week, at the age of 56, Fleming was dead of a coronary haemorrhage. Almost every daily newspaper around the world carried his obituary on the front page. Over 40 million copies of his novels were in print around the globe. In the year following his death, Pan would print almost seven million copies of his books for the UK market; Signet printed almost twice that many in the United States. Even before his death, it must have been clear to Fleming that regardless of whatever happened to him, James Bond would live on.

The impact of *Goldfinger* was nothing short of amazing. No one had ever seen anything like it, and everyone involved in the British film industry wanted to see a lot more.

In 1956, Britain had over 4000 cinema screens. The number had halved by the time *From Russia With Love* opened in 1963. In 1946, cinemas sold 1,600 million movie tickets.

Because of the Fleming connection, there was overt concern on the part of Cubby Broccoli and Harry Saltzman over the series, which filmed its pilot in late November 1963, and was initially entitled *Mr. Solo*. Broccoli and Saltzman pointed out that they had a minor character named Mr. Solo in the script for *Goldfinger*, and so Felton changed the title to *The Man From U.N.C.L.E.* The show's first broadcast on 22nd September 1964 came less than a week after the UK premiere of *Goldfinger*. By then, Bond's influence extended far beyond television.

In June 1964, the producers and Ian Fleming's rights-holding company, Glidrose, authorized Mr. Mervyn Brodie to find licences for James Bond. Initially, Brodie saw a market for James Bond branded clothes; "suits, shirts, ties, knitwear, shoes and coats bearing the 007 or Bond accolade" were under consideration. Wider licences for women's clothing, cosmetics, toys, guns, sports equipment and sweets had been requested from companies in the UK, US, Australia, New Zealand and Japan. This was nearly three months before *Goldfinger* opened.

Clothes were a natural idea for licensing since fashion writer Barbara Henderson had already announced in April, "Out goes the 'Avengers girl' look and in comes the 'golden girl' trend", and the press coverage of Eaton being painted gold started fashion wags speculating on Bond's immediate influence. By the time of the film's release, Honor Blackman and Tania Mallet were posing for fashion spreads in the *Daily Express*. The *Daily Mail* opined on "How to be Pussy Galore… even if there is no James Bond in your life". Within a week, gold-themed women's outfits were showing up in stores, and children's clothes were being pushed with lines like "003 ½ Bond junior and his girl get all dressed up". The *Sunday Mail*'s 'Calling All Women' column announced how to "get that *Goldfinger* look".

Norvic was the first clothing-maker to create an official James Bond-licensed piece of clothing in the UK - the 007 shoe - which appeared in a few different styles, including leopard print. They also manufactured a Pussy Galore shoe for women, which came in zebra stripe and, of course, gold. The first officially licensed mass-market Bond products were designed for a younger age: a book, *007 James Bond*, published by Purnell, and chewing gum cards from Dandy

"It's always struck me that Bond is rather like *The Perils Of Pauline*. It's laughs, it's excitement, suspense, pretty girls, adventure, all the things that when I was a kid, movies were all about." Guy Hamilton

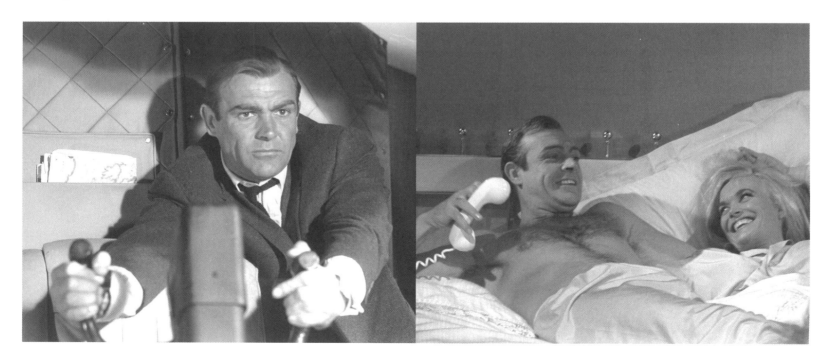

By 1963, with the erosion caused by television, only 400 million tickets were sold. In America, United Artists and other studios had implemented a programme called 'Premiere Showcase' where films ran in multiple theatres in the New York area simultaneously, at premium prices, before wandering out into smaller markets. UA figured that with all the money they spent on promotion, they should play the films in additional theatres. UA decided to introduce the idea to the UK, but they wanted to do it with a film that would justify such an extravagant release pattern. The film, naturally, was *Goldfinger*. The charity premiere had raised over £17,000, but that was nothing compared to the ticket sales. The Odeon Leicester Square did £17,327 in business in the opening week, £2800 more than the previous record, which was held by *From Russia With Love*.

Even before *Goldfinger*'s release, UA was busy shipping out prints of *Dr. No* and *From Russia With Love* to cinemas all over the UK. Even in areas like Devon, far outside the major conurbations, the films played six times between their initial release and the release of *Goldfinger*, each time to strong box office. After *Goldfinger*'s record opening in London, UA decided to put *Dr. No* into a first-run West End house for a week, to be followed by *From Russia With Love*. The film did so well that the cinema booked it for two more weeks. By mid-October, *Goldfinger* completed its official 'Premiere Showcase' run, bringing in almost £200,000, shattering every record in UK cinema history. *Kine Weekly* stated that the film set "a precedent for changing the release pattern for important pictures of the future".

Photos of long queues appeared in the press. The Aston Martin DB5 went on display in several locations, drawing swarms of journalists and crowds at each one. The *Daily Mail*'s investor advice column fielded the question, "Is there a company with a Stock Exchange quote which is making money out of the James Bond films?" The *Mail* recommended investing in the Rank Organization. British Olympic team coach John Le Masurier packed stacks of Bond novels for the athletes to read in Japan in order to keep them inspired and focused.

Everyone seemed to understand the level of success, but no one seemed to understand the incredible impact these films were having on pop culture, the film industry and the collective psyche of a generation. Penelope Gilliatt of *The Observer* decided it was the era. "*Goldfinger* belongs absolutely to our period. So does the command of technology, the stylish brutality, the wit and the nerveless treachery. It is an atmosphere that seems to be everywhere in entertainment and television and conversations and the press, flattening out the old differences between sedate magazines and pop newspapers; an atmosphere that is comic, expert, blessedly derisive and uniquely odious all at the same time."

James Bond's success was gargantuan, but his future could not be predicted by those who had an optimistic self-interest. Cubby Broccoli declared he and Saltzman would continue to make Bond films as long as they continued to be successful, "perhaps five or six more". A guest critic for *The Stratford-upon-Avon Herald* noted that "while Goldfinger is the best in the film series, others will follow to match it". The critic went on to note that the imitators were knocking at the door. "Within a year we will see John Le Carré's Leamas …Len Deighton's Anonymous Agent… James Leasor's Dr. Jason Love, and a neurotic flip-top operative called Boysie Oakes." Nonetheless, the critic stated, "You can be quite certain that no one

Top: Cubby and Dana Broccoli celebrate their wedding anniversary on the set of *Goldfinger* in June 1964 with a Fort Knox cake.

Above: Shirley Bassey with her gold record for 'Goldfinger'. Bassey had previously charted in the UK, with the theme song from *Fire Down Below*, produced by Cubby Broccoli and Irving Allen.

JAMES BOND IS BACK IN ACTION!
EVERYTHING HE TOUCHES
TURNS TO EXCITEMENT!

is ever going to take over from or assume the mantle of the late Ian Fleming". The critic was a spy novelist himself, the creator, in fact, of Boysie Oakes. His name was John Gardner, and from 1980 through 1995 he was the author of the continuation James Bond novels.

To prime the pump for US audiences, UA took an advance print of *Goldfinger* on tour with Shirley Eaton as the host. Glamorous previews took place in Miami, New Orleans, Philadelphia and a host of other cities. In each the reaction was the same - people scrambled for tickets, fans gathered outside the theatre, and local papers covered the event as if Queen Elizabeth II were paying a royal visit.

In the autumn of 1964, the US press virtually existed off reporting the status of British imports - from the Beatles to the Rolling Stones. Bond was no different. *The New York Times*, *Newsweek* and *The Los Angeles Times* all carried stories about Bond's London success, and all expected similar excitement when the film arrived Stateside. United Artists even authorized the production of the first James Bond television special, *The Incredible James Bond*, which was syndicated to local markets. The studio anticipated a huge hit. They were not disappointed.

UA planned a huge New York premiere for 21st December. They shipped the DB5 gadget car via the *SS France*, flew in Honor Blackman and Shirley Eaton, and contacted every Aston Martin DB5 owner in New York to provide the sportiest limo service to the DeMille Theatre (eight agreed to help). The evening continued with dancing at the Astor Hotel, where Shirley Bassey belted out the title song to the VIP guests.

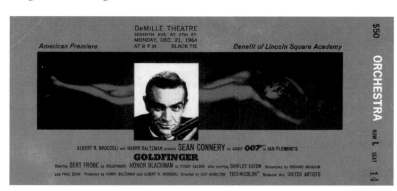

The next day, *Goldfinger* began playing at the DeMille and Cornet theatres in Manhattan. Both were prepared for big crowds, but neither could anticipate the masses of humanity prepared to stand in the cold outside their theatres. On the 22nd, both came close to doubling their house opening-day records. When the final show sold out at both theatres, hundreds left in line begged the management for additional shows. On Christmas Eve, the DeMille officially opened for 24 hours straight, and did not close again until after New Year's Day. At Graumann's Chinese Theater in Los Angeles, *Goldfinger* broke the house record with $50,000 in its first three days. Cubby Broccoli, in Los Angeles for the holidays, went to the theatre to take pictures of the crowds.

The numbers did not drop as the film opened wider. Five weeks into the release, *Goldfinger* had grossed $9 million in 1000 theatres. When the film finally started playing in some second-run houses in the spring, theatres were still packed. In New York 'neighborhood theaters' the film pulled in over one million dollars in one week,

amazing considering that week was in April, and the film had played in the New York area to packed first-run houses for over three months.

Vincent Canby commented, "Whether or not the film's success reflects some anxious fundamental truth about our time, it has already been the cause of important effects throughout the contemporary film world." While some films, like *My Fair Lady*, had grossed massive amounts by playing in roadshow fashion, *Goldfinger* was far and away the most successful standard release film ever made. It was the film that paved the way for studios to believe in the blockbuster mentality.

Internationally, the film swooped through nations like a conquering force. It opened in Rome just after New Year's 1965, and went on to pull in 222 million lire (approximately $2.5 million). This was an enormous increase over the take of *Dr. No* (10 million lire) and *From Russia With Love* (37 million lire). France showed similar exponential growth in revenues. *Dr. No* had grossed 715,000 francs in Paris, and *From Russia With Love* grossed 2.1 million francs. *Goldfinger* out-grossed both films combined in just four weeks. By late April the film opened in Japan, and decimated records. At the Hibiya Theatre, 78,965 tickets were sold in the first week, smashing the record held by *Cleopatra* by 71%. Similar records were set in the Philippines, Germany, Austria and Puerto Rico. The film did not premiere in Singapore until 5th August 1965, but when it arrived it was accorded much the same hoop-la that had greeted the movie in London ten months earlier. Armed guards transported the film to the cinema and record-breaking crowds lined up to see James Bond.

Ticket sales were not the only success for *Goldfinger*. John Barry's score also broke records. The soundtrack, which was released in October, charted even before the film was released. Shirley Bassey's title song made the charts in January 1965, rising to Number Eight in the US and Number Twenty in the UK. Along with 'The James Bond Theme', it became a favourite of jazz musicians, dance bands and (with its raw sexuality) strippers. Two nightclubs in San Francisco - Tipsy's and The Chart Room - started *Goldfinger* floorshows, featuring performers painted in gilt. Both reported booming business - standing room only "nights during the week and turnaway crowds during the weekend", according to *Variety*.

When the Sherlock Holmes musical *Baker Street* premiered at the Broadway Theater in New York on 16th February 1965, a huge billboard over the marquee proclaimed "Sherlock Holmes of Baker Street taught James Bond everything he knows". Another billboard on the side of the Markwell Hotel proclaimed, "Sherlock Holmes makes James Bond look like a sissy - *Baker Street* is a rare musical gem". The show ran for 313 performances - long enough for the publicity department at United Artists to mount their own billboard directly above the one on the Markwell Hotel which said, "'Sherlock WHO?' - James Bond, Secret Agent 007 - and speaking of 'musical gems', have you heard the music from the *Goldfinger* album on United Artists records?" Needless to say, the *Goldfinger* soundtrack far outsold the *Baker Street* original cast album. In fact, in 1965, it replaced the Beatles as the Number One selling album in the country.

Had Cubby Broccoli and Harry Saltzman retired after the global success of *Goldfinger*, they could have lived very nicely for the rest of their days. The producers, though, had more to do than relish their success.

The producers had originally intended to film *On Her Majesty's Secret Service* as the next Bond film; they had scouted locations for *OHMSS* in Switzerland during the shooting of *Goldfinger*, and Richard Maibaum had begun a treatment. But all that went on hold when Saltzman and Broccoli entered into negotiations with Kevin McClory over *Thunderball*. In the week of the *Goldfinger* premiere, the parties finalized a deal. Eon Productions (the company formed by Broccoli and Saltzman) would produce *Thunderball*, with Sean Connery as the star. The deal did not come cheap, both in terms of what would be paid to McClory to keep him from making a full-blown rival production and in terms of a lost project for Broccoli and Saltzman. To make UA's release schedule for *Thunderball*, the producing pair scrapped their plans for a non-Bond film, *The Pass Beyond Kashmir*, a thriller set in India and intended to star Connery. They also had to cut the film from Connery's contract. In the autumn, they approached Guy Hamilton about directing *Thunderball*. Hamilton said he was exhausted of ideas. Terence Young, however, was willing to return for a very handsome salary.

The film started shooting in France at the Château d'Anet on 16th February 1965. The press release announcing the start of principal photography was sent to the US Treasury and the office of the British Exchequer as an acknowledgement of Bond's success (and the taxes both governments earned off the films). At the start-of-

Thunderball was Martine Beswick's third film for director Terence Young. After *From Russia With Love*, she appeared in Young's film version of Daniel Defoe's *The Amorous Adventures Of Moll Flanders*, along with 007 film veterans Bernard Lee, Desmond Llewelyn, Anthony Dawson and her *Thunderball* co-star Molly Peters.

shooting press conference the reporters and photographers mobbed Sean Connery and Claudine Auger. Three days later, *Goldfinger* had its French premiere. Sean Connery was there to promote the film, driving up the Champs Elysées to the cinema in the Aston Martin DB5. As he was pulling the car in front of the theatre, an over-enthusiastic young woman leapt through the passenger-side window, making a grab for the actor. She was wrestled away, but shortly after Connery was mobbed by autograph-seekers. Police arrived on the scene to help restore order and get Connery to safety.

The shooting at the Château included a real gadget developed by Bell Labs for the Army: a rocket pack. The machine actually worked, and two pilots from Bell were brought in to fly the device. The film also featured a hydrofoil disguised as a yacht, the latest twin-engine US Coast Guard helicopter, the new sky-hook sea-air rescue package, a full-size Vulcan bomber reproduction sunk in 50 feet of water, numerous custom-built underwater tow-sleds and wet-subs, 75,000 dollars' worth of diving equipment donated by Voigt, and the return of the Aston Martin DB5.

All the ingredients were the same, but the producers were determined to make this film bigger. Their only yardstick was their own success. Bigger action scenes were only a matter of money, time and imagination. The tone, though, was harder to strike. Richard Maibaum, one of the two writers on *Thunderball*, had the opportunity to compare his work on the 1965 film to the script he had written just four years earlier. "I realize how much we have been influenced by audience reaction." Indeed, *Thunderball* had to find a balance between the sophisticated wit of Fleming's novels and Bond's more recent cultural ubiquity. By the time *Thunderball* went into

production, writer Maibaum was noting, "there is hardly a comic who has not attempted a take-off on him". The result was more self-aware commentary. A villainess in the film mocked Bond as a "sadistic brute", and declared that (unlike Pussy Galore and Tatiana Romanova) she would not turn to the side of right and virtue after sampling the charms of agent 007.

If *Goldfinger* is the film which launched Spymania, *Thunderball* is the movie which acknowledged James Bond's place in popular culture. From *Thunderball* onwards, the Bond filmmakers would be forced not only to make good adventure films, they would also need to react to the public perception of Bond with various background jokes and quips. This 'insider' perspective assumed viewers knew who Bond was, and it granted permission for the casual viewer to laugh at the absurdities of the films while giving more hard-core fans another layer of information to enjoy.

If James Bond were to pull in the box-office of the huge roadshow hits, the filmmakers surmised it should be filmed in the same manner: widescreen. The film format was not the only element which set *Thunderball* apart as an epic. When the crew flew to Nassau in the Bahamas to start shooting on location, BOAC changed the call signal for the flight to '007'. Later, plane-loads of journalists flew in at United Artists' expense, covering the chaos surrounding the filmmaking. The press came from the US, Germany, France, Italy, Austria, Australia, Sweden and Canada. Reports surfaced that crowds from hotels out-numbered those that had watched the Beatles shoot *Help!* there a few weeks earlier. Celebrities came by to watch, including Ringo Starr. Ed Sullivan taped the opening of his next season from the film location. The

press could not help but comment on the circus atmosphere. "Crazes come and crazes go, but the 'Bond phenomenon', as it is now reverently called, is hard to match," wrote William K. Zinsser.

In fact, there was nothing to match Bond in 1965, not even the Beatles. During shooting, according to a press release at the time, Sean Connery spotted "more than 200 young fans" treading water, just out of camera range, around his boat. "Speak to us," one of the bold ones shouted. "You're our leader and we're your people."

Bond novels had sold well over 50 million copies around the globe. Film companies had announced that 20 spy movies were in production or pre-production. Every network in virtually every country with television was prepping or airing spy-related shows. It was a frenzy.

France led the world in Bond merchandise - this at the same time the French and the British were having a very public spat over Great Britain's future membership of the (then) Common Market and France's participation in NATO. During the release of *Goldfinger*, the French bought three million dollars' worth of James Bond tie-in merchandise, which was mostly aimed at adults. There were gold-bordered handkerchiefs, attaché cases, women's undergarments and Bond trenchcoats, among other items.

In the States, products were already rolling off the assembly lines. Colgate-Palmolive marketed 007 men's toiletries. 007 nightgowns appeared in some stores, but did not last long. T-shirts and sweat shirts with the 007 logo abounded. By the summer of 1965, James Bond beach towels were selling at a brisk pace. 007 pyjamas, blankets and sheets graced the aisles at department stores.

In the UK, the emphasis was on the masculine. Anthony Sinclair, the tailor of Connery's suits for the Bond films, announced he was working with Burton's to create a line of Bond clothes for men and boys. United Rum sold 007 vodka (a dismal failure), while Norvic continued to sell 007 shoes at a good clip. Bond ties and suitcases were in the works.

The big market, everyone felt, was children. The toy market was exploding in the US and abroad. Toys were a $100 million industry in America in 1964, and growing rapidly. Big sectors included the slot car racers, which were on-track to bring in more money than all other toy sales combined. Board games sold very well, too, as did model kits. All these markets targeted adults and children. The huge breakthrough toy of 1964 in the US was G.I. Joe, the first doll since Raggedy Andy to sell successfully to boys. Preliminary figures showed sales could reach the eight million unit mark by Christmas 1965. As the grosses for *Goldfinger* piled up, manufacturers planned to bring James Bond into each of these arenas.

The other huge area in the toy market was the sale of miniature cars. A British firm, Matchbox, proclaimed themselves the world's largest car builder. They produced 100 million cars each year, and each one was small enough to fit into a child's hand. Another British firm, Mettoy, wanted to increase their share of the international market in miniature cars.

In the spring of 1965, they developed a plan to do just that. Mettoy owned Corgi, and the company was renowned for making the most detailed and well-crafted die-cast toy cars in the world. The Corgi James Bond Aston Martin would be a feat of engineering all to itself, with multiple moving parts and even an ejector seat. It would also become, on its release in October 1965, one of the best-remembered toys of the generation. The car became an instant hit for Corgi, earning accolades such as 'Best Toy Of The Year'.

On 30th July 1965 a massive meeting took place with over 80 participants representing over 39 companies at London's Film and Fine Arts Theatre. No meeting in the history of film had ever been quite like it. There were the representatives and owners of UK companies which had purchased James Bond licences on one side, and Eon Productions and United Artists on the other. The creators of the cinematic James Bond were scheduled to unveil their game plan to make *Thunderball* the most successful film of 1965/66 and even to screen a portion of the movie.

Those assembled, all of whom had paid dearly for the chance to tie in with Bond, represented a vast array of business interests. They were the manufacturers of bubble gum cards, toy guns, men's accessories, jigsaw puzzles, board games, toy filmstrip viewers, girl's raincoats, carnival hats, luggage, model kits and dolls. They

included publishers of magazines, young adult books, children's books and souvenir programmes. With the information they would be given, each company would plan out a manufacturing programme, develop an advertising strategy and work with retailers to secure shelf space for products. The first key piece of information the licensees were given was the date of the premiere - 21st October 1965. All their preparation and investing went forward from there.

The end of July was also the point where editor Peter Hunt realized he had a problem. *Thunderball* was running long, very long. Publicist Tom Carlile told *Variety* that the film was running "four and a half hours". To make matters worse, Terence Young was soon off to direct a film for the United Nations called *The Poppy Is Also A Flower* (also known as *Danger Grows Wild* and *The Opium Connection*). Whatever fixes to *Thunderball* were needed would happen without Young's participation. In August, Hunt told the producers that the film could not be ready by the scheduled October premiere. The movie had been shot by multiple units with few storyboards. The script had been rewritten during production and there were shots Hunt needed which had simply never been filmed.

At a meeting with Arnold Picker of United Artists, Hunt was asked if there was any way to make the October premiere. Hunt said he could finish the film, but it would not be a good film. Picker let him know this would cost UA millions to delay, and Hunt promised that if he were given the time, he would not only make a good film, he would make the best Bond ever. UA decided to delay the film's UK premiere until December, simultaneous with the US opening.

The delay caused all sorts of problems. Certainly, the cornerstone of success had to be a good film, but now there was a small army of companies counting on Bond. This was the largest merchandising programme in the history of films, and UA had to fight rumours that their film was in trouble. They denied stories of re-shoots in the Bahamas (there were none) and tried to explain that the problem was too much good material, not too little. No one at UA was worried about failure - the investment by UA of nearly $5.5 million in the initial production, plus an additional $1.5 million in studio re-shoots and delays made *Thunderball* more expensive than the three previous Bond films combined, but even if the movie failed to sell one ticket, UA would have more than quadrupled their money on James Bond.

Colgate-Palmolive, though, did worry. In late September, they pulled out of a joint television/cinema ad campaign and declined to mention *Thunderball* specifically in their ads. A memo from Meyer Beck and United Artists to Licensing Corporation of America (the company handling the Bond licences) noted that "it seems as if Colgate is trying to avoid too much tie-up and concentration of their product with *Thunderball* on the basis that *Thunderball* is a one-time situation".

The larger trouble looming on the horizon came in the form of Bond's own success. Everyone wanted to capture their version of it. The glut of secret agent-themed shows in the US began shortly after *Goldfinger*'s grosses with the resurrection of Patrick McGoohan's show, *Danger Man*. The show was called *Secret Agent* in America, where it became an hour-long season replacement in April 1965. John Drake was now a trouble-shooting British M9 agent, who reported to a superior named G. The new theme song - which was a blend of 'The James Bond Theme' and surf music - became a hit single for American pop singer Johnny Rivers.

Danger Man was not the only series to undergo a facelift in an effort to cash in on the James Bond craze. Aaron Spelling had been producing a show for American television starring Gene Barry and called *Burke's Law*. The stories revolved around Amos Burke, a high-living Los Angeles police detective who solved murders. Before the show entered its third season in 1965, Spelling decided to make Burke an international agent for the American government. He presented the idea to ABC, who said "That's our *Goldfinger*! We've always wanted to do James Bond". Overnight, *Amos Burke: Secret Agent* was born. The revamped show lasted 17 episodes before it was cancelled. Other spy shows fared better.

In September 1965, CBS - whose most popular programme for a decade was the Western *Gunsmoke* - premiered a show that was part *Gunsmoke*, part James Bond, entitled *The Wild Wild West*. The main characters, James West and Artemus Gordon, worked for the US Secret Service, using a private train as a base from which to battle a wide assortment of evil geniuses. It rode high in the ratings, but was also one of the most violent programmes on television.

Hedging its bets, CBS also unveiled a more traditional spy series in 1965: *I Spy*, produced by Sheldon Leonard, creator of the long-running *Andy Griffith Show*. Filmed in colour on locations around the world, *I Spy* featured Robert Culp and Bill Cosby as undercover agents Kelly Robinson and Alexander Scott. Robinson posed as a tennis pro, Scott as his trainer. Significantly, this was the first series to feature a black male character on an equal, if not superior, footing with a white counterpart.

The most popular Bond item in the toy market was the Aston Martin DB5. Battery-operated versions and model kits (like the Airfix version seen opposite) sold well, but the best remembered Aston Martin toy was the Corgi die-cast. Corgi's association with James Bond has continued through the 20th Bond adventure, *Die Another Day*, with over 50 different James Bond die-casts released through the years. Before the DB5 model, Corgi's bread and butter sales had been more pedestrian vehicles, including buses and delivery vans. With the Aston Martin, Corgi quickly became focused on the massive sales from film and television tie-ins. Although the toy DB5 sold in the millions, it also drastically raised the bar for all other die-cast toys. Before the Bond car was released by Corgi, the simple fact that the cars rolled across a floor, or had doors which could open, seemed to be entertaining for children. After the Corgi DB5, kids and adults looked at die-casts and inevitably asked, "But what can it do?"

In *Thunderball* the producers wanted James Bond to use the Bell Textron Rocket Pack *sans helmet*, but Bill Suitor, who performed the flight from the Château d'Anet, refused to do the stunt without protective headgear. Consequently, Sean Connery had to don the helmet for his close-ups (**opposite page, top left**).

Claudine Auger, who played Domino, was an inexperienced swimmer. For her underwater interlude with 007, she was doubled by the wife of underwater cameraman, Lamar Boren (**below**). Auger and the other women in *Thunderball* created a press sensation in Nassau (**middle picture, from left**: Martine Beswick, Claudine Auger and Luciana Paluzzi).

The villainous Emilio Largo was portrayed by veteran Italian actor Adolfo Celi (**bottom left**), an actor, writer and director who, prior to *Thunderball*, had made a memorable foil to Jean-Paul Belmondo in the 007-inspired comedy *That Man From Rio*.

To promote *Thunderball*, London store displays featured props from the film, such as the custom-made underwater sleds (**bottom right**).

4. On 24th April 1966, thousands of demonstrators clogged the streets of Paris protesting against American involvement in the Vietnam war. One young man who caught the eye of a photographer was holding a sign of the times - US President Lyndon Baines Johnson posed as James Bond, under the title 'Bloodfinger'.

Spy Versus Spy

After four films, twelve novels, two short-story collections and countless licensed products, secret agent 007 was an iconic figure who represented many aspects of popular culture. The image of Sean Connery in the same pose as the one which was depicted on the protestor's poster sold movie tickets and products to adoring fans. LBJ's image as James Bond succinctly mocked US foreign policy. How could Bond be both the image of the hero *and* the villain? With such broad saturation around the globe, who was James Bond? Was he Sean Connery or was he Ian Fleming's literary creation? Was he an amalgam of jokes, sex, style and action, or just a fad whose days were numbered? Having blazed a trail through the creative process, Cubby Broccoli and Harry Saltzman now had to chart a path for Bond's future. Beset by a host of imitators, besieged by potential partners and threatened with the loss of their star actor, the next two years would mark a drastic change of course for 007, with tremendous impact both on popular culture and the longevity of James Bond.

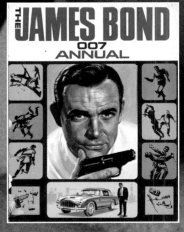

With *Goldfinger* and *Thunderball*, Cubby Broccoli and Harry Saltzman had reinforced and refined the ingredients of the Bond movies - and their particular blend was breaking box office records. Small surprise, then, that as 1966 began, hundreds of movie producers, screenwriters, directors, television executives, toy-makers, musicians and pulp paperback writers thought they knew all the right ingredients, too. Audiences wanted suave, debonair, wise-cracking spies, so these creative minds would deliver. It was inevitable. James Bond was no longer just a fictional secret agent; he was big business.

Once the soundtrack album of *Goldfinger* had reached Number One on the Billboard charts, there was a glut of singles and albums overtly taking 007 as their lead. The years 1965 and 1966 featured, or so it seemed, a never-ending cascade of secret agents. The music charts contained hit songs like 'Agent Double-O-Soul', 'Sock It To 'Em J.B.', 'Secret Agent Man' and 'The Last Of The Secret Agents'.

Albums released during this period included official compilations such as *The Incredible World Of James Bond* and *Music To Read James Bond By, Volume Two*. A Los Angeles jazz musician called Jimmy Bond formed James Bond And His Sextet, and released *The James Bond Songbook*. The Beatles even played a section of 'The James Bond Theme' for the soundtrack to *Help!*

In publishing, books detailing the Bond phenomenon filled store shelves. There was John Pearson's biography of Ian Fleming and various other paperbacks about the life of the late author. Children's annuals appeared in the UK. Kingsley Amis wrote *The James Bond Dossier*, while O. F. Snelling produced *007 James Bond: A Report*. Umberto Eco (later the author of *The Name Of The Rose*) and Oreste del Buono critiqued 007 in *The Bond Affair*. Ann S. Boyd examined the phenomenon's mythology in *The Devil And James Bond*. One of the biggest sellers was *For Bond Lovers Only*, which compiled short articles with photos of Bond women and 007's guns. Even religious groups got into the act, with one publishing *James Bond's World Of Values* - a book which argued Bond has no values worth imitating.

Parodies of Ian Fleming's writing existed in the UK long before the movies. In the US, they first arrived with *The Harvard Lampoon*'s *Alligator* in 1962. During the spy craze, notable parodies included the Israel Bond series by Sol Weinstein (launched in 1965 with *Loxfinger*), the licentious 0008 novels by Clyde Allison, *Pussy L'Amour And The Three Bears* (credited to Ian Phleming) and *Snakefinger* (credited to I. M. Flaming).

Of course, nothing was outselling the original Bond. Pan, the British paperback publisher, released Ian Fleming's novel YOU ONLY LIVE TWICE on 6th May 1966, with a print run of just over one million copies. This was, however, slightly less than the previous year's printing of ON HER MAJESTY'S SECRET SERVICE, the first million-copy paperback printing in Britain (in fact, the first print run was just over one and a half million copies). By the end of May 1965, the month of its release, Pan's sales figures for ON HER MAJESTY'S SECRET SERVICE had topped 1,533,575 copies - almost the entire print run having sold out in just six weeks.

In the light of this level of interest it must have been hard to imagine that anyone could lose money on James Bond, especially during Christmas 1965. Unfortunately, it was this assumption - that Bond naturally equalled profits - which led to the bankruptcy of America's oldest toy company. Gilbert had seen the potential in Bond, and they purchased a licence to make the key toys of the James Bond line in America. The *pièce de résistance* of Gilbert's toy range was the James Bond Road Race Set. At $34.44, the slot-car road race set was the most elaborate and expensive toy carried by Sears, America's largest toy-seller. But it was also the biggest disappointment. Quite simply, it did not work. There was a technical problem with the metal track connectors on the moulded plastic sections. Without good connections, the slot cars

Far left: LBJ gets the Bond treatment during anti-Vietnam War demonstrations in Paris in April 1966.

Left: Numerous unofficial albums announced 'Music from *Goldfinger*' on their cover. An equal number re-interpreted *Thunderball*. Billy Strange released a single of 'The James Bond Theme', and a group called The Menn released 'The Ian Fleming Theme'. Meanwhile, Marty Brill and Larry Foster recorded the comedy album *James Blonde, The Man From T.A.N.T.E.*

As well as annuals and Fleming biographies, one could find racks at any airport, drugstore or bus station filled with writers trying to cash in on the spy craze. Ted Mark created *The Man From O.R.G.Y.* There was the gay-themed *The Man From C.A.M.P.* Adam Diment gave the world McAlpine, the dope-smoking spy, and Bill S. Ballinger introduced a part-Native American spy, Joaquin Hawks, whose rather tired codename was 'Swinger'. *Comrade Spy* by Lev S. Ovalov promised to deliver 'The Russian James Bond'.

Gilbert's James Bond 007 Road Race set spilled across two full-colour pages of the 1965 Sears Christmas 'Wishbook' catalogue, and promised, "an authentic model of his customized Aston Martin DB5". The orders were phenomenal. Bond toys featured exclusively on five pages of the catalogue, and Sears afforded Bond toys premium space in their stores.

"Charlie Feldman is lavish in the Egyptian tradition of lavish. What he's really trying to do is eliminate the Bond pictures forever." Woody Allen

Feldman entertained the idea of making the film on a modest budget of two to three million dollars, without name actors, but then decided that this would be folly. Like Kevin McClory, Feldman knew the public wanted Sean Connery as James Bond - and Connery's 007 belonged to Saltzman and Broccoli.

Always a dealmaker, Feldman approached Broccoli, Saltzman and United Artists with a proposal - that they produce *Casino Royale* together. United Artists offered Feldman $500,000 and a percentage of the profits. The percentage was not large enough to suit him, and he had already invested $550,000 of his own money into developing the script, which by now had been through several writers including, reportedly, Michael Sayers, Joseph Heller (author of the novel *Catch 22*) and director Billy Wilder. UA offered Feldman a deal, but it was not sweet enough; he turned the offer down.

One newspaper hinted that Laurence Harvey would win the part of 007 in *Casino Royale*. Feldman himself had someone else in mind. He told the *Daily Mail* in June 1964, "I want an English actor for the role." He said his "ideal man" would be the star of the television series *The Saint*, Roger Moore. Moore responded, saying, "I've had no approach from Mr. Feldman yet, but this is a wonderful piece of news. I've always fancied myself as a Bond." Negotiations with United Artists continued on and off with Feldman, who was probably unaware that simultaneous talks were going on with Kevin McClory.

In the week *Goldfinger* opened in London, just after Saltzman and Broccoli sealed their deal with Kevin McClory to make *Thunderball*, Feldman announced he had signed actor Terence Cooper as the new James Bond, putting him under exclusive contract for £200 a month.

Variety later quoted Feldman as saying, "We had a deal," but then, "Broccoli and Saltzman told UA that if they made a deal with me, they'd take their films to somebody else." According to Feldman, Saltzman and Broccoli then told United Artists that "if UA doesn't make a deal with Feldman, nobody else will touch the *Casino* deal. It was about five minutes after the UA negotiations broke down that I made my deal with Columbia."

Columbia Pictures approved a budget of between $4.5 and $5 million for *Casino Royale*, which Feldman was now describing as a "high comedy with suspense", as opposed to a spy film with gimmicks. He expected to begin shooting by the middle of August 1965 for a release in the summer of 1966. Seeing that Columbia was serious about pursuing the project, UA and Broccoli and Saltzman again opened negotiations with Feldman which would allow him to feature Sean Connery as 007. United Artists would join forces with Columbia Pictures in the deal, with a hemispheric split of distribution territories.

Variety announced the pending arrangement on 12th May 1965, but a month later it came unstuck. Feldman claimed that the reason was that Broccoli and Saltzman wanted *Casino Royale* to follow their fifth Bond film, which at that time was slated to be *On Her Majesty's Secret Service*, due to begin filming in January 1966 with Guy Hamilton directing. That would mean *Casino Royale* would not go into production until the end of 1966 or early 1967. Feldman, knowing that Broccoli and Saltzman only had Connery under contract for three more films (including *Thunderball*, which was shooting at the time), said, "If I were

willing to wait that long, I might just as well have waited until Connery's contract were up and hire him myself". Indeed, Feldman did ask Connery what he would want to play 007 in a non-Eon film. Connery's reply: "One million dollars."

In his autobiography, Broccoli wrote that the stumbling block in the negotiations was Feldman's insistence that he get 75% of the receipts, with the other 25% going to Broccoli and Saltzman and United Artists. Broccoli's response was that they didn't have any notion of doing that, adding, "On these terms, Charlie, you're going to have to make the picture on your own."

Without Connery, and having just had a smash hit with the 27th June 1965 release of the psychotic comedy, *What's New, Pussycat*, Feldman decided the best way to compete with the Broccoli-Saltzman Bonds was to lampoon them.

He reflected later that he could have done it "the easy way" and made an imitation of the Broccoli-Saltzman films for two to three million dollars. "Then I could grab a million or so profit," he said, "and come out smelling like a rose. But I couldn't make another stereotyped spy film. I wanted something truly different, something on a broad canvas, bold, and way out, a producer's film."

The strain of doing a "producer's film" caused Feldman considerable grief over the next two years and adversely affected his health. Costs spiralled upwards, stars squabbled, scriptwriters and directors came and went, and the film became the talk of the industry, usually with the words "out of control" spoken in the same breath. But Feldman was willing to take the gamble.

Sean Connery, meanwhile, was finding it very difficult to live in a world where the public expected him to be Bond, and only Bond, but he was not eager to leave the role. He simply wanted a larger slice of the pie. Connery was certainly aware of the way other stars were making money off the spy boom, particularly Dean Martin, with his share of the profits from the Helm movies.

Terence Young recalled that after the filming of *Thunderball* was completed, he told Broccoli and Saltzman, "Take Sean as a partner. In future make it Cubby and Harry and Sean. He'll stay with you because he's a Scotsman. He likes the sound of gold coins clinking together. He likes that lovely soft rustle of paper."

There were, indeed, a lot of gold coins clinking at Eon. While *Thunderball* was being filmed, one accountant worked out that the three previous Bond films and their associated merchandising were earning $1000 every hour of the day - day in and day out.

United Artists was making money, Broccoli and Saltzman were making money, and Connery - whose face was the one on the screen and the merchandising products - wanted an equal share.

Ursula Andress (pictured **top right** with Peter Sellers) was reluctant to accept a role in *Casino Royale*, until Peter Sellers arrived with writer Wolf Mankowitz and read the script to her. "He said, Ursula, it's going to be so easy. You just do it with me, it's gonna be fun," remembered Andress. "Then Peter suddenly wanted to change every day the whole script, and every day he had a big fight with the producer, Charlie Feldman. Peter wanted to do another character, he didn't want to do it the way it was written. It didn't stay the film any more. It's not *Casino Royale* like the book. It's completely different."

"I can remember saying 'Look Sean, it's silly not to keep up playing Bond, 'cause whilst you're playing Bond, you can do anything in the world that you want to do. If you say "I want to do *Hamlet*", you could get the money straightaway, providing you're Bond'." Lewis Gilbert

Connery began hinting that the next Bond would be his last. When interviewed by Sheila Graham, he told her, "This is the last one. The sooner it's finished the happier I'll be. I don't talk to the producers. It's been a fight since the beginning. If they'd had any sense of fairness, they could have made me a partner. It would have been beneficial for all. It could have been a very happy thing if they had been fair." Years later, Connery would say, "Had they not been so greedy, today United Artists could belong to Connery, Broccoli and Saltzman". But Broccoli and Saltzman felt that it was they who had initially taken the chance on Fleming's novels and had found the formula for translating them to the screen.

Ultimately, whatever motive they may have had, they made a choice to try an untested premise rather than take on Connery as a partner. They decided it might be his face on the screen, but it was not Connery the public was coming to see - it was James Bond, 007. It would take seven years to prove their thesis.

Also, in Cubby Broccoli's estimation, if there was one thing he didn't need, it was another partner. His association with Harry Saltzman was beginning to unravel. In the beginning, Harry had worked hard to make Bond a success. But once the franchise was up and going strong, Harry, a restless man with a facile mind, began unspooling other projects with great success, including the Harry Palmer films with Michael Caine. While Saltzman was preoccupied with his other ventures, Broccoli felt he was carrying the load of the Bond films pretty much on his own.

On 11th January 1966, production began on *Casino Royale* at Shepperton Studios. Feldman had put together a mammoth cast, including Peter Sellers, David Niven, Orson Welles, Woody Allen, Ursula Andress and John Huston. Huston would also direct, along with Joe McGrath and Val Guest. Sellers eventually had McGrath fired, and Robert Parrish and Ken Hughes came in to shoot other scenes. Richard Talmadge directed the action scenes. More writers came and went, including Terry Southern, Wolf Mankowitz and John Law. Aside from certain character names, there was scant little else about the production that was recognizable as having anything to do with Ian Fleming.

There was trouble almost from the beginning. The mercurial Peter Sellers, recovering from a recent heart attack, was at first enthusiastic about working with Orson Welles, but soon developed a loathing for the legendary director-actor and refused to shoot scenes with him. The soundstages where the film was being made took on a party atmosphere, with show-biz celebrities dropping in to see what all the fuss was about. Some, like Peter O'Toole, were persuaded to make an appearance (O'Toole's remuneration: a case of champagne). Deborah Kerr earned $50,000 for one week's work - which she finished in two days.

Columbia Pictures was not amused with all the expensive cameos. "They keep saying, 'Stop it - no more people'," said Feldman, "but I tell them, 'It's a circus. I can't stop it now'." *Time* magazine dubbed the production *Little Cleopatra*. The budget kept climbing, surpassing the $8 million mark (it

eventually reached $10.5 million). Feldman argued that with below-the-line costs of $2.5 to 3 million, $5 million was not too exorbitant, considering the talent gathered for the extravaganza. Only Peter Sellers was receiving a percentage (and a Park Ward Rolls-Royce that accounted for $23,800 of the film's cost).

The film was scheduled for a Christmas 1966 release, but as production dragged on, it became evident that it would not be ready in time. Columbia put their second Matt Helm film, *Murderer's Row*, into the release slot previously reserved for *Casino Royale*, now scheduled for an Easter release. In the press, Feldman defended the five-director concept as a "stroke of genius" that enabled several scenes to be shot at once, so performers were not idle between scenes. He claimed that if the film had been shot in a traditional manner with the same cast, it would have cost twelve to fifteen million dollars. Privately, however, he was less enthusiastic. When he saw Sean Connery in London after the production ended, he told the actor, "I tell you what, Sean. I wish I'd paid you the million. It would have been a whole lot cheaper."

In February 1966, while cameras rolled on *Casino Royale*, Broccoli and Saltzman left for Japan to scout locations with new Bond director Lewis Gilbert. With two dozen films under his belt, Gilbert was a well-established figure in British cinema.

Gilbert, who had directed two previous films in Asia (*Ferry To Hong Kong* and *The Seventh Dawn*), set about planning the film with the help of William Cartlidge, who had been his assistant director on *Alfie*. "*You Only Live Twice*," said Cartlidge, "was probably, at that time, the biggest movie that had been envisaged in the United Kingdom."

The script for the new Bond was the first not to be written by Richard Maibaum, who was busy with other assignments. In his stead, the producers turned to Roald Dahl. In 1952, Dahl published a famed short story called 'Lamb To The Slaughter', in which a piece of frozen lamb is used as a murder weapon, before being cooked and served to the detective attempting to solve the crime. The idea for the story came from Ian Fleming, who had proposed writing it several years earlier. "It wasn't nasty," Dahl said, "I thought it was hilarious. What's horrible is basically funny. In fiction."

Only in a 007 film will you find women in bikinis in an operating theatre. Said production designer Ken Adam, "They didn't want to see them in surgical scrubs." The scene **above** from *You Only Live Twice* is a reverse of the 1942 Monogram film *Black Dragons*, in which Bela Lugosi plays an evil plastic surgeon who has altered six Japanese men to appear Caucasian so they can become wartime spies in Washington, DC.

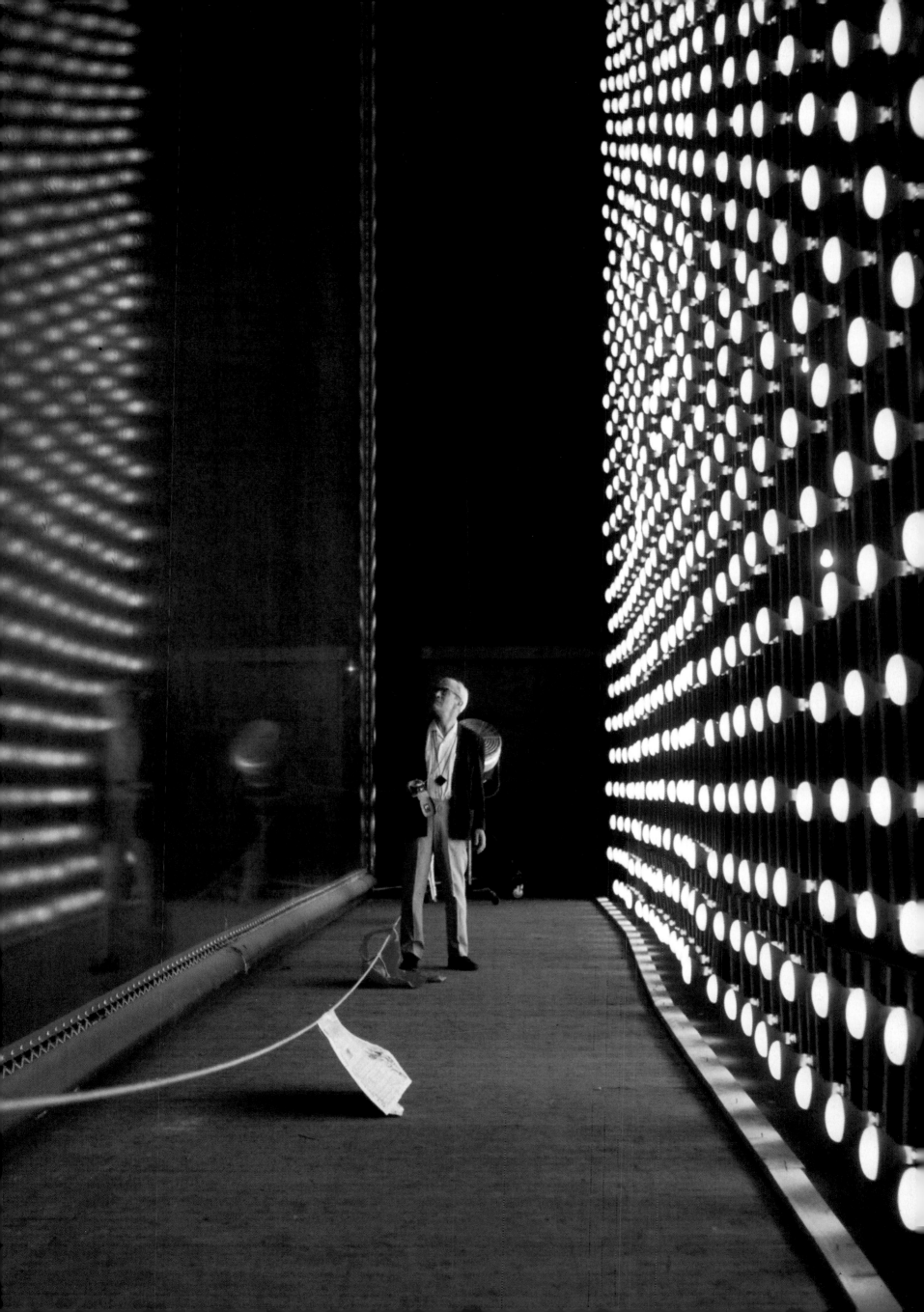

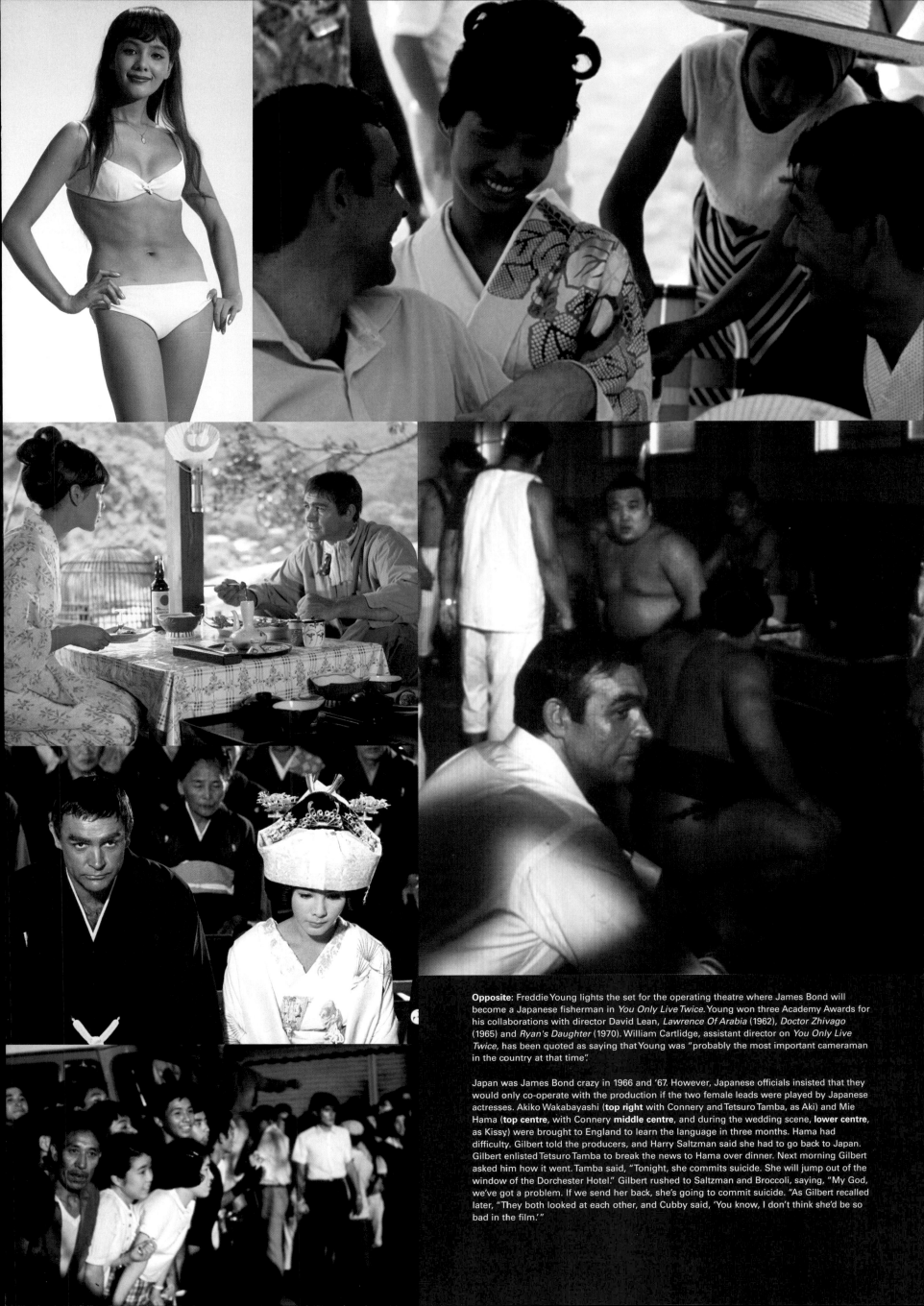

Opposite: Freddie Young lights the set for the operating theatre where James Bond will become a Japanese fisherman in *You Only Live Twice*. Young won three Academy Awards for his collaborations with director David Lean, *Lawrence Of Arabia* (1962), *Doctor Zhivago* (1965) and *Ryan's Daughter* (1970). William Cartlidge, assistant director on *You Only Live Twice*, has been quoted as saying that Young was "probably the most important cameraman in the country at that time".

Japan was James Bond crazy in 1966 and '67. However, Japanese officials insisted that they would only co-operate with the production if the two female leads were played by Japanese actresses. Akiko Wakabayashi (**top right** with Connery and Tetsuro Tamba, as Aki) and Mie Hama (**top centre**, with Connery **middle centre**, and during the wedding scene, **lower centre**, as Kissy) were brought to England to learn the language in three months. Hama had difficulty. Gilbert told the producers, and Harry Saltzman said she had to go back to Japan. Gilbert enlisted Tetsuro Tamba to break the news to Hama over dinner. Next morning Gilbert asked him how it went. Tamba said, "Tonight, she commits suicide. She will jump out of the window of the Dorchester Hotel." Gilbert rushed to Saltzman and Broccoli, saying, "My God, we've got a problem. If we send her back, she's going to commit suicide. "As Gilbert recalled later, "They both looked at each other, and Cubby said, 'You know, I don't think she'd be so bad in the film.'"

Like Fleming, who provided Dahl with several more short story ideas over the years, Roald Dahl had eclectic passions, including orchids, golf, gambling, music, art, antiques and wine. But it was his dark wit and inventive plotting that made him an ideal candidate to script *You Only Live Twice*. "I always thought I would find it a great rush and a pressure, but it's not that at all," said Dahl. "The reason, I think, is mainly because there are such nice people in this bunch." He conferred regularly with the producers and Lewis Gilbert during the script's formative stages. The first two drafts were written in California in early 1966. He was still making revisions to the latest draft while on his way to Pinewood. He found the Bond formula helpful. "You've got your hero ready-made for you. The hard thing was to get a credible plot without going into science-fiction. That is the pitfall."

Dahl, who had known Fleming for 20 years and had always liked his books, nonetheless found *You Only Live Twice* a decidedly un-cinematic story, little more than a travelogue. The producers agreed, and reached a key decision. They would use very little from Fleming's novel. They would create their own James Bond plot. The decision was filled with risks - one of the elements that made Bond stand apart from the host of imitators was the use of Fleming's unique narratives and devices.

In fact, the move away from Fleming pushed the filmmakers to turn towards current events for inspiration, an element which would have a major impact on Bond films in the future. Dahl told the filmmakers that since Bond had already done everything he could possibly do on land, sea and air, he ought to go into space.

1966 proved to be a year of unbridled optimism within the US space programme. The US had doubled the number of manned space flights flown by the USSR (sixteen to the Soviets' eight), and US astronauts nearly quadrupled the cumulative hours spent by Russian cosmonauts in orbit (1993 compared to 507). While the US programme was conducted in full openness to the world's media, the Soviets did not even announce their launch schedules.

The Soviets' veil of secrecy and a growing paranoia about China's role as a burgeoning superpower informed the storyline of *Twice*. While China's brand of Communism had seemed faddish in certain intellectual circles in the early 60s, the events of late 1965 and early '66 changed that. In November 1965, Shanghai newspapers launched an attack against an historian named Wu Han. Han's plays were seen as an attack against Mao Tse-tung. Within weeks, Mao launched the 'Cultural Revolution' in which academics were denounced as 'bourgeois reactionaries', pulled out of classrooms by their students and beaten in the streets. Mao formed a blindly supportive youth organization called The Red Guard, which grew in the autumn of 1966 to number 22 million - a private army capable of toppling any of Mao's political enemies. Many in the West wondered what Mao would do with this new, violent militia he had formed.

During this time, Japan's relationship with China continued to warm - a development which caused concern in the West. Japan also became a cultural fascination for Europe and America. Japanese

technology (with Sony transistor radios) became the rage, monster movies from Toho Studios enjoyed popularity among children worldwide, and Japanese architecture and shipbuilding were the envy of the world. In 1966, spurred by the success of the 1964 Summer Olympics, Japan announced a World's Fair in Osaka for 1970, and won the right to host the 1972 Winter Olympics in Sapporo.

Dahl's script played on all of these elements by creating a story which did not mirror any specific political developments in Asia or the space race, but rather felt as though it was totally in tune with the global pulse. Ken Adam took much of this one step further. Working from the bold palette of Japanese designers of the day and the influence of Mod, Pop Art and Op Art fashions in London, Adam created a design for the film that combined the sleek modern feel of Bond with the more overt jokiness of the times.

The film is ostensibly about SPECTRE's plot to steal Soviet and US space capsules and thus launch World War Three, allowing SPECTRE's sponsor - China - to take over the world. In fact, Dahl and the filmmakers took the viewers on a slightly more psychedelic journey. Dahl's stories were noted for their Freudian imagery, and his script for *You Only Live Twice* proved no less overt with its symbolic 'deaths' and 'rebirths'. The script begins with Bond's apparent death in Hong Kong, his recovery by a submarine, and ejection toward the Japanese coast through a torpedo tube. Once in Japan, Bond follows a beautiful girl through the streets until he eventually falls down a high-tech rabbit hole. What follows are various wild adventures, ruses and disguises for 007 as he pursues the disappearing rockets into a converted volcano. Gadgets fill the film, including the remarkable one-man autogyro dubbed 'Little Nellie', which appears to sport more weaponry than most fighter jets. The result is a story that feels almost dream-like, taking place in the Asian Wonderland of modern Japan. At its core - in place of a bemused Alice - was the imperturbable James Bond.

When the filmmakers arrived for shooting in Japan, though, they found themselves not in Wonderland, but indeed on the other side of the looking-glass.

En route, Sean Connery made an announcement that many had been predicting for some time. At a stopover in Bangkok, Thailand on 27th July, Connery formally announced that *You Only Live Twice* would be his final James Bond film. The Bond image, he said, had

Blofeld's cat (**right**, pictured from *Diamonds Are Forever*), an enduring symbol of languid, emotionless evil, also has a lineage: Dr. No's monkey, which Cubby Broccoli demanded be excised from the final script. Richard Maibaum knew his original idea to give the master villain a pet was powerful. An animal would de-humanize the character and provide a feral air of mystery about him. For *Dr. No*, Maibaum just had the wrong animal. The cat, which first appeared in *From Russia With Love*, became a recurring character, who, like Bond, possessed his own iconography.

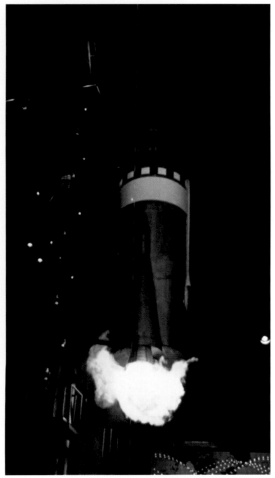

"Your new lair is up and running..."
"Is it a hollowed-out volcano, like I asked for?"

Number Two and Dr. Evil, in *Austin Powers: The Spy Who Shagged Me*

turned into a Frankenstein monster. "It started out as a joke, but things got out of hand - everything became magnified." He later told reporter William Hall, "None of us could have foreseen how it would catch on. I admit it's done more for me than any other character has done for an actor in history. But if you'd been asked the same questions day after day for four years, how would you feel?"

When Connery arrived in Tokyo, he was besieged by the press, who remained unrelenting throughout the exhausting shoot. At one point, a press photographer reportedly followed Connery into the bathroom. For the actor, it was the last straw. The producers intervened, pleading with the press to give him privacy and providing him with a guard detail to keep the press at bay.

But Bondmania, Japanese-style, did not abate. While the crew was filming the Kobe Dock fight scene on location in August, they noted that one cinema was playing a 007 triple-bill daily, with one-hour breaks for lunch and dinner.

On 20th August, Connery celebrated his 36th birthday on the set during the filming of Bond's wedding to Aki. Partly due to the pressures of playing 007, Connery's own marriage was on shaky ground. He and his wife, actress Diane Cilento, had been separated prior to filming. They hoped a quiet working vacation together in Japan would help them iron out some of their differences. The hoop-la was not what either had hoped for.

In the week of 14th-21st September, the unit moved back to the UK for location filming. On the 16th, the *Evening Standard* reported that Sir Alfred Earl, the new Director-General of Intelligence in Britain's Defence Ministry, admitted that he was a 007 fan. "I've read all his books," Earl said, "and thoroughly enjoyed them, too." He added, "Of course, I'm not saying I consider Bond a good operator. But he certainly has a whale of a time."

While *You Only Live Twice* was filming at Pinewood, *Casino Royale* was continuing to roll at Shepperton and other studios. Meanwhile, Roger Moore was shooting the latest round of episodes of *The Saint* at ABP in Elstree, and Stanley Kubrick was directing the landmark *2001: A Space Odyssey* at MGM in Boreham Wood. The sound stages of England were filled with spies and outer space fantasies.

On 26th September 1966, the Bond producers were shaken to learn that Johnny Jordan, an aerial cameraman, had been injured in an accident shooting second-unit footage in Japan. On the same day, the *Evening News* reported that James Bond had been officially declared a possible international menace by the government of Pakistan. The Central Board of Film Censors there warned film importers to be wary of offering spy films because "they are full of crime and bedroom scenes which may have an adverse effect on our international relations".

In October, filming moved to the biggest and most complex film interior ever built in Europe - the volcano interior. Designed by Ken Adam, the mammoth set was large enough for a helicopter to fly around inside. It cost £350,000 to build - more than the entire budget of *Dr. No*. The set, which could be seen from the main London-Oxford road three miles away, required more tubular steel than was used to build the London Hilton.

Even before its release, *You Only Live Twice* impacted on film distribution. United Artists had a long-standing policy that it did not allow 'blind-bidding' of its films. With this policy, no theatre owners could complain they were being hyped into booking a bad film. They had seen the movie first. The exhibitors, though, wanted to change the policy, and wanted to bid on *You Only Live Twice* before

As the box-office receipts of the 007 films ballooned, so did the expectations for the films themselves. Production designer Ken Adam felt the strain on *You Only Live Twice*. "It was quite a strenuous experience until we found this unbelievable volcanic area on Kyushu. There were about six to eight volcanoes, all next to each other, which looked almost like how I imagined a moonscape. We decided that it would be interesting to have the villain live in one of these extinct craters. Cubby gave me a sidelong glance and said, 'Can you do it?' I said, 'Well, give me a chance'. And I started scribbling away.

"When I had done two or three sketches, I presented them to Lewis [Gilbert] and Cubby, and Cubby said, 'Looks interesting. How much is it going to cost?' I knew it was going to be a gigantic set, but I had no idea, and I quoted a million dollars - an enormous amount of money. Cubby didn't blink an eyelid. He said, 'If you can do it for a million, go ahead'. And then my worries started."

Following page, bottom centre: Wing Commander Ken Wallis and Little Nellie travelled to America to be interviewed by Hugh Downs for NBC-TV's *Today Show* to promote *You Only Live Twice*.

"I did **85** take-offs and landings and **46** hours in the air for about seven and a half minutes on the screen. But that's filmmaking, isn't it?" Wing Commander Ken Wallis

the movie was complete. United Artists' policy had inconvenienced them with *Thunderball* when they were not allowed to set their Christmas and New Year's releases far enough in advance. UA relented, and blind bidding soon became the norm in film distribution.

On Pinewood's Stage E on 10th and 11th January 1967, stuntman Bob Simmons was hoisted on wires to film the pre-credits shots of *You Only Live Twice*, showing an American astronaut dying when the SPECTRE intruder rocket closes in on his capsule.

Just over two weeks later, on 27th January, a real-life tragedy claimed the lives of three of America's astronauts. Virgil 'Gus' Grissom, Roger Chaffee and Ed White were killed when the pure oxygen inside their space capsule caught fire during a simulated launch training exercise. White had made the first American space walk as part of the crew of Gemini 4 in June 1965, remaining outside his spacecraft, attached to a tether, for 21 minutes. This was twice as long as the Russian cosmonaut Alexei Leonov, who had performed a ten-minute 'space walk' a few months earlier. Leonov also had a brush with death in 1967; while he was in a limousine on his way to a government reception at the Kremlin, a gunman approached and fired two bullets which grazed his coat and a third which narrowly missed his face. The gunman had mistaken Leonov for Soviet President Leonid Brezhnev, whom he intended to assassinate.

On 19th December 1966, United Artists received an unwelcome Christmas surprise - an official announcement by Columbia Pictures that their mammoth James Bond spoof, *Casino Royale*, would open throughout the United States and Britain in April the following year.

While the films were still in production, Columbia and United Artists had mutually agreed upon a release plan. *Casino Royale* would open during Christmas of 1966, and *You Only Live Twice* would open in the summer of 1967, allowing for six months between the two premieres. However, Christmas came and went with *Casino Royale* still in production. Feldman wanted to hold the release until Christmas 1967, but Columbia, with $9 million invested in the film and interest on bank loans mounting, wanted the film in cinemas ASAP. United Artists were expecting to release *You Only Live Twice* in June, and had put their faith in an earlier announcement that *Casino Royale* would open in October 1967, leaving the summer clear for the latest Sean Connery 007 opus.

When Columbia rushed to get *Casino* out first, it was like a declaration of war to United Artists. Columbia naturally hoped to capitalize on the overwhelming popularity of the Eon-produced James Bond films, which at that point had already racked up the highest box-office grosses of any film series in history - US rentals alone totalled over one hundred million dollars. If *Casino Royale* was as successful as Columbia hoped, it would still be playing when the United Artists film opened.

The battle lines were drawn with the marketing campaigns. Eon and United Artists made it clear that there was only one 007 with the ad-line 'Sean Connery IS James Bond'. Producer Charles K. Feldman and Columbia, whose comedy spoof featured several actors as 007, proclaimed 'Casino Royale Is Too Much For One James Bond'.

After more than a year of press ballyhoo, with pictorials in magazines ranging from *Look* to *Playboy*, there was undeniable demand for *Casino Royale*. The director of the Cannes Film Festival requested it be the festival opener. Unfortunately, Feldman and Columbia were unable to get a print ready and subtitled in time, and were forced to decline the offer. The unavailability of a suitable print also led to the cancellation of a $200-per-ticket charity premiere screening in Dallas arranged by British socialite Lady Sassoon and meant to generate funds for the Southern Methodist University Medical College.

The madcap film barely made its 13th April 1967 London premiere date at the Odeon Leicester Square, which benefited Hurt Minds Can Be Healed, a mental health charity. Rumours abounded that the final cut of the film happened in the Odeon's projection booth. Afterwards, producer Feldman felt the print used for the event was too muddy, and ordered a new one struck for the US premiere. The result was that the film premiered in New York on Friday, 28th April 1967, one day later than planned.

Columbia Pictures spent over a million dollars on *Casino Royale*'s advertising campaign, using the now-famous nude and tattooed woman. Charles Feldman had a history of coming up with iconic images; his contributions to the pop-culture *zeitgeist* included Marlon Brando's torn T-shirt (from *A Streetcar Named Desire*) and Marilyn Monroe's dress blowing up as she stood over a New York subway grate (from *The Seven Year Itch*).

In New York, the roof of Broadway's Screen Building was used as a perch for a 62' by 100' sign of the 'tattooed lady'. Reporters were invited to a luncheon on the roof for the unveiling, where they were served Hebrew National hot dogs and Moët champagne. To help further trumpet the comedy extravaganza, Feldman secured the services of 1967's modelling phenomenon Twiggy. The 17-year-old supermodel was filmed watching the *Casino Royale* trailer for a television spot.

Director Lewis Gilbert discusses a scene with Sean Connery (**top**). In 1966 and '67, the space race was heating up, as America and the Soviet Union each rushed to be the first to land a man on the moon. On 10th April 1966, Alexei Leonov (**bottom**) announced that Soviet cosmonauts were in training for lunar missions. The first US casualties of the space race were Gus Grissom, Ed White and Roger Chaffee (**middle**), who died in the tragic Apollo 1 fire. After the accident, NASA stepped up its testing for future flights. Water impact and flotation tests were conducted by astronauts Jim Lovell, Stuart Roosa and Charles Duke in the Gulf of Mexico on 5th-7th April 1968, using a command service module named 'spacecraft 007'. James Bond's connection with outer space continues. On 4th April 1999, Czech astronomers at the Klet observatory named a minor planet they discovered in 1983, catalogued as asteroid 9007 - 'James Bond'.

United Artists art director Donald Smolen pulled out all the stops to promote *You Only Live Twice*. "The poster lent itself perfectly to a billboard that ran for one entire city block wide," said Smolen. "At one end of one side of the block was the Astor Theater, at the other end was the Victoria Theater. And this big horizontal poster was above all the buildings, from end of the street to the other. We had a little travelling sign at the bottom of the poster that went to one end of the block and said 'HERE' over the Astor Theater, and then it ran down the street to the other end and said 'HERE' over the Victoria Theater. It worked beautifully for about two days, and then all of a sudden one night there was a whole series of sparks, fire started at the poster. All the sparks fell into Broadway, and the whole thing was shut down. The poster remained, but the 'HERE', 'HERE' display sign disappeared."

United Artists countered with a billboard that stretched for an entire New York city block, above Broadway's side-by-side Astor and Victoria theatres, both of which were scheduled to screen *You Only Live Twice*. The billboard was erected in December 1966 - seven months before the release of the film - and featured striking artwork of Sean Connery's James Bond walking along the inner rim of Blofeld's volcano hideaway. Columbia replied with bus and subway posters.

In Boston, an ultra-conservative city with such stringent film censorship that the term "banned in Boston" became a cliché, the ballyhoo over *Casino Royale* boiled over. On 6th May 1967, Columbia Pictures, the Sack Savoy Theater and radio station WRKO decided to have a special early morning 4am screening of the movie. Anyone wearing a trenchcoat or raincoat would be allowed in free of charge. The owners of the theatre, which had a seating capacity of 2,858, reasoned that the hour would prevent the venue from being filled to capacity. They had failed to account for the volatile excitement generated by the combination of the terms "new James Bond movie" and "free admission".

Before one o'clock in the morning, 8,000 teenagers and young adults gathered outside the theatre, some arriving from as far away as Maine and New Hampshire. The start time of the 150-minute film was moved up to 1am, and the theatre quickly filled. The several thousand outside - an ever-increasing number, as many who still thought the showing would be at 4am continued to arrive - demanded a second showing. As word spread that there would not be one, police arrived on the scene to try and contain the trenchcoated mob, which eventually grew to an estimated 15,000. Soon, the scene turned ugly and Boston experienced its first and last James Bond riot.

Inside, the film was kept going throughout the mêlée, but the on-screen hijinks were mild in comparison to what was happening in the auditorium. There were a couple of seat-cushion blazes. Some of the patrons were drenched by a broken fire-hose. There was fighting in the aisles. The female ushers were pushed around until they finally hid in the office. Someone opened a fire door, and the theatre quickly filled far beyond its capacity. The assistant manager, fearing the mob would rip the place down, dared not turn off the projector.

Meanwhile, outside, club-wielding police and police dogs battled enraged youths, who pelted them with beer cans, not all of which were empty. Store windows shattered. Rioters turned over some cars and stole others. A car belonging to a reporter for *The Boston Globe*, parked in front of police headquarters, was painted in stripes. The police called for tear gas and moved on the crowd in full force. By morning, there were numerous looted storefronts, thirty injured, twenty-five arrested and ten hospitalized.

"Charlie learned the hard way that making a Bond film is not a dilettante operation." Cubby Broccoli on Charles Feldman

Later that morning, Justice Elijah Adlow of the Boston Municipal Court called the rioters "idiots", but decided that you do not send idiots to jail. He dismissed the charges against all of the youths except one 24-year-old who was charged with malicious damage to property - a police vehicle. Adlow declared the events "the results of a ridiculous publicity stunt". The event did, indeed, generate publicity, but at a high cost. When it was over, the general manager of Sack Theaters, Alan Friedberg, admitted that the reaction to the promotion went far beyond expectations, adding, "nobody ever dreamed it would create 'A Happening'".

In February, as the final scenes of *You Only Live Twice* were being filmed, *Playboy* magazine featured a pictorial of 'The Girls of *Casino Royale*', with text by Woody Allen. In June, the magazine featured a six-page *You Only Live Twice* pictorial with text by Roald Dahl called '007's Oriental Eyefuls'. That same month, *Popular Mechanics* carried a cover story on Little Nellie - 'How It Works - James Bond's Amazing Autogyro'.

The UA publicity machine again pulled out all the stops for *You Only Live Twice*. There were two TV specials, one for each side of the Atlantic. In March, British viewers were treated to a BBC1 broadcast of Alan Whicker's *Whicker's World* behind-the-scenes *cinema verité* documentary on the making of the film, while on 5th June 1967, American viewers saw NBC's broadcast of *Welcome To Japan, Mr. Bond*, featuring specially filmed segments with Bernard Lee, Lois Maxwell and Desmond Llewelyn.

Along with the 22nd May release of the film's soundtrack, there were major film-specific tie-ins with five leading companies - Colgate, Multiple Products, Milton Bradley, Sony, and Toyota. Colgate created

new TV ads to promote the 007 products originally introduced in 1965. Multiple Products launched a promotional campaign for its Shooting Attaché Case. Milton Bradley began a new campaign to advertise James Bond games and puzzles released years earlier and still selling strongly. Sony touted the communications console inside *YOLT*'s Toyota. The Japanese auto-maker supplied special posters to its dealers to promote the Toyota GT2000. The one seen in the film made its first public appearance in the US on 1st April at the New York International Auto Show. Only two convertible versions of the car were produced, both for the movie. The second car was touring Europe, making the rounds of automotive shows in Brussels, Amsterdam, Helsinki and Geneva. The GT2000 was a 'muscle car' meant to show that Japan could compete with Detroit in the manufacture of powerful sports cars. On 3rd June, *El Diario*, New York's Spanish-language newspaper, began a serialization of the novel YOU ONLY LIVE TWICE, illustrated with photos from the movie.

Then, on 12th June, came the moment everyone had been anticipating - the royal premiere of *You Only Live Twice*, sponsored by the Variety Club of Great Britain to aid the YMCA and the Imperial Cancer Research Fund. In attendance were Dick Van Dyke and Sally Ann Howes, stars of Cubby Broccoli's newest production, *Chitty Chitty Bang Bang*, and Guy Hamilton, then directing Harry Saltzman's *Battle Of Britain*. It was the first London James Bond premiere that Sean Connery had attended since 1963; he arrived sporting a drooping moustache and *sans toupee*. When he was presented to the Queen, she asked him, "Is this really your last James Bond film?" He replied, "I'm afraid so, ma'am." She asked, "Did you feel you were typecast?" He said, "Yes, I think you're right, ma'am".

When the film opened the next day, it broke the opening day record at London's Odeon Leicester Square. In America, it immediately became the Number One film in the nation. After the first weekend, it had grossed $611,074 in New York, Los Angeles, Chicago, Philadelphia, Boston and Baltimore. After its first three weeks of release in 161 theatres nationwide, it earned $6,874,118.

The box-office around the world showed that Bondmania was still strong. In Tokyo, *You Only Live Twice* grossed $51,533 in its first four days of release at the Hibiya Theatre. In the Philippines it shattered the opening-week record previously held by *Thunderball* in Manila, with $112,145 in four cinemas. In Rome, it grossed $116,362 in its first week of release. It set opening day records in Copenhagen, and broke all existing records in its first two weeks in four cinemas in Lima, Peru. By the end of the year, *You Only Live Twice* was the second-highest moneymaker of 1967, after *The Dirty Dozen*.

Just behind *Twice* in global box office was *Casino Royale*. Charlie Feldman's Bond film did only two-thirds the business of Cubby and Harry's Bond. Ultimately, *Twice* did suffer from the competition. The film only sold 36 million tickets in North America, which made it a huge blockbuster, but nothing like *Goldfinger* or *Thunderball*. No one, though, was losing money, and no one thought James Bond films could go on selling exponentially more tickets.

By the summer of 1967, spymania was drawing to a close. The exaggerated sexuality, gadgetry, and sophistication that spawned such rabid interest in the Bond films now felt cliché'd to many. Cultural over-indulgence in all things espionage-related did not keep *You Only Live Twice* from becoming a hit, but the winds of change continued to blow through every aspect of society, even the film industry. While youth groups worldwide asked for world peace, movie audiences lined up to see increasingly violent and raw films.

Broccoli and Saltzman, faced with deepening fissures in their business relationship, also confronted James Bond's identity crisis. With Connery gone, what was the future of 007? Although *Casino Royale* had hurt *You Only Live Twice* at the box office, Cubby and Harry felt they had learned some lessons from the movie. First, *Casino Royale* proved one could sell a lot of tickets to a James Bond movie even without Sean

Connery on board. Broccoli, in particular, felt his old friend Charlie Feldman had blown his chance to make a tremendously successful movie by letting the film's costs run out of control. Thus, while Connery was a plus, Broccoli and Saltzman felt more assured after the summer of 1967 that James Bond the character was the key ingredient for further success. But who was Bond? What made secret agent 007 stand out from the hosts of imitators who parodied his dress, emulated his style, and echoed his exploits?

For Cubby Broccoli, the key was to be found within the words of the man who started it all - Ian Fleming. *You Only Live Twice* had been an exercise in indulgence. The filmmakers constructed an elaborate, entertaining fantasy, but the previously ever-present shadow of the literary Bond seemed barely discernible as parts of the spectacle unfolded. Fleming's Bond was rawer, more dangerous, tinged with a trace of tragedy. For Broccoli and Saltzman, the time seemed right to pull away from the exaggerated elements of spymania and return 007 to his roots.

Above: Sean Connery and his wife, actress Diane Cilento, attend the London premiere of *You Only Live Twice*. After completing filming, Connery told a columnist, "Bond's been good to me, but I've done my bit. I'm out."

5. From October 1962 to May 1967, a period of only four and a half years, Cubby Broccoli and Harry Saltzman premiered five James Bond films which were met with unprecedented box office success and cheered by legions of fans across the globe. They had brought to the world a new kind of hero. They had altered the language and business of the film industry, and had created a pop culture phenomenon. During this time, James Bond had

Calculated Risks

become both a symbol of cinematic innovation and a hallowed tradition, a rite of passage for adolescents. Going to see a Bond movie with the rest of the family became an acknowledgement of maturity. Fathers took their sons and daughters to the films while uttering the words of caution, 'Don't tell your mother'. Getting the more subtle of the sex jokes in the script allowed viewers to feel that they were entering a private club. The real world, though, was changing. The glut of spy films which had been released in response to the Bond phenomenon waned noticeably in 1967, a year which saw the last of the James Coburn Flint films and the Harry Saltzman-produced Harry Palmer movies. The movies were changing direction. They were starting to focus on the growing youth culture in America and, more and more, they were trying to reflect the attitudes, disaffection and discontent of the times.

Across the planet, secret agent 007 could be seen as nothing less than a cultural force, an assertion illustrated by Bond's impact in two unlikely locations. In Jamaica, violent youth gangs - called 'rude boys' - adopted the "licence to kill" motto and took to scrawling '007' on buildings in the slums of Kingston to announce their fearless attitude. Immortalized by Desmond Dekker in his hit song, '007 (Shanty Town)', it was not Bond's elegance or taste that captured the imagination of the impoverished Jamaicans. It was his casual attitude in dispensing violence and death. In Indonesia, the response was totally different. The Jakarta 007 Club became the name of a youth movement which represented an unrepressed enjoyment of popular music, dancing, fast cars and Western fashions. What made the movement so remarkable was that in 1967 no James Bond film had ever been allowed inside the nation.

On 14th April 1967, a film was screened in New York that was to have a major impact on the world of James Bond - *Bonnie And Clyde*. Starring Warren Beatty and Faye Dunaway as the 1930s bank robbers who are gunned down in a blaze of bullets, the film shocked and seduced audiences with its graphic, slow-motion violence. By contrast, the violence of *You Only Live Twice* - with its innovative staging, brilliant sound effects and bravura editing - was anything but seductive. Films like *Bonnie And Clyde*, *The Dirty Dozen* and *Point Blank* showed violence in a new way. They pushed the limits, just as *Dr. No* had done in 1962. These films showed images that were ugly and brutal - like the nightly news footage from the Vietnam War. But the films balanced this brutality by romanticizing the images with glamour and nostalgia. Death in *Bonnie And Clyde* was not heroic as in the old westerns, or ironic as in the Bond films. In *Bonnie And Clyde*, death was both mundane and tragic.

The nature of violence in cinema was changing; so too was the nature of the moral universe portrayed in films. In 1962, the image of Ursula Andress walking out from the sea set men's pulses racing. By 1966, director Michelangelo Antonioni set a different tone in *Blow-Up* when he showed two teenage girls romping naked in bed with a photographer. Where Bond danced on the edge of

moral ambiguity when he fired bullets into the back of Professor Dent, *Blow-Up* questioned the entire nature of right and wrong and moral certainty, distancing viewers from any association with the central characters. The ad-line from the US movie poster almost sounds like it could be describing a Bond film - "Antonioni's camera never flinches. At love without meaning. At murder without guilt." Yet Bond was a hero who vanquished evil. Filmmakers like Antonioni questioned the very premise of the mythology behind characters like Bond.

The fantasy world of Bond had reached a high point with *You Only Live Twice*, and dipped into incomprehensibility with *Casino Royale* and countless spy spoofs.

The mood of the public seemed clear - there was a new direction in modern cinema. Realism and romanticism were merging in complex stories filled with violence and tragedy. The hero was being supplanted by the anti-hero.

While Harry Saltzman and Cubby Broccoli shepherded two big-budget non-Bond films to the screen, 007 took a backseat. It would be two and a half years before the release of the next James Bond film, the longest gap between films up to that date. Saltzman had decided, in May 1966, to become involved with a film being prepared by Polish-born producer Benjamin Fisz (who had produced the early Sean Connery film, *On The Fiddle*, which Saltzman had screened while searching for an actor to play Bond). The project was *Battle Of Britain*, a film intended to be a war epic to rival *The Longest Day*.

While Saltzman was getting his Second World War spectacular underway, Cubby Broccoli completed *Chitty Chitty Bang Bang* - an Ian Fleming story that the spy author had written for his son, Casper. Broccoli wanted to produce a film version in the style of Disney's *Mary Poppins* for his daughter, Barbara. He brought many of the James Bond filmmaking team onto the project. Roald Dahl wrote the script and Ken Hughes directed. Hughes' association with Broccoli dated back to the Warwick pictures *Jazzboat* and *The Trials Of Oscar Wilde*. Like Dahl, Hughes' most recent assignment had been a James Bond film - he was a segment director on *Casino Royale*.

During this time, Peter Hunt was a very busy man. Cubby Broccoli hired Hunt to associate-produce and to film second-unit sequences for *Chitty Chitty Bang Bang*. Shortly thereafter, on 14th September 1967, Eon Productions formally announced that Hunt, who had never helmed a feature, would be directing the next Bond film, *On Her Majesty's Secret Service*. "You have to understand," said Hunt, "I didn't

The mood of America darkened in the spring and summer of 1968 with two tragic assassinations. On April 4th, a bullet felled Martin Luther King Jr. in Memphis, Tennessee. Riots erupted in major cities across the nation. A young politician, Robert F. Kennedy (**above, left**), then a newly announced candidate for President, offered one voice of sanity in the madness which followed King's death. Just two months later, Kennedy was gunned down in Los Angeles. A sense of *déjà vu* pervaded the nation; once again America mourned an idealistic young leader, once again they mourned a Kennedy killed before reaching the full potential of his promise.

Indonesian youths rebelled against the culturally repressive regime of the nation by dancing the Monkey and Watusi (**above, right**) and wearing decidedly European and American clothes. They called their movement 'The Jakarta 007 Club', embracing James Bond as a role model of the modern age.

feel like I was suddenly starting something new. Because I'd been there all the time... so I was extremely experienced."

Majesty's had been in the works for years. Originally planned to follow *Goldfinger*, the film was pushed back to 1966 because of the deal with Kevin McClory to make *Thunderball*. When production of *Thunderball* ran long, Broccoli and Saltzman realized they would need to find a location for Blofeld's hideaway which could be filmed during the late spring and early summer. This proved impossible, and once again, *Majesty's* was shelved in favour of *You Only Live Twice*. This decision did not come without costs. In 1965, United Artists mounted an expensive talent hunt for twelve international beauties to appear in the film with Sean Connery. When the film was cancelled, not only was the talent hunt called off, but early prints of *Thunderball* had to be altered to delete the announcement of *Majesty's* as Bond's next adventure.

After Peter Hunt had been signed to direct, he immediately began working with screenwriter Richard Maibaum to adapt what many considered to be Ian Fleming's best novel. They decided to remain faithful to the source, including the tragic, downbeat ending. It seemed right for the times. "I'll be sticking to the proven Bond formula but, I hope, with a fresh, individual approach," Hunt said.

Given the tenor of the times, and knowing they would be introducing a new actor as 007, the producers and Hunt carefully considered the approach they would take with the new James Bond film. A new actor meant a fresh start, a chance to reinvent the character. "At that time, long hair was coming in, and there were hippie youngsters and that sort of thing," said Peter Hunt. "We went through a whole range of discussions saying, what would the new Bond look like? Should we make him a modern Bond? Should we make him this? Should we make him look like that? And it was agreed by practically everybody in the end that no, what we wanted was another Sean Connery."

While doing a cigarette ad in Germany, one of George Lazenby's fellow actors asked him to go on a blind date in his stead. Lazenby agreed, and found himself in the company of agent Maggie Abbott. A few months later, when Sean Connery announced his retirement from the role of 007, Abbott remembered Lazenby. "I got a phone call in Paris from Maggie saying, 'You gotta come over to London. I think that you're ideal for this role that they can't fill'. And I said, 'What's the role?' She said, 'Well, I can't tell you on the phone'. I said, 'Well, I can't come. Sorry.' Boom. And hung up the phone."

A couple of months later Lazenby heard from a friend that Abbott was still desperately trying to locate him, so he went to her office. "She said, 'I think you'd be right for James Bond'. And I said, 'Why's that?' She said, 'Just your arrogance'."

There were many parallels between Lazenby and Sean Connery. Both came from families with modest means, and both were self-made men. Moreover, both came to the role of Bond with a self-assured attitude and a strong will.

Lazenby, however, came in with the ability to give the producers exactly what they wanted to see. He drove an Aston Martin (purchased with money he had made performing in Big Fry chocolate commercials). He wore a Rolex. He arrived at Eon Productions literally wearing one of Sean Connery's suits (it was sold after Connery failed to pick it up from the tailor). Of course, Lazenby did not have an appointment at Eon. He couldn't get one, as he wasn't a member of the actors' union. Lazenby simply strode past the receptionist to the office of casting director Dyson Lovell.

George Lazenby was born on 5th September 1939, in Goulburn, near Canberra, in Australia. "Canberra was only started in 1900 to be the capital of Australia," said Lazenby. "They built it 90 miles inland, to protect it from attack by the sea. "The only son of a railway worker also named George, Lazenby left home at the age of 15, after receiving an ultimatum. "My mother said, 'Do it our way or get out'. I got out."

At 17, Lazenby finished school and served four months in the Australian Army before National Service was ended. He began work as an apprentice motor mechanic, but switched to car salesman, working in various parts of Australia until a desire to be an entertainer led him to become a guitar player in a band. "I'd never played a musical instrument in my life," said Lazenby, "but I knew 'Guitar Boogie' in every key." Lazenby soon took over the band, which was often hired to play back-up for pop singers touring through the Australian continent. At 20 years old, Lazenby found that he enjoyed being an entertainer. "The only thing that was in the back of my mind, I guess, was to show off, you know. To be somebody."

Lazenby arrived in England in April 1964 and soon found a job doing what he knew best - selling cars. He turned to male modelling after photographer Chard Jenkins entered the showroom and was impressed with Lazenby's 6' 2" frame and virile, masculine look. Within a year, Lazenby became one of the highest-paid male models in Europe.

"When George walks through the office, the secretaries fall off their chairs." Cubby Broccoli on George Lazenby

Knowing he had only one shot, Lazenby had gone to the barber at the Dorchester Hotel and had his hair cut like Connery as Bond. In the chair behind him was 007 producer Cubby Broccoli, who later told the barber, "This guy'd make a good James Bond, but he looks like a successful businessman". With the image complete, Lazenby arrived at Lovell's door, leaned in and casually stated, "I heard you're looking for James Bond". Dyson Lovell was on the phone with Harry Saltzman; he took a good look at Lazenby and said, "Harry, there's someone here that looks kinda like the guy we're looking for."

What followed were four months of screen tests and negotiations. Everyone from minor studio executives to the Fleming Estate was consulted on the choice for the new 007. Eventually, the producers resisted trying to bank on a name star, and went with

their instinct. Lazenby, they felt, was someone they could groom for the role. The turning point came in a screen test with stuntman Uri Borienko. Caught up in the excitement of the moment, Lazenby unleashed a blow that accidentally broke the nose of the stuntman. Saltzman, observing the proceedings, stepped over Borienko and told Lazenby, "We're going with you."

"It was about time," remembered Lazenby. "Because I was very anxious to find out after four months. Even though I was living a life of luxury - they put me up in the Grosvenor House in a private suite - they kept me kind of secret and I stayed out of touch with all my friends."

Secrecy was vitally important for the producers. *Life* magazine expressed interest in placing the new Bond on the cover, provided they could break the story first. Consequently, Lazenby could tell no one he

was so close to being anointed the new 007. As it turned out, he didn't make the cover of *Life* magazine. That same week, the Pope banned the use of the birth control pill by Catholics, and the pontiff took the cover.

Lazenby found that his life changed virtually overnight. Now, he was "immediately accepted by everyone. I mean, you get the best table at restaurants, you get upgraded in airplanes. It's amazing. All the doors open for you." Part of the star treatment involved being fitted for suits appropriate for James Bond, as well as the accompanying Turnbull & Asser shirts. "I wasn't used to wearing such good material, but it felt good," said Lazenby. "The suit felt like you were almost naked. It just hugged your body. And there is a difference, believe me, in having a Savile Row suit and one that you just pick off the peg."

Peter Hunt was determined to take 007 away from the sci-fi fantasy of *You Only Live Twice* and back to the more realistic world of *From Russia With Love*. "I don't foresee any great changes," said Hunt. But there were key changes. To make Bond more realistic, Hunt eschewed the elaborate sets of Ken Adam in favour of Syd Cain's more human scale. Hunt also wanted fewer gadgets, and so did Harry Saltzman. "That's been overdone," Saltzman told a reporter. "We are after a good story now, a good screenplay." Press accounts began referring to the new film as 'James Bond Without Gimmicks'.

Along with taking a back-to-basics approach, Peter Hunt wanted to give his film a posh look, like the melodramas that Ross Hunter produced for Universal Pictures. "I wanted it to be glamorous," said Hunt. "Ross Hunter, all his films looked glamorous. They all looked like they were extremely expensive." Using Michael Reed, the same cinematographer with whom he had shot the second unit work on *Chitty Chitty Bang Bang*, Hunt began filming the new James Bond adventure at Piz Gloria in Switzerland on 21st October 1968. The pair chose a very different approach to the cinematography than that used by Ted Moore and Freddie Young. Reed employed longer lenses, more close-ups, and fewer bold colours.

Hunt also brought in literary critic Simon Raven to give the film's dialogue a finer polish. Hunt wanted Raven "to make the dialogue a little bit sharper and a little better and a little more intellectual". On every level, Hunt was moving to make *Majesty's* more sophisticated and less comic-book.

For the character of Tracy, the woman whom James Bond would marry, the filmmakers decided the part required a performance that would convince audiences James Bond had fallen in love. The role went to one of the most popular actresses in England, Diana Rigg. Rigg had the advantage of following Honor Blackman on *The Avengers*, being familiar to a worldwide audience, and possessing tremendous skills as an actress. By following Fleming's novel closely, the filmmakers walked away from the Bond woman iconography they had so carefully cultivated over the years. Whereas Ursula Andress made her mark walking confidently out of the sea in a white bikini, Rigg's character was introduced attempting suicide, walking into the sea in a shimmering emerald dress.

Director Peter Hunt cast Diana Rigg in *On Her Majesty's Secret Service* at the suggestion of agent Dennis Selinger. "I thought it was a wonderful suggestion," said Hunt. "I was concerned that she wouldn't do it. And I was very concerned about casting Lazenby against her. But I talked with her at length once we decided to cast George and I invited them to my house and took them both out to dinner. I'd already spoken to Diana and said, 'I want you to meet this boy and I'd like you to be very honest with me and tell me what you think afterwards. But, will you come and have dinner with us and we'll make a pleasurable evening?' About four other of my friends came along, too, and we had a lovely evening out... The next day I was delighted because she rang me and said, 'Thank you, it was a lovely evening, and I think he's fine'."

When Tracy and Bond spend the night together, her motivations are complex and she is clearly in a self-destructive state. The encounter leaves 007 confused and intrigued. In this new film, actions and relationships have consequences impacting on James Bond, and Diana Rigg proved to be an actress to make those moral ambiguities feel real.

In addition to this deeper relationship, the film was based on Fleming's most action-packed novel, and Hunt was determined the film would not disappoint even the most rabid action fans. The extended chases - in cars, on skis and down bobsleigh runs - balanced out the heavier dramatic scenes. Despite some throw-away lines, and a section from the novel where an enemy skier is sucked into the turbine of a snow plough, the sequences offer an urgency and sense of desperation which had not been seen in a Bond film since *From Russia With Love*. As Lazenby's Bond states during the film's opening, "this never happened to the other fellow".

Besides introducing a new actor, Hunt and the producers made huge changes to the Bond formula. It was a smart risk to take. The closer *Majesty's* felt to *You Only Live Twice*, *Thunderball* or *Goldfinger*, the more direct the comparison between George Lazenby and Sean Connery. On the other hand, the recipe for success with the Bond films had been proven with five of the most profitable movies ever made. Would audiences want James Bond without gadgets, and without the gargantuan sets? Would they want a Bond who fell in love? It was a tremendous roll of the dice.

Majesty's was the James Bond film in which the filmmakers had to confront Bond's legacy in more ways than simply making changes to the formula. After five films, unprecedented success and a swarm of imitators, it was only natural there would be a backlash in the press. While there had always been a host of critics, it had now been long enough since *Dr. No* for some to say Bond was outmoded, a cultural anachronism.

Because the location was a remote mountaintop accessible only by cable car, the producers and director were able to restrict press access to the set. It was only when the film returned to Pinewood that reporters began flowing through, and they began to pick up scents of discontent. One of the earliest of the negative press articles appeared in *Family Weekly* on 16th March 1969. Written by Peer J. Oppenheimer, it was headlined 'George Lazenby: Arrogant Egotist'. Oppenheimer wrote that all twelve of Lazenby's leading ladies had something to say about him - and all of it bad. Oppenheimer went on to say that Lazenby had infuriated his producers and fellow actors through his indifference and lack of manners. (For the record, Oppenheimer produced and co-wrote the 1965 spy film *Operation C.I.A.*, a movie notable chiefly for being one of the earliest films of Burt Reynolds.)

In August 1969, three months after the completion of principal photography, the magazine *Petticoat* gave a slightly more balanced picture of Lazenby. Reporter Dawn James quoted the actor as saying, "I have worked every day for six months and I'm tired". Lazenby was generous in his assessment of his director and co-star, saying, "I couldn't act at all when I started this film but the director Peter Hunt was most understanding. Working beside a professional like Diana Rigg helped me too. Her timing and reactions seemed to lead me and rub off on me."

By the autumn of 1969, as the film was being readied for release, the British press continued sharpening their pens for the new 007. In the 23rd November issue of the *Sunday Express*, Peter Evans quoted Diana Rigg as saying, "He is utterly, unbelievably... bloody impossible". The article painted a picture of an inexperienced actor whose fame had gone to his head, bickering with his producers, director and co-star. On the eve of the film's UK premiere, an article by Donald Zec, a friend of Cubby Broccoli's who would later help the producer write his autobiography, praised the film but panned its star, concluding dismissively, "Back to the chocolate, George."

The press battle could not mask the truth. The film had been a difficult production. Wherever the fault lay, there was internal conflict within Eon Productions and at United Artists over the finished product. There were also conflicts between Lazenby and the filmmakers and the crew, which may have made him an easy target for the blame.

The biggest row in showbusiness

Dear George ... | *Dearest Diana...*

THE film has opened and is, I hear, making a great deal of money at the box office. This means you have been accepted by the public, which bodes well for your future career. Why, then, do you now persist in dwelling on your petty grievances?

I'm tired of reading those paranoid statements to the Press wherein it would seem you were surrounded lately by hostile people. I agree, by the end of the picture most of the crew were hostile, but only because of your extreme behaviour.

Why else would you persist claiming to be nice to them? Why else would those chauffeurs have run off into a wood? Why else would any member of the unit refused to run a mile for you? No, let's get rid of the genial chauffeur and settle on the sales outcast who was all the girls in the Dairy.

Remember once telling me that you valued honesty highly and that I was 'it' because you haven't? Perhaps you would prefer not to. But let's get rid of the lazy reflection type arriving you silly and insensitive and cross-outburst genial because all the girls in the Dairy.

NO, GEORGE, I did not, as one job do purpose, why would it 'it' make an important issue by both of us? Not, it was lacking together socially, and if you switched on the easy thing then I appreciated and saw every precious moment I could with you.

NO, GEORGE, I was not, as one was, causing chimpanzee to come where we work and we had the row. I was attempting to ease this damage get on a way too soul. You were afraid not when to do - and since you know once about your then I was very fair.

But the matter of telling me—absolutely with thwarts on 'Bull' my way - here it' - one really the best way. I felt it unable to fight back on your score—but I fired.

Later some weeks later you apologised. Does the damage stop...

Neither do I think it nothing (mistake of pity to suggest I was enjoying the row willing. This was your particular pleasure and it is to their embarrassing credit that they treated you throughout with patience and consideration.

Even the cameramen and in to his strike when, after only once a few weeks filming you began to ask him what to do. He was a professional—remember, George?

Yes, I did talk to the crew gaffer. Did you likely simply I preferred their company. And he is Peter Hunt, the director, who does little to tell his temper since the reaction provocation of your stunning off the set, leaving us to our walking.

As for as making it expressed George, on I see, it hours for your first three, with beers flowing in—except I knew dirty money that they found it impossible to trust consider it as....

And concerning you in talking with the producers. I knew dirty money that they found it impossible to trust...

I CANNOT understand what you have written, but I am trying to answer it in the most honest way.

I have dwelt on my present grievances because they may have been petty to you at the time because you have been in the business for 15 years. But I am just a beginner.

My grievances and my "paranoid statements to the Press," as you put it, are all part of some body trying desperately to re-operate and become a good actor. I am, as you know, a raw recruit to show business.

We all make mistakes, and I know I've made mine, so there are in every film. And that includes my dresser. But at the end of the film we're all good mates.

The chauffeurs? The one I had to London, from Eywnham, I took to Portugal to film. Because he was a stranger there he stayed in my guest more than anything. My second chauffeur was a holidaying who drove me a houla.

And if I do young I'd rather drive myself. The little chauffeur was not outside a rediscovered one night. We left and found he car, but there was a rowdy mob of Italians sending me up as James Bond.

The only thing I could do was to walk into the centre of them, rather then let them descend on me.

You warned? I showed the hostess, and I shook the dochester's hand. Then the ten refused I love the hostess out on the street, but said That you think, I crack, but here was a valued home.

I don't remember any solitude walk, speaking of that I would get someone tight enough to want to draw a distance to am. My shore with thing disagreements, but they too, had a ruff bargain, but...

I never said you had ever do no pretend, although it was admittedly my doubtful. The next you good champagne for breakfast I have in the bar. In fact really me most. Give my apple plus any day.

OK, so I said things about your driving, but you don't think I was right, eh?

The flat tyre I experienced, and serve you old other way. It was always the mine like that. I will be hang, but you are going swiss.

I'm sorry it worked on way, too, and there is a challenger a happy man then if I'm but an all I'd and I love them. To get, in am of you, for this is at I you tram it

George

Peace.

THE NEW
BOND

007
AND BRIDE

ALBERT R. BROCCOLI and HARRY SALTZMAN present
JAMES BOND 007
in IAN FLEMING'S
"ON HER MAJESTY'S SECRET SERVICE"
starring GEORGE LAZENBY · DIANA RIGG · TELLY SAVALAS as Blofeld
also starring GABRIELE FERZETTI and ILSE STEPPAT

"The British press tried so hard to make something out of nothing, you know. It's too dull just to make a good film." Peter Hunt

An exhibitors' poll conducted by *Films And Filming* found that it was the most financially successful film shown in Britain in all of 1970 (Harry Saltzman's *Battle Of Britain* came in second).

Reviews of the film were generally favourable. *Newsweek* wrote, "The James Bond craze has ended but James Bond movies live on." The *Los Angeles Times* critic wrote, "It's ironic that Sean Connery, having seen James home through the thinly two-dimensional days, should not be around for the new, higher-interest Bond. George Lazenby handles it very nicely."

As impressive as the reviews and the numbers seemed to be on an initial glance, the film's performance proved to be a deep disappointment to both United Artists and to Broccoli and Saltzman. In North America *Majesty's* ultimately sold less than half the tickets of its predecessor, *You Only Live Twice*, and a quarter of the tickets of *Thunderball*. What had gone wrong? The changes, which seemed palatable to most reviewers, could not overcome the sense among audiences that they were not getting the experience they expected from a Bond adventure. The new actor may have been one factor, but so was the new look and tone. The length - an epic two hours and twenty minutes - did not help.

A month after the release, the verdict was in. While the film made money, *Majesty's* was an experiment that United Artists had no interest in repeating. Bond could do much more, generate better press and, UA felt, still pack in audiences and have them leave feeling good. In January 1970, Broccoli attended two days of meetings in New York to discuss the future of James Bond. Before he went, Broccoli gave his perspective on James Bond's legacy to the film industry to the *Hollywood Reporter*:

"We, in our own way with the Bond pictures, have rejuvenated the bloody industry. Right after we started with the Bond pictures, everyone made a Bond-like picture and made money. Every picture was like it, and there were a bunch of television series that were Bond-like. So it did help rejuvenate the industry."

The white guipure lace dress worn by Diana Rigg for the wedding of James Bond to Tracy di Vicenzo was designed by Marjory Cornelius. Exact copies of the dress, and of the wedding ring, which spelled out 'We have all the time in the world' (**opposite page**), were sold throughout Britain.

"Peter made him more human, more ordinary.
Well, we don't go to the cinema to see ordinary people.
We go there to see things that are larger than life.
We go there to see the gods, the heroes." Simon Raven

Born in Houston, Texas on Christmas Eve 1905, Howard Robard Hughes (**above**) was the son of a man who had become wealthy by inventing a novel oil-drilling bit. The young Hughes was also an inventor; at 13, he built his own radio set. By the time he was 18, Howard Hughes' parents were dead, and he was the 75% owner of Hughes Tool Company, which made him a multimillionaire at the height of the Roaring Twenties. Throughout his life, Hughes indulged his three passions - aviation, movies and women. He romanced Katharine Hepburn, Ava Gardner, Jane Russell and Gene Tierney, among many, many others. Dana Broccoli recalled, "Cubby had known Howard Hughes when they were youngsters together in the early days of Hollywood, and they were great friends".

Cubby Broccoli was also a close of friend of Sammy Davis Jr. (**far right**), who appeared in a brief scene from *Diamonds Are Forever*. Davis, like Bond, was a product of changing times. In the 1960s his tireless work on behalf of civil rights for American blacks won him praise and his stage presence won him notable fans, including Ian Fleming and Roger Moore. Moore, in fact, attended the Hollywood premiere of *Live And Let Die* with Davis.

The question for UA and for Broccoli and Saltzman was not what Bond had done in the 1960s, but where to take 007 in the 1970s. Many thought Bond needed to change even more than he had in *Majesty's* if he were to survive. Despite the changing times, UA felt James Bond could still be profitable, but the studio wanted more involvement. With the January 1970 meetings, United Artists began to assert itself much more into the process of making the Bond films. The studio's president of production, David Picker, decided after the disappointment of *Majesty's* to become a key player in the creative decisions behind the new movie.

To check the relevance of the classic James Bond image, UA launched another double-bill re-release during the summer of 1970. This time they gave 007 a major New York opening and a fair amount of publicity for a joint presentation of *Thunderball* and *You Only Live Twice*. The results were clear - audiences packed theatres and cheered the screen. The conclusion was also clear - filmgoers wanted the classic Bond. UA planned to deliver on that expectation. First, Picker helped in selecting a director. No more first-timers who wanted to give the films an individual stamp. The filmmakers chose Guy Hamilton, director of the film UA most wanted to emulate with the next Bond - *Goldfinger*.

The tone of the new film - called *Diamonds Are Forever* - would be light and breezy, full of humour, in contrast to the darker, more serious tone of the previous 007 adventure. Ken Adam returned as production designer, offering the promise of larger-than-life futuristic sets. And there would definitely be gadgets. Early on, there was even talk of bringing back Gert Frobe to play the villain, as Goldfinger's brother, seeking revenge on James Bond.

Richard Maibaum wrote the new script, but the studio and the producers wanted significant changes, particularly more humour. All agreed to look for a new writer. They wanted him to be young, American, with a good command of the British idiom. David Picker hand-picked Tom Mankiewicz for the job.

"I had just done the book of a Broadway musical of the movie *Georgie Girl*," said Mankiewicz, "and we were nominated for several Tonys, closed in three nights... I got a call from my agent saying, 'How would you like to write the James Bond movie?' I thought he was joking. It was this monstrous joke, because I was still licking my wounds from having flopped on Broadway. They signed me on a two-week guarantee. They weren't all that confident. I was supposed to rewrite 40 pages in two weeks, and then they would see. That went very well, and then I stayed on the picture all the way through."

What Mankiewicz brought to Bond was a sense of pop poetry. He wrote short lines of dialogue often finished by other characters. When the killers Mr. Wint and Mr. Kidd blow up a helicopter, Mr. Kidd remarks, "If God had wanted man to fly..." - to which Mr. Wint answers, "He would have given him wings." Later, Mankiewicz's script revealed a delightfully darker side. The pair of assassins take photos of the corpse of their latest victim, Mrs. Whistler, a missionary school teacher *cum* diamond smuggler, as Amsterdam police recover her body from the local waterways. "Mrs. Whistler did want some pictures of the canals for the children," Mr. Kidd states flatly. "The children will be so thrilled," Mr. Wint replies.

Bond himself gets into the wordplay with Tiffany Case. When 007 arrives at her apartment she changes from a blonde wig to brunette, asking, "Which do you prefer?" Bond replies, "Providing the collars and cuffs match..." The dialogue was, in a word, sparkling. As the plot drifted further away from Fleming's original novel, Mankiewicz's wit kept the narrative moving at such a deft pace there was little time to question the story.

When Mankiewicz arrived, the plot itself had problems. The idea of bringing in Goldfinger's brother was not working, and the filmmakers had a hard time coming up with another villain. That all changed when Cubby Broccoli turned to the continuing saga of one of his oldest friends.

In 1934, Cubby Broccoli had arrived in Hollywood to visit his wealthy cousin, Pat Di Cicco. Pat's friends included actor Cary Grant and a tall, lanky Texan whom Cubby met one night at the Colony Club. The Texan's friends called him Sam. The world knew him as Howard Hughes.

Broccoli befriended Hughes, an aviation pioneer and one of the world's richest men. Years later, when Broccoli began producing his first film, *The Red Beret*, Hughes - then owner of the film studio RKO - agreed to put up the financing (C.J. Tevlin, who was running the studio, later put pressure on Hughes to drop the project, at which point Columbia Pictures picked it up).

After a near-fatal plane crash in 1946, Hughes's mental health began to deteriorate. He became paranoid and developed an obsessive fear of germs. Through the years, he became more and more isolated, running his vast empire from behind closed doors, protected by a coterie of Mormon caretakers.

The last time Cubby Broccoli actually spoke to Hughes was during the filming of *Thunderball*. The billionaire reached him on the set at Pinewood Studios and apologized for not keeping in touch. Cubby's wife Dana remembered, "Howard Hughes asked for every Bond film.

"Vegas opened up for us. They were absolutely wonderful because they decided that Bond was a good thing for Vegas." Guy Hamilton

He ran every single film. And in the end when we asked for the films back, they were just run over and over and over. They were almost worn out. So he really loved seeing these films."

Perhaps Hughes enjoyed the 007 films so much because he saw a reflection of his younger self in them. Like James Bond, Hughes was a tall, handsome womanizer, an adventurer and a technical genius. Though he had never been a secret agent, he enjoyed espionage. He was a major supplier of technology to the CIA through his company, Hughes Aircraft. A pioneer in military electronics, Hughes Aircraft invented the air-to-air missile and provided technology for the space programme as well as for orbiting surveillance satellites. Over the years, Hughes' espionage contracts with the CIA were worth $7 billion.

Hughes also enjoyed intrigue. He very often hired detectives to keep tabs on the activities of his many lovers. And in the early 1960s, when TWA - the airline Hughes had started - set out to serve him with subpoenas for an array of lawsuits, Hughes hired a

double, Brucks Randell, to impersonate him and lead the process servers astray. While Hughes remained hidden in his Bel Air, California home, there were 'Hughes sightings' in Tijuana, Lake Tahoe, Las Vegas and San Francisco.

On 27th November 1966, Howard Hughes moved into the Desert Inn casino in Las Vegas. He took over a ninth floor penthouse, having the windows sealed and fitted with blackout drapes. Two eighth-floor suites became the nerve centre for the millionaire's vast empire. Hughes intended to transform Vegas from a playground for the mob into a sort of adult Disneyland. In a memo to his senior aide Robert Maheu, he wrote, "I like to think of Las Vegas in terms of a well-dressed man in a dinner jacket and a beautifully jewelled and furred female getting out of an expensive car." Soon, he began buying up hotels and casinos all over Las Vegas, and making his dream a reality.

Then, on Thanksgiving Eve, 25th November 1970, Howard Hughes and his Mormon aides vanished from the Desert Inn, much to the dismay of Maheu. The senior aide reported the billionaire's disappearance to the FBI, Nevada Governor Paul Laxalt, and Hank Greenspun, publisher of *The Las Vegas Sun*. On 6th December, Greenspun published a headline, 'HOWARD HUGHES VANISHES!' The article speculated that Hughes had been drugged and kidnapped and was perhaps even dead. Finally, a journalist tracked Hughes down to a luxury hotel in the Bahamas.

Some of Hughes' employees and friends theorized that Hughes had never left Nevada alive, believing he was murdered by his close group of aides, who wanted to gain control of the Hughes empire. Marjel De Lauer, who worked for a Las Vegas television station owned by Hughes, believed the Howard Hughes in the Bahamas hotel was a carefully coached double. For a brief time, columnist Jack Anderson, a friend of Hughes, also suspected that an actor had replaced the reclusive billionaire.

Apparently, the same thought was also in the subconscious of Cubby Broccoli. Early on in the planning of *Diamonds Are Forever*, Broccoli had a dream that changed the direction of the screenplay. Dana Broccoli recalled, "Cubby was always looking for that hook for the story to take off from, and one morning, he woke and said, 'I've had the most fabulous dream'. And I said, 'What? What was it?' Cubby said, 'It was about Howard Hughes'. He said, 'I thought I was outside the penthouse window and he had his back to me and I was knocking on the window and was saying, "Sam..." And when he turned around, it wasn't Howard Hughes at all. It was a total stranger.' He said, 'That's what I've been looking for: this fellow who's kept captive in this penthouse and everything below is still going on as though he exists.' And that was the way the story started."

United Artists made it clear to the producers that there were real limits on the budget for *Diamonds Are Forever*. In a move to cut down production costs, Broccoli and Saltzman decided the entire film would be made in America using studio space at Universal. Also, the production was scheduled to wrap quickly, with a locked shooting schedule of 18 weeks.

Pre-production planning was well underway by 9th February 1971, when the world of the James Bond filmmakers underwent a shake-up, literally. At 6:01am, a magnitude 6.6 earthquake struck Los Angeles, centred on the San Fernando area. It was one of the most devastating earthquakes in California history; 65 people lost their lives. Property damage was estimated at more than half a billion dollars.

The next day, *Variety* reported that Raquel Welch was rumoured to be the next Bond *femme fatale*, but her decision to do the film would depend on who played James Bond. Broccoli had cast Welch once before for the part of Domino in *Thunderball*, but 20th Century-Fox asked him to release her so she could star in *Fantastic Voyage*. Now, Broccoli was reconsidering her. Guy Hamilton, however, felt that Welch's persona might overpower 007. He told Cubby, "Bond and Raquel together is bad chemistry. She's much too animal for this particular role."

Meanwhile, Sydney Korschak, who was helping Broccoli set up deals in Las Vegas, asked the producer if there might be a small role for his friend, Jill St. John. St. John had been married to Woolworth millionaire Lance Reventlow, a Grand Prix racing driver who was killed in a plane crash. She dated Frank Sinatra, Henry Kissinger and George Lazenby (she attended a Los Angeles screening of *OHMSS* with the then 007). Broccoli thought St. John would make a good Plenty O'Toole. Hamilton felt she'd be better as Tiffany Case. He told Broccoli, "With Connery she'd be perfect, but hell, we haven't got Connery".

"United Artists were gung-ho to get Sean back," said Dana Broccoli, "but Harry and Cubby felt they really didn't want to beg a reluctant actor to act." Besides, with UA's budget restrictions, the film could not afford Connery. The question was who could they get? Eventually they began testing some American actors for the role of the quintessential British spy. Guy Hamilton was convinced Bond should be British until he saw an actor on television.

"I thought the guy was terrific," said Hamilton. "He had all the right elements for Bond, he moved beautifully, he had a nice sense of humour. I insisted that Cubby meet him, and it fell like a lead balloon with United Artists. They said, 'He's a TV star'. It turned out to be Burt Reynolds before Burt became famous. He would have made a marvellous Bond, in my opinion." Production manager Stanley Sopel recalled, "We tested about four American actors. There's some marvellous actors in the United States, but there's no James Bond."

The problem was, there was no British James Bond either. Top choice actors were not available. Cubby and Harry decided to look again in the US, to "bend our rule about having to be British," as Broccoli stated in his autobiography. They eventually tested John Gavin, a muscular, graceful, laconic actor who handled action with ease. His dark good looks came from his Hispanic heritage (his mother Delia Diana Pablos was Mexican), but his smooth demeanour and natural elegance gave a British flair to his performances. Soon John Gavin was signed to play James Bond.

Gavin - most famous for his role in Alfred Hitchcock's *Psycho* - had some previous experience in the spy business. From 1952 to 1955 he had served as an air intelligence officer in the US Navy. But David Picker, who had risen to become president of United Artists, felt there was only one actor who could guarantee knock-out box-office for *Diamonds Are Forever* - Sean Connery.

"I'm a big fan of Connery, and I knew one thing: I'm the best Burt Reynolds there is, I don't want to be the next best Sean Connery. I could never do Bond better than he did." Burt Reynolds

"Regretfully, see, one always at that time had to compare anybody we used with Sean," recalled Stanley Sopel. "By which time, Sean was Bond and there could be nobody else. And so there was a big conference in Cubby's house in Beverly Hills. David flew in from New York and we discussed it and we thought, 'Let's see if we can make a deal with Sean'."

To afford Connery, David Picker did some maths. If the film had Connery as its star, and a primarily British crew, it could qualify for the Eady Levy, a refund to studios who made and distributed films in England. With the Eady money the movie was sure to generate, Picker felt the deal with Connery was well worthwhile.

Since Sopel was friends with Sean, the producers dispatched him to London to meet with Connery and his agent, Richard Hatton. They discussed terms over a bottle of Johnny Walker. In the end, Connery was not swayed, but Sopel had agreed to buy a second-hand Mercedes from an East End garage in which Connery had an interest.

The producers tried another tack. "That's when I had to talk to Sean," said Ursula Andress. "Broccoli and Saltzman asked me to come from Paris to London and talk to Sean, to give him the offer and convince him to do the film."

Still, Connery stood his ground. Finally, David Picker decided to take matters into his own hands. A meeting was scheduled at Richard Hatton's offices between Connery and Picker, where the United Artists president made the actor an offer he couldn't refuse. He was prepared to pay Connery $1.25 million, plus 10% of the gross, as well as $145,000 per week if the film ran over schedule. Also, Connery was promised development money and financial backing for two films of his choice, one of which he could direct. Connery, who was well aware that his recent films had not exactly been huge hits, accepted the offer. Five years after leaving the role, he once again agreed to play 007. "I have no real dissatisfaction with the character as such," said Connery. "That would really be stupid. Although I had to take a week to make the decision myself whether I would do it again."

The stunning deal put Connery into the *Guinness Book Of World Records* as the highest-paid actor. It was the beginning of a trend in superstar salaries. Even more stunning was his announcement to donate his salary to the Scottish International Educational Trust. "Sean got no money for the picture at all," said Stanley Sopel. "He donated the whole thing. That is an absolute fact. Some people don't believe that's true but I'm here to tell you it is true. Sean gave all that money away."

The deal with Connery brought celebration and concern. Dana Broccoli remembered, "There was a panic at UA and they called and said, 'Look, we've got Sean. You have to do something with John Gavin'." Gavin, who had a pay-or-play contract, received a payment, and due to Screen Actor Guild rules, still occasionally gets residual cheques from the movie. In 1981, President Ronald Reagan appointed him US Ambassador to Mexico.

A former advertising director for Macy's, Maurice Binder (**opposite top**) joined the army and was stationed on a salvage ship off the coast of California during the Second World War. Making contacts at Columbia Pictures, he began moonlighting as a poster artist.

Among his most famous works from this period of his career was the poster for the Rita Hayworth film, *Gilda*. In the 1950s, he began his association with Stanley Donen, creating the title sequence for *Indiscreet*. He was soon much in demand, creating titles for films in both Europe and the US. It was his work on the James Bond films, however, that made Binder famous.

Connery returned to the role with renewed enthusiasm. "Once back, I must say, he was the real pro," said Dana Broccoli. "Everything went wonderfully well." He was impressed with Tom Mankiewicz's screenplay, agreeing with the emphasis on humour. "At the time I was doing Bond, we had to make sure Bond stopped smoking, that Bond wasn't too much of a thug, and we got into all the political correctness with Bond, but they were very humorous," said

Mankiewicz. "Sean, as it turned out, was so thankful for it. He said this should be a humorous film."

One of the key features of *Diamonds* was the choice by the filmmakers to make James Bond appeal to a wide audience. On 5th April 1971, cameras rolled on the initial scene and the filmmakers were faced with their first creative choice in this area. With the desert outside Las Vegas substituting for South Africa, Bruce Glover and Putter Smith as the homosexual assassins Wint and Kidd begin to close down Blofeld's diamond pipeline. The script called for a lethal scorpion to be dropped into the mouth of the courier, who was a dentist.

There were worries that the gruesome nature of the original version would prove too much for a family audience, so an additional version was shot (the one which was eventually used) in which the scorpion was dropped down the back of the dentist's shirt. The decision was clear - James Bond would break ground in many ways, but he would not be a symbol of the more realistic and horrifying violence in contemporary movies.

The following week, Guy Hamilton filmed the car chase in downtown Las Vegas. "Guy had a very efficient way of running the set, and his own private sense of little prejudices," said Tom Mankiewicz. "I mean, he hated American cars, so in any sequence with American cars - and there are a couple in *Diamonds* - the American cars all had to spin out, they were useless, they were these big, flabby, you know, pieces of tin." Stunt co-ordinator Paul Baxley hired twelve stunt drivers for the chases, including Bud Eakins, the man who performed the famous motorcycle jump credited to Steve McQueen in *The Great Escape*. A total of 55 cars were purchased; 24 of them were totally demolished during filming.

The chase in *Diamonds* had been partially inspired by the highly successful car chase in the 1968 Steve McQueen film, *Bullitt*, but the Bond film added more comedy, à la *Goldfinger*, with a touch of Harold Lloyd. The comic car chases of *Diamonds Are Forever* (and later *Live And Let Die* and *The Man With The Golden Gun*) helped inspire their own genre of films – good ole boy car-crash actioners like *White Lightning*, *Gator* and *Smokey And The Bandit*, which made a superstar out of the American actor Guy Hamilton had briefly considered for 007, Burt Reynolds.

Sean Connery's first scenes were filmed on 2nd April, with Bond encountering Plenty O'Toole in the casino. In make-up as Bond, Connery appeared greyer at the temples and thicker around the middle than he had ten years earlier, but he still had the anarchic exuberance of an impetuous teenager, moving through the various exotic locales and leaving a swathe of destruction in his wake.

Although not in direct contact with Howard Hughes, Cubby Broccoli was able to communicate what he needed through Hughes' friend and associate, Walter Kane. Dana Broccoli remembered that Hughes was called "the Penthouse". "Whenever the production encountered any difficulties, Cubby would make a call to Kane, with the inevitable reply, 'Word has come down from "The Penthouse" that Cubby Broccoli can use anything in any of (Hughes') hotels or anything else that he might need.' And that was a great help."

Left: Apart from in *From Russia With Love* and *Thunderball*, Ernst Stavro Blofeld was never played twice by the same actor. In those two films, Anthony Dawson (Professor Dent in *Dr. No*) provided the on-screen presence of Blofeld, with Erich Pohlmann supplying the voice. After Donald Pleasance and Telly Savalas played the role, it went next to Charles Gray, an actor who had appeared as Dikko Henderson in *You Only Live Twice*. Jill St. John, a chess player, remembered filming with Gray, who played bridge. "I liked him a lot, and I was trying to trade chess lessons for bridge lessons; neither one of us ended up learning to play the other one's game very well."

Above: Putter Smith as Mr. Kidd (**left**) and Bruce Glover as Mr. Wint (**right**). *Diamonds Are Forever* was the first film appearance for Smith, a jazz musician. Glover was an experienced character actor who brought a studied creepiness to the part of Mr. Wint. He won the role when actor/singer/songwriter Paul Williams was unable to reach a deal with the producers.

Sean Connery learned to play golf for *Goldfinger*, and developed an instant passion for the game. Guy Hamilton remarked that during the filming of *Diamonds Are Forever*, "It was more or less in the contract that we could play golf once a week... The stuntman and myself versus Sean and the cameraman, that was our foursome."

"From morning to evening, you heard nothing else but golf," said Ken Adam. Rankled by the incessant talk of golf, Adam - who had never swung a golf club in his life - proposed a challenge. "I said provided I got training for two weeks and a reasonable handicap, I was challenging Sean to a golf match for a hundred pounds bet. Well, that became more important to the whole unit than filming. My assistant was a man called Roy Walker who was practically a golf pro, so every night we used to practise, and I was getting, not good, but quite passable, and with the right handicap, I stood a chance of winning. What I didn't realize is that Sean had specified he was going to play the whole match with a five iron, which apparently is the best iron he could have used, and no other iron. It was raining cats and dogs that evening, and the whole unit was there. Sean was nervous, because he's a bad loser, and he wasn't prepared to lose. And he didn't, in fact, because halfway through the match, I got nervous, and made many mistakes. It became light entertainment which I don't think anyone, Guy or Sean or myself, will ever forget. I know I won't."

It was as if the world of James Bond and the real world of 1971 were merging. Hughes, unbeknownst to all but his closest advisors, was not even in Las Vegas, but was in Nicaragua, running his empire from private phone lines. In the film, Bond steals a vehicle designed to travel across the surface of the moon. The sequence was shot three months before Apollo 15 utilized the first moon buggy. Of course, NASA's vehicle travelled at six miles per hour. Bond's was designed to go sixty.

While on the set of the astronaut training centre, Connery, now an avid golfer, emulated Alan Shepard's golf outing on the moon. The photo, which perfectly captured the Bondian image while updating 007 to the 1970s, was printed in newspapers across the globe.

On 18th May, the merging of Bond and the real world became complete. The unit moved to Palm Springs, where Bond was to search for Willard Whyte. The scene was filmed in a classic Ken Adam set - an 8,000 square foot concrete-and-glass house, with a grand 60-foot diameter circular living room - a room similar in scale and shape to the opium lab set in the opening of *Goldfinger*. Skylights radiated from the ceiling, which was vaulted in a way similar to the interior of the volcano in *You Only Live Twice*. The room featured an indoor/outdoor pool which seemed to hang suspended over the view of the vast valley below, which could almost be viewed as an extension of *Dr. No*'s aquarium. The house, though, had been built in 1968 by designer John Lautner, the man who invented 'Google architecture', so named because of his innovative, spacious designs for the Southern California coffee shop chain, Googles.

While neither Lautner nor Adam consciously influenced the other, their visions of the modern world were similar in scope, line, space and scale. Modern architecture had ventured into wild shapes, new materials and exotic flourishes in the 1960s. Events like the 1964 Olympics in Tokyo, Expo 67 in Canada and Expo 70 in Tokyo showcased remarkable visions

of new types of buildings. More and more often the most elaborate and grand of these structures were described as being like "something out of a James Bond movie".

Fifteen days before the film crew shot scenes with the diamond-encrusted satellite on the Whyte Techtronics Lab set, an important event occurred in the world of espionage. Before 15th June 1971, secret agents were the primary means of gathering intelligence. On that date, the CIA launched the first of a new generation of HEXAGON photo-reconnaissance satellites, and afterwards intelligence agencies turned increasingly to space-based spying. Sean Connery seemed to be leaving the role of Bond just as the real world was leaving 007's behind.

Connery filmed his final segment for *Diamonds Are Forever* on 13th August 1971 - Friday the 13th. Appropriately, the shots were of Bond being placed in a coffin, and the lid closed. With that, Connery closed the lid on his portrayal of 007 in the Eon-produced Bond films.

"Everybody knew he was serious about the fact that he wasn't coming back," said Mankiewicz. "He really wanted to have a career, and a life, other than Bond. I mean, there were so many other things he wanted to do. And as Sean said to me once, 'I keep reading, Boy-o, that I owe it to the audience to come back.' He said, 'I've done seven of 'em, over a period of twelve years. How much do I owe, finally, an audience? Do I owe them 15 of them over 25 years?' He couldn't wait to get on with the rest of his career."

Because of Connery's schedule, and the budget and schedule restrictions put in place by United Artists, the film was rushed by Bond standards. The climactic battle aboard the oil rig had never been properly completed. Some scenes Hamilton would have liked to have augmented or changed could not be fixed. In another move that harked back to *Goldfinger*, Shirley Bassey returned to sing the film's title song, written by John Barry, with overtly sexual lyrics supplied by Don Black. When the cut was completed, however, the filmmakers knew they had made a good Bond film. The larger question was, would anyone care?

Diamonds Are Forever opened in 50 locations in the US and Canada on 17th December 1971. By Christmas, it was at 600 theatres. Around the world, box office take through 2nd January 1972 was $16,238,915. More than $2,000,000 of that came from the 28-theatre New York showcase screenings. After one week at the Odeon Leicester Square in London, the film grossed $88,000, or $33,000 more than the previous record for any cinema in the United Kingdom.

There were reports that in some cinemas, when Connery was first seen in the pre-credits saying, "My name is Bond, James Bond." audiences clapped and cheered. One audience member who would have heard those cheers on the night of the London premiere was the friend who accompanied Connery to the event, a television actor who had been approached for the role of Bond on four separate occasions - Roger Moore.

In his autobiography, *When The Snow Melts*, Cubby Broccoli wrote that once Sean Connery decided to return to the role of 007, he and Harry Saltzman did what they could to keep him happy, including providing a luxury suite at the best hotel in Las Vegas and arranging for him to play golf at the nearby desert golf courses. "If this was to be his last Bond film," wrote Broccoli, "then we wanted to part as friends."

"*Diamonds Are Forever* is really just another strip cartoon for adults, which is why I've never really understood the idea of Bond as a vicious, sadistic killer. There are too many laughs for that." Sean Connery

6. By the early 1970s, the world of espionage was no longer that of the Cold War agents who had risked their lives behind the Iron Curtain to steal secrets and assassinate other agents. It was no longer the grand nuclear posturing of the superpowers in the 1960s. It had morphed into a grotesque reflection of James Bond's world of private global villains, terrorists and extortionists. While billionaires like Howard Hughes could inspire Bond plots and live the life of a reclusive Bond villain, the real global villains were proving

James Bond Saves The World

themselves to be soulless, cold-blooded crusaders who saw random violence as a business venture or a form of political expression. This new generation of villains was soon inflicting more damage than SPECTRE could dream up, and they were doing so with crude, indiscriminate carnage. The worldwide economic boom of the 1960s was over. In Britain sectarian violence in Northern Ireland was tarnishing the ever-shrinking shield of the once-grand imperial power. In the US, the ever-enveloping quicksand of Vietnam had the nation grappling with itself. James Bond's world of sophistication, aplomb and easy solutions seemed simplistic to some critics and downright comic to others. Comedy, as Sean Connery and Guy Hamilton had proved in *Diamonds Are Forever*, was just what the world needed.

Top: An image that shocked the world - a Black September terrorist at the 1972 Munich Olympics.

Middle: Former FBI Special Agent and lawyer G. Gordon Liddy became a White House Staff Assistant in 1971. He resigned his post to become General Counsel of the 1972 Republican presidential campaign and the campaign finance committee. Convicted and sentenced to over twenty years in prison for his role in the Watergate scandal, Liddy served nearly five years. Since his release, he has become a political pundit and radio talk show host.

Below: During the years that he was playing *The Saint* on television, Roger Moore had become acquainted socially with Harry Saltzman and Cubby Broccoli. In 1972, he was their first choice to play James Bond. There was only one problem - they thought he was too fat. "Harry called me, and he said, 'Listen, Cubby thinks you're a little overweight,'" said Moore. "I'd been making *The Persuaders* with Tony Curtis and instead of drinking coloured water, we always had real champagne. And during a year and a quarter of filming, I went from 165 pounds to 185 pounds. So, they said, 'Take a little weight off.' I started working out and dieting. And then, Harry said, 'Cubby thinks your hair's too long.' So I had some of my hair cut off, and went and saw them. Harry said, 'I think you should get a little more cut off, and you should lose a little more weight.' This went on. In the end, I was getting desperate. I thought 'Why didn't they get a thin man who was bald to do the part?'"

Since James Bond's cinematic debut in 1962, the international landscape had altered beyond recognition. No one knew where it would end. In March 1971, the US Capitol was rocked by a bomb blast to protest military actions in Laos. It was just one instance in a long string of dramatic anti-war protests. In February 1972, West Germany paid a five million dollar extortion demand to a group of Arab hijackers. Within a month the extortionists were back. A group planted a bomb on a TWA jet in Las Vegas. They demanded two million dollars, setting off the bomb when the plane was empty. In May, Cunard received a bomb threat against the *Queen Elizabeth 2* ocean liner with a million dollar demand.

At the end of May, the attacks turned deadly. Three members of Sekiguha - a Japanese terrorist organization - landed at the Lod International Airport in Tel Aviv, Israel. They quickly produced automatic weapons and grenades, killed fourteen Puerto Rican tourists, a Canadian woman, and twelve others before Israeli soldiers regained control, killing two of the terrorists. Within months, the anti-Israel Black September group invaded the Munich Summer Olympics. They immediately killed two Israelis, then, when ambushed by the West German police at a military airstrip, murdered the remainder of the hostages. The West Germans captured three of the terrorists before entering into a secret agreement with Black September. The authorities helped Black September stage a hijacking of a Lufthansa passenger jet two months later. In the pre-arranged scenario, the West Germans turned over the three captured terrorists. Under the secret agreement, Black September agreed to refrain from further terrorist action in West Germany. In short, one of the most powerful nations in Europe had capitulated. The bad guys were winning.

Despite the easing of Cold War tensions as the US normalized relations with China and signed the SALT treaty with the USSR, the world did not seem to be a safer place. One madman attacked Michelangelo's *Pièta* in the Vatican while another left the US presidential candidate George Wallace crippled after a failed assassination attempt. A bizarre spate of 31 attempted hijackings in the US (mostly to Cuba) rounded out the year of terror. Understandably, the Nobel committee declined to award its Peace Prize in 1972. Real-life killers sneered at television cameras, and there seemed to be nothing anyone - not even James Bond - could do about it.

In the summer of 1972 a group calling itself CREEP launched Operation Gemstone. As originally conceived, CREEP, through Gemstone, would create a network of spies, eavesdrop on sensitive conversations, utilize prostitutes to extract information from enemies, perform a series of burglaries, and run a number of sabotage raids. CREEP's goals were not unlike that of Sekiguha, the IRA, or the PLO and Black September. CREEP, using extra-legal methods, wanted to humiliate, intimidate, defeat and destroy its political enemies, and as a result, increase its own political power.

If some observers could be excused for thinking of the IRA and PLO as real-life versions of SPECTRE, the men behind Operation Gemstone clearly identified more closely with 007. In fact, some of them were James Bond fans. One leader was an ex-FBI agent and two were ex-CIA agents. The operations were sophisticated, meticulously planned and well financed. The leaders felt they were carrying out their missions for God and country, which justified their actions. Gemstone, though, did not get very far. Budgetary concerns forced many of the ambitious projects to be aborted.

On the night of 16th June 1972, during the third Gemstone burglary, the whole operation imploded when police captured members of the entry team. They were caught inside the headquarters of the Democratic National Committee in the Watergate Hotel in Washington DC. Their parent organization, CREEP, was an acronym for the Committee to Re-Elect the President, and Gemstone had been personally authorized by John Mitchell, the former US Attorney General.

The slow-motion response to the Watergate affair within the United States had a profound effect on the public's diminishing perception of, and regard for, spies. For years, members of the political left had been arguing that the United States' internal and international intelligence networks were abusing their power under the cloak of secrecy. They claimed that the government supported repressive dictators rather than progressive democracies in order to further US political and military dominance around the globe. With the Watergate affair, the left found a group with close links to a sitting president, who were trying to subvert the democratic process and influence the outcome of an election through a well-orchestrated dirty tricks campaign.

During the year between the Watergate break-in and the release of *Live And Let Die* in the summer of 1973, the world began to seriously debate the role of espionage and the rules by which nations spied on each other. The public looked into the face of men who viewed themselves as real-life James Bond figures and did not like what it saw.

Before the Watergate break-in, Cubby Broccoli and Harry Saltzman confronted the challenge of locating a new face for James Bond. United Artists wanted to get Connery back, but despite overtures, Connery remained unmoved. Without Connery, the studio made its wishes clear - UA wanted an established actor with solid professional experience. Broccoli and Saltzman agreed, as did director Guy Hamilton. Somehow, they must have known this choice would have a dramatic impact on the longevity of the Bond series.

One actor who seemed ideal for the role was Roger Moore, but United Artists was not eager to make an offer. His 1969 film, *Crossplot*, had not been terribly successful for UA, and its spy-themed story left much to be desired. Cubby Broccoli felt he owed the Bond role to John Gavin, who had so graciously backed out when Connery became available for *Diamonds*. Harry Saltzman wanted an English actor. Guy Hamilton was pushing for Burt Reynolds, whose star had risen significantly since being considered two years previously. United Artists was interested in Paul Newman. Meanwhile, UA and the producers shot dozens of screen tests throughout the early months of 1972 looking at lesser and unknown actors, just to be sure no stone was left unturned.

Diamonds Are Forever's impressive success at the box office assured the producers that the additional emphasis on comedy was right for the times. Just as Bond had moved away from politics in the 1960s, the character had to continue to move away from the grim world of terror. Now they needed an actor who could pull off that lighter touch, and who could convince audiences not only that he was James Bond, but more importantly, that Bond was not to be taken seriously by those offended by the excesses of the CIA and Nixon's 1972 Presidential campaign. Eventually, everyone came back around to Roger Moore. He was British, carried himself with an air of assured sophistication, and he was known around the world thanks to his TV roles. He also had the right attitude for the times regarding Bond.

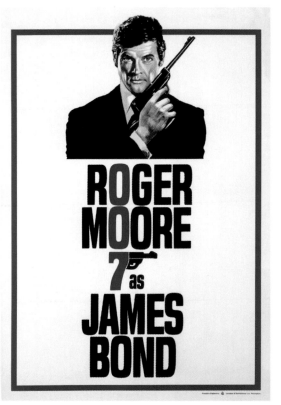

For over ten years, James Bond had been trying to capture Roger Moore. He was on the shortlist of actors considered to star in *Dr. No*, was mentioned for *Casino Royale*, considered again by Broccoli and Saltzman before George Lazenby was cast, and once more when *Diamonds Are Forever* was starting up. But the actor proved as elusive to snare as Ernst Stavro Blofeld, his television and film commitments always getting in the way of his becoming 007. It wasn't until 1972, when pre-production of *Live And Let Die* was underway, that Moore was finally available. There was only one thing Moore had to do before accepting the role - he needed to change his home phone number, which ended with the digits 007.

Moore was good friends with his predecessor in the role, Sean Connery. "I was appearing with Jimmy Tarbuck years ago at the London Palladium in the days when I was The Saint," said Moore. "He asked me if I was friends with Sean Connery, who then played Bond, and Patrick McGoohan, who was Danger Man on television. I said that I was. He then asked whether The Saint and Danger Man and James Bond ever went out for an evening together. I said that we did. Then Tarbuck asked, 'And Pussy Galore?' I replied, 'Well, we don't go looking for it.'"

Roger Moore was born in the Stockwell area of London, south of the River Thames, on 14th October 1927. His father was George Alfred Moore, a police constable. Roger, a rather chubby child, developed his sense of humour as a defence mechanism. When Moore left school, his skills as an artist landed him a job at Publicity Pictures Productions, which specialized in animated cartoons. Moore worked as a tracer and filler-in, ran errands and made the tea. On one memorable morning, he made cold tea, forgot a number of errands and made a mistake on some celluloid. He was fired.

In need of work, he listened to a suggestion that he could make some money as an extra on a film that was being made at Denham Studios, *Caesar And Cleopatra*. "I did this highly pleasurable job for a few days, and on the third day, as I walked through the gates, a car stopped alongside me." Brian Desmond Hurst, the co-director of the film, asked Moore if he was interested in becoming an actor and offered to pay Moore's fees to the Royal Academy of Dramatic Arts.

"Roger Moore was in my class at RADA when we were both seventeen," remembered Lois Maxwell, "and he was gorgeous, he was covered in puppy fat, but he was funny and witty and charming and utterly delightful."

After RADA and a stint in the army, Moore found work on the film *Trottie True* opposite Christopher Lee. Between film roles he supplemented his income as a male model. Michael Caine recalled that Moore did so many print ads for pullover sweaters that they took to calling him 'The Big Knit'.

In the 1950s, Moore went to America, where he appeared in TV plays, including an episode of *Robert Montgomery Presents*, a series produced by Harry Saltzman. Hollywood studios took notice of the handsome young actor, and MGM cast him in *The Last Time I Saw Paris*, with Van Johnson and Elizabeth Taylor. He appeared in *Interrupted Melody*, and starred opposite Lana Turner in *Diane*.

Moore took a starring role in the 1958 TV series *Ivanhoe*, where he worked opposite Christopher Lee on one episode and Robert Brown on another. After a season on the short-lived series, *The Alaskans*, he joined the cast of *Maverick*, a show on which he'd made a guest appearance three years earlier. "They said I wasn't replacing Jim Garner in *Maverick*," said Moore, "but all the clothes had 'Garner' written around the waistband."

Feeling that he was becoming typecast, Moore returned to Europe, looking for fresh opportunities. In Italy, he starred as Romulus in a film about the founding of Rome, *The Rape Of The Sabines*. His co-star was Luisa Mattioli, with whom he fell in love at first sight. Eight years later, after Moore became divorced from Dorothy Squires, he married Luisa. Their union lasted 27 years, producing a daughter and two sons.

While making another film in Venice, Moore's agent phoned to tell him that Lew Grade had purchased the TV rights to Leslie Charteris's *The Saint*. Moore had previously tried to acquire the rights himself, feeling that the part was tailor-made for his persona. Now that Grade wanted him for the role, Moore returned to London.

The Saint became a hit around the world, and allowed Moore the chance to direct as well as act; he also produced the final 47 episodes of the series. When the show ended he tried to resurrect his long-abandoned film career with appearances in *Crossplot* and *The Man Who Haunted Himself*. Then, just as he learned that he was being considered for the role of 007 in *Diamonds Are Forever*, he received a call from Lew Grade in which the television magnate told him that he had sold the TV series *The Persuaders* on condition

Below: *Live And Let Die* director Guy Hamilton at work in New Orleans. Hamilton suggested bringing Bond to the Crescent City because of his love of Dixieland jazz. As in *You Only Live Twice*, many scenes were developed specifically around the choice of location.

"I try to be different in everything but unfortunately I do sort of look like me." Roger Moore

that Moore was the star. Since the original concept for the series had been Moore's, he could hardly refuse. When *The Persuaders* finished its run, Moore was finally available to play 007.

With the role of Bond, Moore had to fight a feeling of fitting into another actor's role. He had been dissatisfied playing a James Garner substitute on *Maverick*, so how would playing a Connery substitute wear on him? For director Guy Hamilton, the worries were of a different nature. Moore's Bond needed to be distinct from Simon Templar, aka The Saint - the role which had catapulted Moore to international stardom. Hamilton wanted no cocking of eyebrows, which had become something of a trademark during Moore's television career. Learning from their experience with Lazenby, they knew that Moore's Bond had to deliver what audiences expected, but they also wanted to avoid too many direct comparisons to Connery.

At the time, Moore remarked, "I have made about 300 television films, each seen throughout the world by about 500 million people,

who will have a preconceived idea about me. There's the same identification of Sean with Bond, and those viewers will have a conception of how Bond should be played. Marrying the two is the problem that niggles and nags away."

Some of the differences between Moore and Connery were purely cosmetic. Moore would smoke cigars rather than Bond's trademark cigarettes. He would not order the signature vodka martini (in *Live And Let Die* Moore's Bond drinks Bourbon, just as 007 often does in the novels). For his first film, the filmmakers would not even dress Moore in a tuxedo.

On a more practical level, Cubby Broccoli and Harry Saltzman realized that James Bond was a role that needed to be played by a leading man. While Bond was the star, the character had to be interpreted by someone who naturally possessed the charm and presence to win over an audience. Leading men - such as Humphrey Bogart, Cary Grant or John Wayne - always brought their own

Above: Jane Seymour was one of the youngest women ever to play a co-starring role in a 007 film. "I was 20 when I started the Bond film," she recalled. "By the time it came out, I was 21, but I was really young. I think it was because they were looking for someone to play a virgin." Seymour took her role very seriously. "Roger Moore actually nicknamed me 'Baby Bernhardt', because I thought it was a very serious acting role, you know, rather like doing Shakespeare or something."

The tarot deck used in *Live And Let Die* (**below**) was designed by a Scotsman, Fergus Hall. The back of the cards featured a pattern comprised of the numbers 007. After the release of the film, the cards were marketed and sold as 'The James Bond 007 Tarot Game'.

Geoffrey Holder (**opposite page**) was a noted Broadway choreographer and actor prior to landing the role of Baron Samedi in *Live And Let Die*. Jane Seymour recalled, "I really bonded with Geoffrey Holder, because I was a ballet dancer before all this, and he of course was a great dancer".

persona to each role they undertook. Thus, the producers decided to let Roger Moore play James Bond as Moore. Bond's charm should be Roger Moore's charm, not an attempt to emulate Connery's. They freed him of the constraints of trying to fill Sean Connery's shoes.

Moore, though, still had to break free from his own worries about Connery's legacy as Bond. "I confessed to Guy (Hamilton) that in reading the script I could hear only Sean's voice saying, 'My name is Bond'. In fact, as I vocalized to myself I found that I was giving it a Scots accent."

The decision to bring Roger Moore in as Bond was paralleled by a decision between United Artists and the producers to continue forward with the budget constraints created for *Diamonds Are Forever*. *Diamonds* sold 25.8 million tickets in North America, which was over ten million more than *Majesty's*, but almost ten million less than *You Only Live Twice*. The studio did not expect Roger Moore's first Bond film to be as successful as Connery's, so they wanted to create a scenario where even if the movie only performed as well as *Majesty's* the studio would still make a handsome profit.

There were some who felt that even *Majesty's* box office numbers were ambitious for a Bond film without Sean Connery. They pointed out that two new Bond-styled television series - *SEARCH* and *The Men* - were running in the US in 1972, and neither gathered high ratings. Even the old stalwart, *Mission: Impossible*, was stumbling. In the UK, *The Adventurer* and *Spyder's Web* were two new espionage shows that were also faltering as spy series slipped off the airwaves.

To hedge their bets on *Live And Let Die*, UA and the producers agreed to sell the US television broadcast rights to the earlier

James Bond films, none of which had ever been aired. ABC won the bidding, paying $17 million for 007. UA's after-tax share of the profits from this sale more than covered their entire investment in the new Bond film. First up was *Goldfinger*, premiering on ABC on 17th September 1972. The film brought in 49% of the viewers across the nation, one of the largest audiences of any film ever to be aired on a US network. Movies on television were huge in the early 1970s, and *Goldfinger*'s record lasted only two weeks until *Love Story* aired on 1st October, but it clearly established that, regardless of the public's perception of spies, Bond was still undeniably big business.

While *Goldfinger* was breaking records on television, Hollywood was watching a new cinematic phenomenon rise in popularity. In 1970 and '71 a trio of films reached cinemas, all of which made tremendous profits, and launched a new genre: blaxploitation films. The films - *Cotton Comes To Harlem*, *Sweet Sweetback's Baadasssss Song*, and *Shaft* - brought the world of the urban black experience to cinema audiences with a decidedly anti-establishment bent. Quickly, every studio began developing films to tap into this market, seeing the movies as modern retellings of 1930s gangster epics. By the end of 1971, when *Diamonds Are Forever* opened, the filmmakers saw the chance to produce the most politically difficult Bond film - *Live And Let Die*.

Ian Fleming wrote LIVE AND LET DIE in 1953, and in doing so, tapped into the racial and political paranoia in the United States. Many whites thought Communists were behind black efforts to obtain civil rights, and Fleming's novel openly toyed with the idea of a large, Communist-controlled underground network in the African-American community. The novel was heavily edited before its publication in the US, and while little in it is openly offensive, its plotline features villains who are exclusively black. Until the release of the first blaxploitation films, the producers could not see a way of realizing the story in any form.

Characters like detective John Shaft (and later Superfly and Cleopatra Jones) were openly compared to James Bond by studios, film critics and moviegoers, despite obvious differences. The James Bond filmmakers, in turn, co-opted the blaxploitation genre. Rather than have the villain, Mr. Big, work for the Soviets, the movie featured the ruler of a small Caribbean nation - Dr. Kananga - cultivating and distributing heroin through his underworld network. Harlem, the Caribbean and New Orleans, where the film was set, were all in the process of cultural upheavals, including rising rates of violent crime. Where the Bond films of the 1960s had taken 007 to places moviegoers could not afford to go, *Live And Let Die* took viewers to places where they *feared* to go.

The filmmakers knew they were courting some small level of controversy by featuring a sophisticated white spy facing off against a small army of black villains so they softened the impact with clever choices. At first there were thoughts of casting Diana Ross as Solitaire, the film's leading lady. Ross had received high praise for her role in *Lady Sings The Blues*, but the producers eventually decided to keep Solitaire white, as she was in the novel.

Bond did find himself rolling in the grass with African-American actress Gloria Hendry, which made the statement that 007 appreciated beauty, whatever the colour. There were concerns within UA about Bond having sex with a black woman, and a photo shoot showing Roger Moore as Bond with Gloria Hendry in a wedding gown caused a few tense moments for the publicity department. Nonetheless, after a series of widely viewed films such as 1967's *Guess Who's Coming To Dinner*, the subject of interracial romance was far from taboo. *Live And Let Die*, however, depicted the encounter as neither poignant nor sensationalistic, which in its own way was a breakthrough. Only the South African censor objected.

In further efforts to balance the racial mix of good and evil in the movie, Bond works with two black colleagues. Also, the filmmakers developed the character of Sheriff J. W. Pepper, who played an important stereotype - the Southern redneck. During the film's extended boat chase, Pepper allowed the filmmakers to show Bond making a fool out of his pursuer. But in this chase, that fool is not the enemy agents but Pepper. Thus, the black villains are rarely the ultimate butt of Bond's jokes - visual or verbal.

The film showcased some wonderful actors, including Julius Harris (**bottom left**), who had to contend with some very hungry alligators using an unfamiliar prosthetic hook. Tommy Lane (**bottom**, **centre left**) appeared in *Shaft* and *Cotton Comes To Harlem*. Geoffrey Holder (**bottom**, **far right**, with Jane Seymour) had actually portrayed Baron Samedi as a dancer in the 1950s as part of his Caribbean dance troupe's New York show. He was later cast as Samedi in the 1957 Truman Capote musical *House Of Flowers*.

On 16th October 1972, stuntman Jerry Comeaux raced his Glastron speedboat at
75 miles per hour toward a specially built ramp to perform a record-setting 95-foot
leap. Eddie Smith and members of the Black Stuntmen's Association contributed to
the scene where the boats dash across a lawn during a wedding. Smith piloted the

Live And Let Die, in a certain sense, turns the Bond image on its head. Although Guy Hamilton toyed with the idea of James Bond as a cultural anachronism in *Diamonds Are Forever* (Bond's conspicuous white dinner jacket in a Vegas casino filled with underdressed tourists), he brings it to the foreground in *Live And Let Die*. When Bond ventures into Harlem, the taxi driver, waiter and a CIA agent who follows him into enemy territory all mock him. Throughout the film, the viewer is reminded that the exotic world into which James Bond ventures is laughing at him - his tastes, his clothes, his British public school affectations. This important element quickly lets the audience know that the filmmakers are under no illusions that these are still the golden days of spy films in the mid-60s. With *Live And Let Die*, James Bond landed squarely in the 1970s, unperturbed by social and political changes.

To complement the lighter touch to the character, the filmmakers chose to raise the level of action in the film. Since car chases in films like *The French Connection* had become a new Hollywood staple, the filmmakers created four chases - one with an out-of-control taxi, another with a private plane virtually destroying New Orleans' Lakeside Airport, one with a double-decker bus, and finally a massive speedboat chase through the Louisiana bayous. The latter chase featured boats sailing over lawns and roads, crashing through a wedding ceremony and slamming into police cars. Staying with the tone of the chases in *Majesty's* and *Diamonds*, the filmmakers relied on daring stunts rather than clever gadgets to make the scenes work.

For the music, the filmmakers teamed up with two icons of the 1960s - George Martin and Paul McCartney. Martin, who had become world-renowned for producing the Beatles albums, wrote the film's score, and McCartney (along with his wife, Linda) wrote the title song. James Bond had mocked McCartney and Martin's music in *Goldfinger* ("My dear, there are some things that are just not done, such as drinking Dom Perignon '53 above a temperature of 38 degrees Fahrenheit. That's as bad as listening to the Beatles without earmuffs."), but now both Bond and McCartney needed to prove their cultural relevance.

Live And Let Die represented a much larger risk for Broccoli and Saltzman than *Diamonds Are Forever*. Connery's absence alone lowered the chances of success. Changing times and public tastes also seemed stacked against Bond. Reviewers came to advance screenings ready to dismiss the film, but the filmmakers made it hard on the critics. *Variety* wrote, "Faced with a real-world crisis in the villain sector... plot lines have descended further to the level of the old Saturday afternoon serial." *The Hollywood Reporter* opened its review stating, "Electronic eavesdropping and the heroic demeanour of a master spy are the by-products of political tactics in serious question these days," but added, "Thanks to Tom Mankiewicz's wry screenplay and Hamilton's efficient, inventive craftsmanship, the movie is a nice piece of fluff."

Others openly embraced the new and clever approach. *The New Yorker* praised the entire Bond canon as "one of the very few phenomena of present-day entertainment that strut around parading viciousness and actually succeed through a peculiar innocence of vice". Vincent Canby of *The New York Times* declared, "*Live And Let Die* is more liberated, more uninhibited, less uptight than any number of contemporary fantasy-feeding black films like *The Mack* and *Cleopatra Jones*." *Films And Filming* simply stated the obvious: "Far and away

the funniest of the James Bond series." Audiences, too, got the point. *Live And Let Die* was a safe film to see in the summer of 1973. The movie, and James Bond himself, were so uncontroversial that the British Milk Board even chose to film an advertisement on the *Live And Let Die* set illustrating the wholesome goodness of milk.

The film indulged in all the excesses of the Bond series, but it revelled in not taking itself seriously. The violence was laced with good humour, and the sex - even the interracial sex - was merely titillating and joyfully uncomplicated compared with the explicit fare playing in cinemas. While other films gloried in the details of drug use, the Bond film used heroin smuggling only as a backdrop. No longer was 007 the hero of the day, but he was the welcomed hero of the not-too-distant past, ever elegant in an inelegant world.

There were few raves for Moore's performance, but nor were there many pans. He was deemed "okay" and "smoothly good-looking", but most reviews barely noted the change from Connery to Moore, which was a welcome turn of events for the studio and the producers. Most critics were busy trying to digest the complex politics within the film, or relishing the total lack thereof. Thus, Moore escaped through escapism, just as the film did, from the harsh critiques that battered George Lazenby.

Audiences delivered the ultimate verdict, and it was far better than the studio had hoped. *Live And Let Die* was an instant smash hit in America. By the end of the year the film had sold more tickets than any other film released in 1973 (three films made more at the box office during the year - *The Poseidon Adventure*, *Deliverance* and *The Getaway* - but they were all originally released in 1972). While the film's 20 million tickets sold in the US were down six million from *Diamonds*, the producers were not concerned because of *Live And Let Die*'s phenomenal performance overseas.

As the summer and autumn of 1973 progressed, Broccoli and Saltzman had to smile. *Live And Let Die* was actually out-grossing *Diamonds Are Forever* in most international markets. Roger Moore, the new Bond, was packing cinemas across the globe. All of United Artists' fears about limiting the budget and the schedule had not hurt the film. In fact, the limited budget only meant more profit for the producers, and *Live And Let Die* quickly became the most profitable Bond film for UA since *Thunderball*.

Only 18 months after Sean Connery's departure, Broccoli and Saltzman felt confident they had reinvigorated the series, answered critics who said Bond was outdated, and staked out a new formula for 007's success. With that in mind, the producers committed to starting work immediately on the next Bond film, scheduled to be released in December 1974. It had taken them just a year and a half to make *Live And Let Die* a brilliant success, and all agreed it was a good idea to strike while the iron was hot.

"United Artists were always asking for a Bond picture they could either open in the summer or at Christmastime, so they didn't care if it was one year, eighteen months, two years, but they certainly wanted them as quick as possible." Michael Wilson

"I thought Roger was wonderful. He could do no wrong in my eyes because I really adored him as a human being. He was such a leader of our production, and he kept us all happy when things were tough."

MAUD ADAMS

Cubby Broccoli and Harry Saltzman first thought of producing Ian Fleming's final 007 novel, THE MAN WITH THE GOLDEN GUN - published in 1965, one year after the author's death - after they completed *You Only Live Twice*. With Sean Connery publicly declaring that he had left the role of James Bond, the producers approached Roger Moore and decided to film the movie in Cambodia. Turmoil in the south-east Asian country, which ultimately led to the rise of a man named Pol Pot and the bloody rule of the Khmer Rouge, derailed their plans.

By the summer of 1973, Moore had established himself as 007, and for his second film, Broccoli and Saltzman returned to THE MAN WITH THE GOLDEN GUN. The novel takes place largely in Jamaica, which was a primary location for *Live And Let Die*, so the producers considered the Middle East.

Tom Mankiewicz, Guy Hamilton and Cubby Broccoli thought they had found an ideal location after seeing a portion of French filmmaker Albert Lamorisse's unfinished movie *The Lovers' Wind*. At the end of the cut the filmmakers watched, a little fox ran across the desert toward an ancient lost city - a spectacular collection of narrow alleys, clay towers and fortress walls rising from the barren landscape. With a little research, Broccoli found out the city was called Bam, and the filmmakers quickly booked a scouting trip.

"We flew to Iran, and it was miserable," said Tom Mankiewicz. "We got to Tehran, and we took off for the city of Shiraz, on Air Iran. Cubby was strip-searched, because they thought his camera was a gun. I mean, it was just a nightmare." The trio next boarded a small plane to fly to the lost city of Bam, but never actually arrived. "We landed in the middle of the desert, people came out to meet us... and it was the wrong city. It wasn't the one in the movie. The mayor had laid on this big lunch for us, and Cubby said, 'Forget it, we're getting back in the plane. It's 140 degrees, I'm not sitting here for three hours...'

"We get back in the plane - absolutely true story - the three of us. We're flying back, the thermal updrafts are absolutely unbelievable in this plane, and we're bouncing, and I just thought 'We're never gonna get out of this'. I said to Cubby, 'You know, when we get back, we should ask Albert Lamorisse where he shot it, we never thought about calling him', and Cubby said, 'He's dead'. I said, 'How did he die?'" Lamorisse, Cubby replied, had died in a flying accident in Iran three years earlier.

"All of a sudden these Phantom jets go by, we're in this little plane, and I said, 'What's going on?' The pilot said, 'Israel has just declared war on Egypt'. The Ramadan War had started...We decided not to go back to Iran to shoot." Little did the filmmakers know, but the war between Israel and Egypt would eventually provide the impetus for the new film's storyline.

Having decided against the exotic labyrinth of Bam, the filmmakers became even more determined to find an appropriate outpost for the film's villain. Guy Hamilton saw footage on television of thousands of limestone mountains rising from the sea in a place called Ha Long Bay, but the filmmakers ruled out a location scouting trip. Ha Long Bay, it turned out, is located in the north-eastern part of Vietnam, near Hanoi. Even though the US and North Vietnamese government had signed a peace accord in January 1973, tensions between the two nations were still too high to consider shooting in the Communist country. However, Hamilton found, there were similar rock formations in Phuket, Thailand. In October 1973, Broccoli and Hamilton conducted a recce of the area and liked what they saw. The decision was made to film *The Man With the Golden Gun* in Thailand and Hong Kong.

Given the south-east Asian setting, the filmmakers again decided to look to a new genre of films. Just as the blaxploitation movies enlivened *Live And Let Die*, the highly profitable martial arts films provided a template for *The Man With The Golden Gun*.

The contemporary fascination with martial arts movies (and the subsequent explosion in karate and judo schools around the globe) could be traced to one man - Bruce Lee. The extraordinarily gifted Asian performer was no stranger to spy films. Born in San Francisco but reared in Hong Kong, he became a child star there before immigrating to Los Angeles, where he taught martial arts while seeking acting roles. On television, he became famous as Kato, sidekick of *The Green Hornet*. Off-screen, he taught his unique fighting techniques to students like James Coburn, star of *Our Man Flint*, who became a close friend. He also choreographed fight scenes for movies, including the Matt Helm film *The Wrecking Crew*. In 1971, Lee left Hollywood, upset not to have been cast in the ABC television movie, *Kung Fu*. Returning to Hong Kong, he made *The Big Boss*, which broke box office records in the territory. Two Bruce Lee films followed in 1972 - both setting Hong Kong records. By the end of the year, the *Kung Fu* television movie aired, and the network turned it into a weekly series, which scored well in the ratings.

In 1973, the Bond filmmakers were not the only ones interested in the growing martial arts phenomenon. George Lazenby's career had hit rock bottom. Unable to get work, he happened to go into the Odeon Cinema in London, where he saw Bruce Lee in *The Big Boss*. Impressed by the forcefulness of Lee's personality, as well as the terrific action scenes, Lazenby decided to make his way to Hong Kong to meet the Asian superstar. He went to Golden Harvest Studios and tracked down producer Raymond Chow, who immediately called Lee in the editing room and said, "George Lazenby's here. Do you want to meet him?"

"No," said Lee. Lazenby went outside to wait for a bus. As he stood there, Lee left the studio to get some lunch. His Mercedes pulled up beside Lazenby, and Lee said, "Get in." Arriving at a restaurant just as a hurricane was beginning, Lee and his entourage sat down with Lazenby. "You got no money," said Lee. "Why?" asked Lazenby. "No one rides a bus in Hong Kong who's got any money," said Lee. Then, turning to Raymond Chow, Lee said, "Raymond, give George ten thousand dollars." When Chow asked what for, Lee responded, "He's going to do a picture with me and that's a deposit."

When Swedish actress Britt Ekland (**above, top left**) heard that *The Man With The Golden Gun* was about to begin production, she went to Cubby Broccoli's office and lobbied for the part of Mary Goodnight. Broccoli politely informed her that sometimes the films did not use all of the characters from the books. Ekland was dejected when she later read that another Swedish actress had been cast in the film. However, Maud Adams (**opposite page**) had been cast as Andrea Anders. When it was decided that Mary Goodnight would be in the film, Ekland was given the role.

Bruce Lee (**above, top right**) became an international sensation in *Enter The Dragon* (1973), released three weeks after the actor's death. Lee had planned for George Lazenby to be in his next movie, and had coerced Raymond Chow to pay the former 007 an advance for his services. Following Lee's demise, Chow found another project for Lazenby - *The Man From Hong Kong* (1974).

Joie Vijjijiva and Cheung Chuen Nam (**above, middle**) portrayed Lt. Hip's nieces, who aid in Bond's escape from the karate school.

For the next two days, Lee and Lazenby talked about the movie they would make together. As Lee saw it, Lazenby could be an important conduit to a Western audience. On the third day, they were having lunch when Lee complained of a headache. That night, Lee failed to show up for a dinner he had scheduled with Lazenby and Raymond Chow. When Lazenby returned to his hotel room, he heard the news - Bruce Lee was dead of a brain oedema. Three weeks later, *Enter The Dragon* was released in the United States to instant acclaim and phenomenal box office.

Enter The Dragon followed a long tradition of Asian films with intricately choreographed fight scenes. The longest-running series featured actor Kwan Tak-Hing, who starred in over one hundred films from the 1940s through the 1970s as the

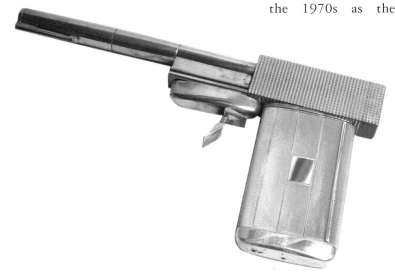

character Wong Fei-Hung, a martial arts master who helped the poor. The films were mostly fictional accounts based on the real-life Wong Fei-Hung (1847-1924), a martial arts master, teacher, healer and revolutionary renowned for protecting the weak and defenceless. To date, there have been over 200 films featuring the character, including the popular series entitled *Once Upon A Time In China*.

While the Wong Fei-Hung series and most other martial arts movies were set in the past, *Enter The Dragon* was set in the present, and featured a very James Bond-style plot. Bruce Lee played a spy who infiltrates the secret island hideaway of a Dr. No-type villain. The finale offered a cat and mouse battle between the villain and Lee. *Time* magazine had referred to Bond as the "spiritual father" of Shaft and Superfly, and Bond had successfully co-opted their genre. Now martial arts films were trying to mine Bond's box office appeal, so the filmmakers decided to utilize martial arts heavily in *The Man With The Golden Gun*.

After completing a draft of the script, Tom Mankiewicz withdrew from the project, feeling that he wasn't giving the producers his best. "This was the third in a row I had done, and I was feeling like I was writing the same scene over and over again," he said.

As Mankiewicz wrote his draft, global events were taking over James Bond's world. As a result of the massive Arab invasion of Israel on 6th October 1973 (while members of the Bond team were flying over Iran) and the subsequent arms sales to Israel by Western powers, the Arab members of OPEC placed an embargo on oil shipments to the United States. Saudi Arabia and the other leaders of the embargo threatened to cut production and sales steadily until Israel evacuated the land it had captured in the 1967 war. The impact of the Arab oil embargo proved to be dramatic and debilitating. To the world's observers, it seemed as if there was a new superpower - the OPEC cartel - that now had the ability to bring the West to its knees without nuclear weapons.

The Bond filmmakers took notice. On 17th November 1973, United Artists announced that 007 veteran Richard Maibaum would write the next draft. The energy crisis became a key element of the film's plot.

The worst day of the energy crisis in the US arrived on 11th February 1974. In New York, the lack of supply caused more than half of the gas stations to close. At some stations, there were lines six miles long. Halfway around the world, on a location recce in Bangkok, Cubby Broccoli was finding that the crisis would have a direct effect on the production of *The Man With The Golden Gun*. Broccoli announced that increased transportation and hotel prices would add 10% to the film's seven million dollar budget. On 13th March, the oil embargo ended, but the Arab nations refused to lower crude oil prices. Since the beginning of the embargo, oil prices had increased by 300%. As a result, the OPEC countries would earn $100 billion in 1974.

Despite an effort to keep the tone of the film light, the Bond filmmakers also found themselves drawn to the development of global terrorism. Fleming's villain, Francisco Scaramanga, was a high-priced assassin. In the film, he is a free agent given nominal protection by the Chinese in exchange for the occasional 'hit'. Assassinations had become an expected part of the news by 1974. On 29th December 1973, for example, Basque separatists set off a bomb, killing Luis Carrero Blanco, the prime minister of Spain. Soon, the fictional Scaramanga had a real-life counterpart: Carlos 'the Jackal', a high-living Venezuelan Communist who years later proclaimed himself a "revolutionary for hire". On 30th December 1973, Carlos tried to assassinate the noted Jewish businessman Lord Sieff. In 1974, Carlos bombed the Israeli Hapoalim Bank in London, followed by bomb attacks on French newspapers.

While Carlos dished out terror on behalf of the Popular Front for the Liberation of Palestine, he had been raised in South America, schooled in London and Moscow, and trained in Jordan. He quickly became the most sought-after terrorist in the world. As *The Man With The Golden Gun* began production, history was again running parallel to the fictional world of James Bond.

As the filmmakers prepped the new 007 movie, they were looking for the hooks - stunts that would grab the public's attention. The ejector seat in Bond's Aston Martin had started the trend back in *Goldfinger*. In *Thunderball*, it was Bond's jet pack and Largo's transforming hydrofoil. *You Only Live Twice* featured a helicopter picking up a moving car with a giant magnet. *Diamonds Are Forever* showed Bond's Cougar driving on two wheels, and *Live And Let Die* featured the world-record boat jump and the shearing off of the top of a double-decker bus.

By 1973, the world's most famous stuntman was an American who dressed like Elvis Presley and, riding a motorcycle, hurled himself across amazing distances. His name was Evel Knievel. On New Year's Day, 1968, Knievel achieved international fame by jumping the fountains at Caesar's Palace in Las Vegas, then crashing upon impact. John Derek, former husband of Ursula Andress, filmed the jump, and his then wife, actress Linda Evans, operated a slow-motion camera near the landing ramp. Her footage, showing Evel tumbling over and over like a rag doll, ignited a worldwide fascination with Knievel. When he awoke from his 28-day coma, he was hailed by some as an American hero. In 1972, George Hamilton starred in a film about his life, and in 1974, Knievel planned to launch himself in a steam-powered rocket cycle contraption across Idaho's Snake River Canyon.

A triumph of ironic casting - Christopher Lee (**opposite**), best known for his film portrayals of Count Dracula, who must shun sunlight or die, starred as *The Man With The Golden Gun*. Herve Villechaize's role as Nick Nack (**below**) led directly to his casting as Tattoo on the American TV series *Fantasy Island*. His signature line from the show's opening - "De plane! De plane!" - became a cultural catchphrase. Three golden guns (**opposite bottom**) were made for the film by Colibri, world-famous for manufacturing cigarette lighters. One was completely solid, another fired a cap, and the third could be assembled and disassembled.

  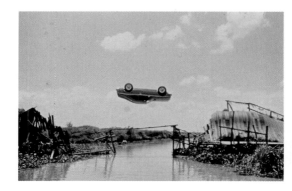

In 1973, stunt show promoter Jay Milligan was sitting in a hotel room in Harrisburg, Pennsylvania having a breakfast meeting with his competitor, Joie Chitwood, who had just finished doing stunts for *Live And Let Die*. Chitwood was telling Milligan he would soon be off to Singapore to perform car stunts for *The Man With The Golden Gun* when Milligan's hotel phone rang. The caller was Cubby Broccoli, who had seen footage of the Astro-Spiral jump which Milligan had performed at the Houston Astrodome. He wanted to know if the same stunt could be performed over a 40-foot wide expanse of water. Milligan excused himself from his breakfast meeting and made the deal to replace Chitwood as the car stunt supervisor on the new 007 film. Chitwood only had himself to blame; he had sent photos of the Astrodome jump to director Guy Hamilton. Astoundingly, the Astro-Spiral jump in the film was performed by Loren 'Bumps' Willert (**above**, with Milligan), a veteran auto show driver, who had never before performed the stunt.

Just prior to the release of *The Man With The Golden Gun,* *Variety* reporter Richard Albarino asked Cubby Broccoli how long he thought Bondmania would continue. He answered, "Until doomsday."

For shots of the flying car actually lifting off and taking to the air, special effects man John Stears constructed a radio-controlled miniature. The full-size flying car never left the ground. Christopher Lee remembers sitting in the full-size mock-up with Herve Villechaize when the diminutive actor said to him in French, "Ah, the things one has to do to be noticed in the cinema."

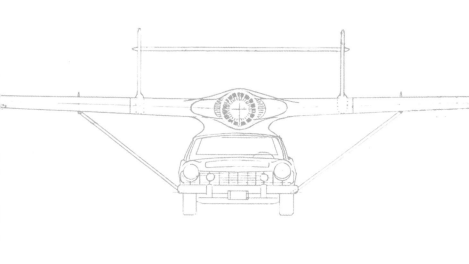

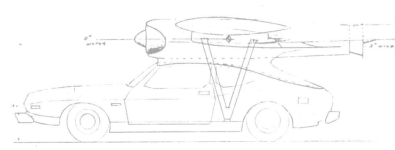

Evel Knievel's fame prompted a slew of stunt show performers, all of whom wanted to thrill race-track and arena audiences without the risk of the shattered bones Knievel suffered with alarming regularity. By 1971, an engineer working on auto accident computer simulations named Raymond R. McHenry designed a new stunt. He called stunt show/demolition derby promoter Jay Milligan, and together the pair tested and staged what would become known as the Astro-Spiral Jump. Milligan debuted the stunt - the safe 360 degree spinning of a car during a mid-air jump - at the Houston Astrodome in 1972. By 1974 Milligan was on his way to Thailand at the request of Cubby Broccoli, who had asked if he could do the stunt for the new James Bond film. The stunt alone cost $300,000 and for Broccoli it was the showpiece of the movie.

The filmmakers also acquired a flying car, which was an actual FAA-approved vehicle being produced in Southern California. Using a Ford Pinto and parts of a Cessna aircraft, one could fly the auto to a destination, detach the wings and avoid renting a car. Alas, the flying in the movie had to be done with a miniature. In late 1973 the airplane-car's inventors, Henry Smolinski and Hal Blake, were flying the vehicle when the wings and engine detached in mid-air. Unfortunately, the wingless Pinto was ill-suited for flight, and the resultant un-aerodynamic nightmare proved fatal for the inventors.

Regardless, the filmmakers felt they had all the right ingredients. The strong cast included Christopher Lee (a cousin of Ian Fleming), two Swedish beauties - Maud Adams and Britt Ekland - and the talented 3' 11' actor, Herve Villechaize. The locations could not be more exotic, the stunts more spectacular, nor the storyline more current. What could go wrong?

In mid-April 1974, *The Man With The Golden Gun*'s first unit flew from London to Bangkok, and from there to Phuket. Principal photography commenced on 18th April, on the beach of Khow Ping Khan Island, with Herve Villechaize's Nick Nack bringing Tabasco to Christopher Lee's Scaramanga. Filming continued in Bangkok, Macao and Hong Kong until the end of June, when the unit returned to Pinewood Studios in England to film interiors. The second unit remained behind in Bangkok to film shots for the car chase scenes. Just as they were finishing, there was an uprising in the country. Gunfire erupted in the streets. The government declared martial law as the second unit crew rushed from Bangkok. But even after the film crews left, James Bond's impact on Thailand continued to be felt, just as it had in many other locations around the globe.

In 1974, the islands near the small resort of Phuket were largely uninhabited and undeveloped. Phuket itself was virtually barren of tourists, but its white beaches and tropical climate, combined with a new bridge from the mainland, soon changed that. The actual location where the filmmakers shot was even more remote. "Phang Nga was this tiny little village with hardly any accommodations at all," said Maud Adams. "The one luxurious hotel that they had put us into was this very, very small hotel that they had found the need to go in and paint before we moved in." Later, the cast and crew discovered that the "hotel" they had occupied was, in fact, the local brothel.

After the towering rock-spire islands received worldwide exposure in *The Man With The Golden Gun*, and travel agents began sending sun-seekers to Phuket, the film location slowly became a tourist destination. When the first adventurous travellers appeared in Phang Nga after the film, they hired local boatmen to take them

to the 'James Bond island'. Soon, a steady stream of visitors ventured from the growing resort in Phuket, and eventually tour operators set up a concession for nearly day-long journeys to the newly christened James Bond Island.

James Bond Island is now populated with souvenir vendors hawking postcards and Coca-Cola. Phuket is a booming resort colony with high-rise hotels and shopping plazas. The once-remote area has now become a tropical playground.

With their exotic globe-hopping, the Bond films have a long history of aiding local tourism. Jamaica, where Ian Fleming wrote his spy adventures, received exposure in the 007 novels and the film version of *Dr. No*. The Orient Express, in turn, benefited from its appearance in *From Russia With Love*. Miami's Fontainebleau Hotel gained a huge publicity boost when *Goldfinger* featured the resort. The Bahamas produced a television ad touting its prominence as the location in *Thunderball*. The use of Japan as a location in *You Only Live Twice* - including key tourist attractions such as Himeji Castle and the Ginza district in Tokyo - helped to promote the nation as a destination.

When the Bond producers set out to film *On Her Majesty's Secret Service* in the Swiss Alps, they discovered a partially completed restaurant atop the 10,000 foot-high Schilthorn. They struck a deal to use it as Piz Gloria, Blofeld's remote clinic. The filmmakers built a helipad on the location, making the restaurant more accessible. Three decades on, the revolving restaurant was still named Piz Gloria and guests could order drinks from the James Bond Bar.

When Bond returned to Jamaica in *Live And Let Die*, he again served as a tourism advertisement, particularly for Ross Kananga's Safari Village - the alligator farm featured in the movie.

"We went down to a place called Phuket, which today is a huge tourist attraction, largely thanks to Bond. I mean, boats take tourists out to see the James Bond Island,

and I think we are largely responsible for an enormous amount of employment down in that neck of the woods." Guy Hamilton

Phuket

Phuket, Thailand, the location of important film sequences for the latest and most exciting James Bond adventure "The Man with the Golden Gun."

Thai International

Richard Nixon's dramatic departure (**far left**) was only one story that defined 1974, a year of denouncement, when heroes fell with alarming regularity. Daredevil Evel Knievel's Snake River Canyon jump failed ignominiously. A coup deposed Emperor Haile Selassie, whose stature as the first internationally recognized black African leader led to the formation of a religion (Rastafarianism) which saw him as the black messiah. Golda Meir resigned as Premier of Israel. Willy Brandt, West Germany's engaging Chancellor, resigned after finding an East German spy among his close staff.

The news headlines also punctuated a year that could only be termed bizarre. Members of a group called the Symbionese Liberation Army kidnapped William Randolph Hearst's daughter, Patty Hearst. She later helped the SLA rob a San Francisco bank (**left**) and changed her name to Tania. The IRA bombed the Houses of Parliament and Harrods in London, while Arab terrorists left a trail of bodies in Israel and Europe. Then there were the crazies - a disturbed man shot and killed the mother of Martin Luther King Jr.; a touched soldier stole a helicopter and tried to crash it into the White House. On Christmas Day, a man drove his car through the gates of the White House and held police at bay for four hours. Yassir Arafat addressed the United Nations General Assembly with a pistol strapped to his hip. It was no wonder that the latest recreational sport, streaking, involved dashing through public spaces without clothes, usually screaming at the top of one's lungs.

Aside from guiding tourists to specific locations, the Bond films tapped into a particular allure associated with tourism - the elegant adventure. James Bond became an emblem for the jet-set lifestyle. One could go anywhere and still experience the best service, dining and lodging. For Bond, travel was effortless. He never elbowed his way through a crowd to lug his baggage off the carousel at an airport, and only in the deepest swamps in *Dr. No* does Bond ever have to swat at a mosquito.

The more subtle appeal of Bond's travel was sex. The mere act of being somewhere else was in itself seductive. For both men and women, the chance to be away from one's ordinary world gave a promise always realized in the Bond films - the opportunity to meet someone exotic and new. Many of us would one day like to find ourselves adrift at sea in the arms of a beautiful stranger, and that simply is not likely to happen during the daily commute to work. Regardless of the destination, by the mid-1970s, 007 helped usher thousands through the travel agent's door.

On 18th June, as filming of *The Man With The Golden Gun* continued at Pinewood, and six months prior to the release of the film, United Artists unleashed a saturation trailer campaign. Seven hundred prints of a 90-second trailer were put into circulation in theatres around the United States. On 31st July, United Artists distributed advance one-sheet posters to theatres in the US and Canada promising 'A Christmas Present From James Bond' and featuring an illustration of Scaramanga's golden gun.

On 7th August, Roger Moore filmed scenes at Pinewood showing Bond in Lazar's workshop and Andrea's hotel suite. That same day, the Chairman of the Republican National Committee, George Bush, gave the President a letter that stated he now felt "resignation is best for the country". The following day, 8th August 1974, Richard Nixon, implicated in the Watergate cover-up, announced his resignation.

In December, *The Man With The Golden Gun* opened in Britain and the US, but the box-office was disappointing, as were the reviews from critics and fans. As 1975 began, the filmmakers began to re-examine their choices. Cubby Broccoli blamed the tight schedule for not allowing the story to be developed fully. Others felt the humour was too rampant - the reappearance of J. W. Pepper and the two kung-fu fighting schoolgirls received particularly cool responses. Critics felt the energy crisis plot already felt out of date, and despite the amazing Astro-Spiral stunt, many found the action tame.

Even Roger Moore felt uncomfortable with some of the rougher violence in the film, which did not mesh with his view of Bond. "It's the second film with Roger Moore," said Michael Wilson, "and I think we were trying to find Roger's voice in the part... He had his own personality and his own strengths and he had to develop those in the role.

"*The Man With The Golden Gun* was sort of exploring Roger as an actor and seeing where we could use him to the best advantage. And his natural gift for humour in the part of James Bond was still being developed."

Whatever the reasons, *The Man With The Golden Gun*, while still making money, failed to reach an American audience effectively. It fared a little better internationally, but it became by far the least successful Bond movie ever released. Amazingly, no one panicked at this news. There was no reason, because, after all, there might not even be another Bond film. For the first time, the future of 007 seemed in serious doubt because of a monumental behind-the-scenes struggle brought on by the collapse of the tenuous partnership of Cubby Broccoli and Harry Saltzman.

7. In 1974, ITV purchased the British broadcast rights for the earlier James Bond films, airing *Dr. No* the following year - it was the seventh-highest rated programme of 1975, attracting an audience of over ten million. The broadcasts of the 007 films in Britain and the United States jump-started interest in James Bond among a new, younger generation of movie fans. Bond appealed strongly to teens in the mid-1970s, but he was also shrouded in mystery. As they watched the films playing on television, parents or older siblings would reminisce about seeing the films in the cinema when they were originally screened. Old toys were pulled from the back of cupboards, soundtracks extracted from dusty record

Nobody Does It Better

collections, and bottles of aging 007 aftershave unearthed from the back of bathroom cabinets. These new fans tried to piece together the history of Bond from the scraps of information they were able to glean in classrooms and playgrounds. Two sources helped. In 1972, the year *Goldfinger* aired on US television, John Brosnan published a book entitled *James Bond In The Cinema*, which detailed the plotlines of all the Bond movies to date. The other source of Bond lore came from second-hand bookstores, which sprang up around the US during the recession years of the mid-1970s. A healthy stack of Bond novels always lined the shelves, along with the occasional gem like *For Bond Lovers Only*.

For Bond fans - both new and old - who had deep pockets, ads could be found in the back of *Famous Monsters Of Filmland* for original James Bond movie posters from *Dr. No*, *From Russia With Love* and *Goldfinger*, but one had to be willing to pay $7.50 for each one. In 1975, a book dealer in New York offered a first edition of CASINO ROYALE for one hundred dollars, but the steep price drove off buyers.

Soon, enterprising teens started publishing fanzines. The first was called *Bondage*, which began when two American High School students, Richard Schenkman and Bob Forlini, frustrated there was no official James Bond fan organization, decided to start one themselves. After a brief conversation with the publicity department at United Artists, where they received permission to use the 007 logo and call themselves "the official James Bond 007 Fan Club", they began creating a mimeographed newsletter, which was followed in June 1974 by the first issue of *Bondage*. Once Schenkman had taken over the Club after high school, the magazine went from publishing fan art to rare articles by Ian Fleming.

For over 15 years, the James Bond 007 Fan Club was a treasure-trove of information for Bond aficionados worldwide. Other newsletters and magazines - with titles like *For Your Eyes Only* and *Mr. Kiss Kiss Bang Bang* - appeared in the 1970s as fans sought to document their enjoyment of the Bond phenomenon and record the elusive history of 007 as it occurred. Many of those who contributed to *Bondage* and published newsletters and fan magazines over the years went on to become deeply involved in the James Bond legacy. Raymond Benson, for example, was eventually selected to write the James Bond continuation novels in 1996. Others, like Schenkman, soon began successful careers in the movie industry.

In late 1975, the fanzines reported a key development in the history of the Bond movies. The partnership between Harry Saltzman and Cubby Broccoli had dissolved.

Harry Saltzman was restless by nature. Although he could have lived a very comfortable life as one of the producers of the 007 films, he wanted to parlay the fortune he had gained from the Bond films into a bigger fortune. Besides producing other films outside the Bond movies, he also invested in business ventures, most notably bids to acquire Éclair Debrie (the French camera manufacturer) and Technicolor. Both ventures cost him dearly.

"As time went on," said Michael Wilson, "Harry got more and more involved in these other projects and then - as his other businesses started to go sour - there became a lot of pressure

financially on him, and therefore on the company. And that's really where the dispute came up. It was not artistic and it was not really a personality dispute. They were both enthusiastic about Bond."

According to Saltzman's assistant, Sue St. John, "The break-up occurred because Harry had pledged his Danjaq shares as collateral to Union Bank of Switzerland to buy Technicolor. And UBS called in the loan." The only way out for Saltzman was to find a buyer for his Danjaq shares. As St. John recalled, "I think Cubby had veto of who he would have as a partner and there were quite a few people interested in buying Harry's share." In fact, St. John's former employer, the Saudi magnate Adnan Kashoggi, was interested and had nine million dollars available, but the deal did not go through as UA did not like the thought of Kashoggi being half partners with Cubby. In addition, Saltzman's wife Jacqueline was very ill with breast cancer and Harry was naturally extremely preoccupied. "He was going through hell on both sides, both in business and at home," said Sue St. John. "It wasn't easy for him. It was horrible."

The banks were unsympathetic to Saltzman's personal problems. "The debt that Harry had with UBS was a long-standing one," said St. John. "Went back years and years. And they had lost patience with him. So they threatened that they were going to take control of Danjaq. All the lawyers thought that this was a real possibility. And Cubby and UA were very worried about it, obviously."

Michael Wilson, who was acting as a legal advisor to Eon Productions at the time, said, "The financial situation that Harry found himself in was gradually deteriorating to the point where the banks in Switzerland wanted to take over his position in the company. They became very hostile; there was one situation that was just Cubby and Norman Tyre (Broccoli's lawyer) and I on one side of the table and about 25 people - Harry, his lawyers, Swiss and otherwise - on the other end, trying to wind up the company, bring it into liquidation, all those kind of things. Everything was going on. Cubby went to United Artists and they said, 'We have a contract and we are insisting that it go forward and Harry is refusing to go forward on the next film. You have to make the film and deliver it to us.'"

The struggle continued throughout 1975. Meanwhile, James Bond rolled on. In 1974, ITV had begun airing the Bond films they had acquired. In the US, *Thunderball* and *Dr. No* appeared on the ABC network in 1974, and *You Only Live Twice* aired in 1975. All three films played to massive ratings.

By the end of 1975, the crisis over Harry Saltzman's debts came to a head. Saltzman felt trapped. He could not sell his shares in Danjaq without Broccoli's approval, and he was reluctant to sell his shares to Broccoli. In 1975, Saltzman made overtures to Columbia Pictures, who expressed interest in his share of the Bond rights. UA, though, did not want another studio involved in the production of the Bond films. In early December, UA and Saltzman reached a deal: the studio would purchase Saltzman's share of Danjaq. With

"It was very sad when that relationship broke up. Cubby was more down to earth. Harry was more of an ideas man. He started in the circus. So they complemented each other." Ken Adam

BONDAGE

BONDAGE NO.1, VOL. 1 MOTTO: " THE WORLD IS NOT ENOUGH"

the agreement, Albert R. Broccoli became the sole producer of the Bond films, albeit with a less than silent partner in United Artists.

UA immediately announced it wanted a rapid production schedule for new 007 films. *Variety* reported that the studio wanted *The Spy Who Loved Me* in cinemas by the end of the year: "*Moonraker* to roll in 1977 and *For Your Eyes Only* in 1978." Broccoli agreed it was time to get back into production, but not without a strong script. For *The Spy Who Loved Me* the story was vitally important - per Ian Fleming's wishes, his estate specified that an entirely new story should be devised for the film version of the title. Danjaq had to agree not to use the novel in any form.

To create a viable story, Danjaq hired a series of writers, including noted author and Bond fan Anthony Burgess, most famous for his novel *A Clockwork Orange*. The question was simple: what tone to take in the wake of the disappointment of *The Man With The Golden Gun*? Stories from the new writers tended to tie into global terrorism with commercial jet passengers being blown up in mid-air, an attack on a convent school, and - with echoes back to Watergate - one proposed scene where a nude President of the United States is forced to "confess his crimes" on television. Broccoli rejected such dark visions of Bond and more writers came and went.

Eventually, the filmmakers decided to use just two tangential elements from THE SPY WHO LOVED ME novel. The first was a pair of villains, named Horror and Slugsy in the Fleming novel. Slugsy was a shorter, stocky, hairless man, and Horror was tall, skeletal, and had teeth that were completely capped in steel.

The second element was SPECTRE. Although the character of Blofeld had presumably been killed at the end of *Diamonds Are Forever*, his limp, lifeless body had never been displayed to moviegoers, and the filmmakers became aware that the fan community still considered Blofeld a viable villain. A small portion of the novel THE SPY WHO LOVED ME concerned Bond trying to close down part of SPECTRE's operation; thus, why not revive the organization in a new form for the 1970s?

The filmmakers dreamed up a dramatic opening where the old guard of SPECTRE was raided and replaced by the new guard - members of Black September, the Red Guard, ETA (the Basque terrorist organization) and others. The idea for this assault had its origins in an unexpected terrorist attack at the end of 1975. For most people in the West, the Arab oil boycott showed implicit support not only for the Palestinian cause, but also for the acts of terrorism committed in the name of that cause. Consequently, the West was shocked when Carlos 'The Jackal' and a group of cohorts stormed into a meeting of OPEC oil ministers, kidnapping the entire group and threatening to kill them if they did not do more to support Palestinians. Many in the press discussed the dreaded consequences of this new breed of bloodthirsty terrorists toppling the governments of oil rich nations and assuming power.

Carlos the Jackal (**below**) made his reputation as the most valuable terrorist fighting for the Palestinians during the summer of 1975. He was living in Paris when another member of the Popular Front for the Liberation of Palestine (PFLP) began co-operating with French authorities. When three officers and the PFLP member arrived to confront him, Carlos whipped out a machine pistol, shot three of the men dead, seriously wounded the fourth, and escaped to Lebanon. It turned out the accuser had been working with the Israeli security service, Mossad, and Carlos was quickly hailed by the PFLP as a killer with nerves of steel.

Left opposite: Harry Saltzman on location for *Live And Let Die*. "I don't think the Bond films would have happened with Cubby or Harry alone. They were a unique partnership," said Sue St. John, Saltzman's former assistant. "They just complemented each other. But I think Harry's contribution was the madness."

BONDAGE NO.1 007 JUNE 1974

As the filmmakers neared production of *The Spy Who Loved Me* in the spring of 1976, a new problem arose. Kevin McClory announced that his non-competition agreement with Danjaq had expired, and that he was now pursuing production of a new Bond film based on the *Thunderball* rights he had secured in 1963 from Ivar Bryce and Ian Fleming. The new script, McClory proclaimed, had been co-authored by himself, noted spy novelist Len Deighton and Sean Connery.

The news could not have come at a worse time for Cubby Broccoli. The new Bond film would not even begin shooting until over 18 months after the release of *The Man With The Golden Gun*, and it would be another year before the film would reach cinemas. The last time Bond had competed against himself (when *You Only Live Twice* and *Casino Royale* duelled in cinemas), both films had been hurt at the box office.

Another problem was the enthusiastic response to McClory's announcement in the growing James Bond fan community. There was disquiet about the new direction for Bond, particularly the emphasis on humour and the perceived lack of energy in *The Man With The Golden Gun*. In America, growing numbers of fans objected to ABC's editing of the Bond films for television. They complained that the best jokes had been cut, the action scenes chopped down, and the advertisements stuck in at all the wrong places. These comments were mostly ignored until 16th and 23rd February 1976, when ABC aired *On Her Majesty's Secret Service* over two nights.

Since *OHMSS*, as it had become known among the *cognoscenti*, had never been re-issued to cinemas, a group of loyal fans were eager to see the movie which many considered to be the most under-rated Bond adventure. It was held up as an antidote to the more humour-laden films. These fans were shocked when the film opened on ABC during the ski chase which begins the action-packed second half of the movie. A voice - which certainly did not belong to George Lazenby - boomed across the airwaves, proclaiming to be James Bond. 'Bond' talked to the viewers and introduced the movie with a variety of wisecracks. By the end of the airing, a week later, James Bond fans were loudly proclaiming the film butchered.

The man they wrongfully blamed for the desecration of 007 was Albert R. Broccoli. He had not seen the airing, nor been told of the changes made to the movie. Nonetheless, fans could not figure out why he would let this happen to one of his films. Many figured he did not care. News of a new Sean Connery Bond film was red meat to this new and vocal group.

On 25th June 1976, Broccoli received another blow. "Soon as our script came out, we were slapped with a plagiarism case by Kevin McClory, who claimed that we'd plagiarized a script that he'd written," said Michael Wilson, "and there was a suit for an injunction on the film." Kevin McClory had asked a London court to enjoin Broccoli from starting production on *The Spy Who Loved Me*. "Finally, the injunction was denied," said Wilson, "and we could go ahead and make the film." The drumbeat in everyone's ears was clear: Kevin McClory was back, and no one quite knew what this would mean for James Bond.

Broccoli had other worries, too. Aside from the older Bond films breaking records in television broadcasts, there was no current model for James Bond's continued success.

There were still spy films, but the hits were paranoid thrillers such as *The Conversation*, *Parallax View*, *Marathon Man* and *Three Days Of The Condor*, which were heavily influenced by Watergate and conspiracy theories surrounding the Kennedy assassination. More traditional Bond-influenced films, such as Clint Eastwood's *The Eiger Sanction*, did middling box office and were trampled by the critics.

The whole nature of the cinematic hero had changed. With political and social disillusionment taking hold, many recent hit films relied on nostalgia. Movies like *American Graffiti*, *The Way We Were* and *The Sting* harked back to an innocent past, while other period films - such as *The Godfather*, *Papillon*, *Robin And Marian*, *Chinatown*, *The Man Who Would Be King* and *The Outlaw Josey Wales* - created complex and fallible heroes from yesteryear. Films set in the modern day seemed remarkably hero-less. The central characters in *Jaws* and *The Exorcist*, two of the highest grossing films of the mid-1970s, were certainly not heroes, but monsters. The most successful spy films were parodies from France - *The Tall Blond Man With One Black Shoe*, its sequel (*The Return Of...*), and *A Pain in the A***.

Right: The miniature Liparus supertanker for *The Spy Who Loved Me* was created by Derek Meddings (not pictured). "You can never miniaturize water," said Meddings, "so the tanker turned out to be 63 feet long. We had a 48-horsepower Evinrude engine, which we didn't put outboard, we put it inboard. That gave us the wash that we needed, because I'd looked at all these shots of supertankers, and you'd get something like a three-mile wash behind it, white water. I wanted to make this look as if it was a totally believable tanker."

"Every time that we've bit the bullet and said,
'We're going to go all out', it has meant that
we've broken out again and re-vitalized the series.
The Spy Who Loved Me was that kind of a picture." Michael Wilson

Television programming offered little better hope. On 7th March 1973, ABC aired a hit television movie, *The Six Million Dollar Man*. The lead character, an Air Force test pilot badly injured in an accident, finds himself outfitted with bionic replacement parts; a government spy agency makes good use of his new-found strength and powers. In the autumn, ABC began airing 90-minute movies, but the ratings quickly sank. Producer Harve Bennett told *TV Guide* in 1974, "This was mostly because the network decreed that Majors should be more of a debonair James Bond character with a lot of glamorous girls and semi-risqué lines". Eventually, ABC turned the show into a one-hour series, and the ratings quickly rose through the roof. Bennett stated, "The elimination of the Bond angle helped a lot". In 1975, ABC also brought Matt Helm to the small screen, but after the failure of numerous secret agent shows, they dropped the entire spy element of the character and turned Helm into a private detective. The next spring, ABC revived Derek Flint in a poorly produced television movie, again disposing of all the Bondian characteristics and modelling the programme after current hit detective shows. In the UK, the two new espionage-themed series airing in 1975 and 1976 (*Quiller* on the BBC and *The XYY Man* from Granada) consciously turned away from the world and mythos of James Bond. The revival of *The Avengers* (entitled *The New Avengers*) lasted only one season.

It was in this environment that Cubby Broccoli convinced United Artists to double the budget on the next Bond film from seven to fourteen million dollars. This figure is remarkable because it meant that the budget for *The Spy Who Loved Me* would increase to far more than the studio had collected in rentals from the US and Canadian release of *The Man With The Golden Gun*. The move was even riskier because by the mid-1970s James Bond merchandising had all but died. Apart from a few jigsaw puzzles in Europe and a toy golden gun produced in Great Britain (which was literally a toy Luger coloured gold), the last film had yielded almost no merchandise licences.

Cubby Broccoli was undeterred. He saw that Bond needed to return to the larger-than-life entertainment that he craved. Instead of rushing the next film, Broccoli insisted on developing a strong script. Rather than see the decline in James Bond's cultural ubiquity as a sign of audience ambivalence, Broccoli pushed to make the new film so big it would be impossible to ignore. It would be, after all, his first James Bond film as sole producer. Broccoli focused on three ingredients: humour, spectacle and fantasy.

During the controversy with Harry Saltzman, Broccoli's stepson, Michael Wilson, joined his company in London as his inhouse business affairs advisor. A trained lawyer and engineer, Michael Wilson worked with writers on the scripts, fighting to raise the level of the new Bond film. As the years progressed, Wilson's contributions would have a continuing impact on the world of James Bond.

Wilson, the son of Dana Broccoli and actor Lewis Wilson (who had played Batman in a 1941 Columbia Pictures serial), had first become involved with the Bond films by working as a production assistant on *Goldfinger*, and doubling Oddjob driving a station wagon during a quick Kentucky shoot. Wilson's background as an engineer proved useful during the development of *The Man With The Golden Gun*, where he provided technical information on solar power. With the legal morass of the break-up of the Broccoli-Saltzman partnership, Wilson became an important right hand to Cubby Broccoli, and Cubby quickly realized that Wilson also possessed a strong understanding of story and the James Bond character.

When Broccoli brought in Lewis Gilbert to direct the film, Gilbert asked Christopher Wood to continue work on the screenplay. Wood's background included a highly profitable series of sex farce books and movies that began with *Confessions Of A Window Cleaner*. Working closely with the filmmakers, particularly Michael Wilson, Wood was finally able to create a coherent feel for the cobbled-together story, something that the previous writers had been unable to do to Cubby Broccoli's satisfaction. Wood recalled, "I think that the shelf life of a writer on that movie must have been about three and a half hours. I came in knowing a script was in existence, but I had no idea so much blood had been spilt."

The finished script proved to live up to Broccoli's vision. It was the most humorous, largest-scale and most fantasy-laden 007 adventure to date. It included a number of elements that came from real-life events and inventions. The story was partially inspired by the real case of Royal Navy Sub-Lieutenant David James Bingham, who sold important photos and technical information about submarine tracking technology to the Soviets in 1970. The idea of Bond and a beautiful Soviet agent teaming together had its roots in the historic Apollo-Soyuz space mission which took place in July 1975.

A villain who wanted to destroy civilization and rebuild a perfect world beneath the sea certainly gave the script an element of fantasy. The concept referred to Captain Nemo in Jules Verne's *20,000 Leagues Under The Sea*, but it was a real Japanese oceanographic research facility and large-scale underwater labs built by the US Navy and ocean explorer Jacques Cousteau that made it seem feasible. It was just this sort of element of reasonable possibility that attracted Broccoli and Wilson.

Bond's underwater Lotus also had its roots in reality, although it became the fantasy fulfilment of engineers who dreamed of cars which were both sea and land-worthy. Like the flying car in *The Man With The Golden Gun*, the underwater Lotus Esprits used in the film were mainly full-sized shells or miniatures, although Derek Meddings and his special effects team did construct one completely operational submarine car. The driver, though, needed to be outfitted in scuba gear since the car was not watertight. Unlike the flying car, though, aquatic cars worked, at least on the water's surface. The most famous of these was the Amphicar, made in Germany and mainly sold in the US from 1961 through 1968. The car made notable appearances in the 1967 spy spoof *The President's Analyst* and in a US Pepsi Cola ad.

Opposite: *The Spy Who Loved Me* was Roger Moore's favourite 007 film. "I don't know whether it was because Lewis Gilbert and I have the same sense of humour, or whether the locations were right, the costumes were right, but everything seemed to work very well on that film," said Moore. "I think it went together. And we had a lot of laughs making it." The underwater Lotus Esprit may have been pure fantasy, but it proved to be a highlight for audiences. The film also showcased remarkable real technology, including the Wetbike (**upper right**) and magnetic levitation devices (**centre right**). In fact, the monorail seen inside Stromberg's supertanker fortress was a genuine magnetic levitation device.

The sketches read (hand-lettered annotations):

Sc. 286 — INT LEPARUS FROM MIDDLE OF BRIDGE (BOW END) 'WAYNE' BEING SWALLOWED BY TANKER WAVE MACHINE TO FORCE WATER AGAINST SUB.

Sc. 286 — THE WAYNE GLIDING INTO ITS BAY

"I can remember walking on this set, and thinking, 'My God, what are we going to do with this?', because it was so huge." Lewis Gilbert

Rounding out the fantasy element was the character of Jaws, the steel-toothed henchman. Originally planned as a more menacing character, Broccoli saw the humour in the idea of a man as dangerous as a killer shark. He pushed for the parody-laced name, and understood how this humour allowed the filmmakers to get away with absurdities.

To give the film scope, it was decided to set a significant part of the action on a supertanker. Supertankers – tankers that carry more than 100,000 tons of oil – came into popular usage in the mid-1960s, but they became famous to the public in March 1967, when the Union Oil tanker, *Torrey Canyon*, crashed against rocks off the coast of England, creating an environmental nightmare. In the intervening decade, tankers had swollen in size, becoming massive structures larger than the tallest skyscrapers. Their oil spills had also continued to make headlines, which helped inspire the filmmakers to pursue a villain who plans to use a tanker in order to wreak vengeance on the polluters of the oceans. The grand scale of the supertanker and public fascination and wariness combined to create a spectacular villain's lair. Originally, the filmmakers hoped to shoot the movie's climactic battle onboard a Shell Oil tanker off the British coast, but safety concerns and costs proved prohibitive. Undeterred, the filmmakers decided to stage the battle on a set that would also contain three hijacked submarines. To build the set, the filmmakers faced the same problem they had encountered a decade earlier on *You Only Live Twice*: no stage was big enough. Rather than building a new, temporary structure, Ken Adam proposed building the world's largest silent stage to accommodate the set. And so was born the $3 million 007 Stage at Pinewood Studios, probably the most famous film stage ever built. As remarkable as the stage's oversized proportions was the fact that the stage was built by Eon Productions, not the studio. It represented Cubby's personal investment in the British film industry.

The stage was inaugurated in a grand ceremony. Former Prime Minister Harold Wilson presided over the festivities. "I think it was a validation of the film industry in Britain," recalled Michael Wilson. "Following on from that, the *Superman* films were made there and the UK film industry became a magnet for *Batman* and *Indiana Jones* because there was this perception that there were talented filmmakers in the UK and they could support the most technologically sophisticated and the biggest films that could be made."

In 1984, after hosting some of the largest films produced in the 1970s and 80s, the 007 Stage burned down during the shooting of

Legend. Cubby Broccoli ordered it rebuilt for *A View To A Kill*, and Pinewood Studios insisted on changing the name of the stage. It is now known as the Albert R. Broccoli 007 Stage, and as of this writing, continues to be one of Britain's most prestigious places to film. The 007 Stage, and the giant supertanker set it housed, were the manifestations of Broccoli's desire to increase the scale of the Bond films. The giant set was expensive, as were location shoots in Egypt and Sardinia, but Broccoli knew he wanted to see the money spent up on the screen.

When the agent of international beauty Catherine Deneuve approached Broccoli with the idea of Deneuve starring as the Soviet spy in the film, Broccoli balked at her fee. He noted most of the leading actresses in Bond films were not stars before appearing with 007, and he emphasized his point when he cast the little-known actress Barbara Bach in the role.

One day, Michael Wilson walked into the production office carrying a copy of *Playboy* magazine. The magazine featured an ad for Canadian Club showing a man skiing off El Capitan in Yosemite National Park. After flying into the void of space, the man, a mountain climber named Rick Sylvester, opened a parachute, drifting into the valley below. Wilson proposed this stunt as the opening of the new film, and the idea excited everyone. "So we went to California and got a hold of Rick," Wilson said, "and it turned out that he'd actually never done it." The photos in the ad, it turned out, had been faked.

Sylvester said that although the stunt had never been done, it *could* be done, if the filmmakers could set up to shoot above the Arctic Circle during a particular six-week window before the winter storms set in. It was a huge gamble - a stunt never performed, a man's life at risk, and an expensive location. Cubby Broccoli weighed the odds, told Sylvester his safety must come first, and after an initial scouting trip, backed the idea.

The stunt showing James Bond sailing into the ether changed the Bond films. As spectacular as the Astro-Spiral Jump had been, Rick Sylvester's ski jump off Mount Asgard was simply the most cinematic stunt ever filmed. The majestic beauty of the location and the long, near silent shot of Bond tumbling through space made every audience member involuntarily hold their breath in anticipation. Then came the *coup de grâce*, Christopher Wood's contribution, the unfurling of the Union Jack parachute. Instantaneously, the world understood the visual punch line. Just as Bond's throwaway lines brought humour to the grimness of death, the Union Jack symbolized the return of the cinematic hero.

The Spy Who Loved Me showcased a new style of Ken Adam design. "I was experimenting with new shapes, because my designs had always been very linear and I wanted to go into more curved shapes. And so the design of Atlantis, which looked like some form of spider or something coming out of the water was all dome and curved surfaces. It gave me an opportunity to design Stromberg's apartment with curve upon curve and so on, which I found very exciting. Some of those sets are some of my favourites sets on Bond. It was a new challenge, and certainly the supertanker set was one of the biggest interior sets ever done."

"I felt, 'This is such a fantastic scene, the ski jump scene, that it's going to make the movie. People are going to talk about it, say 'You've got to see this movie for the ski jump'." Christopher Wood

The world was ready for heroes - desperate, in fact. It was as if the global public had been in a depressive haze for much of the decade. All that changed over the course of 24 hours. On the weekend of 4th July 1976, the United States celebrated the nation's bicentennial. The anniversary was marked with huge patriotic celebrations broadcast worldwide. It seemed as if the nation was finally willing to put the pall of Vietnam and Watergate behind it. Yet for some, the celebration was muted due to the continued shadow of anti-Israeli terrorism. On 27th June, terrorists had hijacked another plane with over 100 hostages. In the following week, the terrorists released 50, but claimed they would kill the rest unless their demands were met. Israel met their demands with a daring raid on Entebbe Airport in Uganda; elite Israeli commandos killed the terrorists and saved all but three of the hostages. It was the first clear-cut defeat for terrorists, and many across the globe saw it as a victory against an insidious war of global fear.

The following year, all the Commonwealth nations celebrated the Silver Jubilee of Queen Elizabeth II and observers across the world agreed: pride was back in fashion.

In the summer of 1977, James Bond was back, too, but changed. Gone were any vestiges of the more brutal and deadly Sean Connery; this incarnation of 007 was all Roger Moore, unabashedly celebrating all the things that made life worth living - adventure, humour, sex, good food and drink, and the promise of a better tomorrow. The latter element came courtesy of Cubby Broccoli's emphasis on fantasy and Ken Adam's futuristic production design, particularly the huge ocean-borne laboratory, Atlantis. Many of the sets were combinations of miniatures and front projection effects, but the result was inspiring, futuristic and upbeat. Everything seemed fantastic yet possible. Adam's use of polished chrome in many of the sets presented a clean world unspoiled by complex motives. The plot, too, was clean, and populated by uncomplicated characters. The story itself could not have been more optimistic, featuring old enemies becoming friends. Even the henchman Jaws proved endearing, and was embraced by viewers at the film's end.

There was no mistaking Roger Moore's character as anyone except 007. The unflappable elegance, indulgent heterosexuality and essential Britishness were all there. Yet everything played counter to the tone of sophisticated ruthlessness of the early Bond films. In *Dr. No*, Bond shoots a man in the back out of a sense of dark anger. In *The Spy Who Loved Me*, Bond swats his tie away from a man holding on for dear life. The result is the same, but where the action in *Dr. No* leaves audiences silent, aware of the stakes for which Bond plays, the murder in *Spy* is committed purely for laughs. Jaws' steel teeth are no less absurd than Rosa Klebb's shoe knife or Oddjob's hat, but the filmmakers in *Spy* relish the absurdity, having Bond electrocute Jaws via the teeth and later trap him with a magnet. In *Thunderball*, Bond fights alongside US aquaparas in the underwater battle, but he acts alone. In *Spy*, Bond is part of an organized military operation, taking orders and preserving a chain of command.

One of the most memorable of all the James Bond stunts is the one that ends the pre-credits of *The Spy Who Loved Me* - 007 skiing off a precipice and opening a Union Jack parachute. The stunt was performed by climber and skier Rick Sylvester. "I'm glad that I did not have to do it," said Roger Moore. "It was a dangerous stunt, because if you look at it, you'll see that the ski almost clips that parachute. Had he gone into it, it could have been the end of him."

The eleven-man camera unit that filmed the stunt - which included future 007 director John Glen - had to wait several days for the Arctic weather to clear up sufficiently for the stunt to be performed. After a night of rain, the clouds parted one afternoon and the wind died down just long enough for the crew to get the stunt in the can. It was filmed from three angles which were going to be intercut, but only the camera to the side was able to keep Sylvester in frame throughout. The use of that one shot, without cutting to the other angles, added to the surreal beauty of the incredible feat.

Even the music signalled a different tone for Bond. The opening blasts of the theme songs for *Goldfinger* and *Thunderball* made it clear these were big, brassy films that pull no punches. For *The Spy Who Loved Me*, the filmmakers brought in Marvin Hamlisch, who gave his song, 'Nobody Does It Better', and much of his score a romantic, graceful feel, as if to say, "Don't worry, you're among friends. Sit back, relax and be entertained". Hamlisch and the filmmakers filled the soundtrack with familiar music, whether it be 'The James Bond Theme', *Lawrence Of Arabia*, 'Lara's Theme' from *Dr. Zhivago* or Laurel and Hardy music. It was as if Bond was consciously taking his place among the classic icons of the cinema, joining an elite group among whom such inside references felt natural.

UA, believing it had a certain hit, spent a record $4.4 million on worldwide publicity for the movie. In the US, the initial teaser trailer for *The Spy Who Loved Me* played during the wide release of United Artists' surprise hit film, *Rocky*. Audiences cheered and clapped when they realized a new Bond film was on the way. United Artists brought in renowned illustrator Bob Peak to create the poster, which also emphasized the fantasy element of the new film. The release trailer featured Moore introducing the film to cinema audiences, a technique not used since Sean Connery narrated a trailer for *Dr. No*.

The film premiered on 7th July 1977 - 7/7/77 - with Princess Anne, her husband Mark Phillips and Earl Mountbatten in attendance at the Odeon Leicester Square in London. Shortly after the film began, the premiere audience went wild. At the end of the pre-credit sequence, moviegoers roared, and the enthusiasm never waned. In the following six days, *The Spy Who Loved Me* shattered the Odeon house record. Within five weeks, the movie had sold a million tickets in Great Britain alone. In early August, scalpers were still buying up tickets early in the day and selling them at healthy profits to latecomers wishing to get into sold-out shows.

"I wanted to make sure that the score didn't sound like it was coming out of the 60s."
Marvin Hamlisch

In the US, two words appeared in review after review: "escapist" and "fun". Critic Arthur Knight noted, "The producer has never stinted on production values. In *The Spy Who Loved Me*, he seems determined to outdo anything he ever attempted before, with enormous sets, elaborate special effects and literally hundreds of extras on camera."

As audiences lined up, others began to try to fathom Bond's 15-year hold on cinema audiences. "Why is it," Richard Corliss wrote, "that three mini-generations of moviegoers... have taken their fantasies bottled in Bond?" Corliss's conclusion is much the same as that drawn by Molly Haskell of *The Village Voice*, "They do what few other films in this area can be said to do: they deliver what they promise, and they adapt to changing times without betraying the basic formula".

The Spy Who Loved Me also delivered at the box office, selling 21 million tickets in the US. The real story, however, was overseas, where the movie broke box office records in Australia, South Africa, Taiwan, the United Arab Emirates, Germany, Italy and the Philippines. The film made 75% of its money in international markets, bringing its worldwide box office to a staggering $186 million. The title song, beautifully interpreted by Carly Simon, rose to Number Two on the Billboard Top 40 pop song chart in the US, and Number Seven in Great Britain. Corgi Toys had a tremendous success with its die-cast Lotus Esprit, which again opened the door for James Bond licensed products.

Cubby Broccoli had bet on a new formula for success and won on a grand scale. James Bond had returned as a pop culture force. In the year of the release of *The Spy Who Loved Me*, the only place on television where one could pinpoint the influence of James Bond was an ABC television movie that co-opted much of the allure of Scaramanga's island in *The Man With The Golden Gun*.

The movie, like the Bond film, featured an island where elaborate illusions awaited visitors. The tall, elegant (and somewhat malevolent) host controlled the situations like a puppet master, and a midget assistant greeted guests with a sly grin. The television movie, which later became a successful series, bore the title *Fantasy Island* and starred Ricardo Montalban and Herve Villechaize. To promote the television movie, ABC aired a long ad on 16th January 1977. The ad played directly after the broadcast television premiere of *The Man With The Golden Gun*.

After the success of *The Spy Who Loved Me*, popular culture embraced Bond in a number of unexpected ways. Most obviously, there was the hope among some that Bond's continued success meant a market for other 1960s-style espionage entertainment. There were a few attempts to capitalize on Bond's box office on television. NBC launched *A Man Called Sloan*, a failed attempt to re-ignite some of 007's magic on the small screen.

In Great Britain, ITC produced *Return Of The Saint* starring Ian Ogilvy, and the next year saw the revival of *Dick Barton*, a 1940s radio (and later movie) hero that many saw as a precursor to 007. CBS picked up the now old *New Avengers* and ran them late night in 1978, even commissioning a pilot for an American version entitled *Escapade*, which aired only once.

On 15th April 1979, ABC aired a TV movie called *The Billion Dollar Threat* that was meant to be the pilot for a Bond-style TV series; the series never materialized. CBS then developed a television movie revival of *The Wild Wild West* which aired in May of 1979 and was followed with another TV film in 1980. Even *Get Smart* attempted to come back with the lacklustre cinema film, 1980's *The Nude Bomb* and two television movies. None of these efforts took hold. Only Bond seemed able to recapture and re-invent the success of 1960s spymania.

The few modestly successful spy efforts - including the BBC's *Omega Factor*, and later the mini-series *Tinker, Tailor, Soldier, Spy* - found audiences by differentiating themselves from the world of Bond rather than emulating it.

Roger Moore visited the composer of *The Spy Who Loved Me*, Marvin Hamlisch (**left**), as he was working on the score. "I can remember being at three o'clock in the morning in an apartment in the West End, you know, in the block behind the Ritz," said Moore, "and Marvin saying, 'And this is what I have done with scene...', and BANGING the piano. I thought, 'Oh, these poor people.' I mean, really, a sort of fourth dimension of sound came hammering out through the West End of London. That's Marvin, who was a very enthusiastic and wonderful writer."

After *The Spy Who Loved Me*, 007 began to appear more frequently as a reference point in music, literature, and non-spy genre films and television shows. Music groups recorded disco versions of 'The James Bond Theme', while the punk band Magazine released a version of 'Goldfinger'. As punk music transformed into new wave, groups copied the surf guitar sounds of the early 60s, creating songs like 'Surfin' And Spyin'' by The Go-Go's, which picked up on the James Bond sound. In Kingsley Amis's novel *Jake's Thing*, Jake decides he would rather watch *Thunderball* on television than sleep with his wife. In films, Burt Reynolds appeared in movies that contained overt Bond references, the first being *Semi-Tough*. Even though the film had nothing to do with Bond, its cast featured Lotte Lenya as a Rosa Klebb-like masseuse with a sadistic streak. In *Hooper*, Reynolds played a stuntman working on a Bond-like film, *The Spy Who Laughed At Death*.

The nature of James Bond's cultural role was beginning to change. No longer was he outdated - the box office receipts showed that. Nor was he the cutting-edge *héros du jour*. The James Bond phenomenon stood at a place where it defied definition. Bond was an accepted part of popular culture, a signpost of quality that refused easy categorization. Everyone enjoyed Bond, but few could imitate his success.

One person who *did* think he could build a better Bond was Kevin McClory, who in 1977, '78 and '79 made a number of attempts to set up his own Bond project. Various studios and production companies took on the project, but time and time again lawyers would advise clients that the risk of losing a legal battle was not worth the potential profits. Ultimately, either because of legal challenges from UA and Broccoli or because of other disputes, McClory was never able to launch his film in the 70s.

A second person who was thinking about James Bond was George Lucas, who had released the most successful movie of all time, *Star Wars*, just a few weeks before *The Spy Who Loved Me*. Attempting to escape the razzmatazz of the movie's release, Lucas went to Hawaii in the summer of 1977 with Steven Spielberg, who was due to release his science fiction opus, *Close Encounters Of The Third Kind*, closer to Christmas.

"We were on the beach at the Mauna Kea hotel in Hawaii," Spielberg told writer Derek Taylor, when Lucas told Spielberg about an idea for a cinematic hero called Indiana Jones who could sustain a series of films like James Bond; Spielberg had previously expressed an interest in directing a Bond film one day. Lucas's pitch convinced him to pursue Indiana Jones rather than 007.

Broccoli, for his part, found it hard to resist the influence of Lucas and Spielberg. The film *Jaws* had an obvious impact on *The Spy Who Loved Me*'s choice of henchman. In 1977 and '78, it was hard to quantify the tremendous impact of *Star Wars* and *Close Encounters* on popular culture, which easily equalled Bond's influence in the mid-60s. A group called Mego had hits with disco versions of *Star Wars* music and the *Close Encounters* score. *Star Wars* toys sold in massive numbers. Magazines such as *Starlog* and *Omni* appeared, devoted to science fiction and fantasy. Science fiction films flooded cinemas, from *Damnation Alley* to *Starcrash*. Even made-for-television movies received theatrical releases, such as the pilot for a new Buck Rogers series.

At the end of *The Spy Who Loved Me*, a title card announced 'James Bond will return in *For Your Eyes Only*'. Broccoli and United Artists decided that film could wait. The public wanted outer-space adventure, and Broccoli felt that in MOONRAKER - Ian Fleming's 1955 novel about an early nuclear-tipped ICBM aimed at London - he had a story and a title that were ripe for the times. Using sections of Fleming's plot about a private industrialist who bankrolls building rockets, Christopher Wood constructed a narrative that had one key element already firmly in place - the film would feature James Bond travelling into space.

In mid-April 1978, Arthur Krim and Robert Benjamin, two of the men responsible for bringing James Bond to United Artists, left the studio along with a host of other executives to form Orion Pictures. During the same year, there was an explosion in the cost of making movies. Budgets soared along with ticket prices around the globe. In Britain, pernicious tax laws made it all but impossible for the wealthy to remain in the country. Cubby Broccoli reluctantly pulled up stakes and moved back to Beverly Hills. He brought back the same team from *The Spy Who Loved Me* to work on *Moonraker*, and set about developing a story which would, he hoped, balance the element of fantasy with the world of James Bond. Broccoli declared that *Moonraker* would not be science fiction; it would be science *fact*.

After a debate about basing the film in Hollywood, the moviemakers decided to take over Paris, a move which required leasing virtually every inch of soundstage space in the city's three studios. Major locations included Venice and Rio de Janeiro, but the scope was, in actuality, much, much larger. Special effects coordinator Derek Meddings occupied the 007 Stage at Pinewood for the film's complex effects, and portions of the movie were shot in locations as disparate as the jungles of Central America, Napa Valley, California and Silver Springs, Florida. At any given point, three separate units filmed, and at times as many as five full crews worked simultaneously around the globe.

THE GREATEST STUNTMAN ALIVE!

Raiders Of The Lost Ark (**above, top**) was a throwback to movie serials of the 1930s and 40s, but there was also a conscious intention on the part of creators George Lucas and Steven Spielberg to create a character who would carry a franchise, à la James Bond.

Above: In *Hooper* (1978), Burt Reynolds plays a stuntman doubling for Adam West, who is starring in a James Bond-type spy film. West had actually once been considered for the role of 007, after the cancellation of his phenomenally popular TV series, *Batman*. This is not the only *Batman* connection to Bond - Michael G. Wilson's father was Lewis Wilson, star of the 1941 Columbia Pictures serial *Batman*.

Opposite: As Dr. Holly Goodhead, Lois Chiles found it challenging to play a "Bond woman" at a time when the feminist movement was at its apex. "At that time, women were protesting their image, how they had been portrayed, and women were burning their bras," Chiles recalled. "Holly was Bond's concession to women's lib. So she could do everything that Bond could do. And I liked that."

"Lewis Gilbert said that he could have made *Dr. No* for the telephone budget on *Moonraker*." Jerry Juroe

The film was massive in scope. The opening sequence, again developed by Michael Wilson, featured Bond being pushed out of a plane without a parachute. The action which followed - a through-the-air chase and mid-air fight - required the use of body-hugging parachute packs, and the development of rip-away clothes to conceal the gear, as well as a lightweight 35mm camera which could be built into a helmet. The sequence proved to be jaw-droppingly amazing because it was clearly not faked. While no one believed that Roger Moore and Richard Kiel had ever jumped from a plane, it didn't matter. The fact that anyone could do this type of action was enough to induce gasping disbelief among viewers.

The film, however, became less believable as it went on, with James Bond eventually taking off in a space shuttle to an orbiting space station. The station, which was massive enough to house dozens of perfect human specimens, but small enough not to be noticed through a telescope, was the lair of Hugo Drax, developer of the Moonraker space shuttle,

who hoped to re-populate the world in his image of perfection. Despite a NASA consultant and an emphasis on the plausibility of the story, the filmmakers delved into pure science fiction by the movie's climax with laser guns and a massive space battle involving Marines and enemy agents.

There were other scenes which, for the first time, pushed the limits of the filmmakers' abilities. When James Bond finds himself trapped in a cable car halfway between the top of Sugar Loaf mountain and the Urca Hill station, the scene relied heavily on effects photography. Later, as Bond escapes a plunge over a giant waterfall via a hang glider hidden in his boat, miniatures and front projection had to be employed to complete the scene, which was originally supposed to be filmed for real.

Because of the complexity of the movie, it was no surprise that it went slightly over budget. Unfortunately, that budget was already twice that of *The Spy Who Loved Me*. No one, though, could argue that the money was wasted. The film

looked spectacular, from Ken Adam's sets to the lush location cinematography. The film successfully created a fantasy reality, pushing even further the wink-at-the-audience jokes of *The Spy Who Loved Me*. Drax calls his pheasant hunt by having an assistant blow 'Also Sprach Zarathustra' on a horn. Later, when Bond is seen on horseback, the theme from *The Magnificent Seven* plays.

The film's summer 1979 release was originally supposed to be tied in to the maiden launch of the actual space shuttle, but NASA postponed that event for nearly two years. It did not matter. *Moonraker* was greeted by eager filmgoers. In London, the film premiered at the Odeon Leicester Square on 26th June 1979, for an audience which included Prince Philip, with a live television broadcast of the event. A party at the London Playboy Club followed with Bunnies and actors in astronaut suits. The film grossed £86,084 in its first week at the Leicester Square cinema, breaking the record held by *Close Encounters*.

From Venice to Brazil to outer space, *Moonraker* is arguably the most globe-hopping Bond adventure. The boat chase sequence at Iguaçu Falls alone involved shooting in seven countries. The falls lie at the borders of Brazil, Argentina and Paraguay. The boat chase itself was filmed in Florida; Derek Meddings shot miniatures in England. Process work with Roger Moore was completed in France, and a crew filmed the sequence's conclusion among the pyramids in Guatemala.

Above: Though the Bondola ride through St. Mark's Square seemed a breeze to 007, capturing it on film was an experience which dampened Roger Moore's ego. Moore said in an interview, "It was really a Ford chassis underneath. So it was fake, but there was the illusion that the thing rose up out of the water. I'm sitting there in a nice grey silk suit, push the button, and the thing starts to rise up out of the water, and WOP! - it throws me into the lagoon. There are 40,000 tourists watching. They think that's rather fun. I don't think it's very much fun at all. I have to go and change my suit again, get made up again, get my hair stuck down, get back into the gondola; it's getting rather squelchy inside now. Five times it tipped over. Luckily, I had five suits. One more take and we wouldn't have been able to do it."

Right: The cable car fight between James Bond and Jaws was filmed on location using stuntmen Dickie Graydon as 007 and Martin Grace as Jaws, and completed with actors Roger Moore and Richard Kiel on a Paris soundstage. Even though the close-ups with the actors were filmed in a relatively safe setting, Kiel still found it nerve-wracking. "It's a whole different world from being inside of the cable car to standing on top," said Kiel, "because the thing would rock, and it's just... It's scary. I do have a fear of that kind of height."

"With *Moonraker* we went pretty far along the track of touching on science fiction. And it was a tremendously successful film." Michael Wilson

In the US, United Artists mounted a lavish premiere at Manhattan's newly re-opened Rivoli Theater on 28th June, which was attended by the likes of Andy Warhol, Frank Sinatra, Robin Williams and Brooke Shields. The premiere was followed by a swank post-premiere party at Regine's. A Los Angeles premiere celebration included a party at Chasen's and such guests as Gregory Peck and Sammy Davis Jr.

To coincide with the New York premiere, the Museum of Modern Art hosted a James Bond symposium, an amazing honour for the film series. Suddenly there was a new tone in some of the commentary on the films - respect for the continued artistry and innovation of the series. Tom Allen in *The Village Voice* wrote, "*Moonraker* is the most expensive avant-garde movie since *Barry Lyndon.*" Allen wasn't joking in his praise. Vincent Canby wrote for *The New York Times,* "What's (*Moonraker*) about? It's about moviemaking of the kind pioneered by Georges Méliès in films like *Voyage To The Moon* (1902) and *20,000 Leagues Under The Sea* (1907)".

Other reviewers were uniformly impressed by the spectacle. Frank Rich wrote in *Time*, "There is at least one course for every conceivable taste… You may as well stuff yourself silly now." Some, however, felt the film lacked the coherent story of *The Spy Who Loved Me* and other Bond adventures. Michael Sragow stated, "*Moonraker*… is especially disappointing because it follows *The Spy Who Loved Me* - one of the most entertaining comic-book movies of all time."

It was at the Museum of Modern Art that Cubby Broccoli began to hear from fans who craved a more serious treatment of 007. During a question and answer session hosted by Judith Crist, Broccoli fielded a number of questions about the tone of the Bonds, ABC's editing of the films for broadcast, and the fate of *On Her Majesty's Secret Service*. Not only were there critics who held Bond in deep respect, but judging from this audience, there were fans who cared a great deal about Bond's future and past.

Moonraker's performance seemed unstoppable. In the US, the film grossed $10 million in four days in 900 theatres. Six days later, the film's box office reached $21 million.

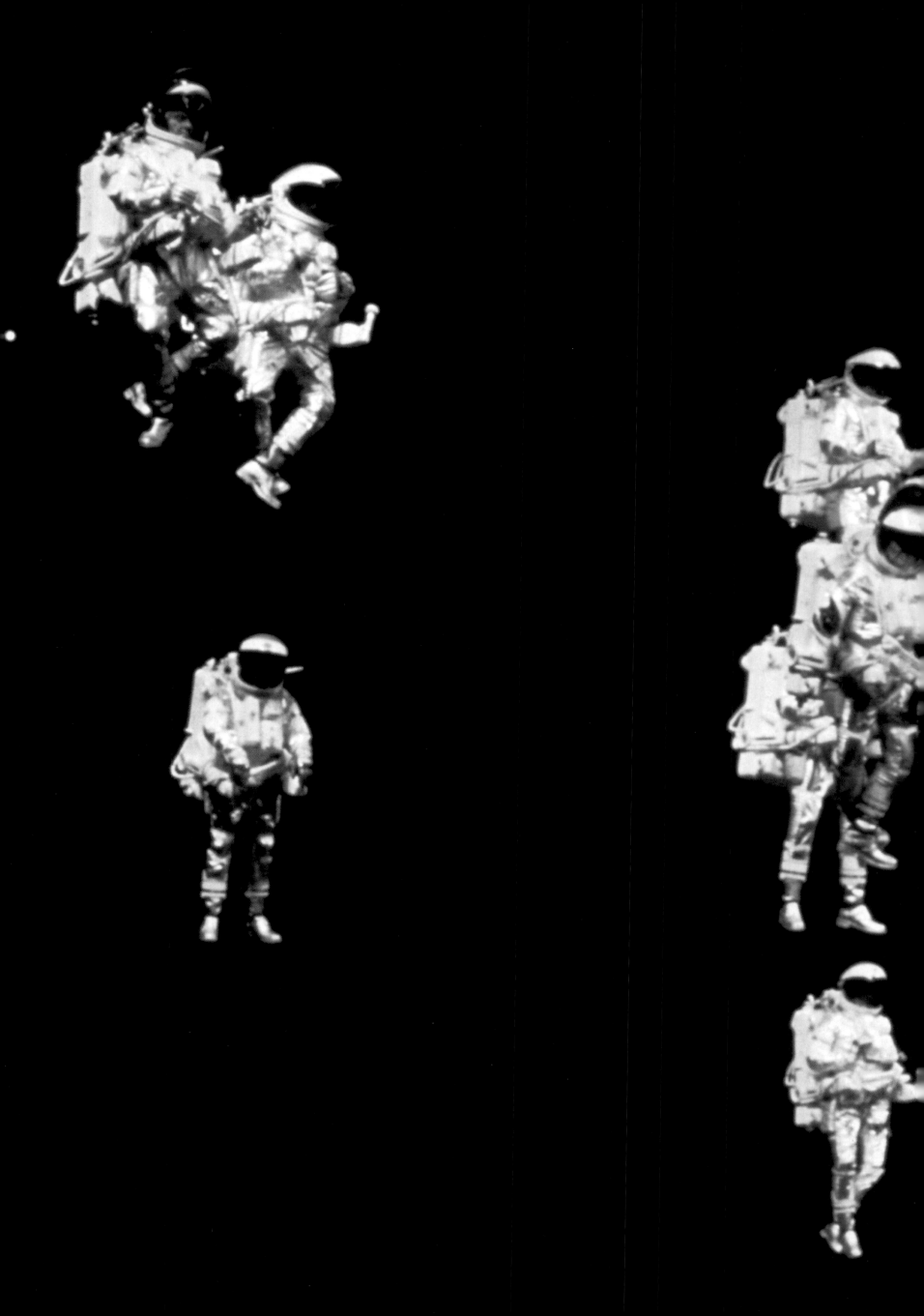

Across Europe, *Moonraker* packed cinemas. In Austria alone, the movie tripled the gross of *The Spy Who Loved Me* in its early weeks. The movie subsequently broke records in dozens of countries on every continent. In Paris, the film sold more tickets in its first week than any previous film ever released. *Moonraker* nonetheless failed to sustain the international performance of *The Spy Who Loved Me*, which played for months in many territories and held the record as UA's highest-grossing film internationally. Even with higher ticket prices, *Moonraker* generated $140 million abroad, almost exactly the same gross as its predecessor. The real success story for the film rested in the US, where *Moonraker* sold millions more tickets than *The Spy Who Loved Me*, which translated into $16 million more in box office. Yet on the basis of worldwide admissions *The Spy Who Loved Me* was still the more successful and profitable film.

Nonetheless, *Moonraker* made sack-loads of money. Tie-in merchandising had brought in additional revenue, even if *Moonraker*-themed toys had not sold well. But there was disquiet in the ranks of the Bond filmmaking family. Michael Wilson discussed his thoughts with Broccoli. Where could they take Bond next? How could they evolve the series? Ultimately, there was one question which had to be answered - who was James Bond? As United Artists revelled in the success of the latest 007 film, Cubby Broccoli decided it was time to read a little Ian Fleming.

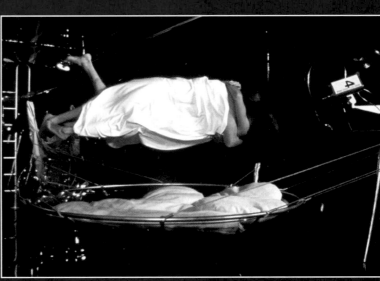

Above: Lois Chiles had fond memories of filming her love scene with Roger Moore. "The fun thing was being in a harness and pretending to be weightless," said Chiles. "When we were free-floating like birds, it was great. The wires were fun. You know, we were pulled up and down like Peter Pan."

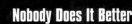

Nobody Does It Better

8. On 7th September 1978, shortly after *Moonraker* began shooting in Paris, a BBC broadcaster named Georgi Markov stood waiting for a bus at one end of Waterloo Bridge in London. Suddenly, Markov felt a sharp pain in his leg. He turned to see a man bending down to pick up an umbrella. The man apologized to Markov for bumping into him, then hailed a taxi and disappeared. Later, Markov's leg began to throb. He noticed a small bloodstain. That night a friend rushed him to hospital where he was admitted with a high fever. The following day he lapsed into shock, and on 11th September, four days after the incident, Markov, a high-profile Bulgarian dissident, died. It turned out that the umbrella he had been jabbed by was actually a gun of sorts. The tip had injected a small pellet into Markov's leg. Someone had bored a number of tiny holes - a mere third of a millimetre in

All Time High

diameter - into the pellet and filled them with a derivative of Ricin, a poison so powerful that one milligram can prove fatal. No one has ever been charged with Markov's murder, but it is believed that he was killed because of his outspoken and effective criticism of Bulgarian Communist leaders. Whatever the reason, a real man equipped by a real government had carried out the task. Many people commented that the assassination was like something out of a James Bond film. It was, except that the Bond films had never been so overtly political.

John Glen, born in 1932 at Sunbury-on-Thames, entered the cutting room at Shepperton Studios in 1947, where he worked on such films as *The Third Man* and *The Wooden Horse* before moving on to Nettlefold Studios. After two years of national service in the RAF, he returned to Nettlefold, then accepted a job at Beaconsfield Studios. Glen became an editor working on documentaries and television series. He both edited and directed episodes of *Danger Man*, and directed a segment of *Man In A Suitcase*. He then received an invitation from director Peter Hunt to become editor and second unit director of *On Her Majesty's Secret Service*, where he supervised the film's thrilling ski and bob run action. Glen went on to edit and direct action sequences for *The Spy Who Loved Me* and *Moonraker*. Impressed with Glen's abilities, Cubby Broccoli rewarded him by offering him the chance to direct *For Your Eyes Only*. Glen performed capably, and remained the director of the next four 007 adventures.

"I suppose in a lot of ways, a Bond director has to be a managing director, as well," said Glen. "Not only does he look after his main shooting unit with all the actors and so forth, he also has to control all the different units you send all over the world. Each evening, when we finish shooting on the floor, I go into the cutting room, and I have to look at all this material coming in from different units all over the world, and I have to speak to the people involved, and tell them whether they're doing the correct thing or whether they have to do something again. And I used to enjoy it. I love all that organizational skill. You get so absorbed in it, and time flies, and you suddenly realize that you've been at work and it's still midnight, and you're going to have to get up again at five o'clock, so you better get home and get your eyes closed for a couple of hours. It's wonderful."

During the mid-1970s, just as James Bond was delving deeper into the realm of fantasy, the real world of espionage was becoming more and more political. The fall-out of the disillusionment in the late 1960s and early 1970s had resulted in a new generation of spies like Christopher Boyce, a young college drop-out who took a job with satellite communications giant TRW. Boyce's work included reading and re-encoding CIA communiqués from across the Pacific. He claimed to have been disturbed at what he saw; the US government was trying to influence a democratic election in Australia. Boyce decided the government was corrupting the very freedoms on which it was built. Soon, Boyce was supplying the Soviets with huge amounts of material on US satellite spying systems, which, in turn, allowed the Soviets to hide their nuclear weapons and their development and testing facilities more efficiently.

While 007 destroyed underwater laboratories and space stations, the deadly war among terrestrial secret agents still raged. Real agents with real licences to kill carried out assassinations, such as the murder of Ali Hassan Salameh by Mossad agents in early 1979 and the so-called 'execution' of Earl Mountbatten by the IRA that August. True-life global villains also emerged, but they were nothing like the wealthy industrialists from the Bond films. In November 1978, the charismatic leader Jim Jones led a mass suicide of over 900 followers in Guyana after ordering the murder of a visiting US congressman and a news crew. In August 1979, as *Moonraker* packed cinemas, the Cambodian government issued death warrants against Pol Pot, the tyrannical ruler who ordered the killing of millions of his countrymen. On 4th November 1979, a group of Iranian militants, supported by the government of Ayatollah Khomeini, stormed the US Embassy in Tehran, taking 52 hostages. One month later, Soviet forces invaded Afghanistan.

During this period, Richard Maibaum and Michael Wilson began working on the next James Bond script, *For Your Eyes Only*. The plan was simple and risky: they wanted to return as much as possible to Ian Fleming for inspiration. Consequently, James Bond would rely more on his wits than Q's gadgets to get him out of trouble. "We figured it was time Bond headed back in a more realistic direction," Michael Wilson told Robert Osborne of the *Hollywood Reporter* a year later. "Next summer we'll know whether or not it was the right decision." It was not just a new direction the filmmakers were considering, it was a wholesale re-examination and re-working of the character of James Bond. As Wilson and Maibaum started to write *For Your Eyes Only*, Cubby Broccoli made another key decision. The new 007 film would again be based at Pinewood Studios; the experiment of shooting in France had proved to be a costly one. The budget would be less than the previous film and held tightly in check.

With this new strategy, Broccoli had to select a new director, someone who innately understood the fine balance of action, humour, sophistication and style required in a Bond film. Broccoli discussed the possibility of bringing back Terence Young, the man who had shepherded three of the first four Bond films to the screen. Broccoli also mulled over the idea of hiring Peter Hunt, the director of *On Her Majesty's Secret Service*. It was a remarkable turn of events that Hunt was even considered. For so many years *Majesty's* had been deemed a failure, despite turning a profit. But for many years, also, fans had pleaded with Broccoli to make another film like *Majesty's*, another film with a more human James Bond.

Peter Hunt was committed to other projects, so Broccoli turned to a first-time director, albeit one who had worked on *Majesty's* as well as the last two Bond films. He was also one of the most experienced second unit directors and editors currently working in Britain: John Glen.

The filmmakers faced another challenge - finding a new James Bond. With *Moonraker*, Roger Moore had fulfilled his contractual obligations and was said to be quitting the role after learning the producers were testing other actors. In fact, the actor, the studio and Cubby Broccoli were all engaged in the difficult negotiations to determine Moore's pay on the new film. Glen was relieved when Moore came to terms with Broccoli; it made his job easier not having to introduce a new 007 to the public.

With Glen at the helm, Broccoli made a commitment to top quality action. Glen had directed the famed ski-parachute jump unit on *The Spy Who Loved Me*, and more importantly, the aerial battle that opened *Moonraker*. While these two scenes existed in the more fantasy-based Bond films, they were audience favourites, and were created for real. That same sense of reality also permeated Glen's work as second unit director for *On Her Majesty's Secret Service*.

For the script, Richard Maibaum and Michael Wilson adapted two Fleming short stories, 'For Your Eyes Only' and 'Risico', combining them into one plot. In doing so, they took 007 into the heat of the Cold War. While Bond had battled villains supported by Communist China (Goldfinger, Blofeld in *You Only Live Twice*, and later Scaramanga in *Golden Gun*), and had brief hostilities with Soviet agents (in *From Russia With Love* and *The Spy Who Loved Me*), the cinematic 007 had never before taken on a master villain who was also a Soviet spy.

Maibaum and Wilson also drew inspiration from two films Cubby Broccoli cited as precursors to the Bond movies: *North By Northwest* and *The Guns Of Navarone*. In *The Guns Of Navarone*, a commando unit must infiltrate a Nazi-controlled Greek island and destroy a set of massive guns concealed in a cliff. Significantly, Maibaum and Wilson set much of the new Bond film's action in Greece. Early on in *The Guns Of Navarone*, a German plane strafes a boat carrying the commandos. Maibaum and Wilson created a similar scene for the assassination of the Havelocks at the beginning of the new Bond film. To penetrate the island of Navarone, the commandos climb a towering cliff, much as Bond scales a pinnacle to reach the villain's lair. *Navarone* also has a gritty and urgent tone. The characters are killers, and their choices weigh on them as they pursue an almost certainly suicidal mission. While Bond films always contained more humour, Wilson and Maibaum wanted to reach a similar level of emotional reality in the story.

Reconsidering *North By Northwest* proved to the writers that they could create a sprawling Bond adventure without a villain cooking up a plot to destroy the world. Wilson and Maibaum returned to a typical Hitchcock plot device. "The only thing that really matters is that in the picture the plans, documents or secrets must seem to be of vital importance to the characters," Hitchcock said to François Truffaut. "To me, the narrator, they're of no importance whatever." In *For Your Eyes Only*, this device was the ATAC - a submarine communicator. The Bond filmmakers expected few viewers to understand the strategic importance of the ATAC, yet the plot redefines Bond's role as a secret agent in the final decade of the Cold War. At the end of the script, Bond vanquishes the villain,

but does not achieve full victory. Rather, he destroys the ATAC. Bond's goal is clearly stated by the action. He is not out to destroy the USSR; his role is to maintain the balance of power.

By 1980 the term 'balance of power' was the watchword phrase in international relations. Observers considered co-existence between the superpowers to be vital. When the US lost key radar stations in Turkey and Iran in the 70s, many worried that the balance of power had shifted. Bond's job in the 1980s consisted primarily of preventing a shift, whether precipitated by rogue Soviet generals or ambitious American arms dealers.

For the story's inspiration itself, Wilson and Maibaum turned back to one of the great high-tech espionage operations of the Cold War, an operation which involved Cubby Broccoli's late friend, Howard Hughes.

On 11th April 1968, a severe explosion sank a Soviet submarine in the Pacific. Seventy sailors died in the tragedy. In *For Your Eyes Only*, the filmmakers had a British spy ship hit a mine in the Mediterranean. The result was the same - the cargo aboard (nuclear missiles and codes on the submarine; the ATAC on the fictional spy ship) was considered too valuable to remain on the ocean floor.

In the case of the Soviet sub, the US Navy located the wreck, but it rested in waters three miles deep. The CIA contacted Howard Hughes, who built a massive ship called *Glomar Explorer* under a secret government contract. The ship would purportedly be able to conduct mining operations on the ocean floor. In reality, it was designed to recover the Soviet sub, a job at which it proved to be only partially successful.

To recover the notebook-sized ATAC, the filmmakers needed less technology than the CIA. An oceanographic archaeologist, Timothy Havelock, mounted an operation on behalf of Her Majesty's Secret Service. Havelock himself was inspired not by Howard Hughes, but rather Jacques Cousteau. Ian Fleming briefly knew Cousteau, and certainly admired his work, which included co-inventing the aqualung as well as undertaking espionage in the Second World War. By 1980, Cousteau had been famous around the world for over 20 years. He had written numerous books and produced many documentaries, three of which earned Oscars. Cousteau's research into mini-subs and deep sea diving equipment laid the foundation for the real-life technology, such as the JIM suit, used in the film.

Part of the story for the new Bond film was mapped out during the winter of 1980, which included a stellar performance by US athletes at the Lake Placid Winter Olympics. Wilson and Maibaum quickly saw the potential of placing James Bond among winter sports like ski jumping and the biathlon. They also recognized the humanizing potential of having the villain sponsor an attractive young figure skater, giving them another opportunity to tinker with the Bond formula. The writers set the winter sports sequence in one of the most cinematic locations on the planet: Cortina d'Ampezzo, site of the 1956 Winter Olympics.

If the planned skiing action and the more realistic tone reminded viewers of *On Her Majesty's Secret Service*, there were other, more overt clues that the filmmakers were tapping back into that film. *For Your Eyes Only* opened with Bond at the grave of his late wife, Tracy, which was a direct nod to the film so many fans felt had been forgotten. Next, Bond did battle with a bald-headed man in a beige Mao suit who petted a white cat. While the character was never named, even casual fans knew this marked at least a symbolic return of Ernst Stavro Blofeld. Perhaps as important as resolving Blofeld's fate, the appearance in the new Bond film represented a move away from the global villainy of recent Bond films and a return to battling potentially more insidious and realistic villains.

Other symbolic changes alerted viewers this was a conscious change in direction. Bond's Lotus Esprit explodes early in the film, and 007 escapes his pursuers in a decidedly unsophisticated Citroën 2CV. It was an obvious attempt to strip away Bond's usual array of gadgets and focus more on the character. Later, Bond finds himself in a typical situation - a beautiful young woman has climbed in his bed. Even though she is close to the villain, Bond refuses to take advantage of her, deciding she is too young.

The filmmakers also removed Bond's veneer of unflappable elegance for the action scenes. In *For Your Eyes Only*, as in the Fleming novels, Bond bleeds, sweats and, with a bitter kick, sends a helpless assassin trapped inside a car over a cliff.

Opposite, top: Countess Lisl was played by Cassandra Harris, then wife of Pierce Brosnan. When introduced to Brosnan, Cubby Broccoli was impressed with him, and kept him in mind as a future 007.

The extensive underwater sequences (**above centre**) required shooting in the Bahamas and in tanks at Pinewood Studios. Amazingly, the underwater close-ups of Roger Moore and Carole Bouquet (**above right**) were filmed on a dry soundstage. The effect was achieved with fans, slow-motion photography, and air bubbles optically superimposed.

Overleaf: Despite tense contract negotiations, Roger Moore and Cubby Broccoli maintained a great friendship, spending hours playing backgammon on set. Michael G. Wilson has appeared in cameos in many Bond films. In *For Your Eyes Only*, he played a priest, which apparently did nothing to appease the Meteora monks.

EON PRODUCTIONS LTD
"FOR YOUR EYES ONLY"
CALL SHEET

Producer: CUBBY BROCCOLI   Date: WEDNESDAY,
Director: JOHN GLEN   Unit Call: 8.30a
Executive Producer: MICHAEL WILSON

Set: (1) INT SUBMARINE (007 STAGE) Sc. Nos: Close Co
         Looking out at Mantis   Mantis
     (2) EXT/INT HELICOPTER)'E'   CUs for Helicopte
     (3) INT SUBMARINE (Dry) Stage 512.515.516.517.
Note: 2nd Unit to work with Main Unit on   522.524.526.528.
007 Stage   ARTISTE   CHARACTER   D/ROOM 588.591.593.596
                                     'F' BLOCK   M/UP

ROGER MOORE   JAMES BOND   74   8.30
CAROLE BOUQUET   MELINA   71   8.15
GEORGE SWEENEY   HELICOPTER   70   To be ad
                   PILOT

Stand Ins: For

ORE   80   8.00
OUQUET   81   To be advised

                                   8.30am

un & Holster with blanks, TV
er, earphones, fall boxes, A
rt, wrist gauge

copter bodies req please, c
Unit, drum & Roller backing

ns to s/by from 8.30am. ple

and Helicopter Sequence to

2nd Unit Call Sheet

h req on 'E' Stage. Practic
es

stes Caravans req on 007 St

Video Playback req please

Wardrobe: ostume for Mantis Operator. Bond

Rushes: Theatre 7 - 5.30pm
Catering: AM & PM Breaks for 70 people please
Transport: Edward - to work to Roger Moore's i
                   Pinewood Car - to collect Scot Fino
                   Dam.
                                              ANTHON
                                              Assist
                                         SIT
                                         ednesday,
                                         oes (all
                                         zes).

The biggest risk with *For Your Eyes Only* was the change in the formula. Why bring Bond into the Cold War after nearly 20 years of keeping him out of politics? Why not let Bond continue to exist in a cinematic fantasy world, which had proved immensely popular?

More than anything it was gut instinct on the part of Cubby and the writers that the time was right for the change. As the film began production in the autumn of 1980, events around the globe began to work in their favour.

In the autumn of 1980, the US elected former actor Ronald Reagan as President. Reagan ran much of his campaign criticizing US relations with the Soviet Union. He felt the country should increase defence and intelligence expenditure and actively fight the spread of Communism. On 4th November 1980, the Cold War ceased to be a secret battle among spies as it had been in the 1970s. With Reagan's election, it became a public declaration. Even before Reagan assumed office, NATO threw down the gauntlet to the Soviets, declaring that if Warsaw Pact troops entered Poland to shore up the Communist regime, grave consequences would follow.

On 20th January 1981, moments after his inauguration, President Reagan announced that the 52 US hostages held in Iran were on a plane flying to West Germany after 444 days in captivity. This event marked a rise in patriotism throughout the West. In mid-April, the US launched the first space shuttle, a remarkable, reusable orbital spaceship. Even a spate of assassination attempts on US soil, including one on Ronald Reagan's life, did not quell the growing sense of pride in the nation.

The situation in Britain during this period proved more precarious. Riots erupted in Brixton, South London, in April 1981, and later that summer in the Toxteth area of Liverpool. Inflation and high unemployment held the country in the grip of economic crisis. In contrast, the romance between Prince Charles and Lady Diana Spencer marked a rise in British pride.

These events occurred after the Bond filmmakers had set out the course for the film, but they contributed to an atmosphere that made Bond's re-appearance as a Cold Warrior seem more appropriate.

Principal photography got underway on 15th September 1980 at the Villa Sylva, on Kanoni Island, near Corfu. The worldwide press reported the start of shooting, and newspapers across the globe published photos of Roger Moore surrounded by a bevy of beauties. Soon the press began to report more news from the Bond film set, including a very public protest against 007.

On 17th October 1980, the *For Your Eyes Only* crew moved to Trinity Rock, Meteora, to film scenes for the climax. Here, they encountered resistance from an unlikely source: the Meteora monks. The monks inhabited monasteries situated atop steep rock masses. Built in the 14th century to bar women and other "unworthies", the monasteries could only be reached by ladder or ropes. Greek authorities and the Greek church granted permission for filming in the area, but the local monks were not pleased with the movie crew's presence.

They protested by hanging signs, sheets and laundry over their buildings in order to disrupt shooting. Undeterred, the art department simply built their own monastery on a barren rock for the long shots, and recreated the setting on a soundstage at Pinewood when the company returned to England.

"Greece had its moments..."
Michael Wilson

"We made arrangements with the church in Athens for us to get permission to use one of the monasteries. And when we arrived, of course, the money that was paid over hadn't reached the local monks so they refused to co-operate. In fact, they went out of their way to sabotage our filming." John Glen

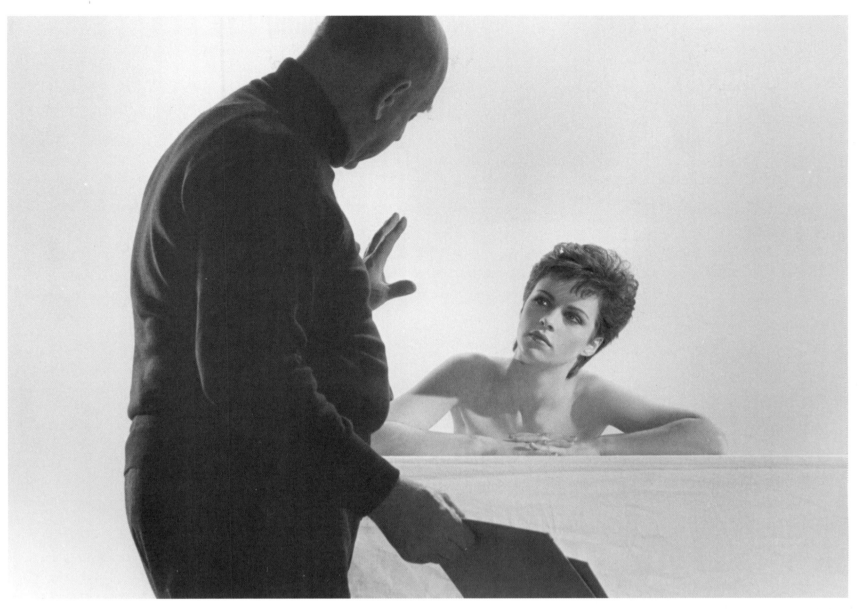

Publicly the monks said they were protesting because the script contained scenes of sex and violence. The Greek legal representative for Eon accused the monks of hypocrisy, saying that they had, in the past, allowed Greek films that included scenes of sex and violence to film on the location, and that the real nature of the protest was that the monks did not receive as large a donation as they felt they deserved. The matter quickly moved to the courts, where the question became whether the local authorities or the monasteries had the right to license filming on the site. Eventually, the case went to the Greek Supreme Court, which ruled that the local government had jurisdiction. The monks learned a valuable lesson: never pick a fight with 007.

When filming wrapped, Maurice Binder, as usual, shot the titles. For the first time, the artist singing the title song appeared in the sequence. "They just thought that I had a commercial appeal and also I think they wanted to do something a little different," said Sheena Easton. "They knew that it would be remarked upon. They knew it would be noticed. And I think it was just luck of the draw really that it all coincided with a time and art and music where you were getting film clips and videos." Indeed, the new title sequence was created just months before MTV was born.

For the first few years, the programming on MTV consisted almost entirely of music videos provided by record companies played in constant rotation. Most of the videos came from Britain, where the tradition of making music promo clips was well developed (the Beatles had filmed promos for several of their songs).

MTV proved its commercial importance when it began airing videos by the band Duran Duran. The band was receiving little radio airplay in the US in 1981, but in markets where MTV was available, their album sales soared. Four years later, Duran Duran would record a James Bond theme of their own, and make an accompanying video.

With their bold use of colour and stylized mix of dance, music and drama, many of the music videos that permeated MTV reflected the influence of the 007 title sequences. "Maurice Binder always felt that he invented the video clip," recalled Harry Saltzman's son, Steven. Philip Dodd, Director of the Institute of Contemporary Arts in London, agreed. "Every time we surf across our channels and hit yet another pop video station," said Dodd, "you can actually see the ghost of Maurice Binder kind of waving to us and smiling."

Champion skier Willy Bogner co-ordinated the ski action for *For Your Eyes Only* (**opposite**). Bogner had previously contributed to the ski sequences of *On Her Majesty's Secret Service* and *The Spy Who Loved Me*.

Sheena Easton (**top**, with title designer Maurice Binder) was always amused that viewers thought she was nude in the title sequence. In fact she was wearing a strapless evening gown.

Lynn-Holly Johnson (**bottom**) won the role of Bibi Dahl after being spotted in the film *Ice Castles*.

For Your Eyes Only premiered at London's Leicester Square Odeon on 24th June 1981. Prince Charles escorted his fiancée, Lady Diana, to the black tie event, drawing a huge crowd in front of the cinema. Thames Television broadcast the premiere live in Great Britain and millions of viewers saw Roger Moore hand Prince Charles a musical wristwatch that played 'The James Bond Theme'. During the following week, there was a rush in London shops to buy the timepiece.

Even the US poster proved to be a break from tradition, using a photograph rather than the action artwork that usually adorned the 007 one-sheets. The photo, showing Roger Moore seen between the bare legs of a model holding a crossbow, proved controversial. The press had a field day as three models claimed that the legs in the poster were theirs. In the end, it was determined that the arm with the crossbow belonged to one of the models, Jane Summer, and the legs were those of Joyce Bartle, who had prior experience as a leg model for Givenchy stockings and L'Eggs. When Bartle put on the required bathing suit, it came down too low, so photographer Morgan Kane asked her to put it on backwards. The amount of skin visible in the finished poster was too much for some markets where newspaper editors pencilled in shorts over them.

Two notable films competed with *For Your Eyes Only* in the US. The first was a Burt Reynolds comedy, *Cannonball Run*, which featured a character obsessed with James Bond who drives a gadget-laden Aston Martin DB5 in a cross-country race. The car used in the film, as it turned out, was the original car from *Goldfinger*. Even more remarkable, the actor playing the Bond-obsessed character was none other than Roger Moore.

The second film was the result of the 1977 conversation between George Lucas and Steven Spielberg in Hawaii. Even though it was a period piece, influenced by movie serials and the novels of H. Rider Haggard, *Raiders Of The Lost Ark* clearly owed much to the Bond adventures, with its use of a pre-credits sequence and breakneck action set pieces. "I consider *Raiders Of The Lost Ark* an imitator of our Bond series," Cubby Broccoli told the *Hollywood Reporter*. "I'm sure there wouldn't have been a *Raiders* if there hadn't been a James Bond. And I love the picture. Spielberg did a masterful job on it." Years later, Spielberg would acknowledge that the character of Indiana Jones was in some ways the cinematic offspring of 007 - he cast Sean Connery as Jones' father.

Aside from Bond and Indiana Jones, the second of the Christopher Reeve *Superman* films also hit US theatres in the summer of 1981. *Raiders* and *Superman* marked a clear change in thinking by filmmakers and studios. The phenomenon of the Bond films had inspired other film series, particularly imitators such as Matt Helm and Derek Flint. Studios generally viewed these movies as programmers, much like the Tarzan, Charlie Chan, Francis the Talking Mule or Sherlock Holmes films. In the 1970s, particularly with the success of *The Godfather Part II*, studios saw the potential for big-budget, high-profile sequels to blockbuster movies. With *Star Wars* and the *Superman* films, studios realized there was a way of trying to duplicate the success of James Bond, not by making spy film imitations, but by creating a sustainable series in another genre. The trade paper *Variety* gave the concept a name from the world of retail - these films became known as 'franchises'. Just as one McDonald's is interchangeable with another, a franchise film delivers a certain anticipated experience to an audience. With a successful franchise, a studio might deliver a new film every two or three years which has a large and ready-made audience, delivers huge profits, and subsequently increases the value of the preceding titles. This had been the model of success for the 007 films, and after nearly 20 years everyone else was finally catching on.

Reviewers mostly embraced *For Your Eyes Only* and applauded the change in tone. Sheila Benson, writing for *The Los Angeles Times*, stated, "Producer Albert R. Broccoli seems to know exactly how to stretch his formula like a cat's cradle in his hands". Peter Rainer of *The Los Angeles Herald-Examiner* noted the prescience of the filmmakers in having Bond battle a Soviet agent. "007, in his heyday, was a Cold-Warrior, and Cold-Warriorism is heating up once again in popular culture."

For Your Eyes Only proved successful in the US, but not quite on the scale of *Moonraker*, selling 22.4 million tickets. Overseas, though, the film was an undeniable smash. The movie grossed $61 million in 21 markets over the course of 14 weeks. Ultimately, the film pulled in $132.6 million internationally, a figure only slightly lower than *Moonraker's* $140 million. Michael Wilson's gamble had paid off. James Bond was back, and back down to earth.

In 1981, the James Bond films were clearly the most profitable series of movies ever produced. The power of the older Bond films to draw an audience had been proven via traditional theatrical re-releases, broadcast television premieres, and screenings on college campuses and in art house markets. In 1980, UA sold 'festivals' to pay cable systems such as HBO, which screened the first eleven films uncut for the first time on television. The response was strong, helping HBO reach more subscribers.

In 1981 the commercial videotape market was still young. The first commercially successful home video recorders had appeared in 1975. Competing systems - Betamax and VHS - crippled the video rental market. Most people who owned VCRs taped shows and movies off television, and studios priced their films between $60 and $120 per tape in the US. The majority of observers could see the potential in the home video business, but no one was certain which formats would prove to be the most commercially viable. RCA decided to introduce a new system into the market: the videodisc. To promote the new technology, RCA spent millions securing the videodisc rights to a wide array of films that were priced attractively compared to video tapes. Key among the titles RCA promoted were the James Bond films, which the company purchased in January 1981 for a reported $1.5 million. Although the films became big sellers, the RCA Selectavision videodisc system was a resounding flop with consumers. Nonetheless, the RCA deal made a statement that the Bond films were an important part of the 'software' for any type of home video system.

In 1982, 20th Century-Fox Home Video released *Goldfinger* on a new video format called the laserdisc, which became a favourite among film aficionados. The following year, it was reissued under the CBS/Fox logo, followed slowly by other Bond titles.

The Bond films began appearing on VHS videotape in the early 1980s, distributed by CBS/Fox in the US and Warner Home Video in much of the rest of the world. CBS/Fox had been an early participant in the home video revolution, licensing many titles from other studios reluctant to begin their own home video operations. However, once the viability of the videotape market had been proved, the studios began releasing their own product. In 1987, the CBS/Fox licence agreements began to expire, and the Bond films reverted back to MGM/UA, who released them on videotapes with a theatrical trailer and a *Pink Panther* cartoon attached.

As 1982 began, Cubby Broccoli had more on his mind than the home video market for James Bond, or the production of the next 007 film. After nearly four decades in the film business, he was about to receive one of the industry's highest honours - one which reminded him of his earliest days on the backlots of Hollywood.

During the height of the Depression, Broccoli had worked briefly as a jewellery salesman. One day, he took his samples to the office of MGM's production chief, Irving Thalberg, one of the most revered figures in the film industry during the 1930s. Tragically, Thalberg died of pneumonia in 1936, at the young age of 37.

The film industry honoured Thalberg by naming one of its most prestigious awards after him. The Academy of Motion Picture Arts and Sciences' Irving G. Thalberg Award is presented to a producer who has made an outstanding contribution to the film industry. In 1982, the award went to Cubby Broccoli. "Hollywood meant a great deal to him, and to receive the Thalberg Award, which was not given out every year, but on very special occasions, it just made him so happy," said Dana Broccoli. "He was delighted with it all, and he couldn't believe that he'd be receiving this wonderful award."

The Academy Awards ceremony of 29th March 1982 featured a spectacular 007 production number, with Sheena Easton singing the nominated song, 'For Your Eyes Only', while various Bond villains, including Dr. No, Blofeld, Oddjob and Jaws (the latter two played by Harold Sakata and Richard Kiel) threatened a dancer playing 007. The production number ended with Easton and 'Bond' blasting off in a rocket. The number served as the preface for the presentation of the Thalberg Award. Clips from the Bond films were shown, ending with the ski jump from the pre-credits of *The Spy Who Loved Me*. The audience cheered.

Roger Moore introduced Broccoli, who gave a gracious speech in which he remembered his former partners Irving Allen and Harry Saltzman. "It meant a lot to all of us," said Tony Broccoli, "because it meant so much to my father. It was a very touching night. It was great. I, along with a lot of people, thought my father deserved some recognition in the business. And even though a lot of people admired the Bond movies and they influenced a lot of producers and directors over the years, to have it all done in public and at a ceremony was, I think, very important and made everyone very, very happy."

For Bill Conti, who had composed the nominated song 'For Your Eyes Only' with Mick Leeson, the evening of the Academy Awards brought a different kind of excitement - he was also conducting the

show's orchestra. "It's unique when you're conducting the orchestra, and you're nominated," Conti remembered. "Now normally, people get a different kind of nervousness. They sit in the audience… and if they win, they're very happy for the rest of the night, and if they lose, they hate being there for the rest of the evening. But when you're conducting the orchestra, you don't have a chance to be nervous. You turn the page until you see your name as part of the nominees. The musicians in the orchestra and myself don't know who the winners will be, so we all have five different pieces of music in front of us.

"During the James Bond nomination, when it got to that time, I turn the page, and there are the nominated songs, and of course one of them was me. And I saw in the eyes of all the musicians, 'Oh, I hope you win'. So, they said, 'And the winner is…', and of course it *wasn't* me. The eyes looked down. 'Oh my goodness, you lost'. And the director's screaming, 'Music!' I said, 'I can't, nobody's looking at me.'"

As well as the celebration of Cubby Broccoli's achievements, the period after the release of *For Your Eyes Only* saw a groundswell of activity surrounding the James Bond fan community. The generation that had first been introduced to 007 on television broadcasts had come of age, and in 1981 they congregated at Bond-themed events around the globe. On 17-19th July 1981, Larry Charet promoted a James Bond Convention in Chicago as part of the Chicago Comicon. The following week, Steven Jay Rubin hosted a James Bond weekend in Century City, California, with George Lazenby and Herve Villechaize among those in attendance. In the UK, a convention of fans included guests such as Peter Hunt and Maurice Binder. The James Bond Fan Club's publication, *Bondage*, had progressed into a slick magazine offering rare behind-the-scenes peeks into the world of 007. In the autumn of 1980, 24-year-old Ross Hendry of Harrow, Middlesex, founded the James Bond British Fan Club. The club distributed two publications, the regular club magazine, *007*, and a newsletter, *For Your Eyes Only*.

The fan community was fed by screenings of the Bond films at art house cinemas, film societies and college campuses throughout the early 1980s. Along with the classics of the cinema, the Bond films always drew enthusiastic crowds. For this new generation of Bond fans these 'one night only' events were often the first chance to see the early films uncut in a cinema. Dealers of 16-millimetre films traded and sold prints of early Bond trailers to a hungry audience.

Top: Roger Moore clowns with John Wells and Janet Brown (impersonating Prime Minister Margaret Thatcher and her husband, Denis) on the 10 Downing Street set of *For Your Eyes Only*.

Above: The 29th March 1982 Thalberg Award was not the first Academy Award experience for the Bond films. On 5th April 1965, Norman Wanstall had accepted the statuette for Best Sound for *Goldfinger*. Visiting America for the first time with his family, Wanstall received the award from Angie Dickinson and said, "This trip will be the most wonderful one of our lives." The following year, the Academy awarded John Stears an Oscar for the special effects of *Thunderball*. On 10th April 1968, Sergio Mendez and Brazil '66 performed the Best Song nominee 'The Look of Love', from *Casino Royale*. *Diamonds Are Forever* was a Best Sound nominee at the Academy Awards telecast of 10th April 1972. Two years later, Connie Stevens performed the nominated title theme of *Live And Let Die*. On 29th March 1978, *The Spy Who Loved Me* had two nominations, one for Best Art Direction, and another for Best Song for 'Nobody Does It Better', which was performed by Aretha Franklin. *Moonraker* was nominated for Best Visual Effects at the 1980 awards show.

In his attempt to produce a rival 007 film, Kevin McClory was facing legal battles pitting him against United Artists, Danjaq (and its production arm, Eon Productions), the literary copyright holders to the Bond novels, Glidrose Publications (now Ian Fleming (Glidrose) Publications), and Ian Fleming's estate. One of the key areas of dispute between Kevin McClory and these parties was the scope of the rights he had obtained in his 1963 settlement with Ian Fleming and Ivar Bryce. McClory maintained that he could expand and change the basic Bond story he had developed in 1959 and 1960 in any number of directions. Others strongly objected to McClory's assertions, feeling his rights were limited to a faithful remake of *Thunderball* and nothing more.

After numerous legal battles in London and Los Angeles courts that extended from 1977 to 1980, McClory found no studio wanted to back his proposed new Bond film. Entertainment lawyer Jack Schwartzman was an executive at Lorimar when that company turned down a chance to become involved in McClory's 007 project. After looking over the legal briefs, Schwartzman felt there was a solution to the problems McClory faced with getting his film made. A year after leaving Lorimar to start his own production company, Taliafilm, Schwartzman and McClory met, and after protracted negotiations, the pair agreed upon a deal in late 1981.

Schwartzman's solution was two-fold. First, he would serve as the film's producer. Second, he would develop a new screenplay that would be a clear remake of *Thunderball*. Schwartzman hired veteran scriptwriter Lorenzo Semple, Jr., who had gained fame as the primary writer of the *Batman* TV series in the 1960s and later wrote scripts for films such as *The Parallax View* and *Three Days Of The Condor*. Schwartzman then contracted with three banks and 26 different distributors around the world, including Warner Brothers, for $30 million in financing. He later told a reporter that he deliberately scattered the money sources, afraid that it would be easier for the legal challenges to cut off the financing if there were just one source. One of Schwartzman's former legal clients, Irvin Kershner, signed to direct. Kershner had previously directed Sean Connery in the 1966 film *A Fine Madness*.

Contacting Sean Connery, Schwartzman found the actor interested in returning to the role of 007... if the price were right. At that point in his career, Connery's film roles netted him about half a million dollars per picture. Roger Moore, meanwhile, was making millions for each of his 007 film appearances. By the time cameras rolled on Schwartzman's Bond film, called *Never Say Never Again* (a title suggested by Connery's wife, Micheline), Connery had negotiated a $5 million payday, as well as a percentage of the profits. The film was set for release in the summer of 1983, head to head with the latest Bond film from Eon.

In April 1981, even before the release of *For Your Eyes Only*, *Variety* reported that United Artists was putting pressure on Cubby Broccoli to keep the costs of the next James Bond film down, as a direct result of the cost overruns on *Heaven's Gate*, which had been one of the most expensive bombs in cinema history. However, UA's global production head Steven Bach said that UA didn't worry that Broccoli's Bond film would have the same kind of dismal box-office as *Heaven's Gate*, because "there's been (a Bond) audience out there for 20 years".

After the release of *For Your Eyes Only*, the cash-hungry studio made its disappointment in the US box office known. Despite the international grosses, they felt Bond could do better, and would have to in order to justify the budget. While *For Your Eyes Only* was the tenth

highest grossing film of the year in the US, it lagged behind many other sequels such as *Superman II, Any Which Way You Can*, and the Gene Wilder and Richard Prior comedy *Stir Crazy*. More galling to the studio was the performance of *Cannonball Run,* with its Bond parody character. Even though no one topped Bond's stunts, the studio felt 007 needed to continue adapting to what audiences wanted to see, and in the summer of 1981 everyone wanted to see *Raiders Of The Lost Ark*.

There was also concern over the title of the new film - *Octopussy. The Los Angeles Times* published an article in which they called the name "obscene". Cubby Broccoli responded, "They're trying to stir up controversy where none exists."

Indeed, Bond's appeal seemed to be so universal that it rendered the otherwise objectionable into something quite palatable. A poll conducted by the National Research Group asked 600 women between the ages of 12 and 49 if they would go to see a film titled *Octopussy*. 37% said no. However, when asked if they would go to see a James Bond film with that title, only 4% said no.

Broccoli hired novelist George MacDonald Fraser, author of the successful *Flashman* novels, to capture a blend of Bond and nostalgic adventure. Later, Richard Maibaum and Michael G. Wilson completed the shooting draft. The finished piece was an intriguing cocktail of the fantastic and the romantic, liberally spiced with classic Bondian elements. The movie kept the Cold War theme, basing its plot on a rogue Soviet general who wanted to stage a nuclear explosion on a West German military base, thus forcing NATO to pull its nuclear weapons out of Europe, allowing for Soviet military expansion. The plotline read like a paranoid commentary from William F. Buckley Jr., but the filmmakers took care to show that the Soviet high command had no interest in dominating Western Europe.

The plot was conceived during a time of tremendous tensions over the nuclear arms situation in Europe, particularly the complex negotiations between the Soviet Union and NATO regarding modernized deployment of Intermediate Nuclear Forces (INF). In 1979, NATO decided to upgrade its nuclear arsenal to Pershing II and Tomahawk Cruise missiles. This brought on waves of protests from anti-nuclear activists.

For many NATO leaders, nuclear weapons provided the only guarantee against Soviet expansion, since the Soviets far outnumbered conventional NATO forces. The point was driven home when US President Ronald Reagan offered to eliminate all US INF weapons from Europe if the Soviets would do the same. European leaders howled at the notion, painting a scenario much like the one outlined by Soviet General Orlov in *Octopussy*.

This primary plot of nuclear sabotage remains in the background for most of the film while James Bond tries to solve the mystery of the death of agent 009 and links between the smuggling operation in Octopussy's Circus and forged Czarist art. The investigation takes Bond to Berlin, where the Cold War still rages, and India, where the film veers into a Rudyard Kipling-esque Never-Neverland. Bond's adventures in India contain few clues of the film's modern-day setting, and include 007 as the quarry in an elephant hunt inspired by the Richard Connell story, *The Most Dangerous Game*.

When Cubby Broccoli chose not to cast Faye Dunaway in the title role of *Octopussy*, the role went to Maud Adams, who had played Andrea Anders, Scaramanga's mistress, in a previous 007 film, *The Man With The Golden Gun*. "I loved the idea of playing in another James Bond movie," said Adams, "and to play the title character, of course, was very, very flattering and fun."

The *Octopussy* crew took over two of the most luxurious hotels in Udaipur - the Lake Palace and the then yet-to-be opened Shiv Niwas Palace (**top left**). The Lake Palace Hotel is commonly referred to as 'the Octopussy Hotel', and, according to a March 2001 article in *The Guardian*, the film is still shown nightly in town.

"One of the great joys of being in *Octopussy* was that a Bond film was coming to India, which is the country where I came from," said Kabir Bedi (**top row, middle** and **middle row, centre**). "It was like going home with the big boys and saying, 'Look what I've come to'. That was a good feeling. And, of course, when the Bond film moves to India, it works with Indian technicians, Indian crews, etc. to supplement the usual (location crew pictured at **bottom right**). Now, the interesting thing here is that India has the largest film industry in the world, so they are technically very proficient. But it is a very disorganized industry. And here you have the organization of the Bond machine coming into India to make a film - on time, on budget. This was certainly a great learning experience for many in India."

Kristina Wayborn (**middle row, left**) recalled an experience which she and Maud Adams had while filming *Octopussy*. "One day in India we decided to go shopping, outside of the compound where we were staying," said Wayborn, "and we found it interesting, because people wanted to touch us. We found out later it was for good luck."

Roger Moore's smile (**middle row, right**) reflects the satisfaction he would later find in his work with UNICEF. The film's use of romantic imagery during the scenes set in India brought a flavour of Rudyard Kipling to the world of James Bond, whether through bizarre weapons (as held by Louis Jordan and Kabir Bedi in the **centre row**), decorated elephants or Octopussy's grand barge (**below**).

Fraser, Maibaum and Wilson also managed to work in elements of three Ian Fleming short stories - 'Octopussy', 'Property Of A Lady', and 'The Living Daylights' - though very little of the Fleming source material remains. More influential was the work of Alfred Hitchcock, particularly the director's pre-war adventures such as *The Lady Vanishes*, which, like *Octopussy*, includes a scene with a magician's disappearing cabinet set aboard a train (as later did the 1989 film, *Indiana Jones And The Last Crusade*).

The Hitchcock influence on 007 had been growing for some time, and *Octopussy* is by far the most Hitchcockian Bond adventure in terms of suspense. One key difference between Hitchcock's heroes and Bond was that Hitchcock made movies about ordinary men in extraordinary circumstances. Bond on the other hand was an extraordinary man. Continuing with the themes begun in *For Your Eyes Only*, the filmmakers brought 007 further back down to earth and placed him in a very realistic world for the Germany-based climax of the movie. As Bond races to disarm a primed nuclear bomb, he is foiled by a woman who will not relinquish a pay-phone and jeered by a carload of youths who pretend to stop to help him but then drive off laughing. As Bond arrives at the US Air Force base where the bomb is set to explode, he can't convince the soldiers or the police of his intentions. To them, 007 is the enemy. To Bond and the audience, the complacent inefficiency of the modern world becomes as insidious as any Bond villain.

After the technological austerity of *For Your Eyes Only*, the filmmakers decided to re-arm Bond with gadgets, but with a twist. Technology never solves Bond's problems, nor do Q's devices work all the time. One transmitter is foiled by the interference of a simple blow-dryer. The gadget which does save 007's skin is the amazing AcroStar mini jet, a small one-man aircraft flown by its creator, John W. 'Corkey' Fornof. Co-owner of the Francis Petroleum Company of Knoxville, Tennessee, Fornof built the jet just for fun. The AcroStar weighed only 450 pounds, with a wingspan of 17 feet and an overall length of just 12 feet. Powered by a single jet micro-turbine TRS engine, the plane offered a top speed of 310 mph, and a rate of climb of 2,800 feet per minute.

Now that the producers had a script with the proper array of elements, there was only one key ingredient missing - an actor to play James Bond.

In the summer of 1982 the media became very interested in the casting of *Octopussy*. With Sean Connery returning as a rival 007, one could almost hear members of the press typing obituaries for the Cubby Broccoli-produced Bond films. The first sign of trouble was that as the start date of *Octopussy* neared, Roger Moore had still not signed on to star in the film. Was Moore scared of the competition? Was he too old? How could anyone compete against Sean Connery's return as Bond?

Broccoli and company hired Louis Jourdan to play the main villain, who was now not going to be Octopussy, but Kamal Khan, an Afghan Prince. Faye Dunaway wanted the title role, which some

observers felt might help compensate for a new Bond. Broccoli had previously thought of casting Dunaway in *Thunderball*. "I wanted her then," he said, "but we weren't able to work it out." Dunaway told Roderick Mann of *The Los Angeles Times*, "I'd love to do this film. I've always admired the expertise of the Bonds."

In May 1982, with Roger Moore's involvement still in question, billboards touting *Octopussy* at the Cannes Film Festival showed what appeared to be Moore as Bond - except the face was blanked out, with a question mark over it. During the first week of June, with negotiations with Moore at an impasse, Oliver Tobias and Michael Billington tested for the role of 007. In late June, an American actor tested for the role: James Brolin. For a short period of time it looked as if Brolin would become the next Bond. The producers and the studio, however, were not anxious to launch a new face as Bond against Sean Connery. At the eleventh hour, Cubby Broccoli struck a new deal with Roger Moore. Moore told *Entertainment Today*, "The poker game is over. We both got tired of dealing so we decided to cut for it. I think we are both happy with the outcome."

With Moore returning as 007, Broccoli decided he had all the star power he needed, and he wanted to put the remaining budget up on the screen. Thus, Broccoli passed over Faye Dunaway (who had asked for a multi-million dollar contract) and cast Maud Adams as Octopussy, a remarkable turn of events considering the actress's prominent role in *The Man With The Golden Gun*. Broccoli knew, though, that Adams had the right kind of self-confident poise and smouldering beauty to hold the screen with Roger Moore. The filmmakers were more interested in international star power, and as such they cast tennis star Vijay Armitraj, an athlete so highly regarded in his native India that a newspaper poll among young readers showed him to be the most popular man in the country.

Never Say Never Again also boasted a cast loaded with international names. Klaus Maria Brandauer, Max von Sydow, Barbara Carrera and Edward Fox led the star-studded ensemble. Newcomer Kim Basinger, who received tremendous press, played the lead female. From all the initial reports, the film would be a high-class affair. The battle of the Bonds looked to some as if it would be no battle at all.

Octopussy began production on 10th August 1982 at Checkpoint Charlie, West Berlin. The filming started amidst an upswing of British pride. Less than two months earlier British forces defeated Argentine troops on the distant Falkland Islands and Prince Charles and Princess Diana welcomed their first child, a healthy boy named Prince William. The summer of 1982 also witnessed increases in East-West tensions as Ronald Reagan's increasingly harsh stance against the Soviets led to the resignation of his Secretary of State Alexander Haig.

The simultaneous filming of *Never Say Never Again* was troubled. Writers continued working on the script during production. Jack Schwartzman complained that the director, Irvin Kershner, "was not the fastest guy in the world". Despite a crew of seasoned professionals, the production seemed disorganized and was plagued by on-set hassles. When filming wrapped in France and moved on to the Bahamas, a week of monsoon-like rain knocked the production severely off-schedule. The foul weather only added to the brooding atmosphere. Sean Connery, knowing that the success or failure of the film would reflect directly on him, took charge. Biographer Michael Feeney Callan reported later that Connery claimed he and the assistant director were the ones who actually produced the film.

Stuntman Martin Grace doubled Roger Moore for part of the train sequence (**opposite**) until, while hanging from the side of the train, he accidentally hit a stanchion and broke his hip. Stuntman Paul Weston finished the sequence. Grace returned as stunt co-ordinator on the following film, *A View To A Kill*.

As General Orlov, Steven Berkoff (**above**) based his portrayal on a character from a Stanley Kubrick film. "I always steal from others," he said, "and that was George C. Scott in *Dr. Strangelove*."

Overleaf: AcroStar jet inventor Corkey Fornof's flight though the hangar in *Octopussy* proved to be an audience favourite. The end of the sequence re-created an event from the real life of the pilot. Once, he lost engine power and had to land on Interstate 85 in North Carolina. "I just coasted the plane down the highway and down an off-ramp to a gas station," said Fornof. "The service station owner leaned over and said 'Am I on *Candid Camera*?' "

"Needless to say, my heart was in my throat.
We had done all the mathematical calculations.

As big as a space looks on the ground, it's a lot smaller when you're moving at 150 knots." Pilot J.W. 'Corkey' Fornof

Jack Schwartzman's wife, actress Talia Shire, told a reporter that *Never Say Never Again* was "a hard production to get through". While it was being shot, Shire went through a difficult pregnancy, and worked on *Rocky III* to make money to keep the Bond film going. Shire was deeply disappointed when Connery grew unhappy with the delays and production problems. "I just didn't know people's buttons can be played with so much," she told reporter Alex Ben Block. "I didn't know there was so much manipulation and game-playing."

In March 1983, after *Never Say Never Again* wrapped, the trustees of the Ian Fleming estate sought an injunction to block the film's distribution, claiming that the finished movie went beyond the bounds of a remake of *Thunderball*. After a hearing that lasted two and a half weeks, the judge ruled that the requests for the injunctions were unduly delayed, saying it would be unfair to hinder a production that was so far advanced. With that hurdle out of the way, the filmmakers needed to resolve much larger problems - the film was not working and needed re-shoots.

Whatever the reasons for the disarray on the set, Jack Schwartzman stood at a disadvantage to Cubby Broccoli when it came to the world of Bond.

The current Broccoli-produced Bond films operated like massive armies, shooting with upwards of five units simultaneously. Broccoli's team knew how to coordinate such complex operations and still achieve a coherent style. Regardless of how formulaic the 007 stories appeared, the films were still tremendously difficult to imitate. It seemed easy, but few musicians, for example, could write a song which would prove to have the quality of a Beatles hit no matter how many times he or she listened to Beatles records. Broccoli also

had use of trademarked aspects of the Bond films on his side - the opening gun barrel sequence and the signature 'James Bond Theme'. These tangible aspects of the Bond films imparted a sense of quality that had been built up in audiences for 21 years. A Bond film without 'The James Bond Theme' had to be able to compensate in other areas.

Broccoli and UA also had years of marketing experience with the Bond films. They could use the past 007 adventures as part of their campaign, and they did. One advance poster for *Octopussy* touted "Nobody Does It Better... thirteen times!" An advance trailer began with titles from previous Bond films moving across the screen. The producers worked with Smith Foods in the UK to create a promotional tie-in, which marketed James Bond contest coupons on over 200 million bags of potato crisps. A deal with Nabisco secured *Octopussy* a place on the front of millions of boxes of Shredded Wheat across Britain. The filmmakers also joined forces with London Weekend Television to produce what would become the most controversial James Bond television special ever made.

The premise of *21 Years Of James Bond* was to have a variety of famous people discuss James Bond as if he were a real person. The opening segment, filmed the previous April at the White House, proved to be a political embarrassment for the Reagan administration. The show opened with the President saying, "I've been asked to state my feelings about a fellow named Bond - James Bond. Well, as I see it, 007 is really a 10." Reagan called Bond, "our modern-day version of the great heroes who appeared from time to time throughout history" and who "put their lives on the line for the cause of good". It was the kind of publicity that couldn't be bought.

In June 1983, as the opening date for *Octopussy* neared, the Metromedia station WTTG-TV in Washington, DC prepared their own promotional spots for the special that began with a voice saying, "A special announcement from the President of the United States," over a shot of the Presidential seal. Then Reagan appeared in a clip from his testimonial, which ended with him remarking, "Of course, some critics might say that Bond is nothing more than an actor in the movies. But then, we've all got to start somewhere." The day after the White House learned of the promos they were pulled from the airwaves.

Sandy Pastoor, programme director at WTTG, defended the promotional announcements, saying he didn't know why Reagan did it, but "obviously, in this town, the President is of some interest, as is James Bond. And if we can marry the two of them to make the programme more attractive to viewers, we'll do that." White House spokesman Mark Weinberg said Reagan never intended his appearance to be part of the orchestrated hype for a Bond movie, particularly one with a title like *Octopussy*, but the defence sounded more like a back-tracking excuse to religious conservatives who did not view Bond as an appropriate subject for presidential endorsement. Liberals critiqued the President's appearance as using his office for the commercial benefit of a for-profit movie. In a few days the controversy passed, and the special, including Reagan's clip, played across the country.

"It's the first time I've been panned for a picture I wasn't in." Roger Moore, after being unfavourably compared to Connery in *Never Say Never Again*

Ronald Reagan helped the film in other ways, too. The Cold War element of the movie could have easily seemed passé had the Soviets and NATO resolved their disputes over European nuclear weapons after Leonid Brezhnev's death in November 1982. They did not, and shortly before *Octopussy*'s release, Reagan raised the level of tension a number of notches. In March 1983, the President made his famous assertion that the Soviet Union was an "evil empire", and denounced the idea of a weapons freeze as "the illusion of peace". As spring wore on, anti-nuclear protests grew in England and West Germany.

On 6th June 1983, while Sean Connery continued to play James Bond in re-shoots in the Bahamas, Cubby Broccoli premiered *Octopussy* at the Leicester Square Odeon, London, with Prince Charles and Princess Diana in attendance.

By all reasoning, the film should have been a disaster. The odd mix of high-tech gadgets, neo-Victorian Indian adventure and Cold War suspense hardly seemed an obvious recipe for success. On top of that, for the film's climax, James Bond dons clown make-up and infiltrates a circus performance. At another point, Bond hides in a gorilla outfit. In certain aspects, the movie challenged and ignored the recipe for Bond's success more than any previous Bond adventure. Regardless, the film did work, especially in America where ticket sales jumped well over the 20 million mark. In international territories, *Octopussy* did not perform as well as the previous three Bonds, but still grossed $120 million overseas.

Exactly four months after *Octopussy* opened, *Never Say Never Again* premiered in Los Angeles, California. Battle scars were evident among the participants. When Connery appeared on *The Tonight Show* with Johnny Carson, Carson asked him who was the best Bond villain. Connery replied, "Cubby Broccoli". Jack Schwartzman was lucky Connery did not name him. There was still friction between the star and the film's producer, and Schwartzman declined to attend some of the European premieres because he knew Connery would be there. Two months after the film's release, Connery was openly critical, telling *Los Angeles Times* reporter Roderick Mann, "Making it seemed as long as all the other six I did put together."

The film also stirred up controversy in the UK, where the Royal Society for the Prevention of Cruelty to Animals urged people to boycott it. The organization objected to a scene in which Bond, on horseback, leaps over a wall and plunges 40 feet into the sea below. The Society claimed the shot subjected the horse to "terror amounting to unnecessary suffering". Warner Bros. cut a half second out of the film, so British audiences would not actually see the horse hitting the water.

By January 1984, *Octopussy* had grossed over $67 million in the US and Canada, compared to roughly $54 million for *Never Say Never Again*. Globally, *Octopussy* outpaced *Never Say Never Again* in virtually every territory. Few observers predicted the extent to which the Broccoli/Roger Moore Bond film would prevail in the box office competition. Connery, though, faced a huge challenge in returning to the role. His Bond film needed to live up to the idealized memory of fans of the early 007 films. Connery had to recapture the very essence of Bond, but the actor himself was only one ingredient of the the success of the early films. He could not design the sets, compose the score or edit the film with the jet-paced sense of movement and action. Moore had the advantage of the experienced crews who had worked on numerous Bond films before. He, too, was one ingredient, but audiences had already embraced the rest of the Bond *mise en scène* that surrounded him.

Never Say Never Again had its highlights, including a campy performance by Barbara Carrera, an exciting hijacking of a cruise missile, and a bizarre video game competition where the participants feel a shock if their opponent scores. The film, though, featured none

of the scope, tension or glamour of *Thunderball*. The gadgets seemed perfunctory and the production design uninspired. Most damning, Connery's 007 seemed slightly uncomfortable, rarely able to capture the schoolboy roguishness which permeated his early Bonds.

The much-touted Battle of the Bonds ended where it began - in court. Even though Schwartzman had won the right to have his film exhibited, his legal troubles were not over. In October 1985, Sean Connery sued Jack Schwartzman for allegedly not paying him all he was owed for his work on *Never Say Never Again*. Taliafilm, in turn, sued director Irvin Kershner in January 1986 for going over budget on the film. The complaint was settled out of court in October 1986.

Octopussy and *Never Say Never Again* both dealt with the threat of nuclear weapons at a time when tensions over the deployment of nuclear-armed Tomahawk Cruise missiles was at its height, and both played into the paranoia of a nuclear weapon falling into the wrong hands. This had been a running theme in the

Bond novels and films ever since Hugo Drax obtained a nuclear warhead in order to destroy London in Ian Fleming's original novel MOONRAKER. With *Octopussy*, the filmmakers created a tale that illustrated the risks of maintaining any nuclear weapons as well as the risks of failing to keep a nuclear deterrent. People on both sides of the political spectrum could watch the movie and feel their views on the subject had been supported. How many of those who camped outside NATO bases in the spring, summer and autumn of 1983 to protest the upgrade in nuclear weapons did so in part because their beliefs had been shaped by works of fiction dealing with nuclear paranoia, including the Bond films? How many of those who worked on the bases as intelligence officers or cryptographers opted for these jobs because of the glamour they associated with fictional spies, including 007?

By the end of 1987, the subject of nuclear deterrence along the West German border was moot. Mikhail Gorbachev and Ronald Reagan signed a treaty that eliminated short-range nuclear weapons from Europe. Despite the superiority of the Soviet forces, the USSR did not over-run Western Europe. In fact, within three years, the Soviet Union itself collapsed.

"We're always looking for interesting women in our films, and Grace is an incredible character." John Glen

After surpassing the rival 007 film at the box office, the Bond producers set out to produce their 14th 007 adventure, *A View To A Kill*. Where *Octopussy* had been infused with a sense of nostalgia, the new film looked to the future, beginning with a timely script that centred on the burgeoning personal computing revolution which would ultimately change the way the world lived, worked and communicated.

The first shot of this revolution was fired in January 1975, when the magazine *Popular Electronics* featured the world's first personal computer, the Altair 8800, on its cover. Young engineers and computer enthusiasts worked on more functional personal computers of their own, including Steve Wozniak and Steve Jobs, who formed Apple Computer in 1976. IBM introduced their PC in August 1981. The company predicted sales of half a million units by 1984. In fact, they sold over two million.

Wozniak and Jobs, not content to let the corporate behemoth monopolize the computer market, began working on a rival personal computer that would be easier for the average person to use. The result was the Apple Macintosh, which was unveiled on 24th January 1984. By 1987, the company was selling Macintosh computers at the rate of one million per year.

The computer revolution would never have been possible without the creation of one of the most important inventions of the 20th century: the silicon microchip. Geoffrey Dummer, a scientist in the British Ministry of Defence, and his small team of researchers came up with the idea of putting an entire circuit on a block of silicon half an inch square in 1952. However, the idea was dropped when a prototype failed.

Six years later, Jack Kilby, a Texas Instruments engineer, demonstrated the first working silicon microchip. In January 1959, Robert Noyce, one of the founders of Fairchild Semiconductor, made his first detailed notes about a solid-state semiconductor. Six months later, Noyce's fellow engineer Jean Hoerni produced an integrated circuit using silicon as an insulating material. Although Kilby was the first to have built a working circuit, it was Noyce's method that ultimately became the standard for the new device.

In 1968, Noyce and two fellow engineers left Fairchild and formed a small start-up company that, three years later, produced the world's first microprocessor, a chip containing all the logic circuits necessary for processing data. The company was called Intel; their microprocessor contained 2,300 transistors and performed about 60,000 calculations in a second. Silicon chips

seemed like miniature miracles. They were cheap to produce, faster than the human brain, and used very little power. Their only weakness seemed remote. In the event of a nuclear blast, the electronic pulse radiating from the nuclear chain reaction would render the chips useless.

With *A View To A Kill*, Michael Wilson received a promotion. "When we got to this film, Cubby said, 'Why don't you just be the co-producer with me?'" said Wilson, who had proved his worth as part of the legal team that advised Cubby Broccoli during the split from Harry Saltzman. He made significant contributions to the next four 007 films as an assistant to Broccoli on *The Spy Who Loved Me*, an executive producer on *Moonraker, For Your Eyes Only* and *Octopussy*, and co-writer of the scripts of *For Your Eyes Only* and *Octopussy*.

The new Bond film presented a familiar challenge to the filmmakers - where to take Bond next? In what direction should they focus the film? These questions of direction and focus had always been key to 007's success. How much to change the series had to be balanced with the need to provide the audience with what they expected. For *A View To A Kill*, with world events turning ever more tragic, bizarre and chaotic, the filmmakers decided to turn away from current events and focus on humour.

In October 1983, just after the release of *Never Say Never Again*, a truck bomb destroyed the US Marine headquarters in Lebanon, killing 216 people. Two minutes later, another terrorist bomb killed 58 at a compound housing French peacekeepers. At the end of the month, the US invaded the small Caribbean island of Grenada in order to oust 'Cuban thugs'. Terrorist battles in the Middle East cost thousands of lives over the next few years, as did CIA-backed revolutions and counter-revolutions in Central America and Afghanistan. In April 1984, Libyan Embassy officials opened fire on protesters in London as global politics seemed to career out of control. With yet another change of power in the Soviet Union, and more changes looming, it appeared to be an appropriate time for James Bond to retreat from the Cold War and return to the type of breezy adventures which marked the late 1970s.

The story for *A View To A Kill* was a total invention of the filmmakers, who developed it as a group. The original Fleming material - a short story entitled 'From A View To A Kill' - involved the assassination of a courier by Soviet spies. It ends with a nice twist, but aside from the Paris location, none of the story was used in the finished script. Rather, the filmmakers pulled together a plot that involved a rogue KGB agent who also happened to be a genetically engineered genius. Now fabulously wealthy, Max Zorin planned to corner the market on silicon chips by destroying Silicon Valley with a massive earthquake triggered by an explosion in a mine he owned. All of those plot elements, however, were secondary. For *A View To A Kill*, what really counted was spectacle.

During the production of *Moonraker*, stuntman B.J. Worth commented to Michael Wilson that he would like to parachute from the Eiffel Tower. Now, with Paris as a potential location, and the successful April 1984 pirate jump by two daredevils, Wilson and Richard Maibaum developed the idea. Stunt driver Rémy Julienne invented a sequence where he jumped a car onto the top of a moving bus. The Bond filmmakers were impressed with what they saw and contracted with Julienne to create a spectacular chase along the banks of the River Seine.

For San Francisco, the filmmakers devised a grand firetruck chase at night and a battle on top of the Golden Gate Bridge. In addition to those set pieces, they decided that Zorin's lair should be housed inside his own corporate blimp, inspired not only by the famed Goodyear blimp, but also the more recent Fuji Film blimp. The Fuji Corporation even allowed the filmmakers to use their colour scheme on the Zorin blimp so that long shots of the real Fuji blimp over San Francisco could be utilized in the movie.

The finished screenplay was gargantuan in scope. The obvious question was whether it could all be captured on film.

Over the course of two decades, the 007 adventures had filmed in some of the most exciting and exotic locations in the world, including Jamaica, the Bahamas, Japan, the Swiss Alps, Thailand, Italy, Brazil, Greece and India. *A View To A Kill* rejected the exotic in favour of the familiar and used some of the world's most famous landmarks (the Eiffel Tower in Paris, and San Francisco's City Hall and Golden Gate Bridge) for major stunt sequences. These key locations provided special challenges for the filmmakers, but the ability to secure them was a testament to the respect garnered by the Bond filmmaking team over many years.

Although originally denied permission to shoot the complex scenes in central Paris, the filmmakers eventually prevailed on both the conservative mayor of the city and the far more left-wing president of France. The granting of the film permits marked one of the few areas of agreement between the two during the mid-1980s. In San Francisco, the filmmakers found a receptive welcome from the city's mayor, Diane Feinstein, and were given *carte blanche* to work within the city. In both locations, John Glen and his team took full advantage of the opportunities.

The sequence at San Francisco's City Hall would have caused controversy for anyone except James Bond. Faking the burning of the landmark building drew the most press attention, but the gas fires essentially posed no danger to the structure. Mayor Feinstein declared that half the people in the city wanted to burn down City Hall anyway, so why not let James Bond do it for real? Another City Hall scene proved more controversial. Prior to the fire, James Bond witnesses the death of a San Francisco city official in his City Hall office. The on-screen shooting eerily echoed actual events that had occurred in the real San Francisco City Hall six years earlier.

In November 1978, Dan White resigned his seat on the San Francisco Board of Supervisors. The Board had eleven members, including Mayor George Moscone, the city's first female Board President, Diane Feinstein, and the nation's first openly gay official elected to a substantial office, Harvey Milk.

On the morning of Monday, 27th November, an enraged White entered City Hall through a basement window to avoid metal detectors. He wanted his position with the Board of Supervisors back and believed Mayor Moscone was not going to allow him to retract

Left: The City of San Francisco gave the 007 production team unprecedented cooperation - including allowing them to stage a fire at City Hall. Months later, the filmmakers returned to thank the city, staging a major press event outside City Hall and holding the world premiere of *A View To A Kill* at the Palace of Fine Arts.

Above: The Zorin blimp mirrored a rise in the use of corporate blimps in the 1980s and 90s. The US military ceased operating blimps in the 1960s, which left Goodyear to dominate the skies until 1981, when Fuji launched its own promotional blimp. So far, only the Zorin blimp has marketed global domination.

"I'm very grateful that I was able to do seven Bonds. Took up fourteen, fifteen years of my life. I had a lot of good times doing it, made a lot of friends." Roger Moore

his resignation. Carrying a loaded gun, White went to Moscone's office and shot the mayor to death. He then walked to the Supervisors' offices at the other end of the building and reloaded his gun. He asked Milk for a few minutes in private, led him into his former office, and killed him. White then turned himself in. With Moscone and Milk assassinated, the President of the Board of Supervisors, Diane Feinstein, became the mayor.

Pleading temporary insanity caused by a sugar rush from eating junk food, White was convicted of voluntary manslaughter instead of murder. The verdict led to the largest incident of gay rioting in San Francisco's history. Called the 'White Night' riots, they were answered by the San Francisco Police Department with an attack on the primarily gay Castro district. Mayor Feinstein's steadiness and command helped calm the city. The following year, Feinstein was elected to the first of two four-year terms.

Even in 1984, when *A View To A Kill* was shooting in San Francisco, the murders of Moscone and Milk were sensitive subjects. After 23 years of success, James Bond, though, was far from controversial. In fact, his integration into popular culture literally allowed him to get away with a cinematic murder that would have at least raised eyebrows for virtually any other film hero. Bond's tenure in San Francisco, in fact, proved to be a celebratory event with large crowds gathering

to watch the film crews at work at some of the city's most beloved landmarks.

On 22nd May 1985, *A View To A Kill* became the first of the Cubby Broccoli-produced James Bond films to have its world premiere held in the US. In return for the cooperation granted to the production by Mayor Feinstein, the producers asked the city of San Francisco to host the event. Stuntman B.J. Worth leapt from a helicopter at a mid-day ceremony in front of City Hall where 500 fans and dozens of reporters gathered. That night the lavish premiere took place at the city's Palace of Fine Arts, complete with 007 ice sculptures and a gourmet buffet set for 1000 guests. Roger Moore, Christopher Walken, Tanya Roberts and Grace Jones attended, but the biggest screams were from the teenage fans of Duran Duran. Crowds packed the sidewalks outside private post-premiere parties, cheering the stars as they entered. It was a grand celebration that seemed fitting for a city that had healed wounds and enjoyed surprising economic growth in just the past year. Mayor Feinstein declared it 'James Bond Day'; it would have been Harvey Milk's 55th birthday.

While Roger Moore's relaxed style gave 007's world a licence for broader humour and greater flights of fantasy, Bond provided Moore with a vast canvas to showcase his urbane charm. Moore was perfectly paired with former Avenger Patrick Macnee, (**below** with Moore and Desmond Llewelyn). The pair had appeared together as Sherlock Holmes and Watson in a 1976 television movie, *Sherlock Holmes 'n New York*.

9. While the fictional character of James Bond had generated a tremendous amount of income over the years, he had never actually saved any real lives or averted any real disasters until the 1980s. By 1985, the future of United Artists rested in the hands of 007, or at least the moviegoers whose patronage would define Bond's box office appeal that year. In the early part of the decade, the studio had reached a financial crisis, and United Artists' parent company sold UA to MGM. However, MGM itself was not in good financial shape. The combined filmmaking operation which was created by the deal needed cash, which precipitated the sale to CBS/Fox of their valuable video distribution licence for studio films, and the quick exploitation of some of the studio's most profitable franchises. New *Rocky* films appeared as fast as the studio could make them. UA released new *Pink Panther* films. The Bond films, with their built-in potential, were

Flirting With Danger

key to the survival of United Artists as a viable studio. Because the solvency of MGM/UA relied on such a small number of film releases, each and every movie was of vital importance to the studio, and none were more important than each succeeding Bond film. The studio wanted - in fact was in desperate need of - another *Goldfinger* or *Thunderball*. In such a climate, *A View To A Kill* could not live up to those expectations.

When Ronald Reagan became President of the US, he approved over 50 major covert intelligence operations in seven years - more than any President since John F. Kennedy. As commentator Bill Moyers has written, while Reagan and his CIA director, William Casey, set the agenda, Oliver North (**top**) was their 007. North lost a 1994 bid to become a US Senator, settling into a career as a host of radio and television programmes.

In 1987, *The Los Angeles Times* reported that Mikhail Gorbachev (**middle**) was a former KGB agent, supposedly trained by Kim Philby. After gaining worldwide fame for his efforts to make the Soviet Union more open and to improve its relations with Western nations, Gorbachev won the Nobel Peace Prize in 1990. Walter Gotell (**bottom**), who first played KGB chief General Gogol in *The Spy Who Loved Me*, not only physically resembled Gorbachev, but his steely charm in his last Bond film, *The Living Daylights*, mirrored that of the new Soviet leader.

Of all the films shown in the US in 1985, MGM/UA distributed only three of the top 40 moneymakers. The studio received $65 million in rental income from *Rocky IV*, which made the Stallone film the third-highest grossing movie of the year in the US. *A View To A Kill* stood at the Number Ten position with $25 million in rentals. It sold seven million fewer tickets in the US than *Octopussy* and nine million fewer than *Moonraker*. Worse, in every major international market except Hong Kong the grosses dropped in comparison to *Octopussy*'s box office. Worldwide, box office fell by $35 million.

While the film was still a hit, no one was satisfied with these results. Michael Wilson and Cubby Broccoli had tried to attract a younger audience to the movie by having the phenomenally popular group Duran Duran co-write and record the theme song. Although the song hit Number One on the US charts, tickets sales did not increase accordingly. The filmmakers had also introduced extreme sports into the film with snowboarding and base jumping (*The Spy Who Loved Me* had had a huge influence on the latter sport, which was at the time in its infancy).

The problem, the filmmakers concluded, was the tone. Humour was right for Roger Moore, but at least part of the audience wanted to take the films more seriously. Even though audiences embraced self-conscious humour like the use of the music from *Lawrence Of Arabia* and *The Magnificent Seven* in *The Spy Who Loved Me* and *Moonraker*, moviegoers did not seem to hold the same warm spot for the use of the Beach Boys hit, 'California Girls', in *A View To A Kill*. Chases filled with jokes always seemed to appeal to audiences, but not the night chase involving a fire truck through the streets of San Francisco. The Bond films had returned to a breezy tone in 1971 with *Diamonds Are Forever*, but with the box office disappointment of *A View To A Kill*, Wilson and Broccoli decided it was time for an extensive reworking of the formula for the next series. They also decided to make the next film without Roger Moore.

In September 1984, while filming the climax of *A View To A Kill* at the Amberley Chalk Pits Museum, Roger Moore told Jacqui Ball of the *Evening Argus*, "I never know from one year to the next what I will be doing. I don't know if this will be the last Bond. I always say it will be the last one." When the film was released, however, many reviewers commented on Moore's age, and one British newspaper ran a particularly unflattering cartoon with Q presenting Moore's 007 with a turbo-charged wheelchair.

In December 1985, Cubby Broccoli called Moore to his Los Angeles home and told the actor that it was time to make a change. Moore, said Broccoli, took the news well, saying, "I agree, Cubby. I think it's time."

During the years that Moore had played the role, a new generation of James Bond fans had come of age who accepted him as 007. Moore chose not to imitate Sean Connery's portrayal, and instead infused the character with his personal brand of charm and light humour. In the process, he claimed the role as his own, and kept the James Bond series thriving for many years.

When Moore first appeared as 007, Watergate and intelligence community excesses had soured the public's perception of spies, the sexual revolution had made Bond's libidinous endeavours appear tame, and the growing blue jean culture made Bond's immaculate dress *passé*. Twelve years and seven films later, the world had evolved into quite a different place, yet Roger Moore had weathered the changes and kept Bond alive as the *least secret* agent on the planet. He had proved to be the perfect Bond for the era.

With Moore's departure from the role, the 007 producers started the process of re-inventing the character, taking some of these societal issues into consideration. Returning to Fleming, scriptwriters Richard Maibaum and Michael Wilson toyed with the idea of showing, in effect, the story of Bond's origin. The script would have featured Bond, an orphan reared by his grandfather after his parents' deaths in a skiing accident, as a young naval officer who was wild and rebellious, living up to the family motto 'The World Is Not Enough'. Through a friend of his grandfather's, Bond would become a sub-agent and redeem himself. Both Maibaum and Wilson thought the idea was a good one, but Cubby Broccoli disagreed. Broccoli felt that audiences did not want to see Bond as an amateur; they wanted to see him as a professional, already in full command of his talents. This had always been one of the series' unique features; because the details of Bond's origins were kept deliberately vague, it was easier for male audience members to project themselves into the Bond character. Broccoli told the writers to try again.

Maibaum and Wilson decided to turn to an Ian Fleming short story, 'The Living Daylights'. This story placed Bond on one side of the East-West Berlin divide, providing cover for an agent escaping back to the West. Bond knows an assassin will try to kill the agent, and his orders are to kill the assassin. When it is time to pull the trigger, Bond sees the assassin is an attractive female member of an orchestra. In a split second, Bond decides to spare her life. He adjusts his aim and shoots the gun out of her hands. The writers used this premise as the jumping-off point for a plot that deeply reflected current events, as well as ancient Cold War history, particularly the twilight areas of espionage and global politics.

Four historical elements served as the background for the plot of *The Living Daylights*. First was the rise of international arms brokers in the 1960s and 70s. Second, numerous changes in Soviet leadership in the mid-1980s had raised international concerns of instability, exacerbated by the Soviet Union's seemingly intractable military involvement in Afghanistan. Third, a major defection of a KGB officer to the UK exposed a large Soviet spy network and caused major tensions between the nations. And on 4th November 1985, the worldwide press reported the bizarre story of a senior KGB officer, Vitaly Yurchenko.

The CIA thought Yurchenko had defected to the US to share KGB secrets, but after a few months Yurchenko slipped away from CIA agents at a restaurant in the Georgetown area of Washington, DC and re-defected to the Soviet Union. Quickly, the West assumed Yurchenko had double-crossed the US - that during his debriefing, he had actually been mining information to give back to the Soviets. While this later turned out probably not to have been the case, the scenario worked in nicely with the Iron Curtain escape in Fleming's 'The Living Daylights'.

Yurchenko's defection also allowed the writers to resurrect the Soviet anti-spy network, SMERSH, which played a part in many of the original Ian Fleming novels. The real life SMERSH, a contraction of the Russian phrase *smert shpionam*, ("death to spies") officially disbanded shortly after the Second World War, but this organization had been blamed for numerous assassinations in the 1950s.

Wilson and Maibaum asked the natural question: what would a KGB defector hope to accomplish by spreading disinformation? For an answer, the writers turned to the recent turmoil after the death of Leonid Brezhnev in late 1982. Brezhnev's replacement, former KGB chief Yuri Andropov, lasted a year and a quarter before he died. His replacement, Konstantin Chernenko, in turn died after only one year and one month in office. Internally, the Soviets seemed beset by political manoeuvring and power plays. In the West, conspiracy theorists wove tales of Shakespearian proportions to explain the rapid successions. Wilson and Maibaum had their story turn on a rogue Soviet General who wants to become KGB chief, a position of unchecked power.

The next question became, what would the head of the KGB do with so much power? The answer proved decidedly capitalist. Maibaum and Wilson developed a plot surrounding the murky world of the Soviet war in Afghanistan, which had begun on Christmas Eve, 1979. Six years later commentators were referring to it as "the Russian Vietnam". Muslim rebels from across the Middle East linked with the Afghani resistance to form a movement called the *mujaheddin* (Persian for "warrior"). The *mujaheddin* received major support from the CIA, but they also supplemented this with the sale of heroin to international markets.

Reportedly, arms traders turned a blind eye to the origins of the drug money as they sold the "freedom fighters" deadly weapons. In 1964's *Goldfinger*, Bond blew up a Central American drug lab, commenting on the lab's owner, "At least he won't be using heroin-flavoured bananas to finance revolutions." Just over 20 years later, Bond was allied with a group who indeed used heroin profits to finance revolution.

If the final plot of *The Living Daylights* - involving rogue military officers, arms dealers and drug money - sounds vaguely familiar, it should. When *The Living Daylights* was in the middle of production in 1986, the biggest story of political corruption since Watergate exploded in the US. Many of the principals involved in the scandal, which became known as Iran-Contra, might have been destroyed if it had not been for one piece of equipment named in honour of James Bond.

On 5th October 1986, in Central America, while the latest Bond film was shooting halfway around the globe, Nicaraguan government soldiers shot down an American cargo plane. Inside the wreckage the soldiers found crates of military supplies obviously intended for the Contra forces that hoped to overthrow the Communist government of Nicaragua. Only one crew member from the plane crash, Eugene Hasenfus, survived. Taken into captivity, Hasenfus admitted that he worked for the CIA. This was a problem because some years earlier, the US Congress had passed a law forbidding the US government from funnelling money, munitions and training manuals to the Contras.

Rapidly, the scheme began to collapse. Not only was there an illegal, co-ordinated effort within the White House to funnel money to the Contras, but the money came from secret arms sales to Iran (which the US had labelled a terrorist state). President Reagan publicly proclaimed that America would "never make concessions to terrorists". In fact, he authorized the sale of TOW and Hawk missiles to Iran in order to gain freedom for American hostages in Lebanon. The man behind the plot appeared to be Lieutenant Colonel Oliver North, a clean cut, square-jawed patriot who some quickly labelled as a rogue working without presidential authority (although North always disputed this characterization).

This plot proved to be alarmingly similar to the illicit scheme run by the villains in *The Living Daylights*. There were even accusations that the CIA had been involved in drug smuggling and drug money-laundering operations on behalf of the Contras. The problem for Oliver North and the Reagan administration was that in Bond's world it was only the villains who were involved in secret arms deals and money laundering. The scandal even had its own Bond woman in the form of Oliver North's disconcertingly beautiful secretary with the vaguely Bondian name Fawn Hall.

On 13th October, CIA Director William J. Casey told Oliver North that the "whole thing was becoming unravelled and that things ought to be cleaned up". North, with assistance from the ever-devoted Hall, took to shredding evidence of the plot. Some later speculated that the destruction of those key documents may have saved President Ronald Reagan from impeachment and many others from jail. The high-speed shredder used by North was an Intimus, *model 007*.

In *The Living Daylights*, Bond inhabits a world that is less black-and-white ideologically than the world of the Roger Moore films. The filmmakers, while clearly taking sides in the Afghan conflict, sought to create a balanced portrayal of the Soviets. General Gogol, the cuddly comic KGB chief played by Walter Gotell since 1977's *The Spy Who Loved Me*, became a minor player, supplanted by the more realistic General Pushkin (John Rhys-Davies). When Bond is ordered to execute General Pushkin, 007 balks, proclaiming Pushkin to be a good man. Eventually, Bond himself becomes something of a rogue, substituting his own judgement in place of M's orders. Pushkin becomes a key ally of Bond's in the effort to ensnare the villains. The balance portrayed is much like that in the real political sphere - while the West abhorred Soviet "meddling" in Afghanistan, it still maintained diplomatic ties and areas of close co-operation with the superpower.

Continuing along the lines begun with *The Spy Who Loved Me*, the Soviet KGB spies are seen as honourable professionals who are enemies only because they subscribe to a differing ideology. As in *Octopussy*, the real villain is a rogue general, but in *The Living Daylights* the general proved to be an avaricious self-serving opportunist rather than a hard-line Communist zealot. In both cases, these generals defy their well-meaning superiors. *The Living Daylights* even sought to balance the equation by having the rogue Soviet general in league

with an amoral American arms merchant, showing that both the Communists and the Capitalists had their bad eggs.

The more balanced and sympathetic portrayal of the Soviet leadership in the Bond films presaged real events. When Mikhail Gorbachev came to power, the country's economy was in decline. In an attempt to modernize it and make it more productive, he proposed two key governmental changes. The first, *perestroika* (literally translated as "restructuring") moved economic control away from the central government, and encouraged limited capitalist ventures. The second, *glasnost* ("openness"), reduced the power of the Communist Party and increased that of elected bodies. Together, these efforts had a profound effect on the world.

In harsh contrast to the bellicose image previously held of Soviet leaders (like Khrushchev pounding his shoe on a podium as he addressed the UN General Assembly in September 1960), Gorbachev seemed, well, like General Gogol: reasonable, co-operative, even cuddly. Instead of threatening Soviet expansion, he worked to improve Soviet relations with Western countries and to reduce tensions and conflicts worldwide, including signing the INF treaty which served as the historical backdrop to the plot of *Octopussy*.

For the Bond producers, the biggest challenge was not walking the tightrope of new political paradigms, but casting.

As with Sean Connery's retirement from Bondage in 1967, the producers were once again faced with the daunting task of selecting a new 007 to take over from an actor who had become hugely popular in the role. Cubby Broccoli and Michael Wilson set about finding a new actor who could place his own stamp on the character of Bond while still embodying the classic 007 style.

A slew of newspapers and magazines upped their circulation over the next year reporting on supposed front-runners in the Bond casting derby. Several stars of American TV series were mentioned, including British actor Simon MacCorkindale, Australian Antony Hamilton, and all-American, 6' 3", 29-year-old John James, star of the popular soap *Dynasty*. In May 1986, the Associated Press and *Entertainment Tonight* reported that Australian model-turned-actor Findley Light had captured the role of James Bond. The rumour, like so many in the past, proved false. Other names touted in the press included Bryan Brown, Michael Nader, Andrew Clarke and Pierce Brosnan, who, because of his role as a well-tailored private investigator on the American television series *Remington Steele*, had often been compared to James Bond.

Casting director Debbie McWilliams remembers, "We would consider lots and lots of people and gradually whittle it down based on their looks, their height, their acting ability. I mean, James Bond has to fulfil a lot of things for a lot of people. So it's not something that's taken lightly. And I think Sam Neill stood a very good chance in those early days." Wilson was keen on hiring Neill, an Irish-born New Zealander who had made an impression in the BBC series *Reilly, Ace Of Spies* (based on the exploits of real-life spy Sidney Reilly). But Broccoli was unconvinced. He favoured an actor named Lambert Wilson (no relation to Michael).

Timothy Dalton, like Pierce Brosnan, was another actor who had gained notice on American television as a James Bond-like figure. In 1979, Dalton had appeared as a jewel thief on *Charlie's Angels*, where he romanced Farrah Fawcett. Fawcett's character fell for Dalton's 'James Bond' style charm. Dalton's connection to Bond went back further. Cubby Broccoli had interviewed him in 1968 when casting for a replacement for Sean Connery. Dalton felt he was

"To look for a new James Bond is one of the most impossible jobs in the entire world." Debbie McWilliams, Eon casting director

too young. In 1980, Dalton was again considered as a replacement for Roger Moore in case Moore left the role.

Dana Broccoli suggested to Cubby that they should once more approach Dalton. The Welsh actor was now very interested in the role, but his obligation to star in *Brenda Starr* precluded him from taking the job. After the *News Of The World* had erroneously reported that Dalton had been fired from the role of 007, Dalton took them to court. In July 1987, he won his case, donating the damages he received to the National Youth Theatre.

With Dalton out of the running, the producers chose Pierce Brosnan as the new Bond. Broccoli had met the Irish actor when Brosnan's wife, Cassandra Harris, appeared in *For Your Eyes Only*. *Remington Steele* was just ending its run. Brosnan, like Dalton, seemed a perfect fit. All the producers had to do was wait 60 days until NBC's option ran out on ordering more episodes of the series. Had Brosnan been waiting for any role other than Bond, the wait would have been perfunctory. With 007, though, it was a daily

media circus. As the frenzy grew, NBC decided Brosnan was suddenly a very marketable commodity. Why shouldn't the network exploit that? At the eleventh hour, the network ordered a series of *Remington Steele* made-for-television movies. Cubby Broccoli declared that Remington Steele would not be James Bond. Suddenly, Brosnan lost one of the most coveted roles in the film industry. He appeared on the cover of *People* magazine with the headline 'Take This Job And Shove It' (referring to his role on *Remington Steele*).

With Brosnan out of the picture, the filmmakers looked again at the schedule and again approached Timothy Dalton. If they delayed production, could he start immediately after *Brenda Starr* completed shooting?

"I wanted to capture the spirit of Ian Fleming." Timothy Dalton

Timothy Dalton filmed his final scene for *Brenda Starr* on a Saturday, flew from America to London on a Sunday, and on Monday, 29th September 1986 arrived at Pinewood Studios for his hair, make-up and wardrobe tests, jet-lagged but enthusiastic.

The British press had announced Dalton on 7th August, but the official inauguration of him as James Bond came on 5th October, with a massive press conference in Vienna. Asked if he was ready for future Bond films should *The Living Daylights* prove successful, Dalton responded, "There is a tide in the affairs of man, and you have to take it at the flood."

Dalton studied the Fleming novels for clues on how to portray Bond, and he imbued his 007 with elements from the literary source. Dalton emerged with a performance that was dark, brooding and edgy. "Bond lives in a world which brings danger to him and to those he loves," he said. "You get this strong feeling that, while he has his life, he wants to live it to the full - not for ostentation or snobbery, but because he needs to touch life in all its forms." Director John Glen welcomed the fresh approach offered by Dalton. "He portrayed all the smouldering qualities that we were trying to introduce into the picture."

What this meant was that for most of *The Living Daylights*, the Bond filmmakers worked to jettison the vast majority of Bond's cinematic past. Dalton's Bond made no jokes about his work, which he took deadly seriously. He was a spy with a dirty job that gave rise to complex emotions. Rather than being ever unflappable, Dalton's Bond often expressed irritation and frustration. Rather than issue a string of witty rejoinders, Dalton's Bond engaged in angry banter. This was a pre-60s, one-woman Bond. Even the references contained within the film pre-dated the Bond films. The scenes in Vienna's famed Prater amusement park directly referred to the 1949 Carol Reed film *The Third Man*. Sequences in Afghanistan echoed epic adventure films such as *Gunga Din* and *Lawrence Of Arabia*.

In other ways, the new movie tried to update Bond through a very modern John Barry score, a new Miss Moneypenny (the role of M had been recast for *Octopussy* after Bernard Lee passed away in 1981) and the latest Aston Martin. The new gadget car was not only a throwback to *Goldfinger* and *The Spy Who Loved Me* but a way of taking back the concept from a host of imitators, such as the KITT car on the NBC action series, *Knight Rider*.

Dalton's strong acting talents matched the filmmakers' desire to make this Bond eminently believable. Dalton was willing to go the extra mile to achieve that verisimilitude. Many critics had complained about the use of stunt doubles for Roger Moore, and Dalton answered by throwing himself into the action. During shooting in Gibraltar, he clung on to the top of a Land Rover speeding down the narrow roads. Dalton loved the action. After seeing a Second World War movie on paratroopers as a kid, Dalton had leapt from stone walls with his friends, imitating the soldiers. The movie, as it turned out, was *The Red Beret*, Cubby Broccoli's first film in the UK.

Timothy Dalton was born on 21st March 1946 in Colwyn Bay, Wales. His father was an advertising executive, but his showbusiness roots were well in place. Dalton's grandfather had been a theatrical manager, and his grandmother a variety performer who had once played music halls with Charlie Chaplin.

At the age of 16, Dalton saw a production of *Macbeth*, and instantly realized that he wanted to become an actor. Dalton's sense of drama, cadence and intensity came from his study of the classics of the stage. He trained at the Royal Academy of Dramatic Arts before breaking into films with the 1968 adaptation of the stage

play *The Lion in Winter*. Dalton held his own alongside Peter O'Toole, Katharine Hepburn and another promising newcomer, Anthony Hopkins.

In 1970, Dalton accepted the role of Heathcliff in a new film version of *Wuthering Heights*, drawing strong reviews and adoring fans. He had become something of a sex symbol. After a role in the film *Mary, Queen of Scots*, Dalton made a decision to concentrate on stage roles rather than movie and TV work. "It paid dividends, because I got some of the best reviews of my life, and came out a much more experienced and mature actor - and person too, hopefully," he said.

In the late 1970s, Dalton again began accepting roles in TV and film on both sides of the Atlantic. He appeared with the legendary Mae West in the 1977 film *Sextette* and showed up in two mini-series, *Centennial* and *Sins*. A strong appearance in 1980's *Flash Gordon* had many observers feeling his star was rising.

By 1986, Dalton possessed all the ingredients he would need to tackle the role of James Bond. Physically he fitted the bill, even resembling Fleming's description of 007. He had talent to spare, and possessed a natural charm and grace vital to the character. The producers and the crew quickly warmed to Dalton as the new Bond.

"James Bond movies have survived so long because you're dealing with the spy world. And with this indestructible character with that English *je ne sais quoi*, that kind of wit, that twinkle." MARYAM D'ABO

Despite statements by Cubby Broccoli, many casual American observers thought that Dalton was merely a second-choice substitute for Brosnan. Besides, they felt that NBC's last-minute order of *Remington Steele* telefilms was mean-spirited. Brosnan's public statements did nothing to dispel these thoughts. Regardless, Dalton's critical reception and worldwide box office meant there were plenty who wanted to see more of Dalton as 007.

As always, the producers had plenty to consider in the cinematic world of James Bond. In the real world, current events had continued to have an impact on the series, including two very different syndromes.

In late 1967, just after the peak of the James Bond craze, John Anthony Walker, Jr. strode into the Soviet embassy in Washington, DC with vital information on the US government's KL-47 cryptographic machine. Walker offered to turn the information over for a price. The KGB gave Walker an envelope stuffed with cash. For the next 18 years, Walker provided the KGB with thousands of classified documents left at dead-drops and collected hundreds of thousands of dollars for his services. One KGB officer commented that with the KGB's ability to decode American cyphers, if there *had* been a war, the Soviets would have won it.

During shooting, the filmmakers scored a major publicity coup. Prince Charles and Princess Diana visited the set at Pinewood Studios, where the Princess shattered a break-away glass bottle over her husband's head. The photo, which looked initially like a bit of bizarre marital violence between the royals, ended up in hundreds of newspapers and magazines, each one mentioning the new Bond film.

With 1987 as Bond's 25th anniversary in the cinema, MGM/UA and the filmmakers planned numerous celebrations. Nightclubs, such as Atlanta's famed Limelight disco, held James Bond nights. MGM/UA television produced a one-hour television special for the film, *Happy Birthday 007*, hosted by Roger Moore. *The Hollywood Reporter* published a special James Bond issue commemorating 007's anniversary and numerous Hollywood celebrations marked the event, including a dinner in Cubby Broccoli's honour which was hosted by the five directors of the Bond films made by Eon Productions.

Timothy Dalton's debut Bond adventure opened in the US on 31st July 1987 on 1,725 screens - the widest ever opening for a Bond film. When the studio tallied up the weekend box-office results, *The Living Daylights* was Number One, taking in $11,051,284 - the highest three-day gross in James Bond history. Audiences clearly responded favourably to the new 007, as did the critics.

In Great Britain, the movie out-grossed *Octopussy* and *A View To A Kill* by over a third, which was also the case in most international territories. In fact, outside the US, the film made $140 million - the same amount as *Moonraker* and over $38 million more than *A View To A Kill*. In the States, however, Dalton's debut ran its course at the box office all too quickly. It ultimately sold fewer tickets than any Bond film since *The Man With The Golden Gun*, almost 1.5 million tickets fewer than *On Her Majesty's Secret Service*. Certainly, the movie was a success, but Dalton and the filmmakers were almost immediately set upon by the Hollywood rumour machine.

In America, the filmmakers faced another silent problem - their audience. Like George Lazenby, Timothy Dalton was relatively unknown to US filmgoers before committing to Bond. Pierce Brosnan, on the other hand, had a large fan following in the US.

Though the KGB cautioned him to keep a low profile, Walker soon had a new MGB sports car and a 24-foot yacht. He and his wife moved into a swank apartment, and he began an affair with a college co-ed that included weekend trips to the Caribbean. In the years to come Walker recruited his best friend and his brother into his spy ring. They, too, liked the money. Walker also recruited his own son, Michael.

When presented with the scheme, Michael Walker asked his father if he had raised him to be a spy. Walker told his son to pull out his social security card. The first three numbers read 007. It was a coincidence (social security numbers cannot be picked) but the psychological power of Bond's Secret Service ID proved so overwhelming that Michael readily agreed to help in the family enterprise.

The end came when Walker's former wife, Barbara, who had landed on hard times, demanded the alimony she had been promised but never paid. Before she called the FBI, she braced herself with a few stiff shots of Scotch; appropriately, it was Johnny Walker Red. After Walker's arrest, many questioned how a low-paid civil servant could have got away with such lavish excesses and high-priced lifestyle without question. A new name was coined for spies who sold out for the money and lived beyond their means: 'The James Bond Syndrome'.

Actor Jeroen Krabbe instigated one of the world's most famous photographs when Prince Charles and Princess Diana visited the Pinewood set of *The Living Daylights* (**top left**). "I said to Diana, 'Why don't you smash a sugar glass bottle on your husband's head?'... I just said it as a joke. And she said to me, 'Good idea.' She tapped one of the guys on the shoulder, said, 'Could I borrow your bottle?' 'Oh sure, sure, your Royal Highness.' So she said to Charles, 'Just turn around.' And he said to her, 'Don't you dare.' She said, 'Oh yes, I do. I do.' Then she lifted the bottle - and this was quite amazing - she waited until all the photographers were ready, waited like an actor or actress: 'Ready?' And then she smashed him on the head. This was front-page coverage the next day. In every paper, every television station, all over the world. And I was in the middle, laughing."

The other syndrome was one of the defining aspects of the 1980s. In 1969's *On Her Majesty's Secret Service*, Ernst Stavro Blofeld held the world hostage with the threat of a virus that would cause global panic. By the mid-1980s, the world was in fact experiencing a panic caused by a fatal virus of mysterious origin which at the time was believed to be transmitted exclusively through sexual contact: Acquired Immune Deficiency Syndrome. Although the earliest known case of death from AIDS occurred in 1959, physicians in New York and Los Angeles identified AIDS as a disease in 1981 after an increase in deaths caused by rare forms of cancer and pneumonia among homosexuals. The disease spread rapidly throughout the US and Europe. Soon, the epidemic reached across sub-Saharan Africa and exploded in south-east Asia.

A few months after the release of *A View To A Kill*, actor Rock Hudson succumbed to AIDS. Hudson, who was privately homosexual, represented a certain type of clean-cut, heterosexual masculinity. His death brought about tremendous public awareness of the disease. His passing also signalled the end of an era of sexual freedom that began with the introduction of the birth control pill and James Bond movies, and reached its apotheosis with the orgiastic atmosphere of disco clubs like Manhattan's popular Studio 54. With the advent of AIDS, safe sex became a necessity and condoms *de rigueur*.

In light of this changing attitude to sexuality, the 007 producers were faced with a dilemma: how would James Bond, whose womanizing was an integral part of his character, react to this new threat?

"There was a feeling that the AIDS epidemic had caught up with us," said Michael Wilson. "Certainly people were thinking about becoming more monogamous. There was this whole idea of safe sex, and all of these issues. And so people commented, is Bond going to become a one-woman man now?"

Long before the public understood the extent of the AIDS crisis, social critics had often assailed Bond for his perceived sexual irresponsibility. In 1984, Dr. David Devlin of Britain's Family Planning Association sounded a typical alarm when he slammed 007 for sleeping with women without caring whether he made them pregnant. The *Daily Express* quoted Dr. Devlin as saying, "If James were a real person, he would have at least 50 children and would probably be suffering from anything from herpes to terminal syphilis." Two years later, as the ability of AIDS to be transmitted through heterosexual sex became better documented, commentators used different language. They said Bond would be dead from AIDS. For the Bond producers, the new health threat meant a slight adjustment. *The Living Daylights*, for example, had portrayed a more romantic 007 and focused on one major relationship.

There was another way in which the world of James Bond intersected the AIDS crisis - paranoia. The Bond stories always played on underlying societal fears, whether it be fear of secret conspiracies hatched deep behind the Iron Curtain or anxiety that stolen nuclear weapons might destroy humanity in the blink of an eye. AIDS caused unease in the public psyche on an even more drastic level than the Red Scare of the late 1940s and 50s. Rather than a Communist under every bed, people worried there was a carrier in every bed. Was that seductive woman or man actually infected with the deadly disease? Was one's husband, wife, lover really faithful? Just as in James Bond's world, AIDS encouraged everyone to trust no one.

Some speculated whether the disease was natural or the man-made creation of secret biological weapons labs run by the CIA or KGB. Long dormant stories - such as Ian Fleming's jokes to JFK about making Cuban men believe they would become impotent if they did not shave their beards - led some to feel that governments (or in some theories, other global villains) had an interest in curbing the sexual revolution and controlling behaviour. Others declared the disease a myth created as a mass mind-control plot. The truth was grimmer; thousands were dying and no one knew where it would end. One thing was certain - in a few short years, AIDS had changed the world, even James Bond's world.

With the recasting of James Bond, the producers also recast Miss Moneypenny. John Glen recalled, "We tested several people and came up with Caroline Bliss (**top left** in *The Living Daylights*). We were hoping to just change the character slightly. It was difficult to accept the change, really. It was a tough one for Caroline to do, I think. She did an admirable job."

Opposite: Talisa Soto and Carey Lowell vied for the attention of 007 in *Licence To Kill*.

"Sometimes Bond reminds me of your classic Westerns. A man rides into town, sorts out the bad guys, and rides out again." Timothy Dalton,

Cubby Broccoli, Michael Wilson and the rest of the Bond filmmaking team felt confident Timothy Dalton was an actor who would carry the franchise into the 1990s, despite the lower than hoped for US ticket sales of *The Living Daylights*. Broccoli and Wilson faced a number of hurdles. First, MGM/UA wanted to keep the costs on the next Bond film under tight control. Although budgets for the Bond films had not risen since *Moonraker*, filmmaking costs had. Broccoli and Wilson were determined to create a visually spectacular adventure and to continue to make certain the money they spent was reflected on-screen.

Second, on a purely technical note, they had to come up with a title for the film that would follow *The Living Daylights*. Ian Fleming had written 14 Bond books, and the only Fleming titles left were short stories - 'The Hildebrand Rarity', 'Risico', 'A Quantum Of Solace' and 'Property Of A Lady'. Although there were new titles from Bond novels written by Kingsley Amis (under the pseudonym of Robert Markham) and John Gardner, the

filmmakers also had the option of creating original Bond titles. While this was sorted out, the film was known only as *Bond 16*.

Finally, Broccoli and Wilson had to come up with a location. In 1987, China hoped to continue to open its film industry to the West. *The Last Emperor*, filmed in 1986, proved to be a cultural and diplomatic boon for the Communist nation, which was entering a tentative period of political openness. Film production also brought in much needed foreign capital. For the Chinese, no film could be seen as more international and more appropriate to the new policies of the nation than the next James Bond adventure. The feelings within the Chinese Communist Party leadership must have been mixed. Certainly, Bond had a global audience and the films continued to be cinematic travel brochures for adventurous travellers, but 007 also meant sex, violence, and the delicate politics of espionage. Nonetheless, the Chinese government extended an invitation to James Bond.

Cubby Broccoli and a dozen colleagues, including Michael Wilson, travelled to China to scout possible locations in late 1987. Over the course of ten days, they toured the studios in Beijing and Shanghai and saw as much of the country as was possible. They discovered, however, that China would not be a bargain. Coupled with stifling bureaucracy and the desire of party officials to have approval over the scripts, there was no set rate for hotels, and no set pricing structure for rentals of film equipment.

While the producers were in China, *For Your Eyes Only* was shown on closed-circuit TV. There was also an invitation-only screening of *The Living Daylights* for Communist Party officials and film dignitaries. In the end, however, the producers chose to go elsewhere. The move proved wise. In the spring of 1989, even before *Licence To Kill* hit screens across the globe, the world was riveted to images from China: one million protesters filling streets with pro-democracy banners, a makeshift 'Goddess of Democracy' statue in Beijing's Tiananmen Square, and a lone student standing in front of an advancing line of tanks. The brutal suppression of the pro-democracy movement in Beijing on 3rd June 1989 left a bitter taste across the world, and James Bond barely avoided being tainted by it.

Whatever the reasons, the China invitation underlined just how fortunate and fortuitous the judgement of the filmmakers had proved to be over the past quarter-century. Despite 15 films produced during a period of constant global change, all had managed to steer clear of geopolitical landmines.

With the costs of producing a 007 adventure mounting, along with studio pressures to keep the budget low, it seemed to Cubby Broccoli that Bond again needed to leave Pinewood Studios. With favourable exchange rates and nearby exotic locations, Broccoli and Wilson chose to base the new Bond film at Mexico City's historic Churubusco Studios.

The 007 crew moved in like an army in the spring of 1988, refurbishing and rewiring much of the studio so it could handle the massive production. The film reflected the more earthy ambience of Mexico rather than the sophisticated polish of England. On 18th July 1988, cameras rolled on an early scene where the villain orders a man's heart cut out of his chest. It was a brutal scene, indicative of the direction of the new film. This was going to be a grittier, tougher Bond.

Licence To Kill gave Desmond Llewelyn his largest role ever in a 007 film. His long association with the role of Q made his a face that the public recognized. "A lot of them don't think it's me, when they see me going on the underground," said Llewelyn. "You can see all these people doing double-takes, and a lot of them are often saying - certainly in supermarkets or on the ferry going to Ireland - 'Has anybody told you how much you look like the man in the Bond films?'" Llewelyn found that the 007 films were a comfort to some of the most unexpected people. "I went to a memorial service of a friend in London, in a big church," he said. "The parson was talking to me afterwards, and he said, 'You know, when I've had a really hard day, and I'm feeling absolutely whacked, I get a drink, sit down and put on a Bond film. For relaxation.'"

"Timothy Dalton and myself, having been the kind of actors that like to do as much research as possible, went back to *Casino Royale*, where Ian Fleming talks about how Bond and the villain are actually mirror images of each other," said Robert Davi (**left**). Davi commented on the ruthless character, "He would be Donald Trump if he was in legitimate business."

Benicio del Toro (**opposite, middle**), future Oscar winner as Best Supporting Actor in *Traffic*, had one of his earliest film roles as Franz Sanchez's henchman, Dario.

With Timothy Dalton, the producers felt they had an actor who could not only embody the qualities audiences expected of James Bond, but one who could also compete with other big-budget action heroes. The 1980s saw the birth of three 'hero' franchises - *Beverly Hills Cop*, which opened in 1984, followed by *Lethal Weapon* (in 1987) and *Die Hard* (in 1988). These films exploited the formula defined by *For Your Eyes Only* - big action set-pieces and heroes who survived by their wits and physical fortitude rather than electronic gadgetry. These films were complemented by the American television series, *MacGyver*, in which the title character, an agent for an organization called The Phoenix Foundation, created Bond-like gadgets out of ordinary items. However, the lead characters in these adventures were more blue-collar; they were working-class heroes who wore scruffy bluejeans instead of tuxedos, and who drove second-hand cars instead of Aston Martins.

There was another film series, though, which resonated with audiences by playing on their fears of a society where laws seemed to protect the rights of criminals more than those of victims. The hero was brooding and vengeful, dispensing brutal justice by embodying judge, jury and executioner in one self-righteous package. He was Dirty Harry, a San Francisco cop with a Magnum .44 and a bad attitude played by Clint Eastwood, who seemed to hiss his lines through clenched teeth. With the release of the fourth Dirty Harry film, 1983's *Sudden Impact*, the character's take-no-prisoners attitude was memorialized when President Ronald Reagan, facing the threat of tax increases from Congress, echoed Dirty Harry's macho challenge, "Go ahead. Make my day."

Dirty Harry was the ultimate establishment anti-hero, a lone law-and-order vigilante who often acted outside the law. Harry was always at odds with his superiors and 'the system'. In the 1970s and 80s 'the system' more and more often became seen as a labyrinth of inefficient bureaucracy which coddled criminals. No one could accuse Dirty Harry of coddling anyone. *Licence To Kill* hurls James Bond into Dirty Harry's world, where well-meaning rules prevent actions and cost lives. Bond echoes Dirty Harry's frustrations and anger in the movie, and like him, Bond quickly chooses to work outside the constraints of his government employers.

Licence To Kill had another parallel with the films of Clint Eastwood. The second half of the film echoes the 'destroy from within' structure of Akira Kurosawa's classic 1961 samurai film *Yojimbo*, which was re-made as Clint Eastwood's first spaghetti western, *A Fistful Of Dollars*. Other elements of the story harked back to Ian Fleming. Parts of 'The Hildebrand Rarity' and the novel LIVE AND LET DIE were worked into the plot. For the villain, though, the filmmakers again looked to the headlines.

Manuel Noriega, like most soldiers, had a hero he idolized. Unfortunately, his was Josef Stalin. Like Stalin, Noriega became

the most feared man in his nation, the small but vital country of Panama. Noriega's rise to power was littered with dead bodies. He helped remove President Arnulfo Arias from his position in 1968, and quickly became head of Panama's intelligence service, which earned a reputation for its brutal tactics. Noriega also began a lucrative drug-smuggling operation. As Noriega's domination grew, so did the voice of his critics, including Dr. Hugo Spadafora. After the grisly decapitation murder of Spadafora in September 1985, many called for a complete investigation. When, in 1988, Panama's newly elected president agreed, Noriega merely removed the man from office and assumed power. After years of using Noriega as a CIA contact, the US government turned its back on the dictator, indicting him on drug charges. Nonetheless, as *Licence To Kill* prepared to start filming, Noriega appeared to have a stronger grip on power than ever before.

The storyline of *Licence To Kill* took James Bond from Key West to the fictional Isthmus City. Locations in Mexico included

THE PETROL TANKER SEQUENCE.

"The major effects challenge on *Licence To Kill* was the work with the tanker chase," said special effects coordinator John Richardson, "where we had all these petrol tankers and they had to crash and blow up with missiles being fired at them. We had aircraft flying over the top. Rémy Julienne and his stunt team were doing all of the driving with the tankers, and they were brilliant. Corkey Fornof was flying the aircraft over the top. And we were doing all the fiery bits in between. It's not often you get the opportunity to do explosions that often and that big. I think we had something like five tankers we had to blow up. That took up a vast portion of the work on the film for us."

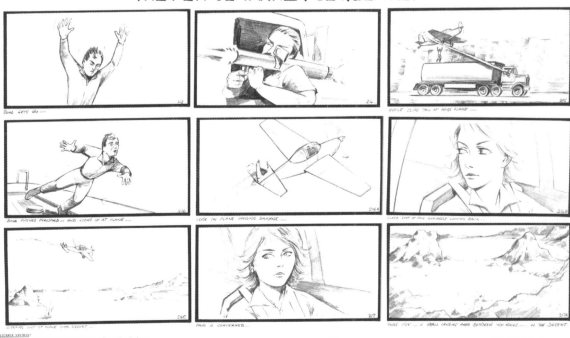

REVISED 4TH JULY '88.   SHEET 26

Otomi, a cultural arts centre that stood in for Sanchez's drug lab, and Arabesque, the Acapulco home of Enrico de Portanova, a long-time friend of Cubby Broccoli, which was the location for Sanchez's villa. Unfortunately, the heavy pollution in Mexico City took its toll on Cubby. After production began, he returned to Los Angeles, leaving the day-to-day management of the film in the capable hands of Michael Wilson and the vastly experienced Bond team.

The climax of the film had the kind of spectacular chase scene audiences had come to expect, except that in this case, the vehicles were tanker trucks, not automobiles. The special effects team created dramatic explosions, while the stunt team choreographed an amazing fight between Bond and Sanchez on the back of a moving tanker truck, which careers off the road and down a long embankment. The confrontation between Bond and Sanchez ends when 007 finally exacts his poetic vengeance using the cigarette lighter given to him as a present by Felix and Della to ignite Sanchez's gasoline-soaked clothes.

The film had its London premiere on 14th June 1989. It was the first 007 film to be rated '15' by the British Board of Film Classification; 38 seconds of violence had to be trimmed from five scenes to keep it from being rated '18' (adults only). In the US, where it opened on 14th July, the film was rated PG-13 (parents strongly cautioned that some material may be unsuitable for children under 13). Previous 007 films had been rated PG (parental guidance suggested).

Licence To Kill also became the only film to carry a Surgeon General's warning in the US, as a result of one of the many promotional tie-ins for the film. The Philip Morris tobacco company paid the producers $350,000 to have their Lark brand cigarettes used as one of 007's secret weapons. Prior to the film's release, US Representative Thomas Luken of Ohio charged that, should it be shown on television, such a promotional tie-in would amount to paid advertising. To ward off potential problems, the health warning was added to the beginning of the film.

In Japan, where cigarettes *were* allowed to be advertised on television, two Lark cigarette commercials aired in 1988 which played on the James Bond image. In one, called 'Masquerade', several revellers, in Amadeus-style masks, pursue a woman across a large square in a European city. Roger Moore helps the woman elude

them with his particular brand of *savoir faire*. In the other, called 'Silhouette', two hired assassins are shown lurking outside a luxury apartment building. Inside, Pierce Brosnan pulls down the blinds and embraces a scantily-clad woman. The assassins open fire with automatic weapons, but fail to hit their targets. When they kick the door of the apartment open, they discover they have been duped by a film projector. Meanwhile, Brosnan and his companion escape by helicopter.

MGM/UA launched more than a dozen promotional tie-ins for *Licence To Kill*, including the first ever 007 lottery. The Kansas Lottery's 'License To Win' scratch-off game offered a bonus prize of $25,000 for collecting each letter in J-A-M-E-S B-O-N-D. In the first entertainment promotion for *USA Today*, the newspaper gave away two Sterling 827SLi cars, touted as having English appointments and Japanese engineering. Sterling took out a one-year licence on 'The James Bond Theme' to promote sales of the luxury sedan in TV commercials, which featured Patrick Macnee asking, "You were expecting someone else?"

Pepsi, Polaroid and Spanish-language TV network Univision teamed up for a contest where the top prize was an all-expenses paid trip for two to Acapulco. Univision created a half-hour programme on the making of the film as one of its *Des De Hollywood* segments; it screened the night before the film's release in Mexico. Martini & Rossi sponsored a 007 cocktail contest in which the winner was sent to the royal premiere in London. Displays in off-licences offered the recipe for the new drink: two parts orange juice, two parts vermouth and a splash of grenadine - shaken, not stirred. For their part, Kenworth offered a limited edition 007 tractor-trailer cab for $100,000. It came with satin sheets, 007 emblems and a tuxedo tailored to fit the buyer. Pan Am, on some of their flights, showed a one-hour salute to Bond.

Despite all these promotions, the film failed to perform to expectations at the US box-office, facing heavy competition from *Indiana Jones And The Last Crusade*, *Lethal Weapon II* and *Batman*. US ticket sales were only 8.7 million, less than *The Man With The Golden Gun* and much less than half the tickets sold for *Octopussy*. In Britain, the movie started strongly, but failed to hold on, eventually pulling in just two thirds of the box office of *The Living Daylights*. Internationally, the film performed better in certain markets, such as South America, Taiwan and France but, overall, even the foreign markets could not alter the perception that the film was a disappointment.

Many factors played into the box office of the film. Cubby Broccoli disliked the ad campaign. Others claimed audiences did not respond to Dalton's Bond. Some pointed to the key changes in the formula, in particular, the violence evident in the film. While the violence was not actually much grimmer than some earlier Bond films, it was not leavened by humour or given the gloss of elegance. The film offered gadgets, but they were presented as intentionally clunky and outdated. Most of all, the filmmakers took a chance by having Bond become a rogue agent. Other British agents fire at him as he runs from M in Key West. Bond's anger also has consequences. His rash attempted assassination of the villain leads to the exposure of an on-going undercover narcotics operation and the death of allied agents. The movie sharply divided critics and fans. Some saw *Licence To Kill* as the ultimate expression of Ian Fleming's Bond. Others wished for the return of the cinematic 007.

For James Bond, 1990 marked the beginning of a period of trials, both legal and creative, which lasted for another five years. During that time the world experienced its most dramatic political shifts since the end of the Second World War. 007, the quintessential Cold War hero, suddenly seemed obsolete to some. Other critics flatly declared that James Bond, after a long life as a popular cultural icon, was finally dead. Those critics, though, forgot to check the pulse of popular culture.

Licence To Kill marked the end of an era. It proved to be the last Bond film for Richard Maibaum and Maurice Binder, two of the creative forces who helped shape *Dr. No*, and had worked on most of the following James Bond films. John Glen, who directed five Bonds and edited and directed second unit on three more, also left the series. Most importantly, *Licence To Kill* was also the final film to feature Cubby Broccoli on the set. Broccoli, Maibaum, Binder and Glen represented almost all the key elements of James Bond's success. The lavish productions, the rapier-sharp dialogue, the stunning and sexy title designs, and the brilliant action scenes all became hallmarks of the Bond films due largely to the efforts and vision of these men. The continuation and future success of the series relied upon Cubby Broccoli's vision to groom successors who could carry on the high standards which had been set since 1962.

"Cubby had a sensibility for making a film that would last. He and Dana always talked about how they would like to put on the Bond films in ten years and not have them feel dated."
Robert Davi

10.

By the end of the 1980s, the Cold War had taken a series of unanticipated turns. A poll of Western Europeans named the man who was considered the greatest threat to world peace. The winner was Ronald Reagan, President of the United States. Reagan was widely viewed as a dangerous hawk who would easily resort to war with the Soviet Union. On the other hand, Mikhail Gorbachev attained near saint-like praise from conservatives and liberals throughout the West. Over the course of four years, Gorbachev turned his back on Soviet expansion and rule through military might. In December 1988, he announced at the United Nations that he had ordered 10,000 tanks removed from the Eastern bloc. In one bold sweep, Gorbachev brought Europe more security than all the spies of the previous 50 years. Less than four months later, the Soviet Union held its most open election since 1917. In May 1989, Hungary removed its barbed-wire border fence with Austria - where some of the scenes in *The Living Daylights* had been set - allowing thousands of refugees to stream into the West. The

Shaken Not Stirred

following month, free elections in Poland brought to power the Solidarity party, founded by Lech Walesa. On 9th November 1989, after millions of citizens protested in the streets, East Germany opened its border with West Germany. The Berlin Wall tumbled as celebrants shattered the huge stone monument to repression.

In the three years after the Berlin Wall fell, the West watched with amazement and often bafflement as the entire Soviet empire fell apart. Just as after the Second World War, map-makers had to scramble to update their atlases as new nations emerged from the old Soviet Union, which formally ceased to exist on Christmas Day, 1991.

The Cold War was over. Even though James Bond rarely fought Cold War battles in the films, he existed, and in fact was created, to be part of the Cold War mythology. If anyone wondered how 007 would respond to the largest upheaval in the global political structure since Ian Fleming first typed the words "James Bond", they were going to have to wait a long time.

In 1989, James Bond's fate seemed less dependent on the battles of the Cold War than the battles for control of MGM. 007 was tied firmly to the studio, once the grand jewel of Hollywood. Unfortunately for Bond, MGM was in trouble - major financial trouble.

Every two years since MGM had purchased United Artists in 1981, the company had counted on a new James Bond film to keep it afloat. Every two years, Bond came through for the studio, until 1989. Although *Licence To Kill* made a healthy profit, it could not single-handedly save the studio. MGM's on-again, off-again owner, the mercurial millionaire Kirk Kerkorian, sold the controlling interest in the company to Italian financier Giancarlo Paretti for close on $1.3 billion in November 1990.

Paretti did not have the actual money to purchase MGM/UA, but he devised a scheme whereby he could use the promise to sell and license MGM's assets, including the Bond films, to pay for the studio before he bought it. Cubby Broccoli felt the rights Paretti promised in order to purchase the studio were undervalued and would drive the studio into bankruptcy, which in turn would devalue the Bond library. Danjaq sued to prevent the sales. Others sued Paretti for different reasons. The studio lapsed into disarray.

The legal turmoil created a myriad problems for Cubby Broccoli, Michael Wilson and the newest member of the core production team: Cubby's daughter, Barbara Broccoli. The studio could not afford to make a Bond film, despite their exclusive contract with Danjaq to produce more. On 8th August 1990, Cubby Broccoli declared Danjaq was for sale and all reasonable offers would be considered.

Selling James Bond looked to the world like a sure sign of low confidence in the future of the franchise. With the ability to make new Bond films in jeopardy and the box office seen as diminishing, James Bond's potential seemed dim. Many predicted 007 would soon be relegated to the world of cable television.

In fact, television in all its forms provided the basis of the resurgence of 007, although throughout the 1980s the growing sub-culture of James Bond had set the stage for 007's return.

In the early 1980s an engineer living near Santa Barbara, California decided to undertake a hobby - collecting James Bond

novels. Michael VanBlaricum searched used bookstores in the US and England for first edition Ian Fleming novels. After obtaining numerous duplicates, VanBlaricum decided to sell some of his extras to finance new purchases. Thus began The Book Stalker, one of a number of small businesses specializing in the growing market for early Ian Fleming editions. Ironically, during the 80s, sales of Fleming's Bond novels in paperback dropped around the globe. In the wide world of popular culture the Bond films and the new John Gardner Bond novels defined 007.

For a select few, though, Fleming's original Bond novels were important literature, a point they defended with academic passion. The first editions of the novels were touchstones for a generation, and VanBlaricum foresaw their iconographic value. Those who paid upwards of five hundred dollars for a first edition of CASINO ROYALE in the early 1980s gave a stamp of importance to the view of Fleming as literature.

Simultaneously, dealers specializing in James Bond movie posters and toys saw a growing market for collectibles from the early films. By the 80s, an original movie poster from *Goldfinger* ran upwards of fifty dollars, a nine-fold increase in value from a decade earlier. Many of these collectors were not the usual Bond fan club members. They appreciated the work of influential illustrators like Robert McGinnis, Frank McCarthy and Bob Peak, and felt Bond posters provided key examples of their work. Baby boomers wanted to recapture some memory from their youth, or even of a particular Christmas Day with a favourite toy. These collectors might not be able to answer a Bond trivia question, but they saw something special, even classic, in the world of 007.

The coolness of Bond extended beyond collectibles. The resurgence of ska music in England in the early 80s produced Bond-inspired hits from groups like The Selector and The Specials. Movies like the 1984 comedy *Bachelor Party* and 1985's *The Goonies* included throw-away references to Bond without the plots having the slightest espionage component. Just as the Bond movies had been sophisticated enough to quote from films like *Lawrence Of Arabia*, these movies tossed off Bond references as a shorthand for elegance and élan.

As the 80s progressed, the growing sub-culture of Bond aficionados grew. The Museum of Modern Art in New York hosted an exhibit of Bond movie poster art. The Museum of the Moving Image in London and the Cinemathèque in Paris included props and design sketches from the 007 films as part of their collections. When legal issues indefinitely delayed production after *Licence To Kill*, it was almost as if popular culture as a singular entity could step back from the Bond phenomenon and begin to assess its impact since 1953. This reassessment started where the Bond phenomenon itself began - with Ian Fleming.

By 1991, a group of Bond authorities led by Michael VanBlaricum became concerned that even with the growing market for Bond collectibles, larger pieces of the James Bond legacy were dropping off the radar screen. From Ian Fleming's professional papers to massive props from the Bond films themselves, Bond's rapid journey through 40 years of literary and cinematic history left little time to catalogue and archive the massive amount of materials and items left in the phenomenon's wake. In 1992, VanBlaricum and his associates formed a non-profit organization, The Ian Fleming Foundation, to preserve the legacy of James Bond.

In the first few months of its existence, the Foundation purchased and saved from oblivion such Bond vehicles as the Neptune submarine from *For Your Eyes Only*, the Lotus underwater car from *The Spy Who Loved Me*, the Blofeld bathosub from *Diamonds Are Forever*, and an underwater tow-sled from *Thunderball*. Teaming up with Reed Exhibitions, the IFF launched a touring exhibition of 007 vehicles which opened in October 1992. Besides the vehicles restored by the IFF, the exhibition featured the original Aston Martin DB5 from *Goldfinger* and the Bell Textron Rocket Pack from *Thunderball*.

The Ian Fleming Foundation also launched an erratically published magazine, *Goldeneye*, which covered developments in the world of Bond as well as in-depth articles on Bond's history. *Goldeneye* appeared during a period of growing press attention to Bond's past, which also saw frequent articles on Bond-related locations in travel magazines and newspapers.

All of these factors created a growing sense among a select but influential group that the James Bond phenomenon was not merely a grand commercial venture that continued to rake in money. Bond was also a form of cultural currency whose value, despite the lack of a new film, was on the rise.

While *Licence to Kill* was still in production, two television films were already being developed focusing on the life of Bond's creator, Ian Fleming. In the US, Turner Broadcasting produced a highly fictionalized film on Fleming's wartime exploits called *Spymaker*. Turner pulled off a casting coup by snaring Jason Connery, son of Sean Connery, to play Commander Ian Fleming. In the UK, Charles Dance appeared in *Goldeneye*, which focused on the story of James Bond's creation and Ian Fleming's personal life. Both films aired in the spring of 1990. While neither was a creative success, *Goldeneye* offered viewers a chance to see Fleming's Jamaican home and featured a brilliant performance by Dance who seemed to capture the writer's unique spirit. The two films marked the beginning of the rebirth of James Bond as a pop culture icon, a resurgence that sprang from the world of video - television, cable, satellite stations, and even laserdisc.

In 1991, the Voyager Company gave the first three James Bond films the deluxe treatment with special edition laserdiscs released through The Criterion Collection, complete with audio commentaries by the original filmmakers. While the discs were later pulled due to legal concerns, they created excitement among cinephiles. The banning of the laserdiscs only added to the allure, with copies soon selling for more than double their original cost.

Superstation TBS offered the first commercial cable airing of the Bond films with *Diamonds Are Forever*, which drew the largest movie audience in cable history. Turner Broadcasting purchased the rights to air Bond films as part of the Paretti deal. The TBS Bond screenings proved tremendously important to 007. A new generation discovered the films through these screenings, much the same way an earlier American generation discovered Tarzan on Saturday afternoon syndication runs in the 70s called *Tarzan Theater*. For those who cared to watch, TBS presented the Bond films in marathon runs that played two to three times a year and were often promoted with sexy ads reminiscent of the Bond title sequences. TBS even ran the 1954 *Climax!* adaptation of CASINO ROYALE in November 1992 (hosted by George Lazenby). Books like Steven Jay Rubin's unlicensed *James Bond Movie Encyclopedia* and the Eon Productions-sanctioned *Incredible World Of 007* provided additional reading for a growing audience of new fans eager to learn more. In October 1992, ITV broadcast *The Living Daylights* along with a 50-minute special, *30 Years Of James Bond*, the first documentary to showcase extensive behind-the-scenes materials on the making of the Bond films.

Television also gave Bond fans a chance to place the world of 007 within the stylistic context of the times. Every night cable television networks seemed to replay the entire history of post-war pop culture. Turner Broadcasting ran *The Man From U.N.C.L.E.*, TV Land played *Honey West* and *Amos Burke Secret Agent*. The Matt Helm movies and the Flint films ran often on various channels. With a few months of dedicated television watching one could quickly feel the pulse not just of the 1960s, but of any decade from the 1950s through to the present day.

Producers of current television shows tapped into the instant nostalgia of the period. Programmes such as *Quantum Leap, China Beach, Tour Of Duty, I'll Fly Away* and *The Wonder Years* harked back to times that shaped the baby boomer generation, often with references to James Bond. ABC tried to re-launch *Mission: Impossible* in 1989 but had little success. Theatrical spy thrillers that attempted to straddle the end of the Cold War - such as *Red Heat, Russia House* and *Company Men* - stumbled at the box office.

Big screen films had better creative success when they used Bond as a reference point for setting the period of the 60s and 70s. *Good Morning Vietnam* from 1987 (in which *Goldfinger* plays at a Saigon cinema), *In The Name Of The Father* (where a character introduces himself as "Bond, James Bond") and *Alive!* (where characters sing 'The Look of Love' to each other), both from 1993, are but three examples. Culturally, spymania did not exist any longer, as the failure of *Hudson Hawk* (a film replete with references to James Bond, *North By Northwest*, and the Flint movies) illustrated in 1991. The cult of espionage seemed to be some intriguing relic of the not too distant past.

While the concept of James Bond nostalgia settled in, the Bond producers were hard at work on a spin-off of the series, an animated show entitled *James Bond Jr.*, which was loosely based on an authorized children's book from 1968 - *003 ½: The Adventures of James Bond Jr.* The worldwide-syndicated series featured the exploits of 007's teenage nephew. Other characters included Q's grandson, Horace Boothroyd, known as I.Q., and Felix Leiter's surfer-dude son, Gordo. Young Bond, Jr. found himself facing danger not only from traditional Bond villains such as Dr. No, Goldfinger and Jaws, but also new creations like Dr. DeRange, Skullcap, and Ms. Fortune. Instead of SPECTRE, the primary criminal organization was S.C.U.M., an acronym for Saboteurs and Criminals United in Mayhem.

Murikami Wolf Swenson, Inc. produced 65 half-hour episodes in association with MGM and United Artists Television. The show began airing in September 1991 with a simultaneous merchandising push. *James Bond Jr.* action figures, storybooks, clothes, videos and computer games appeared in toy stores. The show did not last long, but it was a natural progression. For decades animators had capitalized on the world of 007, and, in fact, Bond had had quite an impact on children's television.

Competing against *James Bond Jr.* in 1991 was a new Disney animated programme, *Double-O Duck*. Also airing was *Pinky And The Brain*, an animated series from Steven Spielberg, featuring a mouse who saw himself as a master of world domination in prototypical Bond villain fashion.

These shows had predecessors from the mid-60s, such as 1965's *Secret Squirrel, Agent 000* (in 1993, Secret Squirrel resurfaced on the Hanna-Barbera programme *Two Stupid Dogs*) and the short-lived *Roger Ramjet*. Bond-themed cartoon series seemed a natural during the 60s. They traded off the James Bond iconography while lampooning 007's suave demeanour. Characters like *Cool McCool*

(1966) set the tone, while programmes like *Spy Shadow* (about a detective whose shadow leaves his body to spy on enemies) appeared to take themselves too seriously for their intended audience.

More established cartoon characters also wanted to associate themselves with the culture of 007 in the 1960s. The Flintstones appeared in the 1966 feature film, *A Man Called Flintstone*, where Fred and Barney were recruited as secret agents. Tom and Jerry starred in a 1967 spoof of *The Man from U.N.C.L.E.*, called *The Mouse From H.U.N.G.E.R.*, in which secret agent Jerry-akin waged a war of duelling gadgets as he attempted to steal a giant refrigerator full of cheese from the clutches of the evil Tom Thrush.

Bond's influence on children's programming continued long after spymania waned. Among the most entertaining and bizarre attempts to parlay the world of Bond into laughs for children appeared in 1970 with a cast of chimpanzees and one orang-utan. *Lancelot Link, Secret Chimp* pitted Lance, an operative of APE (Agency to Prevent Evil) against the villains of CHUMP (Criminal Headquarters for Underworld Master Plan), led by Baron von Butcher. Assisted by Mata Hairi, Lancelot Link faced such CHUMPs as Wang Fu, Ali AssaSeen, Dr. Strangemind, the Duchess and Creto. The series began shortly after the release of *On Her Majesty's Secret Service* with a two-part adventure that featured ski and toboggan action. In the first season, the show ran for one hour, padded out with musical numbers from Evolution Revolution, Lancelot Link's rock band.

One of the most successful of the Bond-themed children's series appeared in the 1980s. Just as the 007 films were moving away from technological wizardry, American television launched a character, simply known as Inspector Gadget, in a show of the same name. Gadget was part James Bond, part Inspector Clouseau, part Maxwell Smart (Don Adams provided the voice) and all Q Branch, with every aspect of his body and clothing convertible to absurd devices.

While these programmes appeared to be part of the past, they were, in fact, very much part of the present from the late 1980s onwards, due to the growth of cable and satellite television. These shows found themselves in constant rotation and airplay over the years on a variety of outlets, once again feeding spymania to a new generation who digested the music, images and iconography without the benefit of the daily headlines and nightly news of the Cold War and sexual revolution.

In 1991 and '92, James Bond's influence seemed to be everywhere, including the music charts. On the radio, heavy metal band Guns N' Roses released a rip-roaring cover version of Paul and Linda McCartney's 'Live And Let Die' in autumn 1991. The video played on MTV in heavy rotation, becoming a major hit. The following year, EMI released a compilation of Bond music that featured a second CD filled with rare and never-before-released music, including the discarded *Thunderball* theme song, 'Mr. Kiss Kiss Bang Bang'. To promote the CD, EMI distributed 'James Bond for President' buttons. The CD, including a slimmed-down version without the rare music, sold very well.

As the 90s progressed James Bond's ubiquity continued to be evident on television comedy shows such as NBC's *Saturday Night Live* and the Fox Network's *In Living Color*. Bond comedy skits had been a staple of variety and comedy shows throughout the 1960s, 70s and 80s. Sonny and Cher performed a notable Bond parody on ABC before the broadcast premiere of *Thunderball* in 1974. Russ Abbot created the running character of Basildon Bond, which was a huge hit in Britain in the 80s. *Saturday Night Live* skits from the 80s included Sting as the villainous Goldsting and Steve Martin as a tightwad Bond. Another episode featured Jimmy Breslin in a skit where Bond villains discussed theories of global domination. Their key suggestion included killing James Bond as soon as he was captured rather than explaining the current nefarious plot to him. Even without current films in the early 90s, James Bond was still popular enough for others to satirize. In 1990, Christopher Walken reprised his role as Max Zorin in a sketch called 'Lease With An Option To Kill'. Building contractors had not yet completed Zorin's secret criminal lair, so when one of his minions captured 007 (played by Phil Hartman), Zorin gave a panicked response: "I'm not ready for him yet!"

In Living Color, the Fox Broadcasting comedy-variety TV show created by the Wayans Brothers, featured two 007-themed skits in 1992-93. One had Alexandra Wentworth as Sue Goober, auditioning to be a Bond titles silhouette girl. The other highlighted an exploit of black spy Darnel Bond, Agent 006, who ordered his malt liquor shaken, not stirred and matched wits with villain Lo Fat, winning Fat's woman, Fat Ho. On *The Simpsons*, Bart placed his James Bond toy figure in the microwave, telling him, "Prepare to die, Mr. Bond."

In 1992, Celine Dion released a new version of 'If You Asked Me To', a song previously recorded by Patti LaBelle for the closing credits of *Licence To Kill*. The tune rose steadily on the Billboard Adult Contemporary and Hit Singles charts, and VH1's video rotation helped rocket Dion to superstar status.

"If there's a James Bond movie on Sunday night, I'm home watching it." Tom Hanks on *The Late Show With David Letterman*, 1993

Above: The voice of Fred Flintstone in *A Man Called Flintstone* was provided by veteran character and radio actor Alan Reed, who created the character's famous "Yabba Dabba Doo" catchphrase. There is a more recent connection between *The Flintstones* and the world of Bond: the 1994 live-action film version featured Halle Berry, who would later star in the 20th Bond film, *Die Another Day*.

"Chaos. That's the new enemy. The restraining hand that the Cold War superpowers exercised is now off."

Michael Wilson,
appearing on CBS-TV's *48 Hours* in 1993

Derek Meddings, a genius at creating special effects in miniature, began his association with the 007 films when he created the exploding poppy fields seen at the end of *Live And Let Die*. He was an Oscar winner for *Superman* (1978), and was nominated for *Moonraker*. *GoldenEye* was a showcase of his talents. As Meddings said when interviewed on the set, "I've got more miniatures to do on this than I think I've ever done on any film."

James Bond returned to comic books in 1992 when Dark Horse Comics launched a new series of 007 graphic novels with *Serpent's Tooth*, which was followed by *A Silent Armageddon*, *Shattered Helix* and *The Quasimodo Gambit*.

In the UK, Corgi toys sponsored the second annual 'World's Biggest Little Motor Show' Convention in June 1993, with full-size and model-scale versions of 007 vehicles. There were also special guests, including Honor Blackman, Desmond Llewelyn and Wing Commander Ken Wallis, pilot of the Little Nellie mini-helicopter in *You Only Live Twice*. During this period, the James Bond Fan Club sponsored luncheons at Pinewood Studios where fans could meet many of the stars and behind-the-scenes creators of the Bond films.

All this activity, which occurred outside any organized publicity campaign or appearance of a new film, primed audiences to re-embrace 007. The filmgoing public did not have to wait long to see a 1990s re-interpretation of the Bond mythos. The first shots at re-launching spymania came in the early 1990s with superstar actors playing secret agents.

As MGM and the Bond producers settled their legal issues during the winter of 1992, other producers had already begun to create present-day spies in the aftermath of the Cold War. Initially the most successful was the cinematic incarnation of Tom Clancy's reluctantly macho CIA hero, Jack Ryan. *The Hunt For Red October* (1990) was set firmly in the Cold War. The two sequels - *Patriot Games* (1992) and *Clear And Present Danger* (1994) - totally ignored East/West tensions and dealt with terrorism and the US war on drugs respectively. The Ryan films, like Bond, were based on a series of best-selling novels, but existed in an entirely different milieu. Some critics cited them as the equivalent of a modern-day James Bond, with Ryan as much of a hero of his time as Bond was a hero for the 1960s. Ryan, though, was a throwback to film heroes of an earlier era. He was

part John Wayne, part Gary Cooper. He fought against well-intentioned bureaucrats as often as he battled his direct enemies. He was a family man who did not seek action but faced any challenge when necessary. In this, Ryan was a 1990s version of the recipe that made 007 so popular.

In 1991 a French film, *La Totale*, drew attention for its comedic story of a James Bond-type character who must keep his daring world secret from his very ordinary family. In the tradition of *The Tall Blond Man With One Black Shoe*, the film turned the Bond mythos inside out.

While the movie was a modest hit in Europe, American filmmaker James Cameron saw the potential to create a film that would provide his answer to 007. Like any project directed by Cameron, the resulting film was produced on a grand scale and filled with visual pyrotechnics. Arnold Schwarzenegger gave the movie star muscle.

Schwarzenegger was another 1980s action star whose career owed much to Bond. While his big hits were largely science fiction and fantasy films, his breakthrough hit as a star of traditional modern-day action movies was 1985's *Commando*, which many critics noted was an assemblage of action sequences obviously inspired by Bond movies. Schwarzenegger, playing a retired special agent, utters dialogue that, in some scenes, virtually copies earlier Bond movies word for word. *True Lies*, however, was a far more complicated return to the turf of 007.

For *True Lies*, Cameron spent more than double the amount previously laid out on any of the Bond movies. He hired Bond veteran Peter Lamont to design the sets and opened the film with a nod to Bond pre-credit sequences, including the classic and oft-imitated image of the secret agent unzipping an outer garment to reveal a tuxedo beneath (the image had become so iconic that around the same time comedian Tim Allen used the gag during an episode of the television comedy *Home Improvement*, introducing himself to his wife as "Bond, James Bond"). Although Cameron's film departed from the Bond formula with its story of family deceit, Cameron presented the action scenes with the spectacle viewers had come to expect from 007 movies. One sequence - where Schwarzenegger in a helicopter rescues his wife from a moving car - echoed a similar scene in *Licence To Kill*. Both scenes were filmed on a disused stretch of US Highway 1 in the Florida Keys. For *True Lies*, Cameron took the location and rescue concept but created a sequence on a much, much larger scale.

1994 saw the appearance of another espionage film that not only owed a lot to its James Bond predecessors, but also helped lay the groundwork for the return of 007. *Terminal Velocity*, starring Charlie Sheen, involves the faked parachuting death of a Russian agent, many aerial freefall action scenes and witty dialogue in the Bond tradition. The film was the first to deal successfully with Russian espionage elements in the post-Cold War world.

When one character discusses the KGB, Charlie Sheen's character offers a sceptical response: "You mean KG *used* to be." Although made on a much lower budget than *True Lies*, the film offered eye-popping stunts in the Bond mould and moved at a brisk, 1990s pace. Many viewers left cinemas after both films wondering if 007 could deliver the same level of entertainment on the same grand scale.

While James Cameron filmed his lavish spy thriller, the Bond producers struggled busily with the question of how to bring 007 into the post-Cold War world. Ultimately, Cubby Broccoli, Michael Wilson and Barbara Broccoli decided not to sell the Bond franchise - if they had ever truly intended to do so in the first place. Michael Wilson has described the proposed sale as an attempt to put a value on the company. Nonetheless, after three years of legal wrangling, James Bond was primed to return to action. There was a collective sigh of relief in the film industry when MGM announced that a new writer, Michael France, had been hired to pen a James Bond screenplay, and that the project was on the fast track for the studio.

The questions facing the Bond filmmakers in 1993 were complex. How would they present 007 in a post-Cold War world? Would he still smoke? Drink? Be a womaniser? A gourmand? An expert in every known thing under the sun?

Who were the new villains? Should 007 now fight terrorists (as Schwarzenegger's character did in *True Lies*), or maybe political idealists (as Robert Redford's character did in *Sneakers*)? The early Bond villains were mythic megalomaniacal figures, but by the 1980s, 007 faced more human adversaries who were based on real geopolitical fears. Should this next Bond try to reflect a new tone of humanity in the character of 007, as movies like *Die Hard* and the Jack Ryan films had done? Or revert to the more fantasy-laden plot-lines of *You Only Live Twice*, *The Spy Who Loved Me* and *Moonraker*?

In their 21st June 1993 issue, the *New Yorker* magazine addressed the problem of James Bond's relevancy in a clever piece of comic fiction by Frank Cammuso and Hart Seely. Entitled 'Oldfinger', the spoof had 007 coming face-to-face with his former nemesis, Goldfinger. Thirty years on from their previous encounter, Goldfinger was now a bartender at a Days Inn hotel, and Bond was fighting eight sexual harassment lawsuits.

The challenges did not daunt screenwriter Michael France. His approach was simple - bring Bond into direct confrontation with the new Russia in all its post-collapse convulsive madness. As for the villain, France concocted a character straight out of the early days of the Bond novels and films - a high-ranking British intelligence officer who has defected, a villain who had been a trusted ally.

The movie, entitled *GoldenEye*, featured a pitched battle between 007 and 006 set in the former Soviet Union and in Communist Cuba. France's script, complete with a plethora of tense action scenes, took a realistic approach, with an emphasis on character. France knew the world of Bond inside and out. He had even published a short-lived Bond fan magazine called *Mr. Kiss Kiss Bang Bang* in the mid-1970s. He gave 007 a chance to symbolically face the demons that haunted him from his 30-year plus legacy by battling traitors and the detritus of corrupt Communism.

If Bond's enemies sprang from 007's legacy, the filmmakers also confronted the nature of Bond himself. Who was this character in a world where the threat of nuclear destruction seemed to grow more remote? Who was James Bond in the 1990s? The filmmakers decided after 30 years that this question needed to be re-examined. They studied the character of Bond and probed every element of 007's nature. Where the Bond films of the 1980s had stripped away Bond's artifice - his gadgets and unflappable nature - the first Bond film of the 1990s promised to challenge Bond's emotional core as a character.

In the spring of 1993, when France was hired, MGM proclaimed full support for the new film, including a $40 million dollar budget. The producers declined to answer who would play Bond, but they referred to Timothy Dalton as "the Bond of record". Nearly a year later, the filmmakers felt they were ready to move forward. Unfortunately it seemed that the filmmaking world was not waiting for James Bond. Pinewood Studios apologized, but said they were too booked up to house the new Bond film (the Sean Connery film, *First Knight*, captured much of the available stage space). MGM made little secret of its strong doubts regarding the box office appeal of Timothy Dalton after such a long gap, and when the filmmakers

finally made a formal approach, Dalton declared he was ready to move away from Bond. The studio also wanted major changes to the script for the new film even though it was scheduled to begin shooting in the autumn. Suddenly, the Bond producers found themselves without a studio, a star or an approved script.

The press immediately speculated about Dalton's replacement. While some likely contenders received attention, such as Mel Gibson, Liam Neeson, Hugh Grant, Daniel Day Lewis and Ralph Fiennes, more hyperbolic articles caused problems. Film critic Gene Siskel proposed Denzel Washington. Another writer wrote a newspaper column proclaiming that US basketball star Michael Jordan should play 007. *Entertainment Weekly* printed a catty article with Hollywood luminaries saying that in order to invigorate the series the new Bond should be Sharon Stone or Eddie Murphy. The article launched a frenzy of rumours of bizarre casting choices, all of which made the actual casting more difficult.

In the end, as they had done with Roger Moore and Timothy Dalton before him, the producers chose an actor they had considered previously, and Pierce Brosnan finally slid into Bond's tailored tuxedo.

"Both Sean Connery and I will be forgotten after everybody sees Pierce." Roger Moore

Roger Moore visited the set of *GoldenEye* (**top**) and reported himself very pleased with his successor. Three of the former Bond actors - Moore, Brosnan and Dalton - later appeared at a memorial for Cubby Broccoli in London.

Brosnan was far and away the public's number one choice for 007. On television, entertainment programmes launched unofficial polls, which Brosnan always won by a landslide. Reporters dogged the actor, asking him if he had been cast. He had seemed perfect for the role in 1986, and now, eight years later, Brosnan's time had come. It only arrived, though, after a tortuous journey.

Just six months after losing out on the role in 1986, Brosnan appeared in a couple of decidedly 007-ish commercials for Diet Coke. The first was broadcast on 25th January 1987, premiering during Super Bowl XXI. On January 24th of the following year, a second commercial aired during Super Bowl XXII, featuring a tuxedo-wearing Brosnan fighting ninjas aboard a moving train. Under threat of legal action from the Bond producers, the commercial was quickly pulled from the airwaves. Later, Kevin McClory and Brosnan discussed the idea of a syndicated James Bond television series based on McClory's limited *Thunderball* rights. Again, legal action forestalled progress, and the series never materialized. For the public, constant coverage of these events in the press only increased the sense that Pierce Brosnan would be a natural choice to play James Bond.

Brosnan's first exposure to 007 had come at age ten (he was born on 16th May 1953), when he and his parents first arrived in London from Navan, County Meath, Ireland. They took him to see his first movie in London - *Goldfinger*. "It was magic," Brosnan recalled in 1995. "Sheer magic." At 16, Brosnan took a job in south London as a commercial artist. He began frequenting the Oval House Theatre Club and became involved in their productions. After spending a few months as a fire-eater in a circus, he decided that formal acting lessons might benefit him and began attending the Drama Centre in London.

After graduation in 1976, Brosnan became acting assistant stage manager at the Theatre Royal, York. Six months later, playwright Tennessee Williams chose Brosnan to create the role of McCabe in the British premiere of *Red Devil Battery Sign*. This led to other stage roles and, in 1980, his first television role, as a trainer in the horse-racing docu-drama *Murphy's Stroke*. He made his feature-film debut shortly afterwards, as an IRA assassin who murders Bob Hoskins in the acclaimed film *The Long Good Friday*. Former James Bond director Guy Hamilton selected Brosnan for a non-speaking bit part in the star-studded *The Mirror Crack'd*, where his role consisted of resting his head on Elizabeth Taylor's bosom.

His American television debut came in 1981, when he appeared in the miniseries *The Manions Of America*. Brosnan then landed the role of Remington Steele, which made him an international star. After *Remington Steele* ended, he appeared in the miniseries *Noble House*, and made a memorable impression as a cold-blooded Russian assassin in the 1986 film *The Fourth Protocol*. Other film work followed, including *Nomads*, *The Deceivers*, *Mr. Johnson* and *Mrs. Doubtfire*.

When his wife, Cassandra Harris, was diagnosed with ovarian cancer, Brosnan put his career on the back burner. Harris succumbed on 29th December 1991. Brosnan became a spokesman for the health concerns of women, and served as Ambassador for Women's Health Issues for the Permanent Charities Committee of the Entertainment Industries. Dealing with his wife's illness and death brought a new sense of *gravitas* to Brosnan's non-comedic performances, an ability to project vulnerability and flinty reserve at the same time. It was a quality that would serve 007 well.

The announcement of Brosnan as Bond, on 7th June 1994, came with a flurry of press coverage, making headlines around the world. Shortly afterwards, challenges mounted for the filmmakers, particularly the grave issue of producer Cubby Broccoli's health. In the summer of 1994, at the age of 86, Broccoli underwent emergency coronary bypass surgery, from which he never fully recovered. The immediate impact of his surgery on *GoldenEye* was personal. Michael

Wilson and Barbara Broccoli had to soldier on with terribly little involvement from the man who had shepherded 16 Bond films to the screen. They would be forced to work in London while Cubby Broccoli convalesced in Los Angeles. Wilson and Broccoli already knew *GoldenEye* was a one-shot chance to re-introduce Bond. After Cubby's operation, they also knew that the fate of the film - and James Bond - rested on their shoulders. The torch had been suddenly and unexpectedly passed.

The first test facing Wilson and Broccoli was securing a director - the first new director of a Bond film in 15 years. The producers considered several top-tier candidates, and finally chose Martin Campbell, who had proved his mettle with the BBC series *Reilly, Ace Of Spies* and the much respected espionage drama, *Edge Of Darkness*. Campbell brought a highly-organized sensibility to the film, carefully mapping out scenes, dissecting shots and allowing single sequences to be compiled from a myriad sources - first unit, second unit, model unit and CGI. He also brought a deep emotional involvement, becoming passionately obsessed with getting the film just right. Campbell totally immersed himself in Bond, constantly challenging everyone to deliver their best.

In mid-summer James Cameron's *True Lies* hit theatres. The film's massive success was both good and bad news for Bond. The movie illustrated the potential audience for 007, but it also raised the stakes. MGM and the producers worried that the new Bond film was not ready, that it needed to be loaded with stronger action, leavened with better humour and focused with sharper dialogue. MGM had counted on releasing *GoldenEye* during the summer of 1995, but the producers wanted more time. Time would cost money. Pre-production was well underway with shooting to begin in the autumn. MGM ultimately decided the filmmakers knew best and the release of the next Bond film was pushed to November 1995.

The continued creative work on the script eventually led to the hiring of Bruce Feirstein, who came in with a two-sentence guide to re-introducing 007: "The world has changed. James Bond has not."

Michael G. Wilson (**top**) had received an engineering degree from Harvey Mudd College and was studying law at Stanford University when, during his summer break, his stepfather Cubby Broccoli asked him to help out with *Goldfinger* in Kentucky. Among his other tasks, Wilson briefly doubled for Harold Sakata in a long shot. After law school, Wilson became a partner in a prestigious Washington, DC firm. In 1972, he joined Eon Productions in a legal/administrative capacity, and went on to become one of the guiding lights of the cinematic James Bond.

A graduate of Loyola University in Los Angeles, Barbara Broccoli (**above**) majored in motion picture and television communications. Only two years old when her father premiered *Dr. No*, she had grown up with the Bond films. She became an assistant director on *Octopussy* and *A View To A Kill*. She was associate producer, with Tom Pevsner, on *The Living Daylights* and *Licence To Kill*. For the latter film, she oversaw the filming of the thrilling tanker truck climax. *GoldenEye* was her first Bond film as a producer.

New Zealand-born director Martin Campbell (**left**) made his debut directing an episode of the TV series *The Professionals* - a show which many considered a hard-edged answer to Bond in the 1970s. After directing more TV series and telefilms, he went to the United States and directed the suspense thriller *Criminal Law*. More film work followed, including *Defenseless* and *No Escape*, before he landed the *GoldenEye* assignment.

In September 1981, Pierce Brosnan and his first wife Cassandra Harris (**inset, opposite**) travelled to Los Angeles looking for work. Brosnan's very first audition was for *Remington Steele*. Before returning to Britain, the couple had dinner at Cubby Broccoli's home. Driving back to their hotel, Brosnan jokingly repeated the famous line, "The name is Bond. James Bond."

With Pinewood Studios out of the frame, the filmmakers needed to find a new production facility. After searching in Europe, Canada and the United States for another studio that would be able to handle the demands of a James Bond production, the producers decided that the best alternative was to create one.

Executive producer Tom Pevsner and associate producer Anthony Waye eventually located an abandoned wartime plane factory and airfield in Leavesden, owned by Rolls Royce. A lease was negotiated, with Rolls Royce giving Eon Productions *carte blanche* in converting the factory into a working studio. Delta Doric, the firm that had rebuilt the 007 Stage at Pinewood following the fire in 1984, were called in. Within five months, they transformed the site into a film facility with 1.25 million square feet of interior space - enough to cover the whole of Pinewood Studios.

Five working soundstages were constructed, as well as a carpenter shop, a prop shop, paint shop, model shop, a special effects stage, dressing rooms and office space. In addition, there was an enormous backlot which could support several major productions simultaneously.

Production designer Peter Lamont, with the experience of fifteen 007 films behind him, made good use of the space that Leavesden

ПОЧТАМПТСКАЯ ул.
14 ← → 20

made available. Soon, the facility housed sets for MI6 headquarters, the Severnaya control station, an opulent Monte Carlo casino, the nerve gas plant infiltrated by Bond and 006 in the film's opening, a lavish Turkish bath and spa where 007 would have a memorable encounter with Xenia Onatopp, Trevelyan's ultra-modern satellite control room, and Valentin Zukovsky's nightclub lair.

Most impressive was the exterior backlot set, which was a recreation of the streets of St. Petersburg for the film's spectacular tank chase sequence. Outfitted with a variety of authentic Russian-style telephone kiosks, statues and street signs, the set intercut seamlessly with second unit action that was filmed on location.

Converting the factory into a studio ended up being a wise and cost-conscious decision on the part of the filmmakers, and a boon to the British film industry. In the years since *GoldenEye* wrapped, Leavesden Studios has housed many other productions, including *Star Wars: Episode 1*, *Sleepy Hollow*, *Longitude*, *The Beach* and the Harry Potter series.

The film also included the requisite lavish locations audiences had come to expect in a Bond film, including Puerto Rico, Monaco, France and Switzerland, in addition to St. Petersburg. In every

The tank chase in *GoldenEye* was partially filmed on the backlot at Leavesden, where production designer Peter Lamont and his skilled artisans recreated the streets of St. Petersburg. It took 175 workmen just over six weeks to complete the set, constructed over an area of two acres with 62 miles of scaffolding supporting the fabricated buildings. For the shot of the tank bursting through the wall (**opposite**), portions of the set were built with brick-size thermalite blocks.

Delta Doric, the company that rebuilt the 007 Stage after the disastrous fire in 1984, spent five months converting the abandoned wartime Rolls Royce plane factory and airfield at Leavesden (**top**) into a film facility large enough to hold the elaborate sets demanded by a James Bond film.

With its distinctive cowling, Alec Trevelyan's private locomotive (**middle**) earned a nickname on the set - 'Darth Train'.

Soon after the completion of *GoldenEye*, Derek Meddings (**bottom**) succumbed to cancer. Special effects supervisor Chris Corbould said, "We were nominated for a BAFTA Award for *GoldenEye*. You know, it would have been nice to have sat at that table with him. He was just such a sweet, sweet man."

aspect, there was a push for the best production value and an effort to make certain the final product would reflect the care and expense taken to make the film.

The key to *GoldenEye*'s success would not be the clever sets, elaborate model work, nor even the spectacular locations. This film's ability to make an impact relied on presenting an incarnation of James Bond movie-goers could embrace. When Bruce Feirstein came on board after a rewrite of the Michael France script by Geoffrey Caine, he worked closely with the filmmakers to deliver the James Bond audiences knew and loved at every turn. Feirstein and Martin Campbell made certain Brosnan's first turn as 007 was filled with every Bond touchstone imaginable. Bond would drive an Aston Martin DB5. He would wear a tux. He would gamble at a casino and win a high-stakes game of *chemin de fer*. Unlike Timothy Dalton, Pierce Brosnan's Bond would not throw away the signature introduction "Bond, James Bond." Brosnan's 007 would deliver the classic line in full close-up. Feirstein and Campbell knew they had to create classic scenes between Bond and Q, Bond and Moneypenny, as well as Bond and M. For the latter two scenes, the filmmakers were faced with the need to hire new actors. Feirstein and Campbell twisted the relationship between Bond and Moneypenny, making her the one female who patronizingly disregards his incessant flirting, which brought a layer of 90s sophistication to the on-screen repartee.

For the scene between Bond and M, Campbell and Feirstein pushed the boundaries even further. Somewhere in the Roger

Moore era, M had become little more than a foil for 007. By the Dalton films, the head of MI6 seemed to be a doddering oaf. The filmmakers decided to take a huge risk: to cast a woman to play the role of Bond's chief. Many feared this meant a politically correct, watered-down Bond. However, as written by Feirstein, this M was every bit as tough and steely as her male counterparts; perhaps more so. She set the tone of the film by calling Bond a "sexist, misogynist dinosaur, a relic of the Cold War". Feirstein's M may have been the new head of MI6, but she was also telling the audience exactly who James Bond was. In this the filmmakers continued down the path marked by Michael France of directly confronting the Bond legacy, embracing it and re-focusing the character for a new decade.

The largest convergence of fiction and reality came from the casting of Dame Judi Dench as M. The historical precedent for making the intelligence chief in the new Bond film a woman came in 1992 when Stella Rimington became the Director General of MI5, Britain's internal spy agency. She was the first woman to attain the post, and the first head of the agency to be officially identified. During her tenure, she sought to make the agency more open, even publishing a brochure that explained MI5's duties and functions.

After being cast as M, Dench said, "I was absolutely delighted when I got the call because I've been a huge Bond fan for years, and Bernard Lee was a great friend of mine. I can now refer to myself as a Bond woman, and will indeed for the rest of my career."

During the course of the film virtually every character discusses the popular culture image of James Bond. A CIA agent calls him a

decades. The name of the satellite and the movie referred to Ian Fleming's Jamaican home where he wrote the Bond novels.

More recent events mirrored the villain's use of the GoldenEye satellite via a hostile takeover. Early in the development of surveillance satellites, governments realized that an unmanned orbiting piece of equipment, much like a parked car, could be stolen or, to use the term of the intelligence community, spoofed. Satellite spoofing involves taking control of the craft's functions, which might include one nation

"I have no doubt that the fact M became a woman was directly related to the fact that I became Director General of MI5." Stella Rimington

"stiff-assed Brit". A Russian gangster mocks his penchant for martinis "shaken, not stirred". His main love interest complains that Bond is immature, just playing around like "boys with toys". The harshest words come from the villain, the former 006, Alec Trevelyan, who asks if "the vodka martinis silence the screams of all the men you've killed". The filmmakers also decided not to pull back on the sexuality in the film. After all, the hedonistic attitude was a key aspect audiences expected from the character.

"Bond is Bond. He is a sexist. Completely," said Pierce Brosnan. "And if you don't make him that, then you don't have a Bond movie. And people want a Bond movie."

The new Bond film also took 007 behind the Iron Curtain. Although overtures had been made in the mid-70s, bringing Bond into the new Russia was the ultimate statement about James Bond in the post-Cold War world. Even so, in the end the filmmakers only sent in a second unit crew to St. Petersburg to shoot location shots and some amazing stunts for the tank chase.

The story for the film had its roots in reality, and not just the world of post-Cold War Russia. The film opens with a sequence during the Cold War where 007 and 006 raid a Soviet chemical weapons plant. During and after the Gulf War, both Russia and the United States had come under heavy criticism for stockpiling large quantities of chemical weapons despite the fact that both countries had long ago signed a global treaty proclaiming they would never use them.

Orbiting weapons in space had also long been banned by treaties, but films, including the Bond movies with *Diamonds Are Forever*, had often used the concept of a killer satellite. The GoldenEye satellite concept - a nuclear pulse weapon which would render the enemy's electronics useless, and therefore would make retaliatory missile launches impossible in the case of nuclear war - had been discussed for

forcing a foreign country's spy satellite to transmit its high-resolution images to the spoofer's receivers. Even private citizens have managed to spoof telecommunications satellites. The most famous spoofing incident occurred in 1986 when a mysterious message from one 'Captain Midnight' appeared over HBO's eastern US feed via the Galaxy 1 satellite. That incident sent shockwaves through the communications industry and the government. The same technique used by 'Captain Midnight' could have disrupted sensitive US Defense Department transmissions, zapped errant information to monitoring banks at NORAD, or redirected encrypted CIA communiqués. Government officials were not comforted when the mastermind was found to be a 25-year-old satellite TV dealer in Ocala, Florida. Appropriately, the film he interrupted on HBO was *The Falcon And The Snowman*, a movie about the Christopher Boyce espionage case.

The real 'Captain Midnight', John MacDougall, was not too different from *GoldenEye*'s Boris in certain respects. Both were smart, young, and felt under-appreciated for their knowledge. Boris, though, possessed the skills to be able to spoof satellites and computers into wiring billions of pounds sterling to hidden bank accounts, not to mention the ability to target and fire the lethal GoldenEye weapon.

Dame Judi Dench (**opposite**) won high praise for her portrayal of M. "I enjoy playing M," said Dench. "She adopts quite a tough line in this movie, but, then again, how would you become head of MI6 by being anything but tough?"

When asked if she had any trepidation about taking the role of Moneypenny, Samantha Bond (**above**) said, "Because I do such a lot of classical work in the theatre, I'm quite used to taking on roles that have been played by other people. In that sense, it's not more daunting than any other job that I spend my life doing. Having said that, the problem with Moneypenny is that she's kind of this sort of fantasy next-door girl that everyone has a very clear idea of. So that's a little troublesome to one's mind."

"I think every man wants to be James Bond... and it's always been my secret desire, too." Famke Janssen

Opposite: Famke Janssen (**top left**, **middle left** and **bottom right**) was thrilled to land the part of Xenia Onatopp. "Xenia gave me a great opportunity to be all the things I would sometimes like to be, but could never get away with," she said. "She loves men - in her own way. There's a kind of animal attraction between her and James, because Xenia's definitely an animal."

Sean Bean (**top middle**) had been rumoured as a 007 contender before landing the role of Alec Trevelyan. "The villain has always been an integral ingredient to the success of the Bond films, and Trevelyan is a good adversary to Bond in this adventure," said Bean. "They are a good match - each knowing that the other can be a totally professional, ruthless killer when he wants to be - so the final confrontation between them is powerful and very spectacular."

Rounding out the cast of *GoldenEye* were Alec Cumming (**middle right**), Gottfried John (**bottom right**) and Robbie Coltrane (**bottom left**), who also appeared in *The World Is Not Enough* as Russian arms dealer Valentin Zukovsky. Coltrane enjoyed his dialogue in *GoldenEye*. "I do get to say the immortal line when the gun comes up, 'Walther PPK, 7.65 millimetre. I only know three men who carry these, and I believe I've killed two of them.' I mean, I would pay to say a line like that!"

"The only reason I do Bond is because I'm a fan of Bond, and not because I particularly like doing title sequences." Daniel Kleinman

As producers, Michael Wilson and Barbara Broccoli faced the daunting task of striking the right balance between new and old both creatively within the film and with the team which would make the movie. One crew member who seemed irreplaceable was Maurice Binder, whose imagery was essential to the Bond film-going experience. They turned to a commercial and music video director who had long admired Binder's work and received amazing results.

In 1989, Daniel Kleinman had directed the music video for Gladys Knight's 'Licence To Kill'. He didn't hesitate to take the job. "I grew up watching Bond," said Kleinman. "I always loved the title sequences." The video was an homage to Maurice Binder, and Wilson and Broccoli remembered the respect and talent evident in Kleinman's work.

Using state-of-the-art computer graphics, Kleinman created a beautiful Bondian title sequence for *GoldenEye* in the Binder

tradition. "We had a bit of a discussion at the beginning as to whether we should carry on some of the classic motifs of the girls and guns and what have you," said Kleinman. "And I was very much of the opinion that, yes, one should stick with some of the formula and just sort of update it and freshen it up a bit."

Part of that freshening-up included giving the opening gunbarrel a more three-dimensional appearance. "I had a James Bond gun when I was a kid," said Kleinman. "I collected the bubble gum cards. You know, I was a fan and it's a great buzz to be part of the family of it and work on it."

Kleinman's titles were designed for the new title song, which was written by U2 band members Bono and The Edge and performed by Tina Turner. Turner followed the long line of classic *chanteuses* who belted out Bond songs, plus she, like Bond, was a survivor of the 60s who retained her popularity in the 1990s. Bono and The Edge had their own reasons for writing the title song. They had often stayed at Ian Fleming's Jamaican home, Goldeneye, as guests of Chris Blackwell, the current owner. They thanked Blackwell for letting them use Goldeneye in the liner notes on the CD release of the song.

The score was composed by Eric Serra, best known for his music for *La Femme Nikita*. Serra wanted to try a very 90s score, steering clear of the big brass sound of John Barry. The result proved to be a controversial one. Another composer, John Altman, was brought in to rescore the tank chase sequence, basing it on 'The James Bond Theme', which many felt was underused in Serra's score.

A key change in the direction of the series came in the globalization of 007's character through the nature of his iconography. Bond had always carried a German gun, but now, in addition to his personal Aston Martin, he would drive the German BMW Z3. Though he would still wear finely tailored suits, they would be from

Though Daniel Kleinman got his start directing music videos, he rarely did them again after *GoldenEye*. "Partly that's because I feel like the Bond title sequence is almost like the greatest music video in the world, and it's seen by more people," said Kleinman. "It is the greatest title sequence to do in the world. I think anything else would have to be pretty special not to be an anti-climax after that."

Brioni of Italy instead of Savile Row. In place of a Rolex, 007 would wear a sleek Omega watch. The linking of top brands to 007 also reinforced the idea of Bond as the ultimate statement in masculine style.

As the film completed shooting, a massive and remarkable publicity campaign began. During the summer of 1995, teaser trailers announced the return of James Bond in cinemas across the globe. In the autumn, BMW launched a $10 million media blitz tying their new car to James Bond. Print ads for Church's shoes and Yves Saint Laurent cosmetics touted their appearance in the new Bond film. In the US and Great Britain, networks screened hour-long specials on James Bond. Saks Fifth Avenue's flagship store in Manhattan featured clothes from *GoldenEye* in their store windows. All in all, MGM and companies who wanted to be a part of the re-introduction of 007 spent $55 million to promote the new film.

Creation Entertainment, which had sponsored a James Bond convention in Los Angeles in the autumn of 1994, held a convention in New York to coincide with the launch of *GoldenEye*. On 13th November 1995, MGM staged the largest James Bond premiere in history at New York's Radio City Music Hall. The event became a media frenzy. BMW launched the Z3 with a major press show in Central Park, and held an exclusive pre-premiere party at the famous Rainbow Room at Rockefeller Center. The premiere itself opened doors to fans and celebrities, including Kathleen Turner, Molly Ringwald, Gary Sinise and Lauren Bacall. Onlookers clogged the Avenue of the Americas to see the stars, and traffic in mid-town Manhattan came to a standstill. Inside, after brief introductions of the filmmakers, the lights dimmed. Barbara Broccoli and Michael Wilson watched as the giant curtains parted in the cavernous cinema. Would *GoldenEye* work? Had they delivered a movie that was a cultural anachronism, or an exciting cinematic experience?

Within moments, the producers had their answer. The audience roared, cheered and applauded during the pre-credits sequence, first at the mind-boggling bungee jump from high off a dam, then at Brosnan's first close-up, and finally when Bond managed to catch an out-of-control plane in a mid-air motorcycle-freefall stunt. Even after 33 years, no one knew how to open a film like James Bond. The excitement continued throughout the movie. At the exclusive post-premiere party at the Museum of Modern Art, the enthusiasm was palpable. The film, filled with exotic characters, felt at once both new and fresh while delivering the classic ingredients of Bond's past successes.

The re-introduction of Bond was not, in fact, a re-invention of the character. Instead, the filmmakers had bet that unapologetically delivering 007 to the audience would make Bond stand out in a world of human-scale cinema heroes and testosterone-driven action films. *GoldenEye* did not stint on the action, but Martin Campbell allowed Pierce Brosnan to seduce the audience with cool confidence. Brosnan's Bond was sexy, sleek, and very much of the moment. He might be, as M declares, "a relic of the Cold War", but he never seemed more comfortable with himself, his vices and his victories.

For MGM/UA, the new Bond film signalled a massive investment for the still cash-strapped studio. They needed a hit film, and booked *GoldenEye* onto more than 2,700 screens in the US and Canada, 10% of the total movie screens available. On Friday, 17th November 1995, *GoldenEye* opened nationwide in the US. Audiences packed theatres as cinema managers booked special late-night shows to accommodate the overflow crowds. Fans embraced the new film, the new star and the new style. Four days after the US opening, the film premiered in London with a grand party at the Imperial War Museum following the screening. The film continued to open to cheering crowds. When Pierce Brosnan refused to attend the French premiere to protest against French government nuclear tests in the South Pacific, the event was cancelled, but the resulting worldwide publicity seemed to bolster the notion of a very current-thinking, 1990s Bond. Ticket sales in France did not appear to suffer as a result, more than doubling the box office of *Licence To Kill*.

In the US the film sold over 24 million tickets, launching Bond back to the box office heights of *Moonraker* and *Diamonds Are Forever*, and almost three times the number of tickets sold for *Licence To Kill*. As importantly, the film cracked the $100,000,000 mark in US box office, a key benchmark for blockbuster status. Internationally, *GoldenEye* more than doubled the take of the previous Bond film.

In the years since 007 had last appeared on cinema screens, the market for movies had changed. While *GoldenEye* raked in a staggering $355 million worldwide, films no longer made the majority of their revenue from ticket sales. In the following year, *GoldenEye* was released on video and special edition laserdisc. The film played on pay-per-view systems and pay cable outlets like HBO. Each new market appealed to different types of viewers, and in each one *GoldenEye* proved to be a huge success.

The movie's winning combination of humour, action and elegance proved that James Bond was not bound by the confines of the Cold War. He was a hero every bit as relevant in the 1990s as he had been in the 1960s. In fact, *GoldenEye*'s success helped launch a new wave of spymania.

Opposite: Wayne Michaels performed the bungee jump that opens *GoldenEye*, leaping off the 750-foot high Contra Dam near Lugano, Switzerland. The stunt set a world record for a leap against a fixed object. "It's pushing the limits of what can be physically done," said Michaels, who performed the leap twice. "You're trying desperately to hit a pocket of air that will take you away from the wall, and the winds that are whipping around the bowl of the dam toss you like a leaf."

11. During the summer of 1995, while *GoldenEye* was wrapping production at the converted Leavesden aircraft factory, scenes for another spy film were being shot on the Albert R. Broccoli 007 stage at Pinewood Studios: a big-screen re-interpretation of the television series *Mission: Impossible*. The film, which starred Tom Cruise - the biggest box office star in the world at the time - was originally scheduled to compete directly with *GoldenEye* during the winter of 1995, but re-shoots delayed the premiere until the summer of 1996. Despite generally lacklustre reviews, the movie played to huge audiences and ultimately outgrossed *GoldenEye* by nearly one hundred million dollars worldwide. Spymania was back, but with a twist. In the 1960s, James Bond had been the undisputed ruler of the universe of cinematic espionage. He was the *sine qua non* of secret agents, untouched in the scope and scale of his adventures and unmatched at the box office. Cubby Broccoli and Harry Saltzman had gambled that audiences saw James Bond as the star - and not the actor who portrayed 007. Consequently the producers had been able to perpetuate the series through five different actors and changes in the creative team. For many years, the Bond

Return Of The Classic

films were a genre unto themselves. In the 1980s and 90s, top-tier actors and filmmakers who had grown up on the Bond films began moving into the territory of 007 with tremendous success.

The sarin gas released by the Aum Shinrikyo cult in the Tokyo subway in March 1995 (**top**) killed 13 people and injured several hundred. The cult had also used sarin undetected in the Japanese city of Matsumoto in June 1994.

In June 2000, the US 9th Circuit Court of Appeals dismissed charges against an FBI sniper involved in both the Waco (**above**) and Ruby Ridge incidents, citing "Supremacy Clause immunity" as its rationale. Judge Alex Kozinski wrote a dissent in which he castigated the court for creating a "007 standard", saying "Because the 007 standard for the use of deadly force now applies to all law enforcement agencies in our circuit - federal, state and local - it should make us all feel less secure."

Jonathan Pryce (**opposite page**) achieved his Bond villain look in a suit by Kenzo. "We went through elaborate well-tailored business suits, colours and ties and everything, and that suit had always been in the background, because it looked a bit like a Bond villain suit. We tried it, and it does look good."

In 1981, Brian DePalma, the director of *Mission: Impossible* and the creator of many Hitchcock pastiches, had directed a film entitled *Blow Out*, which featured John Lithgow as a white-haired killer who draws on a black glove before strangling his victims with a garrotte wire concealed in his watch. The character was a clear reference to Red Grant from *From Russia With Love*. With spy films back in vogue in the 1990s, filmmakers like DePalma and stars like Tom Cruise and Arnold Schwarzenegger could compete for box office dollars on a par with 007 like no cinematic spy could have done in the 1960s.

With *Mission: Impossible*, DePalma and Cruise tried to turn the entire superspy genre inside out, making the hero of the 1960s series a villain in the film. Traitorous figures were a re-occurring theme in the spy films of the mid-1990s, and for good reason. While there was no shortage of larger than life rogues from current events - such as Libyan dictator Muammar al-Qaddafi, Saddam Hussein, president of Iraq, and Slobodan Milosevic, the Serbian nationalist who spearheaded the bloody conflict in Bosnia Herzegovina in the early 90s - those villains, like the Communist rulers of the 1960s, seemed almost too real for most filmmakers (an exception was 1997's *Peacemaker*, with George Clooney as the Bond-esque secret agent and a plot centred around terrorists from the Balkans). More and more, during this period, the cinematic enemy seemed to come from within. Both *GoldenEye* and *Mission: Impossible* dealt with this issue, as did 1996's *The Rock*, starring Sean Connery, in which disgruntled US Marines threaten to launch chemical weapons onto the city of San Francisco. Connery's character in the film is a former MI6 agent held in prison for 30 years, a nod to his Bond legacy.

In the real world, with no superpower left to fight, the West seemed to be at war with itself. In February 1994, Federal agents arrested Aldrich Ames, a 52-year-old CIA employee turned traitor. Ames seemed to define the banality of evil. He sold secrets for money, drank too much and often received poor evaluations from his superiors. Despite flimsy explanations, Ames's ever-expanding wealth over the previous decade was rarely questioned. He proclaimed that he had become a traitor because he believed the CIA had become little more than a sham that worked only to justify its existence. Because of Ames's position, he gave the Soviets (and later the Russians) the names of key double agents who were summarily executed. When National Public Radio reported on a government auction of Ames's personal belongings, the reporter claimed, with tongue in cheek, that a cassette deck contained a tape of 'The James Bond Theme'. Indeed Ames, like the Walkers in the 1980s, was accused of falling into the James Bond Syndrome.

Treachery existed worldwide - and was often unrelated to espionage. In Japan, a religious sect called Aum Shinrikyo launched an attack on the Tokyo subway system, releasing deadly sarin nerve gas in March 1995. Another nerve gas attack in Yokohama followed in April. Both events seemed to defy logic or rational motivation. In the US in April 1995, an embittered ex-soldier named Timothy McVeigh drove a Ryder truck filled with crude explosives into downtown Oklahoma City. McVeigh parked the truck, walked to a nearby car and drove off. A short while later, the truck exploded and the blast shattered the Alfred P. Murrah Federal building, collapsing much of the structure and killing 167 people inside. Many of the victims were children.

The attack, by an American on Americans, was partially inspired by a siege two years earlier in Waco, Texas, where Federal agents were unable to get members of an armed religious sect led by a gun-loving zealot named David Koresh to surrender. The government eventually used armoured vehicles to knock down walls and pump tear gas inside. The sect leaders chose martyrdom over arrest, and started to kill each other or themselves, as well as burning down their own compound. Over 80 died.

The world suddenly seemed to become a very perilous place. The likes of Shoko Asahara (leader of Aum Shinrikyo), Timothy McVeigh and David Koresh revealed a dangerous, messianic, *fin de siècle* trend in global terror. These were people who were not only misguided, but who, with religious fervour, embraced evil, mocked justice, and who had no regard for human life. They also existed in a time when their particular acts of terror took on operatic proportions.

Those events shared a common thread with other major cultural touchstones of the era: the Los Angeles riots, the bombing of the World Trade Center in 1992, the Russian military attack on the Moscow parliament building, and the seemingly never ending saga of O.J. Simpson. The link? Each of these events was afforded non-stop, 24-hour coverage on CNN and other newsmedia outlets. The populace at large watched the horrors unfold in near real-time, narrated by a crew of glossy-looking news anchors. Each tragedy was often given its own logo and title - 'Oklahoma City Bombing', 'Tokyo Subway Attack', 'Siege At Waco'. Increasingly, the media began to latch on to stories which captivated viewers by developing a strong dramatic arc. Drama, sex and violence were what sold both in news reporting and entertainment. Two US presidential hopefuls - Senators Gary Hart and Joe Biden - found themselves forced to drop out of the 1988 race because of media revelations. In 1992, right-wing groups worked hard to unearth damaging personal information on Bill Clinton as he

ran for President, although their efforts were so transparent that they proved futile. In England, various factions of the Royal family seemed to court the press with damaging stories about the state of the marriages of both the Prince of Wales and the Duke of York.

The media obsession with the British Royal family quickly became a daily horror show. Newspapers lined up as pro-Princess Diana or pro-Prince Charles. Photos of Princess Diana, one of the most photographed women in history, were so valuable as to entice the owner of the gym she frequented to allow hidden cameras to be secreted in the ceiling. The results were mundane shots of a woman using a weight machine. Because that woman happened to be Princess Diana, the photos ended up on the front page of newspapers. Nothing was sacred. Tapes of mobile phone conversations found their way to the media and were played on the air, transcribed and printed. Neither the media nor the public could seem to get enough.

Sagas of private sex lives seemed to capture and sway public opinion, whereas other stories, such as the massive genocide in Rwanda and deadly bombings in India, garnered little media attention. Some observers raised the question: if news outlets like CNN were deciding what was newsworthy based on ratings, could they also manipulate events for their own potentially more nefarious purposes? During the post-production of *GoldenEye*, as the filmmakers thought about the next Bond movie, Bruce Feirstein decided the question was worthy of further exploration. The concept was simple: a media mogul as the villain. Feirstein boiled down the essence of the concept to one line, which he wrote on a card: "Words are the new weapons; satellites are the new artillery."

Feirstein's idea resonated with Michael Wilson. In Britain, the press barons had long held massive power, which they often used to support political parties and candidates with unvarnished abandon. In the US, newspaper tycoons such as William Randolph Hearst helped define yellow journalism. Hearst has been credited with forcing the US into the Spanish-American War before the beginning of the 20th century with lurid stories of Spanish abuses of American prisoners in Cuba and accusations that Spain had sunk the *USS Maine*. The more recent incarnations of Hearst-like moguls included Ted Turner, the

founder of CNN; Rupert Murdoch, the Australian owner of Sky Broadcasting, Fox Studios, and dozens of newspapers; and Robert Maxwell, who in 1970 was deemed by Britain's Department of Trade and Industry to be unfit to run a public company.

Maxwell, in particular, was a fascinating character, born in Czechoslovakia, family killed in the Holocaust, war hero. Maxwell built his empire through hard work, but his business practices drew fire. Despite the Department of Trade's efforts, Maxwell eventually owned one of the largest media empires in the world. Maxwell was also alleged to have links to the Israeli intelligence service - Mossad. In 1991, when his media empire, loaded with debt, began to crumble, Maxwell raided the pension funds of the companies he controlled in an effort to save his business. When the pension funds proved to be too little, Maxwell apparently committed suicide off the Canary Islands.

Media tycoons always seemed to want a greater voice in public policy. Rupert Murdoch seemed to be bent on giving his news a right-wing slant. Robert Maxwell had actually served in Britain's Labour government during the 1960s. In 1994, Italy elected a media tycoon, Silvio Berlusconi, as prime minister.

Originally, Feirstein wanted his new Bond villain to use his media empire to launch a war over Hong Kong as part of a plot of personal revenge. The handover of Hong Kong from Britain to the Chinese was scheduled for the summer of 1997, which was months before the release of the new Bond film. The filmmakers realized the film could seem outdated before it hit cinemas, and a new, less political plot developed, with the villain now devoted to launching a war between Britain and China in a complex scheme to secure satellite transmission rights in China.

Other changes followed. Feirstein originally named his villain Elliot Harmsway - a name which had its own connection to James Bond's creator, Ian Fleming. Fleming's wife Ann had previously been married to the press magnate Esmond Cecil Harmsworth, otherwise known as the 2nd Viscount Rothermere, publisher of the *Daily Mail*. The name was deemed too close for comfort, and thus was changed to Elliot Carver.

"**Coming around to the role for a second time, it had a comfortable air. I think the pressure was more on Roger Spottiswoode than on me.**" Pierce Brosnan

Bond waits for Paris (**top**) in a scene that refers back to *Dr. No*, when 007 watched for the arrival of Professor Dent. The scene has another, less obvious connection to an early Bond film - it was shot at the clubhouse at Stoke Poges, the golf course used for the famous match between Bond and Auric Goldfinger.

Munich-based actor Gotz Otto (**right and opposite**) won the role of Stamper when he went to the office of producer Barbara Broccoli, who was on the telephone to casting director Debbie McWilliams. Broccoli told McWilliams, "Hold on, I have a good-looking German guy here - I'll be back to you in a minute." She then turned to Otto and said, "OK, you have 20 seconds to introduce yourself." Otto, who had had all his hair cropped for a television production he had just finished, said, "I'm big, I'm bad, I'm bald, I'm German. That's five seconds." Otto later recalled, "She grinned at me and went back to her call. I think that is what got me the part."

The final story of the new film, called *Tomorrow Never Dies*, featured a world steeped in 90s cutting-edge technology. Carver's plot involved the manipulation of the global positioning system, the US satellite system which can pinpoint the location on the planet of any person or vehicle with a receiver. In the film, Carver also owns a massive stealth ship which is invisible to radar. Although it seemed a flight of Bondian fantasy, stealth boat technology had, in fact, been around for 20 years. The US Navy commissioned a ship called the *Sea Shadow*, which was built by Lockheed Martin under CIA supervision in the 1980s. In 1993, the programme became declassified, and the first photos of the ominous-looking craft surfaced in the press.

Despite finding an inventive villain and intriguing technology, the development of the story for the new Bond film proved difficult due to many factors. The filmmakers had reintroduced Bond in 1995 after careful groundwork. Now they needed to repeat the trick without the benefit of *GoldenEye*'s director. To replace Martin Campbell, Wilson and Broccoli hired Roger Spottiswoode, who reportedly had some creative disagreements with the producers during development and shooting.

Like Peter Hunt and John Glen before him, the Canadian-born Spottiswoode began his career as a film editor, working on Sam Peckinpah's *Straw Dogs* and *Pat Garrett And Billy The Kid*, as well as Walter Hill's *Hard Times*. Peckinpah had left a huge legacy in the way his films were edited, which was almost the antithesis of the Bond films' quick, elegant cutting. Peckinpah shot his violence like it was a ballet, and his editors often worked to slow down action in his movies, in contrast to Peter Hunt, who used cutting to speed things up. Spottiswoode made his directorial debut with *Terror Train* before graduating to more upscale fare such as *Under Fire*, *Shoot To Kill*, *Turner & Hooch*, *Air America* and *Stop! Or My Mom Will Shoot*. His editorial background was a factor in his hiring, and the marriage of the Bond style with Spottiswoode's Peckinpah training created one of the most tightly edited Bond films in thirty years. The achievement is remarkable since MGM/UA had set a release date for the film of 19th December 1997, which meant there would be a very short post-production schedule.

The filmmakers also faced similar problems to those on *GoldenEye*. Even though they carried out significant shooting at Pinewood Studios, the facility once again could not house the entire production. To make matters worse, Leavesden Studios was busy with George Lucas's *Star Wars: The Phantom Menace*. Once again, the filmmakers found a huge industrial space (this time an abandoned grocery warehouse) which they duly converted to a film studio, dubbed 'Frogmore'.

The world of Bond was equally active off the set as on during 1996 and 1997. There was the legitimate fan/historian side of Bond - and the fans and historians, many who had not been born when *Dr. No* was filmed, were having a major impact on the world of 007. In March 1996, Raymond Benson, author of *The James Bond Bedside Companion*, was chosen to become the new author of the James Bond novels; though honoured, he also admitted to being "ecstatic and terrified". Ian Fleming's name stayed in the press with the release in 1995 of Andrew Lycett's definitive biography of the author. On 14th April 1996, Desmond Llewelyn and the family of Ian Fleming attended a ceremony for the unveiling of a special commemorative English Heritage Blue Plaque

outside the author's former London home in Ebury Street, Belgravia. The First Edition Library of Shelton, Connecticut made available exact replicas of all of the original British first editions of Fleming's 007 novels for the collector market.

Bond film historians constructed *The Ultimate James Bond: An Interactive Dossier* on CD-ROM in the autumn of 1996. An encyclopedic overview of the Bond films, it featured over 55 minutes of full-motion video, 22 minutes of audio clips, 1800 stills and 850 detailed articles. In October 1996, London's Institute of Contemporary Arts held a one-day seminar that sought to address the James Bond cultural phenomenon. Simultaneously, a licensed five-day event, The James Bond Jamaica Festival, entertained fans and the press at the Jamaican Grand Hotel in Ocho Rios. The one-off festival included tours of Ian Fleming's home, Goldeneye, and events with celebrities such as George Lazenby, Ursula Andress and Maud Adams. In addition to these official activities, there were hosts of other fan events, including Bond Fan Club luncheons at Pinewood Studios and a James Bond cruise in January 1997.

Regardless of the number of fan events, fan clubs or Bond-themed seminars, the real impact of 007's legacy existed in the wider popular culture. In 1996 and 1997, James Bond's legacy rumbled through cinemas worldwide. In *Executive Decision*, a taut 1996 airplane hijacking thriller, Kurt Russell rushes into action straight from a black tie party, prompting his colleagues to call him James Bond. At the other end of the spectrum, *Trainspotting*, a brilliant film about heroin addicts in Scotland, contains numerous Bond references, as one of the characters is a Bond buff. The soundtrack even included the song 'Closet Romantic' by Damon Albarn, the lyrics of which consisted solely of titles from James Bond movies. The children's comedy *Dunston Checks In* featured a trailer which began as a parody of the trailer for *GoldenEye* (a marketing device later used for print ads for the 1997 film *Mouse Hunt*, which parodied the print ads of *Tomorrow Never Dies*).

San Francisco Chronicle   A13

007 Skywriting Seen As Sign From God

If James Bond seemed to be everywhere, one cult went to extremes. On 13th December 1997, MGM hired a skywriter to trace the number 007 above Los Angeles. Some members of God's Salvation Church proclaimed the number in the sky to be an unmistakable sign from the Lord that the end was nigh and that they should move to Garland, Texas, where they hoped UFOs would pick them up in 1998. No UFOs showed up, and they moved to New York awaiting nuclear war in 1999. Alas, some dreams are made to be shattered.

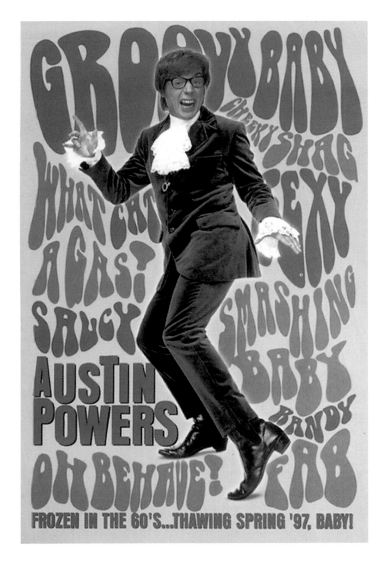

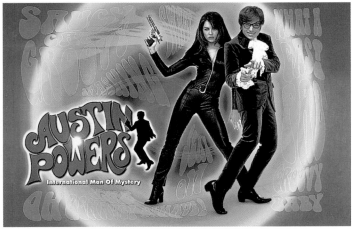

Mike Myers (**above**) has said in interviews that Austin Powers' impossibly hairy chest was inspired by Sean Connery (**opposite, top right**). By the time Myers began production of his third Austin Powers film, it was rumoured that Connery was being approached to play the randy spy's father. Eventually, the role went to another 1960s spy icon - Michael Caine.

The sexual appetite of Austin Powers also seemed a throwback to womanizing spies of the 1960s, such as George Lazenby's 007 in *On Her Majesty's Secret Service* (**opposite, centre**), who beds several women at Piz Gloria while on his mission to save the world from Blofeld.

Everyone seemed to be getting in on the act. In 1996, Leslie Nielson starred in *Spy Hard*, which began as a full-on parody of the Bond films. While the film failed to capture the magic of some of Neilson's other parody roles, the titles and title song by 'Weird Al' Yankovic showed an inventive way to send up the 007 films. The Bond parodies continued the following year with *The Man Who Knew Too Little*, starring Bill Murray not as a spy but as a bumbling tourist who believes he is pretending to be a spy in a role-playing 'living theatre' experience. These films seemed like minor blips on the cultural radar, however, when New Line Cinema released its spy film parody in the summer of 1997.

One day in the mid-1990s, comedian Mike Myers was driving to hockey practice when 'The Look Of Love' came on the radio. Along with the song came Mike's memories of being a boy in Toronto, Canada staying up late with his father and watching spy films on television - spy films his late father loved.

From James Bond to bad Italian quickies, from Harry Saltzman's Harry Palmer films to the over-produced madness of *Casino Royale*, Myers at once understood the absurdity and allure of the spy movies of that era for his generation and those younger than him.

"I thought, 'I wanna be in a movie with this song, and everything that it implies.'" Myers told the *UCLA Daily Bruin* in 1997. "All the 60s swinger, sexual revolution stuff. We live in such an uptight politically correct time. It makes me laugh to think that at that time, people were just unabashedly, publicly horny, which nobody is now."

Austin Powers was created then and there.

For the generation of teens who flocked to *Austin Powers, International Man of Mystery* the spies of the 1960s were even more distant than they were to Myers, who was born in 1963. Spy films and television shows were part of pop culture history, something which existed mostly before they were born. Spy films came to represent their parents' or grandparents' whacked-out vision of style and entertainment in the era before the internet, computer games, CDs and microwave ovens.

Austin Powers represented an amazing cultural synthesis. Over the years, through the endless television broadcasts and video releases, the classic iconography of James Bond became part of the youth culture.

It was a reference point to some not too distant past when things were somehow better, more sophisticated in a naïve way, sexier and yet innocent. But the iconography of 007 altered its meaning, much as it had for Jamaican youths and Indonesian teens in the late 60s. Here was a hero beloved by parents and grandparents - the very sort who railed against gangsta rap for its values - yet their hero carried a gun, which he used to kill at will, smoked and drank with impunity, and celebrated his prodigious heterosexual libido with a host of willing partners. Bond was too absurd to be taken seriously, but too serious to be taken simply as absurd. Among the teens and twenty-somethings of the 1990s, the classic 1960s image of James Bond joined the Rat Pack, Tony Bennett and Tiki bars as ironic symbols of boundless optimism.

By 1994, there was a name for the movement - 'Lounge' - which seemed to encompass every aspect of pop culture from the late 40s to the late 60s. Lounge encompassed a culture that had been considered endlessly un-cool by the ultra-hip in the 70s and 80s. The swinging bachelor pad lifestyle from the days of scandalous sex and smoking jackets was back. Music stores filled bins with Lounge Music collections, which often included tracks from Bond soundtracks, and even more often from rare, off-beat re-recordings of Bond soundtrack music from the 60s. Lounge music both laughed at and embraced the past, and no part of that past received more attention than 007.

Lounge music had its 1990s counterpart, the hypnotic, ethereal Trip Hop and Techno music that was created almost exclusively from samples, synthesizers and overdubs. Once again, James Bond played a key role in this trend. John Barry and the Bond soundtracks of the 1960s provided many samples for the leading artists in the movement, such as England's Grantby (on tracks like 'Timber'). Soon, more accessible pop groups like Pulp and Portishead started playing with the Barry/Bond sound, stretching and twisting it into something new. The John Barry/Bond sound, which so excited fans of film music in the 60s, was now some of the hottest music around. The impact of 007 in music and movies seemed to reach its zenith in 1997 when the song 'Six Underground' by the Sneaker Pimps was featured in the film *The Saint*. The song showcased a haunting riff sampled from the *Goldfinger* soundtrack. The result was that *The Saint*, a film that itself was both a re-interpretation of the 1960s spymania television show, and an attempt to capture the 1990s spymania audience, ultimately featured part of the soundtrack to *Goldfinger* in the film.

Other musicians lined up to compose songs that played off the coolness of Bond around the world and across the cultural spectrum. The influential Japanese pop group Pizzicato Five recorded 'Twiggy, Twiggy, Twiggy vs. James Bond', which was a hit in both Japan and cutting edge dance clubs around the globe. The gay band Pansy Division released a semi-pornographic song entitled 'James Bondage', which turned many Bond double entendres into triple entendres. When a television ad campaign in Britain featured the original recording of 'We Have All The Time In The World' from *On Her Majesty's Secret Service*, the song, which had done little as a single in 1970, suddenly raced up the charts.

A young composer named David Arnold could see a movement. He had been swept away by the sound of John Barry's score for *You Only Live Twice* when just a kid at a children's party. Even over the twittering sound of a 16mm projector, Arnold knew he was hearing something special. Two decades later, he was ready to release *Shaken And Stirred, The David Arnold James Bond Project*. Arnold collected some of the most diverse and talented names in music and worked with them to re-record James Bond classics with a personal stamp. When Arnold sent some of the tracks to Barbara Broccoli and Michael Wilson, he suddenly found himself part of the new Bond film. The lessons learned producing *Shaken And Stirred* were a tremendous help. "We spent a lot of time deconstructing Bond music and understanding what made it work," said Arnold.

Arnold continued the trend of Bond fans who turned pro. His project featured work by The Propellerheads, who also created overdubs for the new Bond score, and later worked with Shirley Bassey on a very Bondian song for the group's

album, *Decks Drums And Rock And Roll*. Arnold infused his work with cutting-edge sounds and sweeping orchestras in the style of John Barry. His score for the new Bond film, now entitled *Tomorrow Never Dies*, paid homage to almost every Bond score from the past, from *Dr. No* to *GoldenEye*. Arnold added a layer of his own unique sound and arrangement, truly bringing the Bond sound into the 1990s.

Meanwhile, the filmmakers were too busy to enjoy the warm embrace of Bond by the world of popular culture. They had tried to film part of *Tomorrow Never Dies* in Vietnam, but were unable to break through the Red tape (pun intended) to secure permissions. Instead they filmed the south-east Asia scenes in Thailand, even returning to the waters near James Bond Island close to where *The Man With The Golden Gun* had been shot. Although the film did not contain a breakthrough location, it did break ground in other ways.

"It's a small role, but it motivates James's actions in a way.
I guess it's one of the few times in a Bond film that there has
been some sort of past emotional relationship between Bond and
a woman. She has to make a choice: be loyal to her cruel and
unscrupulous husband or help her former lover. Her decision is
an integral part of the movie." TERI HATCHER

"I'd already decided that we weren't going to have a Bond girl, we were going to have a Bond woman. We were going to have a new kind of woman, reinvent the whole thing." Roger Spottiswoode

By the time *Tomorrow Never Dies* began production, the filmmakers had had time to digest the reactions of critics and fans to *GoldenEye*, and what they heard was encouraging. There was an immediate acceptance of Brosnan in the role of 007; many said he was the best Bond since Connery. Like all the actors who had taken on the role, Brosnan was a Bond well suited for his time. In the new film, he wanted to push the character farther. "Pierce always wanted to have a closer look at the character's inner life - the brooding that's so much a part of the Fleming novels," said Bruce Feirstein.

To accomplish this, Feirstein introduced a character named Paris into the story. Paris was Elliot Carver's wife, but more importantly, she was an ex-lover of James Bond's. "That was something that came from me in the sense that I wanted the woman to mean something to Bond," said Brosnan. "This was a woman he loved, and there's no reason you can't go there with these kind of emotions with the character… When you read the books, (Bond) conceals so much fear. I mean, this guy is shit-scared the whole time. He's got to be. But he's the ultimate hero. But to see the crack, to see the flaw, and to let the audience in just for that brief moment, then that's what I find exciting about doing it."

The role of women in Bond films has been controversial ever since 1962. From *The Spy Who Loved Me* onwards there seemed to be a conscious effort to address the issue. The publicity for each new film took pains to explain how the female character was more than just a beautiful woman in a bikini. Feminists often expressed outrage at the role of women in Bond movies, and just as often, other feminists embraced the independent spirit of the female characters. Like so many aspects of Bond's world, there was truth in all the arguments. The women in Bond films were self-sufficient and dependent. They were both strong and pliant, expendable and necessary. Their complexity rested in the dichotomy of their role in the James Bond universe.

As heroic tales built on mythic structures, the Bond movies were no more character studies than *Cinderella*. The characters were iconoclasts in the 1960s who became iconic as the films progressed. These were not inner examinations of the emotionally complex lives of spies. The characters - male and female - would always be given just enough backstory to justify their skills and actions, but little more. With *The Spy Who Loved Me* the filmmakers made an effort to equalize the playing field, developing female characters who had key technical skills important to Bond's mission. But the filmmakers had to balance the desire for sexual sparks with the desire to create female characters who served as little more than eye candy. There was still an effort until *GoldenEye* to have at least one scene where James Bond walked past a pool or beach filled with gorgeous models in bikinis (a tradition begun with the poolside scenes in *Goldfinger*). With *Tomorrow Never Dies*, the filmmakers asked themselves whether they could create a female character who was Bond's equal on every level. The answer was found not only in the writing, but also in the casting of actress Michelle Yeoh as Chinese agent Wai Lin.

"The producers recognize that the audience is changing," said Michelle Yeoh. "They're much more sophisticated, and they want to deal with women who are strong… Also, it makes Bond a man of the 90s, going into the next millennium, you know. It was fantastic. I loved it when M was Dame Judi Dench. It was, like, about time. And now, with this, it firmly endorses him as a man of the 90s who is strong as well, who is confident of who he is, and he doesn't have a quarrel about working with a woman." In fact, the filmmakers ended up having Bond virtually begging Wai Lin to be his partner on the mission. She is far from bowled over by 007, and Bond continually finds himself just two steps behind his Communist counterpart, constantly playing catch-up.

Despite the rushed production schedule and creative tensions, *Tomorrow Never Dies* proved to be a strong follow-up to *GoldenEye*. The film delivered all the key Bond ingredients with a 1990s twist. Brosnan seemed more relaxed in the role, less tense, which worked with some clever editing tricks on the part of director Spottiswoode. In fact, the editing was a stylistic highpoint of the film along with the music. Spottiswoode was able to create moments of seamless movement and to tighten the film below a two hour running time - the first Bond film to run less than 120 minutes since *Diamonds Are Forever*.

Michelle Yeoh's performance was also a high point with both audiences and critics. Her action scenes were a direct nod to the influence of the Hong Kong action cinema of stars such as Jackie Chan and directors like John Woo, who were finding new ways of presenting cinematic thrills in the 1990s. While Hollywood increasingly relied on computers, Hong Kong's inventive film industry re-ignited in the late 1980s with daring and complex stunt work often performed by the stars themselves. Although Yeoh did not perform the dangerous stunts in *Tomorrow Never Dies* herself, she was totally believable as a woman of action. Her sex appeal came from her confidence in movement and her physical strength just as much as her beauty.

Tomorrow Never Dies was the second Bond movie to carry a dedication (*GoldenEye* was dedicated to the memory of Derek Meddings). At the end of the film a title appeared in honour of the man who had guided Bond through the first 17 screen adventures and reinvented action filmmaking in the process: Cubby Broccoli. On 28th June 1996, Albert R. Broccoli died in Beverly Hills at the age of 87.

At a press conference for *Tomorrow Never Dies*, Michael Wilson said, "The thing about Cubby and our films - and he's sorely missed, obviously, it's the empty place at the table - but Barbara and I did spend an enormous amount of time working with Cubby over the years. I started full time in '74, and she started in 1981 when she got out of school, just on the floor, working her way up. Through being mentored, and by osmosis, we've certainly absorbed a lot of Cubby's views, so we think we're carrying on the films as he would see it. And one of our major functions is to protect the character against writers and directors and studios who say 'Let's try this, and let's try that'. In some ways, we're the guardians of the gate."

As a further tribute to Cubby, *Tomorrow Never Dies* was the first 007 film to carry the credit "Albert R. Broccoli's Eon Productions Presents." Although Michael Wilson and Barbara Broccoli had inherited the mantle, they wanted to ensure that the man whose vision sustained the series for so long would never be forgotten.

On 3rd December 1997, a couple of weeks before the release of *Tomorrow Never Dies*, Pierce Brosnan became the 2,099th person to be honoured with a star on the Hollywood Walk of Fame. Desmond Llewelyn was the first to address the crowd of adoring fans. As they yelled "Q! Q!", he approached the podium and said, "Alright, pay attention!" When the applause died down, he continued by saying, "I had a certain amount of difficulty making my way down Hollywood Boulevard not treading on the stars of old friends, like Cubby Broccoli. And I'm sure Cubby would be absolutely thrilled at what is happening today."

When a reporter at the *Tomorrow Never Dies* press junket asked Pierce Brosnan if he was excited about receiving a star on the Hollywood Walk of Fame, Brosnan replied with amusement, "I'm a different man. I expect more respect. I'm a star, guys. I've arrived. And that is it. I'm gonna go up at lunchtime and polish it."

"Cubby Broccoli created not only the Bond franchise, but the big-event action-adventure picture itself, and changed the movie business. He did something unique, and did it well, for a very, very long time." Bruce Feirstein

When Pierce Brosnan was introduced, he remarked, "It's an honour to be joining all the great artists already on this Walk of Fame, and to have so many friends here for this occasion. I should acknowledge a few who have contributed to this occasion, to the great opportunity they offered. First of all is the man himself. You know the name. It's Bond. James Bond. There is certainly the late and very lamented Cubby Broccoli, as well as Barbara Broccoli and Michael Wilson, who have maintained the Bond dynasty with the quality and care they brought to each production, and were kind enough to invite me on board, to make this movie, two years ago."

The celebratory mood belied the tension that the Bond filmmakers were feeling. The American opening was just a couple of weeks away, and they were going to be facing a box-office juggernaut, James Cameron's much-hyped *Titanic*. Produced with a budget of nearly $200 million, twice the cost of *Tomorrow Never Dies*, *Titanic* had already opened in the UK on 18th November, to staggering results. In America, the film would open on 18th December, the same day as *Tomorrow Never Dies*.

Though threatened by the competition, Bond did not get lost in the tidal wave of *Titanic* hype. In the end, the new 007 film grossed over $125 million in the USA, and over $200 million in the rest of the world. It was helped by a massive marketing campaign which included promotional tie-ins with Avis Rent-a-Car, Brioni suits, Heineken beer, Smirnoff vodka, BMW, Ericsson phones, Omega watches and Visa credit cards. Visa had participated in innovative ad campaigns before, but *Tomorrow Never Dies* marked the first time they had ever become a full marketing partner with a film studio, including a stylish television ad which starred Brosnan as Bond. Liz Silver, advertising vice president for Visa USA, told the *Wall Street Journal*, "If we're lending our brand to be associated with something, we want it to be an entity that also has a quality brand."

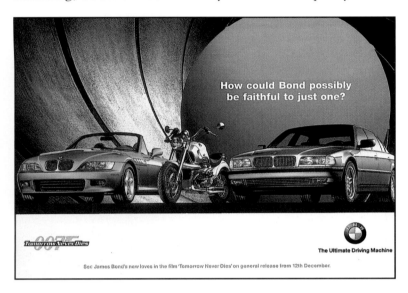

How could Bond possibly be faithful to just one?

Tomorrow Never Dies   The Ultimate Driving Machine

See James Bond's new loves in the film 'Tomorrow Never Dies' on general release from 12th December.

Besides the promotional push, BMW had also supplied several $13,000 R1200 motorcycles and ten $92,000 750iL sedans to the production. The company was eager to continue their association with James Bond, after the introduction of the Z3 roadster in *GoldenEye* helped the car have the most successful car launch in history, with 10,000 advance sales of the $30,000-plus vehicle.

The film's success was important to MGM. In 1995, the studio was owned by Credit Lyonnais SA, who had to sell the company by early 1997 to comply with US banking legislation. The success of *GoldenEye* made MGM more attractive to potential buyers, but film production ground to a halt while the studio was being prepared for sale. Eventually, in October 1996, a group led by billionaire investor Kirk Kerkorian, who had owned the studio twice previously, and Australia's Seven Network engineered a $1.3 billion management-led buy-out of MGM. The first important release under the new ownership was *Tomorrow Never Dies*. Its success insured that MGM would survive, and that James Bond would return.

Before *Tomorrow Never Dies* reached cinemas, Kevin McClory once again appeared on the scene. In October 1996, McClory announced that he was planning to make yet another alternate 007 feature based on his rights to *Thunderball*, to be titled *Warhead 2000 A.D.* McClory told *Variety* that an unnamed lead had been chosen and the financing was "as good as" in place. After reading the article, Gareth Wigan, co-vice chairman of Columbia-TriStar, a division of Sony Pictures, asked *Variety* reporter Eric Boehm for McClory's phone number. Sony Pictures/Columbia had taken a $3.2 billion write-off in 1995 to cover its losses. Unlike other studios, Sony/Columbia did not have a franchise series that could be used as a 'tentpole' to generate enough income to guarantee a certain level of cash-flow for the company. It needed its own James Bond, and Wigan intended to deliver just that.

The behind the scenes strategies at Sony/Columbia included a key player - former MGM/UA executive John Calley. When

MGM/UA was sold to Kirk Kerkorian, John Calley, who had shepherded many of the studio's successes - including *GoldenEye* - to the screen, was left out of some very lucrative dealmaking. In 1996, Calley left for Sony where he learned of the approach to McClory. Calley had dealt with McClory before. In the 1980s he worked as a consultant for Warner Brothers when they were involved with *Never Say Never Again*.

Negotiations with McClory took time; the deal finally closed on 9th October 1997, one year to the day from Calley's hiring by Sony. McClory told *Weekly Variety* that he expected "some noise" over the new Bond film, but all the potential players were "aware that there are no legal problems whatsoever". In fact, McClory's rights were defined by legal problems. Soon, a flurry of lawsuits hit the courts, including a claim by Sony/Columbia and McClory that the United Artists Bond films had exploited elements of "the cinematic James Bond" which McClory had created. If Kevin McClory won this battle, his claim could be worth many, many millions.

The legal battle that followed pointed up the dilemma of the Bond producers. 007's continued success relied on the cultural ubiquity of James Bond. For 35 years, the Bond producers and hundreds of filmmakers worked to define, hone and re-define 007. With each success, Bond's value as a commodity rose.

A measure of that success could be seen in Bond references in the media, spy-themed television shows and parodies. Increasingly, though, the Bond producers found themselves having to fight to maintain control over the imagery and iconography of 007.

Back in the 1960s, when parodies and spy films were rampant, the Bond producers sued to keep overt knock-offs out of US cinemas, such as an Italian spy film entitled *Goldsinger*. In the late 70s and early 80s, the producers fought to keep book publishers from using James Bond movie stills without permission. When spymania came again in the mid-90s, the filmmakers needed the ability to work with marketing partners such as BMW to obtain the maximum promotional benefit for the minimum costs. But if BMW's competitors could make an ad which traded off the James Bond imagery just as easily, then why would BMW bother to officially associate with 007? This was the case in 1994, just as the BMW deal for *GoldenEye* was being secured, when American Honda Motors Co. released a television ad for the Honda Del Sol featuring a James Bond-type character being attacked by a henchman dangling from a helicopter. In that case, a federal court in Los Angeles ruled that Bond was owned by MGM and Danjaq and that the Bond character was unique and copyrightable.

On the other hand, there appeared to be fall-out from too much commercial exploitation. The official tie-in advertising for 007 that accompanied *Tomorrow Never Dies* as well as the product placement in the film drew criticism, including a satirical skit by US talkshow host Jay Leno. Pierce Brosnan later admitted he felt less than fully comfortable about his decision to participate in so many marketing campaigns associated with the film. Meanwhile, unofficial, but clear, references to Bond in advertising continued - a 1999 documentary entitled *20 Dates*, for example, featured artwork of the star in a classic James Bond pose holding roses rather than a gun.

One of the complex matters facing the Bond team and MGM was the tremendous success of Austin Powers. The second film, *The Spy Who Shagged Me*, was scheduled to be released during the summer of 1999. Although the first Powers film had grossed a solid $50 million, New Line Cinema knew from market research and the video sales of the first film that there was a huge audience waiting to see the second movie. It was obvious where the inspiration for the title came from, especially considering that when Myers was a film student, he wrote a monograph entitled 'Joseph Campbell's Cosmogenic Monomyth Cycle and *The Spy Who Loved Me*'. The Bond producers and MGM, however, felt the title seemed too close to Bond for comfort. Movie titles are not copyrightable in the classic sense, but rather are self-policed by the Motion Picture Association of America, the film industry group which also administers movie ratings in the US. Rather than fight over the title, MGM and New Line negotiated an agreement which allowed *The Spy Who Shagged Me* to retain the title without objection if each print of the film shipped to movie theatres in the US included the trailer for the new Bond film, *The World Is Not Enough*, scheduled for release in the autumn.

The film, which was less of a Bond parody than the first, was as inventive as it was derivative, and went on to become one of the year's biggest hits. Besides a title inspired by a previous 007 film, the sequel also launched a James Bond-size merchandizing campaign, with TV specials, action figures, soundtracks, milk ads, and Virgin Airways billboards with the slogan, "There's only one Virgin on this billboard, baby." For Halloween 1999, the grey Mao suit of the villain of the films, Dr. Evil, proved to be one of the biggest-selling costumes on the market. The outfits were, in essence, Blofeld costumes circa 1967. The Austin Powers films were proving to be funhouse mirror versions of the Bond films, and although they certainly stood as Exhibit A in the case for 007's long-term cultural impact, they also represented the threat of parodies to usurp the marketing potential of the 007 brand.

By March 1999, Sony/Columbia still had no Bond film in development. The studio was now being perceived in the film industry as playing potentially dirty pool in its efforts to create a competing Bond franchise. Regardless of how energetically Sony defended their plan, the Bond franchise had come to represent a somewhat cherished ideal among filmmakers - a clearly identified film series of impeccable quality, created for over 35 years by a small family of key filmmakers. Why would someone want to sabotage that? Many speculated on John Calley's bitterness or felt the original Sony announcement was designed to undercut MGM's public offering of stock in 1997. The reaction was markedly different from when McClory fought to make a new Bond film in the late 1970s and early 1980s. Now, even most Bond fans failed to support the idea of a Columbia Bond series. Faced with these realities and with a ruling by a Los Angeles judge that MGM was likely to prevail on the merits of the now complex legal case, Sony decided to settle.

The settlement resulted in MGM obtaining the distribution rights to the 1967 film *Casino Royale*. Earlier the studio had purchased the distribution rights to *Never Say Never Again*, and now MGM and the Bond producers controlled all of the James Bond films. This consolidation, along with other rights negotiated in the 1980s, gave the filmmakers greater control over the cinematic James Bond, tie-in merchandise, and spin-off characters such as James Bond Jr. The settlement with Sony precluded the studio from ever developing a James Bond film in the future. The case effectively shut Hollywood's doors to Kevin McClory, but Mr. McClory decided he would not let Sony decide his fate. McClory decided to continue his suit against Danjaq and MGM alone.

While facing the threat of the Sony/McClory developments, the Bond producers were hard at work on the 19th film of the series. Continuing with Pierce Brosnan's desire to explore the inner workings of 007, and continuing the focus on more developed female characters, the filmmaking team created a story which was a tremendous departure from the Bond formula. They decided to entitle the movie *The World Is Not Enough*, a title which had its origins in the James Bond novel, ON HER MAJESTY'S SECRET SERVICE, where it is mentioned as the motto on the Bond family crest. As in the film of *Majesty's*, Michael Wilson, Barbara Broccoli and the filmmaking team decided to push the boundaries of Bond's traditional relationship with women: what if James Bond fell in love?

From the beginning the clear determination was to develop the most complex and interesting lead female for the film. The first draft script was written by Neal Purvis and Robert Wade, who had earlier penned the critically acclaimed drama *Let Him Have It* and the 16th-century heist adventure *Plunkett & Macleane*. Michael Apted took over the directing reins. Apted had developed a reputation for getting strong performances from actresses with memorable films such as *Coal Miner's Daughter*, *Nell*, *Gorillas In The Mist* and *Blink*. "I'm inheriting a successful franchise," said Apted. "Successful because it works, so I have to decide which elements to change, just a little, to keep the film fresh and modern."

The plotline features Bond falling in love with Elektra King, the daughter of a British oil tycoon. Elektra had once been kidnapped and held hostage by the terrorist, Renard. What Bond fails to realize, until it is almost too late, is that she is still Renard's lover.

Elektra is originally believed to be a victim of a psychological phenomenon called 'the Stockholm Syndrome'. The phrase was coined in 1973, after four Swedes - three women and one man - were held in a vault of Stockholm's Sveriges Kreditbank for six days by two ex-convicts. Upon their release, the captives displayed a strange association with their captors. Some of them later testified on behalf of, and raised defence money for, the bank robbers.

The Stockholm Syndrome has been described as an emotional attachment that develops when a captor threatens a hostage's life, deliberates, and then decides not to kill them. The feeling of relief caused by the removal of the threat of death generates a feeling of gratitude in the hostage. It is, in essence, a survival mechanism; those who fall victim to it are fighting for their lives. The Bond filmmakers reversed the concept. Rather than have Elektra fall in love with Renard, it is the terrorist who falls for the victim.

Renard, the first fully-fledged terrorist villain of a Bond film, had many similarities to Carlos the Jackal, the international terrorist who seemed to adopt a James Bond lifestyle. By the time of the Jackal's arrest in the autumn of 1997, he was considered something of a pathetic figure. French authorities arranged with Sudanese officials for his capture while the playboy terrorist was in hospital recovering from surgery to increase his sperm count.

The emotional storyline of *The World Is Not Enough*, though, mirrored the strange political developments in the United States during 1998 and early 1999. In early 1998, President Bill Clinton gave a deposition in a civil sexual harassment case which had been openly financed by the President's political enemies. As the President answered questions under oath he did not know that a special prosecutor was waiting to launch an investigation into a rather tortured affair between Clinton and a White House intern named Monica Lewinsky. The 'Lewinsky Affair' seemed to be the antithesis of James Bond. Every aspect appeared to unfold in broad daylight. Any information that parties sought to keep secret was soon leaked to the press. Camps on both sides debated every legal manoeuvre virtually non-stop on television news channels.

Robert Carlyle (**above**) and Sophie Marceau (**opposite page** and **below, left**) were the villains of *The World Is Not Enough*. "It's a piece of history," said Carlyle. "This is number 19 and you look at all the great actors that have played villains over the years. Robert Shaw, Christopher Walken, folk like that. It's an honour to be part of that."

John Cleese's wife, Alice Faye, was a longtime friend of 007 title creator Maurice Binder, and through him also became friends with the producers of the James Bond films. Over the years, Cleese (**below, right**) had expressed interest in playing a Bond villain, but when the producers finally called, they wanted him to be a Q in waiting. As Alice Faye watched her husband film his scene with Desmond Llewelyn, she had tears in her eyes. "When he shot that take, I said to my husband afterwards, 'Desmond's leaving. You know, this is going to be a very powerful scene in the movie.' And if you've seen the movie, it is. The audience absolutely picks up on that goodbye."

"With regard to the topical aspect of the Bond stories,
it's nice to put the film on the cutting edge of the news."
Michael Apted

With all the media furore surrounding the Bill Clinton-Monica Lewinsky affair (**far left**), numerous commentators sought to draw analogies to James Bond, including the suggestion in *Time* magazine that to raise money for his legal defence, Clinton should take to wearing an Omega watch as product placement, à la 007.

The Millennium Star (**left**) was one of twelve diamonds that an armed gang attempted to steal from a display at London's Millennium Dome in November 2000. Police were tipped off and replaced the jewels with crystal replicas the day before the attempted robbery.

In the early days of the scandal, before the moment-by-moment details were dumped into the lap of the public, there was widespread speculation that Lewinsky had been set up to trap Clinton in a compromising position. It turned out that she had been shamelessly manipulated by a woman named Linda Tripp and a host of unseen advisors to Tripp, and the result was more sympathy for the all-too-human President than for his pious enemies. Nonetheless, the story was filled with seductive figures who seemed to be wounded innocents but later turned out to have very specific malicious agendas. Elektra King was neither Linda Tripp nor Monica Lewinsky, but her character's hidden agenda and relentless seduction of 007 reflected both.

The risk for the filmmakers in exploring such complex territory was that Bond films have always featured clearly identifiable villains. *The World Is Not Enough* fell into murky territory on that count. Ostensibly, Elektra is the central villain, but this does not become apparent to Bond until late in the story. As a result of this, Bond moves through most of the film not trusting his own instincts, and Brosnan gave a tense, more angry performance that reflected 007's situation in the film. At the movie's climax, Bond had to cold-bloodedly shoot Elektra, a moment that concerned some members of the creative team. It marked a significant shift from Brosnan's preceding two Bond films, and the changes were cause for some justifiable worry. On two previous occasions when the filmmakers had seriously altered the Bond formula - in *Licence To Kill* and *On Her Majesty's Secret Service* - the result had been disappointing box office.

The filmmakers were keenly aware of the timing of the new film. It would be the last Bond film of the second millennium, and the production team wanted it to feel very much like the first film of the new century. Filming got underway at Pinewood Studios on 11th January 1999, after the script had undergone rewrites by Dana Stevens, whose work was uncredited, and Bruce Feirstein. While the first unit filmed scenes of Pierce Brosnan on the MI6 sets, the second unit went to the ski resort of Chamonix in the French Alps, which would double for the Caucasus Mountains in the finished film.

In early February, a massive snowstorm caused a vast avalanche, which inundated a town near the location. The Bond team chose to help with search and rescue operations, despite the expensive delay of production. "(The mountain crew) are all specialists and we were glad to lend them to the rescue effort," said Michael Wilson. "Money is not an issue here. Our team will stay at the avalanche site as long as they are needed." The crew's helicopters were vital, and for once Bond actually helped save the day.

In mid-February, the first unit crew travelled to Bilbao, Spain, to film locations near the Guggenheim Museum, one of the major architectural structures of the 1990s, which seemed to single-handedly turn the Basque city into a key destination for European travellers. The pre-credits sequence ended with action taking place around another architectural marvel, the Millennium Dome in London. The idea for the Dome was born in 1992, when National Heritage Secretary Peter Brooke proposed an exhibition to mark the end of the century. The structure was designed by Richard Rogers, the architect responsible for the Pompidou Centre in Paris and the Lloyd's building in London. Construction work was still continuing as *The World Is Not Enough* filmed there.

In November 2000, the Dome became the scene of the most ambitious robbery ever attempted on British soil. Many news outlets reported the story as like "something out of a James Bond film". A gang of thieves used an excavator to break into the Dome, which housed a dozen of the most valuable diamonds on the planet, including the 203-carat De Beers Millennium Star. Unfortunately for the robbers, Scotland Yard had been tipped off before the raid and replaced the diamonds with fakes. Detectives captured four of the thieves immediately. Two others tried to escape via a speedboat down the Thames, but were quickly captured; five others were rounded up in raids in south-east England. Observers were quick to point out that the attempted escape method - speedboat down the Thames - seemed to have been inspired by the pre-credits scene of *The World Is Not Enough*, which was released over a year earlier. The robbery was on the scale of *Goldfinger*, as the diamonds were valued at £200 million. Had the robbers been successful, it would have been by far the largest heist in British history. Instead, in February 2002, the gang were sentenced to prison terms of between five and eighteen years.

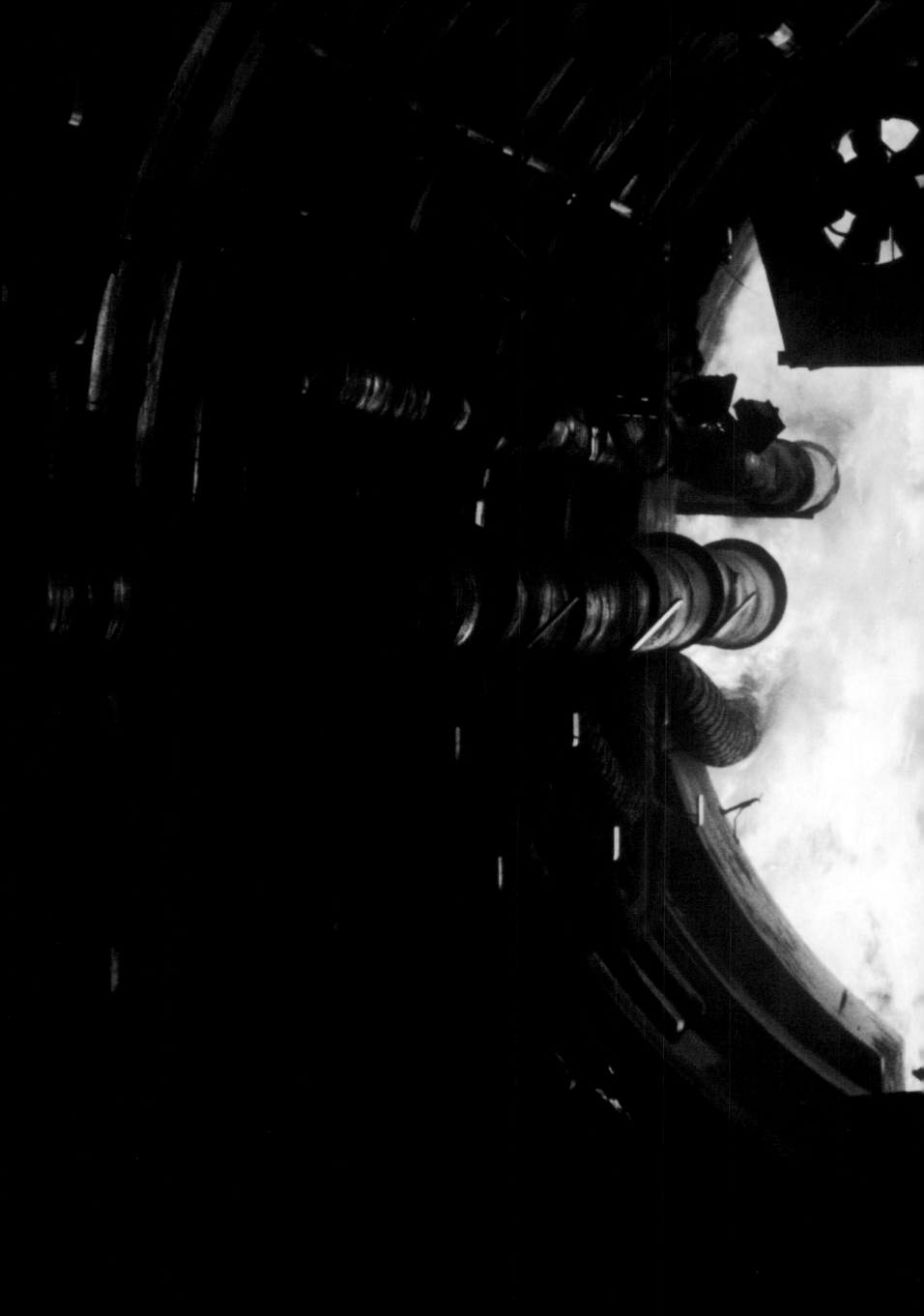

For the title song, the filmmakers decided to continue the trend of *Tomorrow Never Dies*, where cutting-edge artists contributed to the soundtrack. For the previous film, three well-respected performers had given their talents - Sheryl Crow, Moby, and k.d. lang. For composer David Arnold, it was a somewhat frustrating experience. Only k.d. lang worked with Arnold on her song. Crow and Moby (who was re-recording 'The James Bond Theme' in his distinctive style) worked separately from Arnold. For *The World Is Not Enough*, Arnold lobbied to write the film's title song with lyricist Don Black, who had previously contributed to theme songs for *Thunderball*, *Diamonds Are Forever* and *The Man With The Golden Gun*. Black had collaborated with Arnold on 'Surrender', the song recorded by k.d. lang that was used over the end titles of *Tomorrow Never Dies*. To perform the new film's title song, Arnold contacted one of the hottest bands around at the time - Garbage. The band's vocalist, Shirley Manson, had been telling the press for some time that they wanted to do a Bond theme. Other movie producers approached them to perform theme songs for their films, but Garbage held firm: it would be Bond, or nothing.

When it was time to record the song, Garbage were on a world tour. The producers hired a private jet to fly the band from Portugal to London, where they spent two days in a studio with a full orchestra working with Arnold. Butch Vig said later, "This was the first time we ever recorded with a 60-piece orchestra and that was a most excellent experience."

"We're a bunch of geeks. We're not cool at all. We're the geekiest band out there, let me tell you, so it's an honour to do the theme song for such a cool international spy."
Garbage co-founder and drummer Butch Vig

Denise Richards (**opposite top**) enjoyed working with director Michael Apted. "He's one of the reasons why I really wanted to do the movie," she said. "I think he really brought a nice element to Bond. He focused on the relationships with the actors and of all the characters, and really wanted to keep all the women in the movie very strong. Still sexy, but with a point of view and something to do. I loved working with him, and I think he did a wonderful job. He really brought something different to it."

In 1986, after a New York exhibition of his graffiti art, Goldie (**above right**) moved to Florida, where he started a business selling engraved gold teeth. In 1990, he moved to London, where he became a popular club DJ and rising pop star.

The blades destroying Bond's new BMW (**top right**) belong to a helicopter rig that the producers had hoped to use in *GoldenEye*. The idea had been filed away and was resurrected for the elaborate caviar factory scene.

"Q's such a tiny part, it always astonishes me that I'm so well-known." Desmond Llewelyn

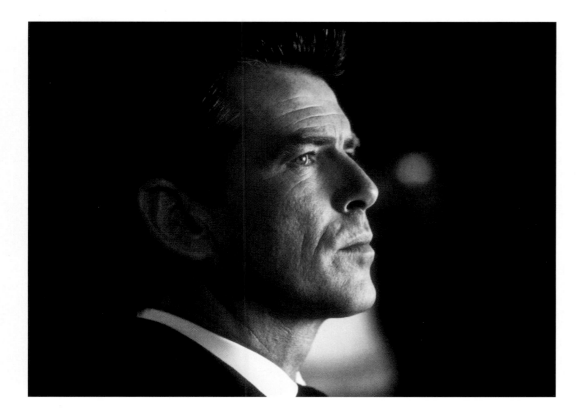

As the film was nearing its premiere date, MGM and MTV entered into a huge, multi-million dollar deal to promote the 007 adventure with shows featuring the stars of *The World Is Not Enough*, specials and airings of the music video of the title theme. Aside from the standard advertising, a hundred hours of special programmes were prepared to reach MTV's global audience. In the US, Europe and Asia, MTV viewers were given a chance to win the new BMW Z8 featured in the film. Pierce Brosnan and Denise Richards featured prominently in the 1999 MTV Europe Music Awards show which was aired globally on 11th November, eight days prior to the US premiere. Among other activities, a programme on the making of the music video was aired in all markets, and a half-hour behind-the-scenes special on the making of the movie shown on MTV Europe. MTV Asia's popular movie series, *MTV Screen*, put out a 30-minute special on the making of the film and MTV Latin America broadcast a two-hour programme featuring interviews with Bond stars, movie clips, footage from the Los Angeles and London premieres, and 007-style videos from favourite MTV artists.

Pierce Brosnan, Desmond Llewelyn, Serena Scott Thomas, Robbie Coltrane and Michael Apted were on hand for the American premiere in Westwood, California on 8th November. Two weeks later, on 22nd November, the London premiere was held at the Odeon Leicester Square. Apart from the stars from the film, former Bond women Shirley Eaton and Maryam d'Abo attended the event. Ex-Beatle and Bond title song performer Paul McCartney was also on hand. The premiere benefited Children's Promise, a charity which asked everyone in the UK to donate the value of one hour's earnings so that children might have a better future.

The film's promotion extended into the home video market as MGM prepared special edition DVDs of all of the Eon-produced Bond films, featuring over one hundred interviews with the talents behind the Bond legacy. The Bond DVD project resulted in the production of 26 new documentaries and featurettes on almost every aspect of the 007 films. Noted film author, Iain Johnstone, wrote a book on the making of the movie. The central question remained: would audiences respond to the film, despite its unusual level of complexity?

The answer came in the form of tremendous box office grosses, which were on a par with *GoldenEye* and *Tomorrow Never Dies,* topping the $350 million mark worldwide. This result showed a clear pattern of solid success for the James Bond of the 1990s, and it proved that audiences were willing to accept a more complex vision of James Bond's world in these complex times.

Times, though, were changing. The world of Bond was created on the ideals of the last half of the 20th century. By 2001, Bond's Western values, which had been refreshingly shocking to film audiences in 1962, now appeared tame and chivalrous. Bond indulged in the pleasures of life and embraced the risks. In this, 007 represented something of the culture, a culture that had won the Cold War and prospered with the victory. On the morning of 11th September 2001, both that victory and the prosperity of the post-Cold War world seemed to vanish in a sickening cascade of ash and flames.

The 20th century was over. A new era had begun.

Less than a month after the London premiere of *The World Is Not Enough*, the 007 cast lost one of their most treasured members - Desmond Llewelyn (**opposite**), who played the armourer, Q, in 17 James Bond films. The 85-year-old actor was returning from a book signing near his home when his car was involved in a head-on crash on the A27 near Firle in East Sussex. Llewelyn was taken to Eastbourne District General Hospital, where he succumbed to his massive internal injuries a few hours later. Three months later, a memorial service at St. Paul's Church, Knightsbridge was attended by former 007 Roger Moore and Samantha Bond.

Llewelyn's death was mourned by Bond fans around the world. He was the only cast member to have appeared in films with all of the actors who played 007, from Sean Connery through to Pierce Brosnan. With his passing, the films would no longer have a visible link to their past. At the US premiere of *The World Is Not Enough*, E! reporter Ted Casablanca asked Llewelyn how many more Bond movies he planned to do. Llewelyn responded, "That's up to God."

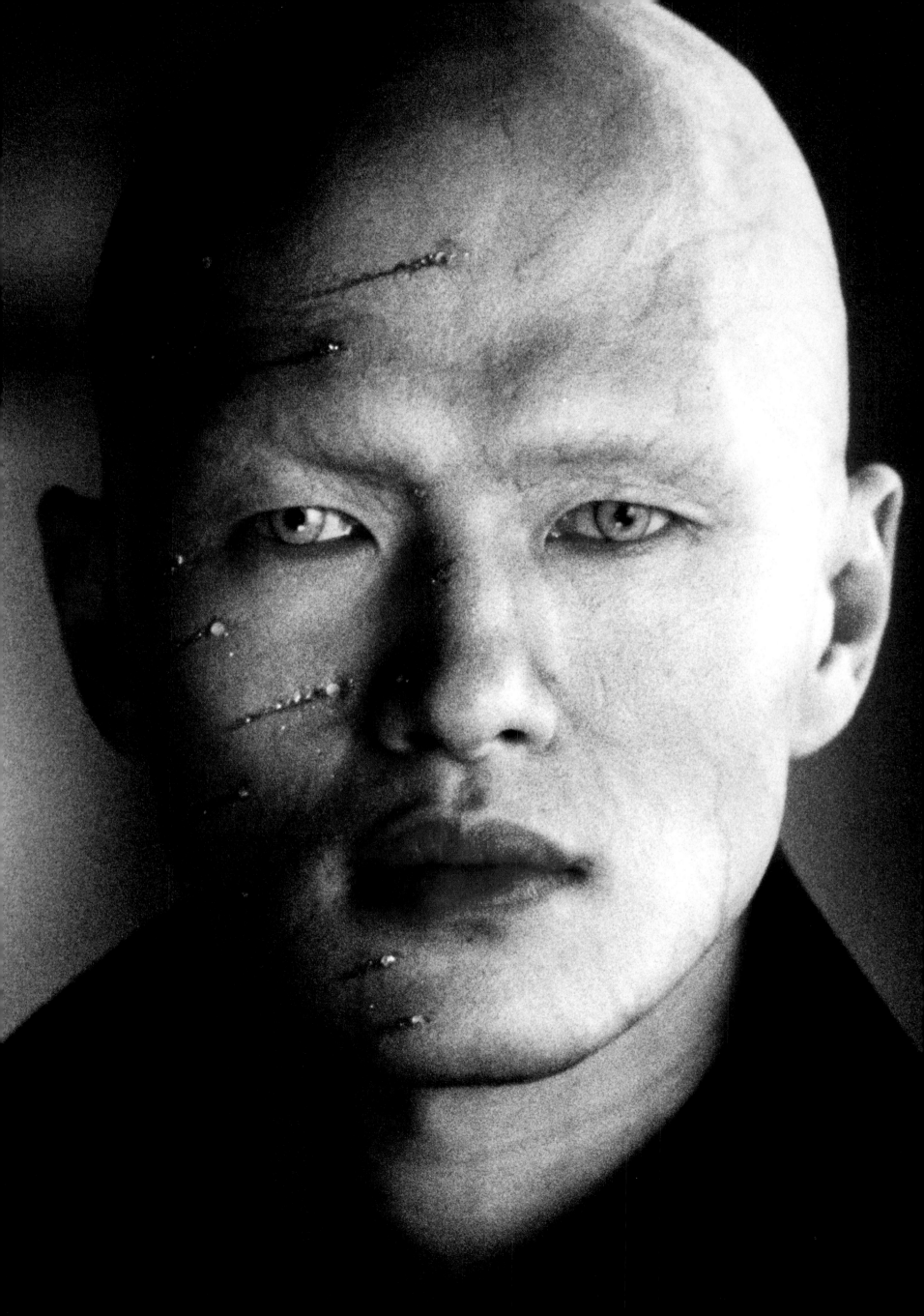

12.

One billion dollars. The spreadsheets at MGM told the story dispassionately, but the number itself was nothing short of astounding. The three 007 films featuring Pierce Brosnan had sold over one billion dollars in tickets by the end of the millennium. Additional revenues from video, DVD, cable, broadcast and pay-per-view revealed a pattern of unbridled triumph. James Bond, the literary hero of the 1950s, the cinematic phenomenon of the 60s, and cultural icon of the 70s and 80s, had conquered the 90s. Continued commitments by rival studios to launch spy-themed films and TV shows confirmed the notion that this incarnation of spymania was far more than just a passing fad. The Bond filmmaking family reacted to the steady drumbeat of success in an unorthodox fashion. Rather than envisioning a limited window of time to capitalize on Bond's continued popularity, they decided to step back and reassess. Just as the box office numbers told their story, Michael Wilson and Barbara Broccoli saw other numbers up ahead. The next Bond film would be the 20th in the series. 2002 would mark 50 years since Ian Fleming began typing CASINO ROYALE, and the 40th anniversary of the release of *Dr. No*. While Ian Fleming understood the almost mystical appeal of 'double-0 seven', the filmmakers were able to appreciate the alignment of anniversaries. If they waited three years to premiere the next Bond, they could celebrate all of these multiple milestones.

Two Minutes Into The Future

In the aftermath of the deadly attacks on the World Trade Center **(top)** and the Pentagon of 11th September 11, 2001, the Western nations rallied to battle global terrorism. Within months, British and American troops were fighting side by side in Afghanistan. The new enemies were not all external. Just a few months before the terror attacks, US authorities arrested the most dangerous spy in the history of the FBI, Robert Philip Hanssen **(above)**, who sold secrets to the Russians after the fall of Communism. Outwardly, Hanssen appeared to be a religious family man, but appeared to have an all-too-real James Bond fantasy life. Apart from spying, he carried on an expensive relationship with a stripper. Adrian Havill wrote, "To him she was a Bond girl come to life on the arm of a real 007," although Hanssen refused to sleep with the woman and often tried to convince her to attend church.

Previous spread: Rick Yune as General Zao in *Die Another Day*, the first Korean henchman in a James Bond film since Oddjob in *Goldfinger*.

In one sense, the fates appeared to be on the producers' side. Pierce Brosnan's Bond continued to be tremendously popular with the public. Despite the delay between films, 007 had never seemed so ubiquitous. The life of *The World Is Not Enough* extended far beyond the cinemas. Bond movies, like almost all films, followed a pattern of distribution that took years to play out before the broadcast premiere on domestic television networks. The special edition DVDs, a number of books examining aspects of the Bond films and novels, and a growing amount of merchandising also kept James Bond in the limelight.

No one, however, could predict the future, particularly the global shift that would occur with the terrorist attacks of 11th September, 2001. The shockwaves of the devastating suicide assaults rocked the world, and the impact in the entertainment industry was immediate. For a week in the US, television networks disrupted programming schedules, trying, as commentators noted, "to find the right tone". At film studios, armed guards and barricades appeared amidst concerns over the possibility of further terrorist strikes. Within studio and network offices, release patterns for films and television broadcast schedules were changed due to worries over insensitive content.

Observers noted that Osama bin Laden had been trained by the CIA back in the days when the West supported the Afghan 'freedom fighters' who had battled against Soviet occupation. In the fictional world of *The Living Daylights*, James Bond had been aided by Kamran Shah, the wealthy *mujaheddin* leader. Shah, like the real-life bin Laden, was university-educated and both were fearless fighters, natural leaders and born survivors.

For the Bond filmmakers, 11th September and the resultant war on terrorism occurred far into the process of preparing Bond 20, which would become known as *Die Another Day*. As so often in the past, the producers and writers had diligently avoided religion and politics, although there were vague similarities between the proposed storyline and current events. Osama bin Laden used 'sleeper' agents, assimilated into ordinary lives in another country until 'awoken' by their control, to carry off the World Trade Center and Pentagon attacks. Sleepers (both good and bad) played a role in the *Die Another Day* script. More pointedly, the climax of the new film took place in a giant out-of-control aircraft destined for a fiery demise. If there were concerns about the impact of 11th September on the new Bond film, the producers did not reveal them.

Meanwhile, the media and US politicians began using 007 as a verbal shorthand when discussing the war on terror. At a briefing on 15th November 2001, US Department of Energy Secretary Spencer Abraham led reporters on a tour of some of the high-tech weapons the US had developed to combat terrorism. Giving the demonstration made Abraham feel, he said, "a little bit like Q in those old James Bond movies, with (Director of Homeland Security) Governor Ridge, as our James Bond".

Three months later, reporter Georgie Ann Geyer questioned US Vice President Dick Cheney about security surrounding his location, often described in the months after the terrorist attack as simply "undisclosed". "There's a certain level of speculation, sir, in Washington... that you have been James Bond-ized. We don't know where you are, we don't know what you're doing. I would just like to ask, are you enjoying this? And has it changed your personality? And can you give us any insights?"

Cheney obviously enjoyed the comparison. "I'm just sitting here thinking about the analogy to James Bond," he said, eliciting laughter from the reporters. "There are certain features of this lifestyle that I have not been able to avail myself of, to put it in those terms. Although I am hopeful."

These remarks by US leaders illustrated the way Western society continued to embrace James Bond after 11th September. Dick Cheney was obviously happier being compared to 007 than being attacked for spending so much time in secret locations. The Bush administration preferred to comfort Americans with the thought that figures like Q and James Bond were fighting against future terrorist attacks.

In fact, just as Bond's Western values provided a counterpoint to the Spartan Soviet aesthetic during much of the Cold War, they also stood in stark contrast to the values of Osama bin Laden and his Al-Qaida terrorists.

In the 1960s, Western intelligence services had studiously avoided comparisons between the cinematic 007 and the work of real spies. Yet by the 1990s, James Bond was an acknowledged inspiration. In November 1997, the CIA actually set up a recruiting booth at a Virginia movie theatre during the opening weekend of *Tomorrow Never Dies*. In 1998, the agency decided it was lagging behind in implementing information technology, particularly innovations related to the internet. It funded a new corporation, formally launched in 1999, devoted to providing solutions for the intelligence community. The corporation's name, In-Q-Tel was inspired by the technological mastermind of the Bond films, Q. With this choice of name, the CIA paid tribute to James Bond's position as a leading force in the cult of espionage.

The real world's fascination with 007 continued to influence actual developments, such as the US Army's 'smarTruck', unveiled on 5th March 2001. The Army's own press release declared, "Check out the Army's 'James Bond-like' concept vehicle." The smarTruck was designed to transport troops through hostile urban territory. For inspiration, the design team first watched a few James Bond films, then outfitted the vehicle with oodles of gadgets. While the smarTruck did not feature an ejector seat, it did have a smokescreen similar to the one seen in *Goldfinger*. It also included a sophisticated set of voice-activated accessories and door handles wired to give an electric shock to unwelcome intruders - both inspired by Bond's car in *Tomorrow Never Dies*.

Despite worries in some quarters that 11th September might reduce the public's interest in the fictional adventures of 007, the public showed an unfailing devotion to James Bond, as two UK publishing ventures illustrated. *The Little Book Of Bond*, a compendium of movie quotes, sold far beyond expectations over Christmas 2001. A new magazine for younger fans, *The 007 Spyfiles*, flew off newsstands in early 2002, the first issue selling half a million copies in Britain alone.

For the Bond producers Michael Wilson and Barbara Broccoli, an apparently seismic change in the balance of global politics did not alter their commitment to the next Bond film or their belief that James Bond would still prove relevant to an audience. During the early months of 2001 the creative team behind the series had quietly developed the script for the 20th Eon Productions 007 adventure. Neal Purvis and Robert Wade wrote the first draft of what would become *Die Another Day*. New Zealand-born director Lee Tamahori, known for hard-hitting dramas like *Once Were Warriors*, helped the writers shape later drafts. Tamahori possessed a deep knowledge of the early Bond films and spoke of his great respect for directors like Terence Young, Guy Hamilton, and Lewis Gilbert. That sense of respect did nothing to diminish Tamahori's desire to place his own unique stamp on the series.

For Tamahori and the filmmakers, the script for *Die Another Day* would become a synthesis of many current themes running though the Bond films of the 1990s - the push to add dramatic weight to the film plots, the extensive melding of action with the storyline, and the delicate balance between Bond's 40-year cinematic past and his current adventure.

Following the pattern of the other recent films, the script attempted, as Pierce Brosnan said, to "peel back the layers" of the character of 007.

The movie opens not with a triumphant Bond, but with the capture of 007 by the North Korean military and his imprisonment. When 007 is traded back to Britain (in a scene reminiscent of the Francis Gary Powers/Rudolph Abel exchange in February 1962), Bond discovers that because of the gruelling interrogations by the North Koreans, MI6 now suspects he could have been unwittingly compromised. He is deemed 'damaged goods', a risk. In *GoldenEye* the filmmakers had Bond confronting a changed world; in *Die Another Day* it is the world that fears that Bond himself has changed.

In order to locate one of his original captors Bond has to break away from British government confinement in Hong Kong. Like *Licence To Kill*, the film portrays Bond as a rogue agent. Tamahori described the tone as "darker" than previous Bond films. "Bond is betrayed right at the beginning and spends much of the film without the resources of MI6." This element of the plot only tells part of the story, for this is also the most gadget-laden Bond since the 1970s.

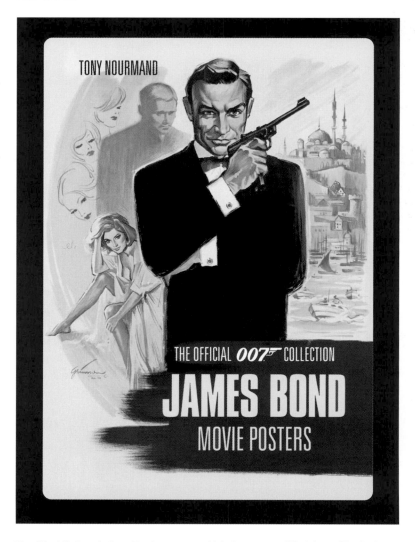

Top: The US Army's SmarTruck concept vehicle is not a modified Aston Martin, but a re-tooled Ford F-350 which includes a rear oil-sprayer (à la *Goldfinger*) and a tack dispenser (as seen in *Tomorrow Never Dies*). It also has biometric fingerprint identification for the driver and a night-vision display for driving without lights after dark.

Above: Tony Nourmand's *The Official 007 Collection James Bond Movie Posters* was the first book to draw widely on rarities from the archives of Eon Productions, including unused artworks from the Bond movies.

Above: The real Aston Martin V12 Vanquish incorporates technology worthy of Q's lab. The car manages to perform in temperatures ranging from -48°C to 81°C (or -40°F to 178°F). Although the car may include cutting-edge features, Q's offsite lab is filled with many references to Bond's past, including even the Player's cigarette poster in the background. In the novel THUNDERBALL, the heroine Domino concocts an enchanting biography for the portrait of the sailor who appears on the Player's box, claiming him as her "one true love.., the first man I ever sinned with".

Sin will cross many minds at the sight of Halle Berry (**right**) walking out of the surf just as Ursula Andress did in *Dr. No*. Berry's looks earned her many beauty pageant awards, including the title Miss Ohio, and the chance to compete in the Miss Universe and Miss World competitions. Her considerable acting skills can be seen in many powerful dramas, including *Introducing Dorothy Dandridge*, *Jungle Fever*, *Bulworth*, *Monster's Ball* (her Oscar-winning performance) and *Losing Isaiah*.

In fact, *Die Another Day* is a film wrapped in technological wizardry, from surfboards filled with lethal weapons to a host of autos armed to the teeth. Key among the cars is a fully kitted-out Aston Martin V12 Vanquish, replete with a few old tricks and a remarkable array of new devices. The Vanquish is a great match for Bond: a blazingly fast, inherently exotic sports car. There is nothing either mass-market or consumer-oriented about this machine. It is every bit as individualistic as Bond himself. The return of James Bond to a new Aston Martin marks a decision to link 007 with his past while still keeping Bond very much on the edge of the present.

The film offers a tremendous sense of fun by playing with the 40-year legacy of Bond, whether in a quick reference to the early movies when Miss Moneypenny listens in on M via her desk intercom or a quick tip of the hat to Desmond Llewelyn when John Cleese as the new Q declares, "I never joke about my work."

The references, which are almost an anniversary present to long-time fans, fill the movie, but like the gadgets, the references never take over. When Bond meets Cleese's Q in *Die Another Day*, the lab is filled with past gadgets. As Bond darts out of a room in a clinic, he pauses to sample a grape, à la *Thunderball*. The many visual cues and snippets of dialogue are designed to intrigue Bond fans, including such familiar sights as a laser beam threatening to slice a human in half, a body being sucked out of a hole in a plane as it depressurizes, and a Union Jack parachute, although each is presented with a twist. Even Ursula Andress's iconic bikini-clad entrance from the sea in *Dr. No* is given a nod.

The wink-and-nod to Bond fans belies the sense of sweeping change evident in the script. *Die Another Day* feels bigger in scope and scale than any of the previous Brosnan Bond adventures. The homage to Bond's past seems to mark a fond farewell to the 007 of the previous millennium, a salute as the filmmakers begin to chart a new course.

None of the core ingredients have been altered - this is still the same James Bond - but there is a breathless quality to the story, a tonal shift first experimented with in *The World Is Not Enough* but now solidified.

The North Korean aspect of the plot is intriguing, since Kim Jong II, the nation's leader, is reportedly a big fan of the Bond movies, and the British *chargé-d'affaires*, Jim Haore, told the *Financial Times* in 2002 that most of the North Korean men he met had seen a James Bond film. It was also a political hot potato, with Korean groups announcing before the film even began production that they would object to any storyline that appeared to vilify Koreans. The filmmakers, however, had - as usual - made the villains self-obsessed individuals, not nations.

During the early development of the script, the Bond producers and MGM had continued to battle Kevin McClory's ongoing lawsuit, which claimed that McClory was owed part ownership of the cinematic incarnation of James Bond due to his contributions to the story that became *Thunderball*. In March 2000, a judge ruled that he was dismissing McClory's claim, agreeing with Danjaq and MGM that he had waited too long to file his lawsuit. McClory appealed the decision, but the Federal District Court of Appeals for the 9th Circuit upheld the earlier ruling. Marc Becker, an attorney representing MGM and Danjaq, said, "We certainly hope that this will end it all. It should."

The ruling honoured the decades of commitment to James Bond and the careful development of the series undertaken by the producers who had guided the Eon 007 films, all of whom had each spent years working with writers, directors, production designers, composers and hundreds of skilled actors and technicians in constructing the adventures of James Bond. They had based the films on the successes of Ian Fleming's novels and built from there. Considering the depth and length of the accomplishment, it would have been a tragedy had the credit and success afforded the producers and the studio been mitigated by a contrary ruling. With the legal battle out of the way, and with all the Bond films, including *Casino Royale* and *Never Say Never Again*, now owned by Danjaq and MGM, the filmmakers and the studio had even further motivation to make the 20th Bond film a movie to remember.

The scale of *Die Another Day* was not the only impressive change in the world of 007. Ever since the release of *GoldenEye*, manufactures and marketers had become increasingly interested in capturing some of the Bond magic, but with the focus on the films, little had been done in the way of creating a large-scale marketing strategy. After the release of *The World Is Not Enough*, the film producers decided to address that situation. Working with marketing guru Keith Snelgrove, the filmmakers created a new company, Bond Marketing, Inc., to develop and license a new wave of Bond merchandise within a co-ordinated strategy.

"I think James Bond represents worldly omnipotence — someone who is on top of things and who always beats the 'bad guys' - no matter what the odds. With, of course, all the latest technology available to mere mortals. As children, we dream of being heroes, and as adults, that dream is still with us. What can be better than always winning? Absolutely nothing. That's why we like James Bond." Donald J. Trump

A design team helped create a uniform guide to 'the Bond style' that would reach across a variety of merchandise, unifying the James Bond product line with a definitive look and feel. The merchandising licences focused on key areas directly related to the James Bond image, including highly detailed replica and radio-controlled cars, specially designed watches, playing and trading cards, spy-themed toys for children, and action figures aimed at the adult collectors market (including a Bond girl Barbie and a Ken figure as Bond).

The plan to develop James Bond as a marketing and merchandising brand was on a scale not attempted since the mid-1960s. Certainly there had been merchandising pushes in the recent past, including the amazing successes of Neiman Marcus's limited edition James Bond BMW Z3s and the Corgi and Johnny Lightning die-cast Bond vehicles designed for the collectors market. But there had also been numerous companies who had been unable to capitalize on their Bond licences. Bond Marketing, Inc. was designed to work closely with licensees, helping behind the scenes with design, promotion and marketing strategies for their products.

The impetus for this new focus on merchandising originated a few months before the premiere of *Tomorrow Never Dies* with the release of the most successful James Bond product ever. In fact, it was more than just a product, it was the launch of a new incarnation of 007. Since 1953, when Jonathan Cape first issued the novel CASINO ROYALE, 007 had conquered the worlds of publishing, film, music, television and home video. On 25th August 1997, James

Bond revolutionized the world of interactive video games.

The release of the *GoldenEye 007* game for Nintendo 64 changed the gaming industry forever. Many critics could barely hide their excitement, and *GoldenEye 007* was quickly deemed "the best computer game ever". One critic noted, "It's very difficult for me to describe a game that is so close to perfection." Another stated that *GoldenEye 007* was "easily the surprise hit of the decade." The game topped sales lists, selling over 2.1 million copies in the US in 1998 alone, earning the Game of the Year award from the Academy of Interactive Arts and Sciences. *GoldenEye 007* was so big that Nintendo credited it as a driving force behind the success of the Nintendo 64 platform during the Christmas 1997 sales season. "No game in history took the world over by storm like this one, and no game will probably ever do it again," wrote Anthony Eaton in 2001.

The *GoldenEye 007* game was an important milestone in the history of Bond, because, like the novel CASINO ROYALE and the film *Dr. No*, it represented a new viable franchise for 007. While film studios were looking towards video games as the source for new film concepts, the Bond producers had successfully taken a cinematic hero and transformed him into the most popular video game hero on a monumental scale.

The game brought in more revenue than the theatrical release of the film on which it was based, and transformed a generation of computer game aficionados who soon described themselves as James Bond fans even though they had never seen a 007 film. Colleges and

fraternities hosted *GoldenEye 007* tournaments. By the summer of 2001 the game had sold over eight million copies worldwide, making it far and away the top-selling video game of all time. While eight million might not sound an astounding number compared with the number of worldwide admissions to the films, consider that the games originally sold for $61.00 apiece, and that among boys aged seven to fourteen in the US, 73% had played the game within the four-year period since its release. To them, 007 was cool, cutting-edge, high-tech. While they probably did not even know that Dom Perignon was a brand of champagne, the youngest computer game fans understood that James Bond represented quality and sophistication.

The impact of *GoldenEye 007* on the computer gaming industry was immediate and controversial. *GoldenEye 007* popularized its format – a design called 'first person shooter' - which quickly became the most imitated in the video game industry. However, at a time when there were concerns about the impact on children of violence on television, in movies and in video games, the designers of subsequent Bond video games made an even greater effort to downplay random violence in favour of strategy and careful choices. Players are rewarded for non-lethal confrontations in *007: Agent Under Fire*, and bloodletting, just as in the Bond films themselves, is minimized. The changes have not seemed to slow the enthusiasm for Bond among game players. *007: Agent Under Fire* was securely ranked in the Top Ten games sold during the 2001 Christmas season in both the US and Great Britain. *007: Agent Under Fire* proved remarkable for other reasons. Unlike the games based on *Tomorrow Never Dies* and *The World Is Not Enough*, *Agent Under Fire* was not modelled on any Bond films. The game created new characters and new adventures. The next Bond computer game, *Nightfire*, would also be an original scenario with clever plot twists.

The unprecedented success of the new video games not only illustrated the merchandising potential of James Bond, it also justified the commitment of resources to insuring that James Bond represented the best in all areas of the consumer marketplace. James Bond was now more than just a fictional character. He was a brand, and every James Bond creation - whether a movie, computer game or wristwatch - needed to reflect the allure and feel of the unique world of 007.

Cars continue to play a strong role in Bond's world, as the stunning chase across the ice in *Die Another Day* (**top**) demonstrates. The iconographic nature of the 'Bond car' has also been a key to Bond's merchandising success, from the original Corgi Aston Martin DB5 to the new film, where even the villain's car gets the Bond treatment with this 1:18 scale Jaguar XKR Roadster convertible (**middle**). With the success of the *GoldenEye 007* video game (**bottom**), Bond merchandising entered a new era. The focused campaign is designed not only to provide Bond products to the legions of fans but also to enhance the appeal and value of 007.

By the formal start of production of *Die Another Day* in January 2002, all the elements for the 20th Bond adventure seemed to reflect this quest for the best. The technical crew again read like a who's who of the film industry, with numerous Academy Award winners in key positions. Longtime collaborators, like production designer *extraordinaire* Peter Lamont, costume designer Lindy Hemmings and special effects supervisor Chris Corbould (to name a few) returned. Continuing a tradition begun with *GoldenEye*, the producers and the director gathered together a cast of world-class actors, including Halle Berry as Jinx and the return of Dame Judi Dench as M.

Halle Berry won the 2001 Best Actress Oscar for her role in *Monster's Ball*, becoming the first African American actress ever to win the category (Dame Judi had won the Best Supporting Actress award in 1999 for her performance in *Shakespeare In Love*).

For the role of Gustav Graves, the filmmakers cast Toby Stephens, whose mother, Dame Maggie Smith, was also nominated for an Oscar in 2001 (as Best Actress in a Supporting Role).

To interpret the title song, the producers snagged the most successful female singer/composer of the past twenty years - Madonna. David Arnold, fresh from the acclaim surrounding his innovative work for *Changing Lanes*, returned to create the score. Producers Michael Wilson and Barbara Broccoli also continued to bring members of their family into the world of Bond. Michael Wilson's son, David, who had joined the team on *GoldenEye*, took on the position of Vice President, Global Marketing. Greg Wilson, David's brother, also began working on the production as script

supervisor, along with one of Cubby Broccoli's granddaughters, Heather Banta in the wardrobe department.

The worldwide press covered the production in minute detail, while the producers prepared to celebrate the 40th anniversary of the Bond legacy. In March 2002, the National Museum of Photography, Film & Television in West Yorkshire, England launched an exhibition of Bond props, artifacts and production art. The interactive exhibit was scheduled to arrive in London at the Science Museum just a month before the Royal premiere of *Die Another Day*.

In April, Penguin reissued all the original Ian Fleming James Bond books in hardcover, paperback and audiobook formats. The release made a big splash in the UK, where London storefronts offered displays and newspapers published appreciations of Fleming's contributions to modern popular literature.

James Bond continued to be a significant part of the fabric of global culture, a continuing traveller down the twisting road of the *zeitgeist*. During the years since Brosnan had taken over the role, a constant flow of espionage-themed films had filled cinemas, creating and extending this new era of spymania with movies that were every bit as whacked out as the spy films of the mid-1960s. Consider the following list of big-budget studio releases - *The Avengers* (1998), *Wild Wild West* (1999), *Inspector Gadget* (1999) and *Mission: Impossible 2* (2000) - each of which was based on a long-ago cancelled television show that owed its very existence to the James Bond phenomenon. Without 007, it is unlikely that espionage comedies like *Spy Kids* and *Zoolander* (both 2001) would ever have been born.

"It's a leviathan of a movie. They've thrown everything at it but the kitchen sink." Pierce Brosnan

Opposite, left: Director Lee Tamahori and Halle Berry both share a multi-cultural background. Tamahori is a Maori New Zealander with significant European blood, whose breakthrough film dealt with issues of assimilation. Berry's parents were an inter-racial couple, although Berry sees herself very much as an African American. Both the director and the actress have embraced their cultural heritage in their public lives, and both brought with them interesting and broad personal perspectives on the world of Bond.

Above: A weathered, hirsute Bond after his confinement in a North Korean prison, an image in stark contrast to Bond's reputation as a cinematic hero who never has a hair out of place.

Left: Gustav Graves' ice palace was inspired by the real Icehotel in Jukkasjärvi, Sweden. Construction of the amazing structure takes place annually, starting in November, utilizing over 30,000 tons of snow. By mid-May, the hotel has to close for the season because it has melted away. For the film set, production designer Peter Lamont used plastic resins to re-create the look of real ice. The plastics needed to be strong since the set provided the location for a high-speed car chase.

Overleaf: Rosamund Pike as Miranda Frost and Toby Stephens as Gustav Graves. Prior to appearing in the 007 film, Stephens had taken the title role in a 2001 television production of *The Great Gatsby*.

More serious spy movies included 1998's *Enemy Of The State* and *The Art Of War* (2000), which featured Wesley Snipes as the first successful attempt at a black James Bond-type character, in this case a spy for the UN. The film opened with a very Bondian scene featuring Snipes in the requisite tuxedo, and later showed an underworld club with nude women painted gold. *Spy Game* (2001) brought Brad Pitt and Robert Redford together in an elaborate espionage tale set over a 16-year time-span.

The Tailor Of Panama, released in 2001, was based on the novel by John Le Carré. It used the premise of a British spy who had been booted from a good assignment for the very Bondian political sin of sleeping with the wrong woman. Director John Boorman managed to secure Pierce Brosnan for the role of Osnard, the spy who uses a delusional expatriate in Panama to help him construct an elaborate plot for revolution. Eventually, the revolution is revealed to be nothing more than an excuse for Brosnan's character to embezzle millions in aid to the non-existent insurgents.

The Tailor Of Panama put a fresh spin on the Bond mythos by placing a misanthropic Bond-like character in the delicate strictures of the real world. Osnard's serial seductions seem more pathological than sexual; his self-assured, lone eagle form of espionage proves to be totally self-serving and leaves a wake of tragic deaths in his path.

The Tailor of Panama exemplified the remarkable cultural polarity of 007. On one side was the extreme parody offered by Mike Myers with the Austin Powers films. On the other was Le Carré's attempt to deflate the Bond image through serious drama. Surrounding both extremes was a world seemingly filled with the debris of the Bond mythology.

By the 2001 television season, US networks featured three new spy shows - *Alias*, *The Agency*, and *24* - each influenced by the legacy of 007 in its own way. Film studios released a plethora of spy-themed film titles in the summer of 2002, including *Undercover Brother*, *XXX*, *Enigma* (from Bond director Michael Apted), *Sum Of All Fears*, *Bad Company*, Austin Powers in *Goldmember*, *The Bourne Identity*, *Spy Kids 2* and even *Crocodile Hunter: Collision Course*. Musicians, from established stars to obscure jazz quartets, continued to re-record Bond theme songs, with titles like *Casino Royale*'s 'The Look Of Love' once again appearing on the Billboard charts.

Above: Dame Judi Dench brings back the coldness of character of M which she exhibited in *GoldenEye*. In the years since she took over the role, she has been nominated for four Academy Awards, winning once.

Right: The hovercrafts used in the opening sequence of the film are able to travel over the land-mined demilitarized zone separating North and South Korea. In recent years activists have tried to develop similar hovercrafts to detect such dangerous weapons.

The community of collectors of Bond memorabilia came of age during this time. Christie's hosted its first auction devoted solely to James Bond in 1998, featuring, among other items, Oddjob's steel-rimmed hat. Eon Productions became an important bidder at the auction, purchasing the lethal hat and numerous other items for its growing collection. Another Bond auction followed in 2000, by which point vintage Bond posters were commanding prices of hundreds, sometimes thousands of pounds. The inflation in the prices of 007 items could be most clearly seen in the amounts paid for Fleming first editions - in 2001, a pristine, unsigned copy of CASINO ROYALE sold for over $20,000.

Of course, Bond's impact has travelled far beyond entertainment. 007 has shaped the way news is reported. A typical headline in the UK announced, "Top mafia chief seized in 'James Bond' hide-out." The article revealed a reinforced door, a hidden escape hatch in the back, and nothing else. On CNN, a reporter commented that Peru's former spy chief, Vladimiro Montesinos, had lived "like James Bond". It turned out that during a search of Montesinos's beach house authorities found a few hidden cameras and an escape tunnel beneath a false bathtub. Why not report that both men had houses "suitable for hiding Anne Frank", or "hideouts similar to those used

by 1920s Prohibition gangsters in the US"? The descriptions are probably more accurate. The *Los Angeles Times* reported in 2002 that "in Japan, professional 'breaker-uppers' employ James Bond-like tactics to divide lovers, spouses and even corporate partners". The "James Bond tactics" boiled down to standard private detective tricks: hidden cameras and attractive decoys hired to lure someone into a compromising position. This mythology of 007 is so prevalent that when we see one element - a secret hideout, a hidden camera - we extrapolate the glamour, the sophistication, the lethal dangers.

Why has James Bond entertained us for so long when we have cast aside so many popular culture icons during the past 40 years? James Bond's survival throughout the last half of the 20th century can be attributed to many factors, but luck is not one of them. 007 may have been created at the right place and time in history, but his continued resonance with the worldwide movie-going public has little to do with chance. Bond has lasted because of the enduring mythology of the character and the continued relevance of his

Above, left and right: Three steel-rimmed hats were made for *Goldfinger*. Only one of them survived, which was sold by Graham Rye, president of the James Bond 007 International Fan Club, at auction at Christie's in 1997 . The hat later went on show in the UK at The National Museum Of Photography, Film & Television in Bradford, as part of a touring exhibition celebrating Bond's 40th anniversary which later moved on to the Science Museum in London. *The Times* reported that there was "enough in the exhibition to please diehard 007 anoraks as well as casual fans who only ever watch Bond on a rainy bank holiday afternoon."

fictional universe. This mythology has - with relatively few adjustments - survived for 50 years since Ian Fleming created 007, and throughout 40 years of cinematic adventures.

The character of James Bond defies one of the key romantic tenets that identify the mythic hero. Bond does not exist in the distant past. In this, Bond is unlike Sherlock Holmes, a character clearly tied to the temporal popular culture of his era. Sir Arthur Conan Doyle's original Holmes literary adventures were published over a 41-year span, but Holmes existed in a Victorian and Edwardian world where the character's iconography and traits were clearly defined by a time and place. Despite some Hollywood films where Holmes pursued Nazi agents on gas-lit London streets, the march of history, particularly the advent of the Second World War, made Sherlock Holmes irrelevant as a modern hero. Holmes, in essence, matured from a pop culture icon into a period-piece hero.

James Bond survived the first decade of his biggest test: the end of the Cold War. During the 1990s, Bond existed both as an icon of an era now past and as a modern hero. Most critics would say Bond's world is essentially our world, but Bond's world is dramatically different, seen through a magical looking-glass that exaggerates beauty, elegance and danger. For 40 years, Bond's cinematic world

has continued to be relevant to film-watchers around the globe. It is close enough to our world for us to continue to embrace 007 as a modern hero, while still accepting him as part of our popular culture.

The art of creating mythic stories set in the present is particularly difficult because the present constantly changes, as the events of 11th September illustrate. Yesterday's technological innovation becomes tomorrow's outdated trinket. Fashion tastes and music styles shift into self-parody with alarming speed. Morality changes, too, offering no respite for storytellers. The quaint tales of yesterday so quickly seem uncomfortably patronizing or insensitive. Bond, though, does not, in fact, exist in the present. He exists in a more rarified time and place that the filmmakers refer to as "two minutes into the future".

Many wise men have gone broke trying to predict the future, yet the Bond mythology seemingly requires such prescient abilities from those who craft his adventures. When *Dr. No* premiered in London, the filmmakers could not have known that the Cuban missile crisis was about to erupt. Nor were there hints of the Profumo scandal when *From Russia With Love* started shooting in early 1963. In January 1966, a US plane with a hydrogen bomb disappeared in the Atlantic Ocean off the coast of Spain, which struck some observers as eerily similar to the theft of the NATO bombs in *Thunderball*, released just weeks earlier. The tragedy of Apollo 1 preceded *You Only Live Twice*, and its tale of astronauts dying and being kidnapped in space, by mere months. In *Diamonds*

Are Forever, Blofeld stole the identity of a reclusive Howard Hughes-type billionaire; as the film played in cinemas, Hughes himself called reporters to announce that a purported autobiography by Clifford Irving was a hoax. Irving, it seems, had tried to steal the real Hughes' identity.

This unscripted connection between the Bond films and current events continued with the more recent movies. The plot of 1995's *GoldenEye* centred around the robbery of British banks through electronic transfers. Just a few months earlier, Nick Leeson managed to destroy Barings Bank, and the media seized on the idea that Leeson had, in the process, pulled off an elaborate electronic robbery. Daiwa Bank of Japan revealed a billion-dollar fraud loss under similar circumstances just two months before *GoldenEye* premiered. The Clinton-Lewinsky affair broke just over a month after the film's release, and with it came credible charges of media manipulation by reporters, prosecutors and persecutors who were doggedly pursuing impeachment of the US President.

On the date of the US release of *The World Is Not Enough*, papers around the globe carried the news of the launch of a US-backed pipeline from Baku in Azerbaijan to the Turkish port of Ceyhan. The fictional battle over just such a pipeline was the very focus of the new Bond film. In addition, the climax of *The World Is Not Enough* featured the deliberate sinking of a Russian nuclear submarine. In August 2000, less than a year after the film opened, a real Russian sub - the *Kursk* - sank in mysterious and tragic circumstances in the Barents Sea.

The Bond films have also been prescient when it came to events many years after the film's release. This was particularly true for *Goldfinger*, certainly the most iconic of the Bond movies. In the early 1970s when gold prices soared, many openly speculated that the US government itself had raided Fort Knox, leaving empty vaults. Reporters were eventually taken inside the depository, and many expressed disappointment that the interior looked nothing like Ken Adam's glittering version. In the late 1970s, *Goldfinger* was again cited when the Hunt brothers of Texas tried to corner the market on silver - not through robbery, but through aggressive purchases. Whereas Auric Goldfinger hoped to cause financial chaos through his control of the metal markets, the Hunts caused havoc when they lost control. The situation became so dire that US banks propped up the pair with an emergency $1.1 billion credit line.

Many other Bond films seemed to foreshadow future events. Blofeld's spacecraft-eating rocket in *You Only Live Twice* bore a close resemblance to NASA's own Delta Clipper craft, tested between 1993 and 1996. The satellite-based laser weapon of *Diamonds Are Forever* preceded Ronald Reagan's Strategic Defense Initiative programme by over a decade. Blofeld's system deserves credit for working perfectly with far less than 20 years of research and development. Nearly two decades after *Live And Let Die*, conspiracy theories abounded that the CIA (and not drug lords like the fictional Dr. Kananga) developed crack cocaine as a cheap way to turn a significant percentage of the American black population into addicts.

By the late 1970s, environmentalists were openly accusing oil and coal companies of squelching research into solar power, although they did not go as far as accusing them of hiring an assassin - like Francisco Scaramanga - to obtain key technological components. In 2001, China and the US tussled over the downing of a spy plane that the Chinese argued had entered Chinese airspace, an echo of the opening of *Tomorrow Never Dies* where a British warship is guided into Chinese waters by the villain, who proceeds to provoke his own international incident. The prescient nature of the films continued with *Die Another Day* when, well after the Korean elements of the plot was firmly established in the script, George W. Bush proclaimed to the world that North Korea was part of "an axis of evil", causing speculation about further conflict.

James Bond has not shaped history so much as given us a fictional context for our social changes over the past many decades. Bond has represented the virtues of our consumerism and materialism.

We want the best cars, finest clothes, most reliable watches, just like 007. Bond has allowed us to embrace our hedonism, even if we only live out such fantasies vicariously through 007's adventures. For both women and men, Bond has served as an example of sexual emancipation, a hero who enjoys and embraces the moment without guilt.

Bond has also given us a language to define our enemies, and not just the usual Cold War suspects. 007's adversaries have represented the deadly sins - from Goldfinger's greed to Blofeld's snobbery in *On Her Majesty's Secret Service*. The Bond villains have lusted for power, been trapped by their own pride, lashed out in anger, and found themselves unable to quench

Top: Just as James Bond's legacy in literature and films has spanned 50 years, so too has the legacy of the Cambridge spy case, culminating with the release of Miranda Carter's biography of Anthony Blunt in 2001. If Fleming hoped CASINO ROYALE would address the issue of betrayal raised by the case of the 'missing diplomats', then 007 has more than accomplished his creator's initial goal.

"The British have become noticeably less impressed with their supposed superiors over the past half century", Julian Barnes wrote in the *New Yorker* in January 2002. "The social class that took for granted its right to rule and administer no longer commands automatic respect. One key factor in that loss of respect is the case of the Cambridge spies."

After the defection of Kim Philby, the 'third man', in 1963, and the confession of one-time American communist Michael Straight in 1964, M15 confronted Anthony Blunt, offering him immunity if he confessed everything. Blunt agreed, but few feel he ever told the entire truth. Blunt was not publicly unmasked until 1979, when Prime Minister Margaret Thatcher announced Blunt as a traitor. The British had good reason to keep Blunt's role secret. By 1964, Blunt was the pre-eminent art historian in England; he had been knighted, and worked for the Queen.

James Bond, on the other hand, has built up all the institutions that the Cambridge spies tore down. If Burgess, Maclean, and later Kim Philby, Anthony Blunt, and John Cairncross, who became known as the 'fifth man', represented all that was wrong with the British system, the literary Bond made a case for all that was right. Later, the cinematic 007 became a global ambassador who did much to promote the image of a royal and worthy Britannia: consider the unfurling of the Union Jack parachute in 1977's *The Spy Who Loved Me* alone.

For many around the world, James Bond *is* Britain. He is certainly the personification of the quintessential British spy. In this respect fact has been over-ridden by fiction. When President Bill Clinton made Sean Connery an honorary citizen of the US in 1999, he remarked, "After all, we couldn't have won the Cold War without you." When we think of sophisticated, public school-educated British spies, we do not think of the Cambridge gang. We think only of James Bond.

"It's the women, the gadgets, the sex, the romance, the fantasy world, the ultimate hero." Pierce Brosnan, on why the world loves James Bond

their gluttonous appetites. They embody the excesses of our times. It seems almost comical, but certainly appropriate, that one of the last ongoing efforts at the much-vilified, now-bankrupt, energy-trading firm Enron was named Project Thunderball.

Despite the fact that we never see James Bond helping little children, or shepherding old ladies across busy streets, Bond is a humanist. He lives life to the full, but does not intoxicate himself with excess. Bond enjoys the challenge, expects the best and gives his best back to the world in return. Bond clearly loves his fictional universe. He is not out to change the world, but, more importantly, to save the world. In the Bond adventures, it is the villains who are agents of change, who bring chaos and uncertainty.

"The world has changed. James Bond has not." Writer Bruce Feirstein's approach to bringing James Bond into the 1990s also defined Bond's lasting appeal and the key to the future success that awaits the character. Audiences expect new exploits, gadgets, villains, women, theme songs, and even new actors portraying Bond, but for 40 years, they have wanted 007 to remain essentially unchanged. However, Bond has had to evolve through the years, sliding with the times from cold, rebellious killer to comedic, self-assured sensualist. The success from film to film has often depended on the filmmakers' ability to find the right pulse of the times. With each new film after the initial blush of success in the 1960s, the producers have faced the same question—where to take 007 next?

As 007 walks ever so nonchalantly into our new, uncertain

millennium, he should be aware that the deck has been stacked against him. The villains have changed, the gadgetry has become more sophisticated and deadly, the women are decidedly more complex, and the scope has expanded to a truly awe-inspiring scale. It is indeed a new era, and all the stops have been pulled. But don't bet against Bond. Despite the changes sweeping through our world, James Bond does not slide into his lethally equipped Aston Martin V12 Vanquish alone. 007 is accompanied by an array of talented filmmakers, skilled technicians, and legions of loyal fans. We cannot predict the future, but we can safely bet that James Bond will be part of it.

From a simple portable typewriter on a desk in Jamaica, Ian Fleming created a character that quickly became a legend. Bond's remarkable journey from the mind of Fleming to the consciousness of succeeding generations illustrates our fantasies and our nightmares. We live in a world that enjoys James Bond because we live in a world where we believe we need 007. We need his calm elegance, his spirit of adventure, his courage and verve. We need his ability to say just the right thing at just the right time, his understanding of how to push the boundaries without ever going too far. We need Bond to re-introduce us to the exotic nature of our own world, the excitement and intrigue in our own lives.

Let us hope that as long as our society values sophistication, grace, adventure, and sensuality, we will continue to be enthralled with the adventures of Commander James Bond, C.M.G., R.N.V.R., secret agent 007.

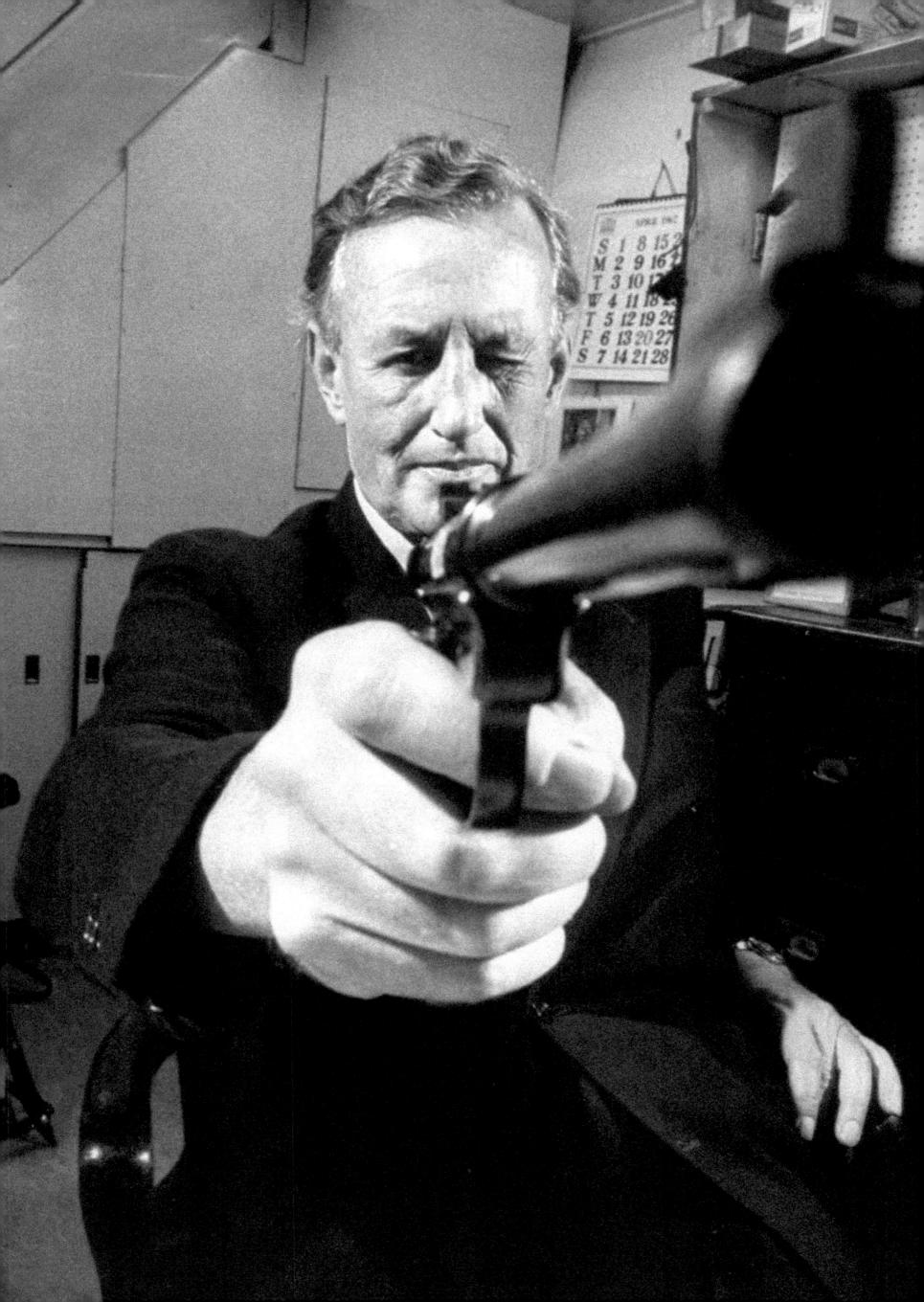

James Bond: The Numbers

James Bond is known by his number, 007, and his impact on popular culture can be illustrated by the dates and numbers that document his 50-year career. What follows is the raw data off the constantly running Bond ticker tape, the statistics that can be used to settle bets, confound your friends and irritate your enemies - use with caution. Financial data is generally presented in US dollars, as that is the way in which film studios tend to immortalize their box office successes.

Date of publication of CASINO ROYALE: 13th April 1953
Number of copies printed of first edition of CASINO ROYALE: 4,750
Number of copies of Fleming's 14 Bond books printed since 1953: over 70 million
Date of CBS-TV broadcast of *CLIMAX!* **Episode 'Casino Royale':** 21st October 1954

Dr. No

Worldwide box office: $59.5 million
World premiere: 5th October 1962 at the London Pavilion
US release date: 8th May 1963
European release dates: Denmark - 5th April 1963; Finland - 29th March 1963; Sweden - 29th April 1963; West Germany - 25th January 1963
US box office: $16.067 million
US admissions: 19 million
Hit singles: UK - 'The James Bond Theme' (performed by John Barry & His Orchestra; composed by Monty Norman) reached 13 on sales chart
US - 'The James Bond Theme'(performed by Billy Strange) reached 58 on *Billboard* Pop Singles chart (in 1964)
Soundtrack album: US - reached 82 on *Billboard* Album sales chart
Awards: Nominated for two Laurel Awards, given by *Motion Picture Exhibitor* magazine
Number of sold-out shows during first week at the New Empire Theatre, Bombay, India: 28
Date of television premiere: 10th November 1974, on ABC
Date of first broadcast in UK: 28th October 1975, on ITV
Ranking among most-watched programmes of the year: 1st
Number of homes watching first UK airing: 9.2 million
First broadcast on 'late night' television in US: 26th December 1978, on ABC
Date of first pay cable broadcast: 7th June 1980, on HBO
Date of return broadcast during prime time in US: 20th July 1983
Ranking among most-watched programmes of the week: 1st
Date of first basic cable television telecast: 4th March 1991, on TBS
Ranking among most watched movie broadcasts in UK in 2001: 12th

From Russia With Love

Worldwide box office: $78.9 million
World premiere: 10th October 1963, London Pavilion
US release date: 8th April 1964
European release dates: Denmark - 20th December 1963; Finland - 14th August 1964; Sweden - 31st March 1964; West Germany - 14th February 1964
US box office: $24.8 million
US admissions: 26.8 million
Hit singles: UK - 'From Russia With Love' (performed by Matt Monro, composed by Lionel Bart) reached 20 on singles chart
US - 'From Russia With Love' (performed by The Village Stompers) reached 81 on *Billboard* Pop Singles chart
Soundtrack album: UK - reached 39 on sales charts; US - reached 27 on *Billboard* Album sales chart
Awards: BAFTA – Best Cinematography (colour):Ted Moore; British Society of Cinematographers – Best Cinematography: Ted Moore; Golden Globe nomination for Best Song. Two Laurel Award nominations
Date of television premiere: 14th January 1974, on ABC
Date of first broadcast in UK: 2nd May 1976, on ITV
Ranking among most-watched programmes of the year: 7th
Number of homes watching first UK airing: 9.2 million
Date of first basic cable television telecast: 4th March 1991, on TBS
Ranking among most watched movie broadcasts in UK in 2001: 22nd

Goldfinger

Worldwide box office: $124.9 million
World premiere: 17th September 1964, Odeon Leicester Square, London
US release date: 25th December 1964
European release dates: Denmark - 26th December 1964; Finland - 29th January 1965; France - 18th February 1965; Sweden - 5th February 1965; West Germany - 14th January 1965
Asian release dates: Japan - 9th April 1965; Singapore - 5th August 1965

US box office: $51.1 million
US admissions: $50.6 million
Hit singles: 'Goldfinger' (performed by Shirley Bassey, composed by Leslie Bricusse, Anthony Newley, John Barry)
UK - reached 21 on singles chart
US - reached 8 on *Billboard* Pop Singles chart
'Goldfinger' (performed by Billy Strange)
US - reached 55 on *Billboard* Pop Singles chart
'Goldfinger - Instrumental' (performed by John Barry & His Orchestra)
US - reached 72 on *Billboard* Pop Singles chart
'Goldfinger' (performed by Jack LaForge, His Piano & Orchestra)
US - reached 96 on *Billboard* Pop Singles chart
Soundtrack album: UK - reached 14 on sales chart
US - reached 1 on *Billboard* Album sales chart
Awards: Won Academy Award for Best Sound Effects, awarded to Norman Wanstall. BAFTA - nominated for Best British Art Direction (Colour). Nominated for Edgar Allan Poe Award for Best Mystery Screenplay. Won two Laurel Awards
Amount grossed in 41 US cities, 64 cinemas in two weeks: 2.9 million
US cities reporting record opening week grosses: 41 (ie all cities where film was playing)
US cinemas reporting record opening week grosses: 64 (all the cinemas where film was playing)
Ranking among fastest grossing films in US history as of January 1965: 1st
Date of television premiere: 17th September 1972, on ABC
Percentage of US television viewers who saw premiere broadcast: 49%
Ratio of New York City televisions tuned to *Goldfinger*: 3 out of 5
Date of first UK broadcast: 3rd November 1976, on ITV
Ranking among most-watched programmes of the year: 1st
Date of first basic cable television telecast: 5th March 1991, on TBS
Ranking among most-watched movie broadcasts in UK in 2001: 27th

Thunderball

Worldwide box office: $141.2 million
World premiere: 9th December 1965, Hibiya Cinema, Tokyo, Japan
US release date: 21st December 1965
UK release date: 29th December 1965
European release dates: Denmark - 17th December 1965; Finland - 25th December 1965; Ireland - 10th February 1966; Sweden - 17th December 1965; West Germany - 17th December 1965
US box office: $63.6 million
US admissions: 58.1 million
Hit singles: 'Thunderball' (performed by Tom Jones, composed by John Barry, Don Black)
UK - reached 35 on singles charts
US - reached 25 on *Billboard* Pop Singles chart
Soundtrack album: US - reached 10 on *Billboard* Album sales chart
Awards: Won an Academy Award for Best Visual Effects, awarded to John Stears. BAFTA – nominated for Best British Art Direction (Colour). Nominated for Edgar Allen Poe Award. Won two Laurel Awards
Percentage by which *Thunderball* **out-grossed all other films during opening week in US:** 400%
Number of box office records set during London opening weekend: 11
Date of television premiere: 22nd September 1974, on ABC
Date of first broadcast in UK: 26th February 1977, on ITV
Number of viewers watching broadcast: 16.6 million
Ranking among most-watched programmes of the month: 1st
Ranking among most-watched programmes of the year: 14th
Date of first basic cable television telecast: 5th March 1991, on TBS

Casino Royale

World premiere: 13th April 1967, Odeon Leicester Square, London
US release date: 28th April 1967
European release dates: Finland - 22nd December 1967; France - 22nd December 1967 (France - 20th February 2002 [re-release]); Sweden - 22nd December 1967; West Germany - 21st December 1967
US rental: $10,200,000
Hit singles: 'Casino Royale' (performed by Herb Alpert & The Tijuana Brass, composed by Burt Bacharach)
UK - reached 27 on sales chart
US - reached 27 on *Billboard* Pop Singles chart; reached 1 on *Billboard* Adult Contemporary chart
'The Look Of Love' (performed by Dusty Springfield, composed by Burt Bacharach and Hal David)
US - reached 22 on *Billboard* Pop Singles chart
'The Look Of Love' (performed by Sergio Mendes & Brasil 66)
US - reached 4 on *Billboard* Pop Singles chart (in 1968)

'The Look Of Love' (performed by Isaac Hayes)
US - reached 79 on *Billboard* Pop Singles chart (in 1971)
'The Look Of Love' (performed by Diana Krall)
US - on *Billboard* Pop Singles chart in 2002
Soundtrack album: UK - reached 35 on sales chart
Awards: Nominated for Best Song Academy Award for 'The Look Of Love'.
BAFTA – nominated for Best British Costume (Colour), and one Laurel Award

You Only Live Twice
Worldwide box office: $111.6 million
World premiere: 12th June 1967, Odeon Leicester Square, London
US release date: 13th June 1967
European release dates: Denmark - 11th September 1967; Finland - 15th September 1967; France - 20th September 1967; Norway - 18th September 1967; Sweden - 15th September 1967; West Germany - 14th September 1967
US box office: $43.1 million
US admissions: 36 million. The film set opening day records at the Chinese Theater in Los Angeles and the Fox Theatre in Philadelphia.
Hit singles: 'You Only Live Twice' (performed by Nancy Sinatra, composed by John Barry and Leslie Bricusse)
UK - reached 11 on sales chart
US - reached 44 on *Billboard* Pop Singles chart
Soundtrack album: US - reached 27 on *Billboard* Album sales chart
Awards: BAFTA – nominated for Best British Art Direction (Colour). Nominated for Edgar Allen Poe Award
Date of television premiere: 2nd November 1975, on ABC
Date of first broadcast in UK: 20th November 1977, on ITV
Ranking among most-watched programmes of the year: 4th
Date of first basic cable television telecast: 6th March 1991, on TBS
Ranking among most-watched movies broadcast in UK in 2001: 13th

On Her Majesty's Secret Service
Worldwide box office: $64.6 million
World premiere: 18th December 1969, Odeon Leicester Square, London
US release date: 18th December 1969
European release dates: Denmark - 18th December 1969, Finland - 19th December 1969; Norway - 18th December 1969; Sweden - 18th December 1969; West Germany - 19th December 1969
US box office: $22.8 million
US admissions: 14.7 million
Hit singles: 'We Have All The Time In The World' (performed by Louis Armstrong, composed by John Barry and Hal David)
UK - reached 3 on sales chart (in 1994, 25 years after first release)
'On Her Majesty's Secret Service' (performed by David Arnold and The Propellerheads)
UK - reached 7 on sales chart (in 1997)
Soundtrack album: US - reached 103 on *Billboard* Album sales chart
Awards: George Lazenby nominated for a Golden Globe as Most Promising Newcomer
Number of cinemas at which *OHMSS* opened on 18th December 1969: 1700
Date of television premiere: 16th and 23rd February 1976, on ABC
Date of first broadcast in UK: 4th September 1978, on ITV
Ranking among most-watched programmes of the month: 1st
Date of first basic cable television telecast: 10th March 1991, on TBS

Diamonds Are Forever
Worldwide box office: $116 million
US release date: 17th December 1971
UK release date: 30th December 1971
European release dates: Denmark - 17th December 1971; Finland - 25th December 1971; Norway - 26th December 1971; Sweden - 20th December 1971; West Germany - 14th December 1971
US box office: $43.8 million
US admissions: 25.8 million
Hit singles: 'Diamonds Are Forever' (performed by Shirley Bassey, composed by John Barry and Don Black)
UK - reached 38 on sales chart
US - reached 57 on *Billboard* Pop Singles chart
'Diamonds Are Forever'(performed by David Arnold and David McAlmont)
UK - reached 39 on sales chart in 1997
Soundtrack album: US - reached 74 on *Billboard* Album sales chart
Awards: Nominated for Best Sound Academy Award
Number of major US cities reporting record opening week grosses: 8
Number of countries reporting record opening week grosses: 13
Date of television premiere: 12th September 1975, on ABC
Ratio of televisions tuned to ABC broadcast out of all TVs in the US: 1 in 5
Ratio of televisions watching third ABC broadcast on 26th December 1976: 1 in 4
Date of first broadcast in UK: 25th December 1978, on ITV
Ranking among most-watched programmes in UK in 1981: 2nd
Date of first basic cable television telecast: 6th March 1991, on TBS

Ranking among most-watched movies on basic cable up to that date: 1st
Ranking among most-watched movies broadcast in UK in 2001: 23rd

Live And Let Die
Worldwide box office: $126.4 million
US release date: 27th June 1973
UK release date: 6th July 1973
European release dates: Denmark - 17th December 1973; Finland - 21st December 1973; Sweden - 22nd December 1973; West Germany - 19th December 1973
US box office: $35.4 million
US admissions: 20.1 million
Hit singles: 'Live And Let Die' (performed by Paul McCartney & Wings, composed by Paul & Linda McCartney)
UK - reached 9 on sales chart
US - reached 2 on *Billboard* Pop Singles chart
'Live And Let Die' (performed by Guns N' Roses)
UK - reached 5 on sales chart in 1992
US - reached 33 on *Billboard* Pop Singles chart
US - reached 19 in terms of US single sales
Soundtrack album: US - reached 17 on Billboard Album sales chart
Awards: Nominated for Best Song Academy Award for 'Live And Let Die'
Estimate of worldwide viewership of all Bond films as at end of 1973: 700 million
Date of television premiere: 31st October 1976, on ABC
Ratio of televisions tuned to ABC broadcast out of all TVs in the US: 1 in 4
Date of first broadcast in UK: 20th January 1980, on ITV
Ranking among most-watched programmes in UK in 1980: 1st
Number of viewers who watched 1980 UK broadcast: 23.5 million
Date of first basic cable television telecast: 7th March 1991, on TBS

The Man With The Golden Gun
Worldwide box office: $97.6 million
World premiere: 19th December 1974, Odeon Leicester Square, London
US release date: 19th December 1974
European release dates: Denmark - 19th December 1974; Finland - 20th December 1974; Norway - 20th December 1974; Sweden - 21st December 1974; West Germany - 19th December 1974
US box office: $20.1 million
US admissions: 10.25 million
Date of television premiere: 16th January 1977 on ABC
Ratio of televisions tuned to ABC broadcast out of all TVs in the US: 1 in 4
Date of first broadcast in UK: 25th December 1980, on ITV
Date of first basic cable television telecast: 7th March 1991, on TBS

The Spy Who Loved Me
Worldwide box office: $185.4 million
World premiere: 7th July 1977, Odeon Leicester Square, London
US release date: 13th July 1977
European release dates: Denmark - 12th August 1977; Finland - 23rd September 1977; France - 12th October 1977; Norway - 16th August 1977; Sweden - 17th September 1977; West Germany - 25th August 1977
Asian release date: Hong Kong - July 1977
African release date: South Africa - 9th December 1977
Oceanian release date: Australia - 9th December 1977
US box office: $46.8 million
US admissions: 21.0 million
Hit singles: 'Nobody Does It Better' (performed by Carly Simon, composed by Marvin Hamlisch and Carole Bayer Sager)
UK - reached 7 on sales chart
US - reached 2 on *Billboard* Pop Singles chart. Held number 1 position on *Billboard* Adult Contemporary chart for 7 weeks
Soundtrack album: US - reached 40 on *Billboard* Album sales chart
Awards: Won ASCAP Film and Television Music Award for Most Performed Feature Film Standard for 'Nobody Does It Better'. Nominated for three Academy Awards for Best Art Direction, Best Original Score, and Best Song. Nominated for two BAFTAs – Best Production Design and the Anthony Asquith Award for Film Music. Nominated for two Golden Globes. Nominated by the Writers Guild of America for Best Comedy Screenplay Adapted From Another Medium. Nominated for two Saturn Awards from the Academy of Science Fiction, Fantasy & Horror Films
Estimate of worldwide viewership of all Bond films as at end of 1977: 1 billion
Date of cable television premiere: 12th November 1978, on Home Box Office
Date of television broadcast premiere: 9th November 1980, on ABC
Date of first broadcast in UK: 28th March 1982, on ITV
Date of first basic cable television telecast: 8th March 1991, on TBS

Moonraker
Worldwide box office: $202.7 million
World premiere: 26th June 1979, Odeon Leicester Square, London
US release date: 29th June 1979

European release dates: Austria - 31st August 1979; Denmark - 13th August 1979; Finland - 17th August 1979; France - 10th October 1979; Netherlands - 12th July 1979; Sweden - 18th August 1979; West Germany - 31st August 1979

Asian release dates: Hong Kong - 1st August 1979; Japan - 8th December 1979

African release dates: Kenya - August 1979; South Africa - July 1979

Oceanian release date: Australia - August 1979

Percentage of seats sold on opening day in Hong Kong: 97%

Amount of rain in inches dumped on Hong Kong on opening day due to Typhoon Hope: 8"

Percentage of seats sold during entire opening week in Opera Theatre, Bogotá, Colombia: 100%

Percentage of seats sold during first three days at 20th Century Theatre, Nairobi, Kenya: 100%

Ranking in box office gross among all films to play in Lebanon through 1979: 1st

US box office: $62.7 million

US admissions: 24.9 million

European box office: UK - $19.4 million; West Germany - $12.9 million; Netherlands - $6.7 million; France - $5.9 million; Switzerland - $3.9 million; Italy - $3.6 million; Sweden - $2.67 million; Denmark - $2.1 million; Spain: $2.07 million

African box office: South Africa - $1.9 million

Latin American box office: Brazil - $1.9 million

Oceanian box office: Australia - $3.9 million

Awards: Nominated for Best Visual Effects Academy Award

Per screen average during first week of US release: $30,643

Date of television premiere: 22nd November 1981, on ABC

Date of first broadcast in UK: 27th December 1982, on ITV

Ranking among most viewed shows in UK in 1982: 8th

Date of first basic cable television telecast: 8th March 1991, on TBS

For Your Eyes Only

Worldwide box office: $194.9 million

World premiere: 24th June 1981, Odeon Leicester Square, London

US release date: 26th June 1981

European release dates: Austria - 7th August 1981; Denmark - 10th August 1981; Finland - 21st August 1981; Netherlands - July 1981; Norway - 21st August 1981; Sweden - 22nd August 1981; West Germany - 6th August 1981

African release date: South Africa - July 1981

Asian release dates: Japan - July 1981; Philippines - July 1981

Middle East release date: Israel - July 1981

US box office: $52.3 million

US admissions: 22.4 million

Hit singles: 'For Your Eyes Only' (performed by Sheena Easton, composed by Bill Conti and Michael Leeson)

UK - reached 8 on sales chart

US - reached 4 on Billboard Pop Singles chart

Soundtrack album: US - reached 84 on Billboard Album sales chart

Awards: Nominated for Best Song Academy Award and Best Song Golden Globe. Nominated by the Writers Guild of America for Best Comedy Screenplay Adapted From Another Medium. Won the ASCAP Award for Most Performed Feature Film Standard and a German Golden Screen

Percentage of seats sold for all shows, opening week at Rex Theatre, Helsinki, Finland: 95%

Number of opening day box office records set during release in Spain: 6

Box office records set in UK: 27

Date of television premiere: 27th January 1985, on ABC

Date of first broadcast in UK: 31st August 1986, on ITV

Octopussy

Worldwide box office: $183.7 million

UK release date: 6th June 1983

US release date: 10th June 1983

European release dates: Austria - 5th August 1983; Denmark - 15th August 1983; Finland - 12th August 1983; France - 5th October 1983; Norway - 19th August 1983; Sweden - 23rd July 1983; Switzerland - 5th August 1983; West Germany - 5th August 1983

Asian release dates: Hong Kong - 1st July 1983; Japan - 2nd July 1983

African release date: South Africa - 24th June 1983

Oceanian release date: Australia - 24th November 1983

US box office: $67.9 million

US admissions: 21.5 million

European box office: Germany - $15.65 million; France - $9.11 million; Netherlands - $5.79 million; Sweden - $5.44 million; Switzerland - $4.17 million; Italy - $3.41 million

Asian box office: Japan - $15.07 million; Taiwan - $2.86 million; India - $2.14 million; Hong Kong - $2.05 million

African box office: South Africa - $3.69 million

Latin American box office: Mexico - $1.50 million; Brazil - $1.03 million

Oceanian box office: Australia - $4.68 million

Number of box office records set during first three days of release in West Germany: 35

Number of box office records set during first three days of release in South Africa: 28

Number of box office records set during first three days of release in Sweden: 17

Hit singles: 'All Time High' (performed by Rita Coolidge, composed by John Barry

and Tim Rice)

UK - reached 75 on sales chart

US - reached 36 on Billboard Pop Singles chart. Reached 1 on Billboard Adult Contemporary chart

Soundtrack album: US - reached 137 on Billboard Album sales chart

Awards: Nominated by the Guild of British Film Editors for Best Film Editing

Date of television premiere: 2nd February 1986, on ABC

Date of first broadcast in UK: 30th January 1988, on ITV

Ranking among most viewed programmes in UK in 1988: 15

Never Say Never Again

Worldwide box office: $137.5 million (estimate)

World premiere: 6th October 1983, Mann's National Theater, Los Angeles

UK release date: 15th December 1983

European release dates: Denmark - 20th January 1984; Finland - 16th December 1983; France - 30th November 1983; Norway - 26th December 1983; Sweden - 16th December 1983; West Germany - 20th January 1984

US box office: $55 million

US admissions: 17.5 million

Awards: Nominated for a Golden Globe for Best Supporting Actress, Barbara Carrera

Box office for opening weekend in US: $9,725,154

Ranking of first weekend box office among all films ever released in autumn in US through 1983: 1st

Date of television premiere: 2nd November 1986, on ABC

Date of first broadcast in UK: 25th December 1986, on ITV

A View To A Kill

Worldwide box office: $152.4 million

World premiere: 22nd May 1985, Palace of Fine Arts, San Francisco

UK release date: 13th June 1985

European release dates: Denmark - 9th August 1985; Finland - 9th August 1985; France - 11th September 1985; Norway - 16th August 1985; Sweden - 12th July 1985; West Germany - 9th August 1985

Asian release date: Japan - 6th July 1985

Latin American release date: Brazil - 27th June 1985

US box office: $50.3 million

US admissions: 14.1 million

European box office: Germany - $11.72 million; France - $8.16 million; Sweden - $5.35 million; Netherlands - $4.86 million; Italy - $4.54 million; Switzerland - $3.11 million

Asian box office: Japan - $9.06 million; Taiwan - $2.43 million; Hong Kong - $2.21 million; India - $1.77 million

African box office: South Africa - $1.74 million

Latin American box office: Brazil - $1.23 million; Mexico - $0.87 million

Oceanian box office: Australia - $3.01 million

Hit singles: 'A View To A Kill' (performed by Duran Duran, composed by Duran Duran and John Barry)

UK - reached 2 on sales chart

US - reached 1 on Billboard Pop Singles chart

Soundtrack album: UK - reached 81 on sales chart

US - reached 38 on Billboard Album sales chart

Awards: Nominated for Golden Globe for Best Song. Nominated for a Razzie Award, worst actress, Tanya Roberts

Number of box office records broken in Taiwan, Thailand, Hong Kong and South Africa: 33

Date of television premiere: 5th November 1987, on ABC

Date of first broadcast in UK: 31st January 1990

Ranking among most viewed programmes in UK in 1990: 7th

The Living Daylights

Worldwide box office: $191.2 million

World premiere: 29th June 1987, Odeon Leicester Square, London

US release date: 31st July 1987

European release dates: Denmark - 14th August 1987; Finland - 31st July 1987; France - 16th September 1987; Norway - 5th August 1987; Sweden - 10th July 1987; West Germany - 13th August 1987

US box office: $51.185 million

US admissions: 13.1 million

European box office: Germany - $19.52 million; France - $11.44 million; Netherlands - $8.82 million; Italy - $4.45 million; Sweden - $7.65 million; Switzerland - $5.73 million

Asian box office: Japan - $12.59 million; Taiwan - $3.00 million; Hong Kong - $1.92 million; India - $1.25 million

African box office: South Africa - $2.30 million

Latin American box office: Brazil - $1.16 million; Mexico - $0.67 million

Oceanian box office: Australia - $3.83 million

Hit singles: 'The Living Daylights' (performed by a-ha, composed by Pal Waaktaar and John Barry)

UK - reached 5 on sales chart

'If There Was A Man' (performed by The Pretenders, composed by John Barry and Chrissie Hynde)

UK - reached 49 on sales chart

Soundtrack album: UK - reached 59 on sales chart

Date of television premiere: 15th April 1990, on ABC
Date of first broadcast in UK: 3rd October 1992, on ITV

Licence To Kill

Worldwide box office: $156.2 million
World premiere: 13th June 1989, Odeon Leicester Square, London
US release date: 14th July 1989
European release dates: Denmark - 7th July 1989; Finland - 21st July 1989; France - 16th August 1989; Norway - 7th July 1989; Sweden - 7th July 1989; West Germany - 10th August 1989
US box office: $34.67 million
US admissions: 8.7 million
European box office: Germany - $14.22 million; France - $12.36 million; Netherlands - $8.68 million; Sweden - $8.55 million; Switzerland - $4.36 million; Italy - $2.56 million
Asian box office: Japan - $8.79 million; Taiwan - $3.87 million; Hong Kong - $1.78 million; India - $0.89 million
African box office: South Africa - $1.87 million
Latin American box office: Brazil - $2.16 million; Mexico - $1.06 million
Oceanian box office: Australia - $2.67 million
Hit singles: 'If You Asked Me To' (performed by Patti LaBelle, composed by Diane Warren)
US - reached 79 on *Billboard* Pop Singles chart
'If You Asked Me To' (performed by Celine Dion)
UK - reached 57 on sales chart in 1992
US - reached 4 on *Billboard* Pop Singles chart. Reached 3 on Airplay chart. Reached 1 on Adult Contemporary chart
Date of television premiere: 24th February 1993, on Fox
Date of first broadcast in UK: July 1991, on Sky
Date of first commercial broadcast in UK: 3rd January 1994
Ranking among most-viewed programmes of the month: 8th
Ranking among most-viewed programmes of the year: 16th

GoldenEye

Worldwide box office: $350.7 million
World premiere: 13th November 1995, Dorothy Chandler Pavilion, Los Angeles
US release date: 17th November 1995
UK release date: 24th November 1995
European release dates: Austria - 29th December 1995; Belgium - 20th December 1995; Denmark - 26th January 1996; Estonia - 9th February 1996; Finland - 15th December 1995; France - 20th December 1995; Germany - 28th December 1995, Greece - 12th January 1996; Iceland - 15th December 1995; Italy - 12th January 1996; Luxembourg - 22nd December 1995; Netherlands - 7th December 1995; Norway - 26th December 1995; Poland - 26th December 1995; Portugal - 8th December 1995; Slovenia - 10th December 1995; Spain - 20th December 1995; Sweden - 8th December 1995; Switzerland - 15th December 1995
Asian release dates: Hong Kong - 21st December 1995; Japan - 16th December 1995; Korea - 16th December 1995; Malaysia - 22nd December 1995; Singapore - 7th December 1995
Middle East release date: Israel - 8th December 1995
Latin American release dates: Argentina - 7th December 1995; Mexico - 15th December 1995; Panama - 25th December 1995
North American release dates: Canada - 16th November 1995
Oceanian release dates: Australia - 21st December 1995; New Zealand - 26th December 1995
US box office: $106.4 million
US admissions: 24.45 million
UK box office: £17.393 million (as of 21st January 1996)
European box office: Germany - $43.55 million; France - $27.28 million; Switzerland - $10.27 million; Netherlands - $9.68 million; Sweden - $8.45 million; Italy - $6.33 million
Asian box office: Japan - $19.68 million; Taiwan - $5.57 million; India - $3.88 million; Hong Kong - $2.82 million
African box office: South Africa - $2.99 million
Latin American box office: Brazil - $2.70 million; Mexico - $2.26 million
Oceanian box office: Australia - $10.74 million
Hit singles: 'GoldenEye'
(performed by Tina Turner, composed by Bono and The Edge)
UK - reached 10 on sales chart
US - reached 71 on US singles sales chart
Awards: Nominated for two BAFTA awards for Best Special Effects and Best Sound, and nominated for two MTV Movie Awards for Best Sandwich In A Movie and Best Fight
Date of television premiere: 27th September 1998, on NBC
Date of first commercial broadcast in UK: 10th March 1999
Ranking among most-watched movies broadcast in UK in 2001: 15th

Tomorrow Never Dies

Worldwide box office: $335.3 million
World premiere: 9th December 1997, Odeon Leicester Square, London
US release date: 19th December 1997
UK release date: 12th December 1997
European release dates: Austria - 19th December 1997; Czech Republic - 1st January

1998; Denmark - 19th December 1997; Estonia - 26th December 1997; Finland - 19th December 1997; France - 17th December 1997; Germany - 18th December 1997; Greece - 9th January 1998; Hungary - 18th December 1997; Iceland - 12th December 1997; Italy - 23rd December 1997; Netherlands - 18th December 1997; Norway - 19th December 1997; Poland - 16th January 1998; Portugal - 19th December 1997; Russia - 19th December 1997; Slovakia - 1st January 1998; Slovenia - 18th December 1997; Spain - 16th December 1997; Sweden - 19th December 1997, Switzerland (French-speaking region) - 17th December 1997; Switzerland (Italian-speaking region) - 18th December 1997; Switzerland (German-speaking region) - 19th December 1997
Asian release dates: Hong Kong - 22nd January 1998; Japan - 14th March 1998; Singapore - 24th December 1997; South Korea - 24th January 1998; Taiwan - 24th January 1998; Thailand - 6th March 1998
Middle East release dates: Israel - 19th December 1997; Kuwait - 17th December 1997; Lebanon - 18th December 1997
Latin American release dates: Argentina - 15th January 1998; Brazil - 16th January 1998; Mexico - 16th January 1998
North American release date: Canada - 19th December 1997
Oceanian release dates: Australia - 26th December 1997; New Zealand - 26th December 1997
US box office: $125.332 million
US admissions: 26.7 million
UK box office: £19.884 million
Hit singles: 'Tomorrow Never Dies' (performed by Sheryl Crow, composed by Sheryl Crow and Mitchell Froom)
UK - reached 10 on sales chart
'The James Bond Theme (Moby's Re-version)' (performed by Moby)
UK - reached 8 on sales chart
Awards: Nominated for a Golden Globe, a Golden Satellite, and a Grammy for Best Song, 'Tomorrow Never Dies'. Won Best Sound Editing - Foreign Feature from the Motion Picture Sound Editors, USA. Won an International Monitor Award for Best Electronic Visual Effects In A Title Sequence. Nominated for two MTV Movie Awards for Best Action Sequence and Best Fight. Academy of Science Fiction, Fantasy & Horror Films awarded Pierce Brosnan a Saturn Award for Best Actor
Date of television premiere: 13th October 1999, on ITV
Date of first commercial broadcast in US: 14th January 2001, on CBS

The World Is Not Enough

Worldwide box office: $352,030,660
World premiere: 8th November 1999, Bruin & Fox Theaters, Los Angeles
US release date: 19th November 1999
UK release date: 26th November 1999
European release dates: Austria - 10th December 1999; Belgium - 1st December 1999; Bulgaria - 25th December 1999; Croatia - 16th December 1999; Cyprus - 24th December 1999; Czech Republic - 13th January 2000; Denmark - 10th December 1999; Estonia - 17th December 1999; Finland - 3rd December 1999; France - 1st December 1999; Germany - 9th December 1999; Greece - 7th January 2000; Hungary - 25th November 1999; Iceland - 26th November 1999; Italy - 14th January 2000; Malta - 8th December 1999; Netherlands - 2nd December 1999; Norway - 3rd December 1999; Poland - 7th January 2000; Portugal - 3rd December 1999; Romania - 28th January 2000; Slovakia - 13th January 2000; Slovenia - 20th January 2000; Spain - 3rd December 1999; Sweden - 8th December 1999; Switzerland (French-speaking region) - 1st December 1999; Switzerland (German-speaking region) - 2nd December 1999; Turkey - 14th January 2000
Asian release dates: Hong Kong - 16th December 1999; Japan - 5th February 2000; Indonesia - December 1999; Malaysia - 18th November 1999; Philippines - 5th January 2000; Singapore - 18th November 1999; Taiwan - 1st January 2000; Thailand - 3rd December 1999
African release date: South Africa - 26th November 1999
Middle East release dates: Egypt - 9th January 2000; Israel - 25th November 1999; Kuwait - 5th January 2000; Lebanon - 2nd December 1999; South Africa - 26th November 1999
Oceanian release dates: Australia - 25th November 1999; New Zealand - 26th December 1999
Latin American release dates: Argentina - 23rd December 1999; Brazil - 24th December 1999; Chile - 23rd December 1999; Colombia - 25th December 1999; Ecuador - 24th December 1999; Mexico - 24th December 1999, Panama - 25th December 1999; Peru - 24th December 1999; Trinidad and Tobago - 24th December 1999; Venezuela -15th December 1999
US box office: $126.93 million (as of 23rd April 2000)
UK box office: £28.577 million
Awards: Won a Blockbuster Entertainment Award for Favourite Actor - Action, Nominated for Favourite Actress – Action and Supporting Actress - Action. Won an Empire Award for Best Actor. Nominated for a Saturn Award for Best Action/Adventure/Thriller. Nominated for a Golden Satellite for Best Song. Nominated for Best Sound Editing In A Foreign Film by the Motion Picture Sound Editors. Won a Razzie Award for Worst Supporting Actress, nominated for a Razzie for Worst Screen Couple, Pierce Brosnan and Denise Richards
Date of television premiere: 14th November 2001, on ITV
Ranking among most-watched movies broadcast in UK in 2001: 5th

James Bond: The Adventures

This section includes a breakdown by film of: the villains, both major and minor; their evil plots; the Bond women (the ones with some romantic involvement with 007); Bond's allies on his mission; Bond's team (the re-occurring characters working with Bond across a number of adventures, each introduced during an actor's first appearance in the role); Bond's gadgets (the ones actually used by 007 in the course of the film), and the locations (the identifiable places where the story takes place, not where the filmmakers shot the movie). This is not an exhaustive list of every character or every beautiful woman to appear in a Bond film, but rather a handy thumbnail guide to the world of 007.

IN LITERATURE (Dates refer to first publication in book form, novelizations of film scripts have been excluded)

By Ian Fleming

CASINO ROYALE - 1953 • LIVE AND LET DIE - 1954 • MOONRAKER - 1955 •
DIAMONDS ARE FOREVER - 1956 • FROM RUSSIA WITH LOVE - 1957 • DR. NO - 1958
GOLDFINGER - 1959 • FOR YOUR EYES ONLY - 1960 ('FROM A VIEW TO A KILL',
'FOR YOUR EYES ONLY', 'QUANTUM OF SOLACE', 'RISICO', 'THE HILDEBRAND
RARITY') • THUNDERBALL - 1961 THE SPY WHO LOVED ME - 1962 • ON HER
MAJESTY'S SECRET SERVICE - 1963 007 IN NEW YORK (published in the US edition of
Thrilling Cities) - 1964 YOU ONLY LIVE TWICE - 1964 • THE MAN WITH THE GOLDEN
GUN - 1965 OCTOPUSSY AND THE LIVING DAYLIGHTS - 1966 ('OCTOPUSSY', 'THE
LIVING DAYLIGHTS', 'PROPERTY OF A LADY' (first published 1963 in *The Ivory Hammer
- The Year At Sotheby's*; collected in US paperback editions, included in edition published in
2002 by Penguin), '007 IN NEW YORK' (included in edition published in 2002 by Penguin)

By Kingsley Amis

COLONEL SUN - 1968

By John Pearson

JAMES BOND – THE AUTHORIZED BIOGRAPHY OF 007 - 1973

By John Gardner

LICENCE RENEWED - 1981 • FOR SPECIAL SERVICES - 1982 • ICEBREAKER - 1983
ROLE OF HONOUR - 1984 • NOBODY LIVES FOREVER - 1986 • NO DEALS MR. BOND - 1987
SCORPIUS - 1988 • WIN LOSE OR DIE - 1989 • BROKENCLAW - 1990
THE MAN FROM BARBAROSA - 1991 • DEATH IS FOREVER - 1992 • NEVER SEND FLOWERS - 1993
SEAFIRE - 1994 • COLD - 1996 (published under the title COLD FALL in the US)

By Raymond Benson

ZERO MINUS TEN - 1997 • THE FACTS OF DEATH - 1998 • HIGH TIME TO KILL - 1999
DOUBLESHOT - 2000 • NEVER DREAM OF DYING - 2001 • THE MAN WITH THE RED TATTOO - 2002

Uncollected short stories

'BLAST FROM THE PAST' - *Playboy*, January 1997, 'MIDSUMMER NIGHT'S DOOM' - *Playboy*, January 1999, 'LIVE AT FIVE' - *TV Guide*, 1999

ON FILM

Dr. No - 1962
Produced by Albert R. Broccoli & Harry Saltzman
Directed by Terence Young
Screenplay by Richard Maibaum, Johanna Harwood, Berkley Mather
James Bond played by Sean Connery

THE VILLAIN: DR. NO (*Joseph Wiseman*) - half-German, half-Chinese implacable genius, lost hands in radiation experiments, replaced them with powerful metal hands, works in the service of SPECTRE

SUB-VILLAINS: MR. JONES (*Reginald Carter*) - operative for Dr. No, poses as a chauffeur, takes cyanide rather than reveal information
PROFESSOR R. J. DENT (*Anthony Dawson*) - local operative working for Dr. No, metallurgist, well-connected in Jamaican society
MISS TARO (*Zena Marshall*) - secretary working in Government House in Kingston, Jamaica
THE PHOTOGRAPHER (*Margaret LeWars - credited as Marguerite LeWars*) - attractive Dr. No operative assigned to photograph 007

VILLAIN'S PLOT: Interferes with US rocket launches by means of an atomic-powered radio beam which overwhelms ground control instructions

BOND WOMEN: HONEY RYDER (*Ursula Andress*) - beautiful orphaned daughter of a marine biologist killed by Dr. No
SYLVIA TRENCH (*Eunice Gayson*) - wealthy woman whom Bond meets at a London casino across the *chemin de fer* table

BOND'S ALLIES: FELIX LEITER (*Jack Lord*) - Bond's CIA ally
QUARREL (*John Kitzmiller - credited as John Kitzmuller*) - local fisherman working for

secret service station chief John Strangways during the time of Strangways' murder, and later for Felix Leiter and James Bond
PLEYDELL-SMITH (*Louis Blaazer*) - Principal Secretary working for the British government

THE BOND TEAM: M (*Bernard Lee - in* Dr. No *through* Moonraker) - head of the British Secret Service, an authoritative father figure who sends James Bond on his missions
MISS MONEYPENNY (*Lois Maxwell - in* Dr. No *through* A View To A Kill) - M's secretary, who, for many years, enjoys a flirtatious relationship with 007
MAJOR BOOTHROYD (*Peter Burton*) - the Armourer working for the British Secret Service, replaces Bond's Beretta pistol with a Walther PPK

BOND'S GADGETS: None, save for Bond's Walther PPK and a Geiger counter

LOCATIONS: London; Jamaica; Crab Key

From Russia With Love - 1963
Produced by Albert R. Broccoli & Harry Saltzman
Directed by Terence Young
Screenplay by Richard Maibaum, Johanna Harwood
James Bond played by Sean Connery

THE VILLAINS: ERNST STAVRO BLOFELD (*Anthony Dawson; voice of Eric Pohlmann*) - head of SPECTRE
ROSA KLEBB (*Lotte Lenya*) - former KGB Colonel now working for SPECTRE as Number Three, Director of Operations
DONALD 'RED' GRANT (*Robert Shaw*) - homicidal paranoiac, convicted murderer who escaped from Dartmoor prison, recruited by SPECTRE as a professional killer

SUB-VILLAINS: KRONSTEEN (*Vladek Sheybal*) - Chessmaster, Director of Planning for SPECTRE, aka Number Five
MORZENY (*Walter Gotell*) - SPECTRE agent in charge of SPECTRE Island, later kills Kronsteen and sent personally to stop James Bond
KRILENCU (*Fred Haggerty*) - Bulgarian killer working for the Soviets

VILLAIN'S PLOT: Using a Lektor decoding machine and a beautiful Russian cipher clerk as bait, SPECTRE hopes to lure 007 to his death

BOND WOMEN: TATIANA ROMANOVA (*Daniela Bianchi*) - Corporal of State Security at Soviet Embassy in Istanbul, she is lured into SPECTRE's operation against Bond believing Klebb still works for the KGB
SYLVIA TRENCH (*Eunice Gayson*) - back from *Dr. No*; Bond's date for a picnic

BOND'S ALLIES: KERIM BEY (*Pedro Armendariz*) - head of Station T, Turkey, former circus performer, an expansive, resourceful Southern European agent working for the British

THE BOND TEAM: Q (*Desmond Llewelyn - in* From Russia With Love *through* Diamonds Are Forever *and* The Man With The Golden Gun *through* The World Is Not Enough) - the creator of Bond's lethal gadgets, aka Major Boothroyd

BOND'S GADGETS: Bond's briefcase, which holds an AR-7 folding sniper's rifle, 40 rounds of ammunition, an exploding tear gas cartridge disguised as a tin of talc, trigger mechanism for tear gas in trick latches, 50 gold sovereigns, and a throwing knife; Bond also uses a pager, a radio car phone, a telephone bug detector, and a Rolleiflex camera with a concealed tape recorder

LOCATIONS: SPECTRE Island; Venice; London; Istanbul; Eastern Europe aboard the Orient Express through Yugoslavia, with stops in Belgrade and Zagreb; the Aegean Sea

Goldfinger - 1964
Produced by Albert R. Broccoli & Harry Saltzman
Directed by Guy Hamilton
Screenplay by Richard Maibaum, Paul Dehn
James Bond played by Sean Connery

THE VILLAIN: AURIC GOLDFINGER (*Gert Frobe*) - British immigrant gold baron in league with the Chinese, obsessed with gold

SUB-VILLAINS: ODDJOB (*Harold Sakata*) - Korean killer who has a lethal metal-rimmed hat, working for Goldfinger
KISCH (*Michael Mellinger*) - lieutenant working for Goldfinger
CAPUNGO (*Alf Joint*) - Mexican thug sent by Mr Ramirez to kill Bond

VILLAIN'S PLOT: Goldfinger, with the help of the Chinese, plans to detonate an atomic bomb inside the gold vault of Fort Knox, thus irradiating the US gold stocks, sending the US economy into chaos and increasing the value of his own gold holdings

BOND WOMEN: BONITA (*Nadja Regin*) - tarantella dancer working with Mr. Ramirez to trap Bond
JILL MASTERSON (*Shirley Eaton*) - Goldfinger's beautiful paid companion; dies of skin suffocation when painted gold after she betrays Goldfinger's card-cheating scam to 007
TILLY MASTERSON (*Tania Mallet*) - Jill's sister, killed by Oddjob's deadly hat
PUSSY GALORE (*Honor Blackman*) - criminal pilot working with Goldfinger who ultimately decides to help 007

BOND'S ALLIES: FELIX LEITER *(Cec Linder)* - Bond's CIA ally.

BOND'S GADGETS: Seagull snorkel device; grappling hook gun; homing devices (large and small, the latter concealed in 007's shoe); Aston Martin DB5 with bulletproof windscreen, smoke screen, oil sprayer, front-wing machine guns, rear bullet-proof shield, tyre-slashing blades, homer tracking screen, and ejector seat

LOCATIONS: Mexico; Miami; London; Goldfinger's golf club in Kent; Switzerland; Kentucky; Washington DC

Thunderball - 1965
Presented by Albert R. Broccoli & Harry Saltzman
Produced by Kevin McClory
Directed by Terence Young
Screenplay by Richard Maibaum and John Hopkins, based on the original story by Kevin McClory, Jack Whittingham and Ian Fleming
James Bond played by Sean Connery

THE VILLAINS: ERNST STAVRO BLOFELD *(Anthony Dawson; voice of Eric Pohlmann)* - head of SPECTRE
EMILIO LARGO *(Adolfo Celi)* - Italian, Number 2 in the SPECTRE hierarchy, in charge of the ambitious plot to steal two nuclear weapons, has only one eye

SUB-VILLAINS: JACQUES BOTIER *(Bob Simmons/Rose Alba)* - SPECTRE agent who fakes his own death. Bond makes the ruse real
COUNT LIPPE *(Guy Doleman)* - SPECTRE agent at Shrublands who tries to kill Bond
FIONA VOLPE *(Luciana Paluzzi)* - SPECTRE agent who uses her potent sex appeal as a weapon
ANGELO PALAZZI *(Paul Stassino)* - operative hired and trained to replace Domino's brother and hijack the NATO bomber
VARGAS *(Philip Locke)* - cold-blooded killer working for Largo

VILLAIN'S PLOT: SPECTRE hijacks a NATO bomber and steals the nuclear weapons onboard, demanding a ransom from the US and UK

BOND WOMEN: DOMINIQUE DERVAL *(Claudine Auger)* - called 'Domino' by her friends, she is the 'kept woman' of Emilio Largo, and sister of the NATO pilot whom Largo has killed and replaced to carry out his plot
PATRICIA FEARING *(Molly Peters)* - physical therapist at Shrublands health clinic

BOND'S ALLIES: FELIX LEITER *(Rick Van Nutter)* - Bond's CIA ally
PAULA CAPLAN *(Martine Beswick {credited as Martin Beswick})* - local secret service field liaison for 007 in Nassau
PINDER *(Earl Cameron)* - Nassau local who runs the Bahamas station for the British secret service

BOND'S GADGETS: Bell-Textron jet pack; Aston Martin DB5 with bulletproof shield, high-pressure water jets; miniature underwater breathing apparatus; miniature Very light; radioactive homing pill; watch with concealed Geiger counter; camera with Geiger counter; underwater propulsion unit armed with exploding torpedoes and 'smokescreen'

LOCATIONS: France; Shrublands Health Clinic; London; Nassau, Bahamas and out-islands; Miami

Casino Royale - 1967
Produced by Charles K. Feldman, Jerry Bressler & John Dark
Directed by Val Guest, Kenneth Hughes, John Huston, Joseph McGrath, Robert Parrish
Screenplay by Wolf Mankowitz, John Law, Michael Sayers
(Sir) James Bond played by David Niven

THE VILLAIN: LE CHIFFRE *(Orson Welles)* - gambling mastermind, operative of Smersh
JIMMY BOND/DR. NOAH *(Woody Allen)* - nephew of James Bond, Smersh agent, megalomanical madman with an inferiority complex

SUB-VILLAINS: VESPER LYND *(Ursula Andress)*: richest woman in the world, also working with Smersh
AGENT MIMI/LADY FIONA *(Deborah Kerr)* - Smersh agent who poses as M's wife, becomes a nun and later helps Sir James Bond
MISS GOODTHIGHS *(Jacqueline Bisset)* - Smersh agent sent to seduce Evelyn Tremble

VILLAIN'S PLOT: Dr. Noah is going to replace all world leaders with robot replicas, then unleash a bacillus which will make all women beautiful and destroy all men over 4'6"

BOND WOMEN: BUTTERCUP *(Angela Scoular)* - another female Smersh agent who poses as M's daughter
THE DETAINER/LADY JAMES BOND *(Daliah Lavi)* - British agent trapped and interrogated by Dr. Noah

BOND'S ALLIES: EVELYN TREMBLE *(Peter Sellers)* - Baccarat expert asked to pose as James Bond
COOPER *(Terence Cooper)* - another agent recruited to pose as James Bond
MATA BOND *(Joanna Pettet)* - daughter of James Bond and the late Mata Hari

BOND'S GADGETS: X-ray eyeglasses which allow the wearer to see through the back of playing cards; television watch

LOCATIONS: Paris; Scotland; London; India; Berlin; Monte Carlo

You Only Live Twice - 1967
Produced by Albert R. Broccoli & Harry Saltzman
Directed by Lewis Gilbert
Screenplay by Roald Dahl, Additional Story Material by Harold Jack Bloom
James Bond played by Sean Connery

THE VILLAIN: ERNST STAVRO BLOFELD *(Donald Pleasence)* - head of SPECTRE

SUB-VILLAINS: MR. OSATO *(Teru Shimada)* - SPECTRE operative, chairman of Osato Chemicals and Engineering
HELGA BRANDT *(Karin Dor)* - seductive SPECTRE agent, aka Number 11, works with Mr. Osato
HANS *(Ronald Rich)* - Blofeld's personal bodyguard

VILLAIN'S PLOT: Blofeld, under contract to the Chinese, abducts both Soviet and American spacecraft in order to launch World War III

BOND WOMEN: AKI *(Akiko Wakabayashi)* - Japanese secret agent working with Tiger Tanaka
KISSY *(Mie Hama)* - orphaned Ama girl and Japanese secret agent
LING *(Tsai Chin)* - Chinese girl in Hong Kong who aids in the (fake) killing of Bond

BOND'S ALLIES: TIGER TANAKA *(Tetsuro Tamba)* - head of the Japanese Secret Service
DIKKO HENDERSON *(Charles Gray)* - British station chief in Tokyo, killed by a masked SPECTRE agent shortly after meeting Bond

BOND'S GADGETS: Pocket-sized safe-cracker; Little Nellie gyrocopter armed with two synchronized machine guns firing incendiary and high-explosive bullets, forward-firing rocket launchers, rear-firing flame guns, heat-seeking air-to-air missiles, smoke ejectors and aerial mines; helmet camera; suction devices for climbing walls; cigarettes with rocket-powered darts

LOCATIONS: Alaska; Hawaii; Hong Kong; Tokyo; Kobe/Osaka; Cape Kennedy; Star City, USSR; Japanese fishing village near Island of Matsu; Blofeld's volcano; outer space

On Her Majesty's Secret Service - 1969
Produced by Albert R. Broccoli & Harry Saltzman
Directed by Peter Hunt
Screenplay by Richard Maibaum, Additional Dialogue by Simon Raven
James Bond played by George Lazenby

THE VILLAIN: ERNST STAVRO BLOFELD *(Telly Savalas)* - head of SPECTRE

SUB-VILLAINS: IRMA BUNT *(Ilse Steppat)* - companion/Personal Secretary of Blofeld
GRUNTHER *(Yuri Borienko)* - thug working for Blofeld

VILLAIN'S PLOT: Blofeld has brainwashed young women to release germ warfare agents unless his demands, including total amnesty for all of his past crimes, are met

BOND WOMEN: COMTESSE TERESA DI VICENZO *(Diana Rigg)*: known as Tracy, tragically beautiful, widowed, suicidal daughter of Marc Ange Draco
RUBY BARTLETT *(Angela Scoular)* - English farm girl being treated by Blofeld for allergies to chickens
NANCY *(Catherine Von Schell)* - Italian girl being treated by Blofeld for allergies to potatoes

BOND'S ALLIES: MARC ANGE DRACO *(Gabriele Ferzetti)* - head of the Union Corse, one of the largest European crime syndicates, father of Tracy
SIR HILARY BRAY, BARONET *(George Baker)* - Sable Basilisk of the Royal College of Arms, allows Bond to adopt his identity in approaching Blofeld
CAMPBELL *(Bernard Horsfall)* - Secret Service agent in Switzerland

BOND'S GADGETS: A combination safe-cracker and photocopying machine; miniature camera

LOCATIONS: London; Portugal; Geneva and Berne, Switzerland; Swiss Alps

Diamonds Are Forever - 1971
Produced by Albert R. Broccoli & Harry Saltzman
Directed by Guy Hamilton
Screenplay by Richard Maibaum and Tom Mankiewicz
James Bond played by Sean Connery

THE VILLAIN: ERNST STAVRO BLOFELD *(Charles Gray)* - head of SPECTRE, creator of various identical doubles, has kidnapped billionaire Willard Whyte and is using Whyte's empire for his own purposes

SUB-VILLAINS: MR. WINT *(Bruce Glover)* & MR. KIDD *(Putter Smith)* - pair of homosexual killers working for Blofeld
BERT SAXBY, *(Bruce Cabot)* - supposedly Willard Whyte's right-hand man; in actuality a top operative for Blofeld
PETER FRANKS *(Joe Robinson)* - diamond smuggler who serves as part of Blofeld's diamond pipeline
MORTON SLUMBER *(David Bauer)* - mortuary owner, part of Blofeld's diamond smuggling operation
SHADY TREE *(Leonard Barr)* - Las Vegas comic, part of Blofeld's diamond smuggling operation
PROFESSOR DR. METZ *(Joseph Furst)* - idealistic scientist, world's leading expert on laser refraction, designer of Blofeld's satellite weapon

BAMBI (*Lola Larson - credited to Donna Garrett*) & THUMPER (*Trina Parks*) - female bodyguards assigned to keep Willard Whyte trapped in his house

VILLAIN'S PLOT: Blofeld holds the world hostage with the threat of a diamond-encrusted, laser-firing satellite

BOND WOMEN: TIFFANY CASE (*Jill St. John*) - diamond smuggler who serves as part of Blofeld's pipeline
PLENTY O'TOOLE (*Lana Wood*) - casino gold-digger who almost beds Bond

BOND'S ALLIES: FELIX LEITER (*Norman Burton*) - Bond's CIA ally
WILLARD WHYTE (*Jimmy Dean*) - multi-billionaire casino/aerospace magnate

BOND'S GADGETS: Pocket mousetrap-style clamp to crush prying fingers; artificial fingerprints; voice-altering device; piton gun; inflatable plastic sphere which allows Bond to walk on water

LOCATIONS: Japan; Cairo; Spain; London; South Africa; Amsterdam; Los Angeles; Las Vegas; outer space; North Dakota; China; Baja California

Live And Let Die - 1973
Produced by Albert R. Broccoli & Harry Saltzman
Directed by Guy Hamilton
Screenplay by Tom Mankiewicz
James Bond played by Roger Moore

THE VILLAIN: MR. BIG/DR. KANANGA (*Yaphet Kotto*) - Caribbean island dictator, who also acts as an underworld boss and heroin distributor in the US

SUB-VILLAINS: BARON SAMEDI (*Geoffrey Holder*) - ruler of the Kingdom of the Dead in the voodoo religion, the man who cannot die ; a mythical spirit working with Kananga or a mere mortal?
TEE HEE (*Julius Harris*) - grinning killer who lost an arm to a crocodile and now sports a lethal prosthetic pincer in its place
WHISPER (*Earl Jolly Brown*) - fat, soft-voiced henchman working for Kananga
ADAM (*Tommy Lane*) - thug working for Mr. Big
CAB DRIVER 1 (*Arnold Williams*) - comedic henchman/taxi driver working for Kananga

VILLAIN'S PLOT: Mr. Big uses Fillet of Soul restaurants and voodoo shops as fronts for distributing two tons of free heroin, thus doubling the number of addicts in the US while forcing all the competitors out of business

BOND WOMEN: MISS CARUSO (*Madeline Smith*) - Italian agent in Bond's home when M and Moneypenny arrive
ROSIE CARVER (*Gloria Hendry*) - a CIA agent under the control of Kananga
SOLITAIRE (*Jane Seymour*) - Kananga's virgin voodoo priestess who has the power to see the future… as long as she remains chaste

BOND'S ALLIES: FELIX LEITER (*David Hedison*) - Bond's CIA ally
QUARREL JR. (*Roy Stewart*) - son of Quarrel (see *Dr. No*), fisherman/agent on the island of San Monique

OTHER: SHERIFF J.W. PEPPER (*Clifton James*) - Southern redneck whose world is destroyed by James Bond

BOND'S GADGETS: Magnetic watch with facing that acts as a circular saw; radio receiver disguised as automobile cigarette lighter; bug detector in toilet kit; signalling device in hairbrush; hang glider; shark gun and high-pressure capsules

LOCATIONS: London; New York; New Orleans; San Monique

The Man With The Golden Gun - 1974
Produced by Albert R. Broccoli & Harry Saltzman
Directed by Guy Hamilton
Screenplay by Richard Maibaum and Tom Mankiewicz
James Bond played by Roger Moore

THE VILLAIN: FRANCISCO SCARAMANGA (*Christopher Lee*) - the world's most expensive hit man

SUB-VILLAINS: NICK NACK (*Hervé Villechaize*) - midget personal assistant to Scaramanga
LAZAR (*Marne Maitland*) - Portuguese gunsmith based out of Macau, provides golden bullets to Scaramanga
HAI FAT (*Richard Loo*) - Thai industrialist working with Scaramanga to harness the secret to solar power
CHULA (*Chan Yiu Lam*) - martial arts expert who faces off against Bond

VILLAIN'S PLOT: Scaramanga has stolen a Solex agitator, which harnesses solar power, and used it to create a prototype solar energy plant, of which he is going to offer the plans to the highest bidder, giving them a monopoly on solar power

BOND WOMEN: SAIDA (*Carmen du Satoy*) - Beirut belly-dancer who has one of Scaramanga's golden bullets
ANDREA ANDERS (*Maud Adams*) - Scaramanga's kept woman, who solicits Bond to kill her lover
MARY GOODNIGHT (*Britt Ekland*) - British Secret Service agent in Hong Kong

BOND'S ALLIES: COLTHORPE (*James Cossins*) - ballistics expert working for Q

LT. HIP (*Soon-Taik Oh*) - British Secret Service agent in Hong Kong
BILL TANNER (*Michael Goodliffe - uncredited*) - Chief of Staff, first appearance in a Bond film
SHERIFF J.W. PEPPER (*Clifton James*) - Southern redneck from *Live And Let Die*, thrown together with Bond

BOND'S GADGETS: Homing device disguised as clothing button; fake superfluous nipple

LOCATIONS: London; Beirut; Macau; Hong Kong; Thailand; Scaramanga's Island

The Spy Who Loved Me - 1977
Produced by Albert R. Broccoli
Directed by Lewis Gilbert
Screenplay by Christopher Wood & Richard Maibaum
James Bond played by Roger Moore

THE VILLAIN: KARL STROMBERG (*Curt Jurgens*) - shipping magnate with webbed hands and an obsession with the world beneath the sea

SUB-VILLAINS: SERGI BORZOV (*Michael Billington*) - KGB agent killed by Bond at opening of film, lover of Major Anya Amasova
JAWS (*Richard Kiel*) - looming, indestructible killer with metal teeth
SANDOR (*Milton Reid*) - killer working for Stromberg
AZIZ FEKKESH (*Nadim Sawalha*) - intermediary in the sale of submarine tracking plans
MAX KALBA (*Vernon Dobtcheff*) - Egyptian nightclub owner who has obtained the submarine tracking system plans and offers them for sale
NAOMI (*Caroline Munro*) - secretary to Stromberg, and lethal helicopter pilot
LIPARUS CAPTAIN (*Sydney Tafler*) - Stromberg operative manning his submarine-eating supertanker

VILLAIN'S PLOT: Stromberg intends to destroy above-ground civilization by using stolen nuclear submarines to ignite World War III among the superpowers and create his own kingdom beneath the sea

BOND WOMEN: LOG CABIN GIRL (*Sue Vanner*) - KGB agent who is in an embrace with Bond at film's opening
FELICCA (*Olga Bisera*) - beautiful woman helping to trap Bond when he goes to meet Fekkesh, warns 007 before Sandor can shoot him
MAJOR ANYA AMASOVA (*Barbara Bach*) - KGB spy who joins forces with 007, unaware that he killed her lover

BOND'S ALLIES: ADMIRAL HARGREAVES (*Robert Brown*) - Royal Navy Admiral, flag officer, submarines
SHEIK HOSEIN (*Edward de Souza*) - Cambridge-educated Egyptian with intelligence contacts who helps Bond on his mission
CAPTAIN BENSON (*George Baker*) - liaison at Polaris submarine base in Scotland
CAPTAIN CARTER, USS WAYNE CAPTAIN (*Shane Rimmer*) - US Navy officer who transports Bond to the Liparus via submarine
COMMANDER TALBOT, HMS RANGER CAPTAIN (*Bryan Marshall*) - Royal Navy officer whose submarine is the first to be captured by Stromberg

BOND'S TEAM: GENERAL GOGOL (*Walter Gotell - in* The Spy Who Loved Me *through* The Living Daylights*)* - unlikely ally and sometimes adversary in the age of *détente*
SIR FREDERICK GRAY, MINISTER OF DEFENCE (*Geoffrey Keen - in* The Spy Who Loved Me *through* The Living Daylights*)* - stern British government cabinet minister

BOND'S GADGETS: Wristwatch with ticker-tape message readout; rocket-firing ski pole; cigarette case that converts into a microfilm viewer; Lotus Esprit outfitted with a rear-firing cement sprayer, submarine transformation package for underwater use, equipped with sea-to-air missiles, torpedoes, underwater 'smokescreen' and sea mines; Wet Bike

LOCATIONS: Moscow; People's Rest & Recuperation Centre in Soviet Union; Austria; London; Scotland; Egypt; Sardinia; Atlantic Ocean

Moonraker - 1979
Produced by Albert R. Broccoli
Directed by Lewis Gilbert
Screenplay by Christopher Wood
James Bond played by Roger Moore

THE VILLAIN: HUGO DRAX (*Michael Lonsdale*) - emotionally cold aerospace mogul whose company, Drax Industries, builds the space shuttle

SUB-VILLAINS: CHANG (*Toshiro Suga*) - Drax's laconic Asian manservant/killer
JAWS (*Richard Kiel*) - steel-toothed killer who now works under individual contract

VILLAIN'S PLOT: Drax plans to destroy all life on earth via space-launched globes filled with lethal chemical compounds and begin a new civilization created from his physically perfect specimens of humanity aboard his space station

BOND WOMEN: HOLLY GOODHEAD (*Lois Chiles*) - NASA/CIA operative assigned to watch Drax
MANUELA (*Emily Bolton*) - agent working for station VH in Rio de Janeiro

BOND'S ALLIES: CORINNE DUFOUR (*Corinne Clery*) - a pilot in the service of Hugo Drax

BOND'S GADGETS: Wrist dart gun with armour-piercing and cyanide-coated darts;

cigarette case X-ray device for safe-cracking; cigarette lighter camera; high-speed gondola/hovercraft; speedboat equipped with bullet shield, mines, homing torpedo, hang glider concealed in roof; Seiko watch with concealed plastic explosive and detonator

LOCATIONS: Yukon Territory, Canada; in the air returning from Africa to London; London; Los Angeles; Southern California; Venice; Rio de Janeiro; Rio Tapirapé, Brazil; outer space

For Your Eyes Only - 1981

Produced by Albert R. Broccoli
Directed by John Glen
Screenplay by Richard Maibaum & Michael G. Wilson
James Bond played by Roger Moore

THE VILLAIN: ARISTOTLE KRISTATOS (*Julian Glover*) - Greek smuggler who formerly fought with the Greek resistance alongside Columbo, now working with the Soviets, a double-agent pretending to be loyal to the British

SUB-VILLAINS: BALD-HEADED MAN WITH WHITE CAT (*John Hollis*) - unnamed incarnation of Blofeld who appears for one last go at 007
HECTOR GONZALES (*Stefan Kalipha*) - Cuban hit man hired to kill Melina Havelock's parents before they can recover the ATAC; killed by Melina Havelock
EMILE LEOPOLD LOCQUE (*Michael Gothard*) - enforcer in the Brussels underworld, convicted murderer, a cold killer working for Kristatos who leaves small dove pin on the bodies of his victims in order to implicate Columbo
ERIC KRIEGLER (*John Wyman*) - East German biathlon champion and henchman working for the KGB and Kristatos
APOSTIS (*Jack Klaff*) - hood working for Kristatos
GENERAL ANATOL GOGOL (*Walter Gotell*) - although Gogol is an ally on this mission, his efforts encourage the deadly methods of Kristatos

VILLAIN'S PLOT: Kristatos plans to sell the Soviets an ATAC (Automatic Targeting Attack Communicator) system, which emits a coded transmission to order nuclear submarines to launch Polaris missiles

BOND WOMEN: MELINA HAVELOCK (*Carole Bouquet*) - daughter of murdered marine archeologist, Sir Timothy Havelock, out to avenge the death of her parents
COUNTESS LISL (*Cassandra Harris*) - not a real countess, an ally of Columbo, poses as an Austrian but actually English from Liverpool
BIBI DAHL (*Lynn-Holly Johnson*) - champion skater, a *protégée* of Kristatos who is rejected by Bond when she climbs in his bed

BOND'S ALLIES: SIR TIMOTHY HAVELOCK (*Jack Hedley*) - noted marine archeologist; although Bond never meets Havelock, his work on behalf of the British Secret Service prior to his murder aids Bond in recovering the ATAC
BILL TANNER, CHIEF OF STAFF (*James Villiers*) - runs the Secret Service operations 'while M's away', assigns Bond to Operation Undertow
MILOS COLUMBO (*Topol*) - warm, pistachio-eating Greek smuggler with a personal vendetta against Kristatos, known as 'the Dove'
FERRARA (*John Moreno*) - the British Secret Service's man in Northern Italy
JACOBA BRINK (*Jill Bennett*) - former champion skater training Bibi Dahl

BOND'S GADGETS: Lotus Esprit Turbo with self-destruct device; binocular camera; identigraph computer (matches descriptions of suspects to database of photos); digital radio watch

LOCATIONS: London; Ionian Sea; near Madrid; Corfu; Cortina d'Ampezzo, Italy; Albania; Meteora, Greece

Octopussy - 1983

Produced by Albert R. Broccoli
Directed by John Glen
Screenplay by George MacDonald Fraser and Richard Maibaum & Michael G. Wilson
James Bond played by Roger Moore

THE VILLAINS: KAMAL KHAN (*Louis Jourdan*) - exiled Afghan Prince, sportsman, gambler, smuggler of jewels with Octopussy, and cohort of General Orlov in massive scheme which brings Kahn riches from the Kremlin's art treasures
GENERAL ORLOV (*Steven Berkoff*) - unstable Soviet military hawk eager to see the USSR invade Western Europe

SUB-VILLAINS: COLONEL LUIS TORO (*Ken Norris*) - Bond impersonates this officer on assignment to destroy a spy plane in the Caribbean
GOBINDA (*Kabir Bedi*) - towering killer working for Kamal Kahn
MISCHKA (*David Meyer*) & GRISCHKA (*Anthony Meyer*) - twins who perform a daring knife-throwing act in Octopussy's circus and also act as assassins for Kamal Khan
THUG WITH YO-YO (*William Derrick*) - low-caste thug working for Gobinda

VILLAIN'S PLOT: Kamal Khan joins with rogue Soviet General Orlov to utilize Octopussy's circus in order to smuggle and detonate a nuclear bomb on an American military base in Germany, which will lead to Western forces being withdrawn and pave the way for a Soviet invasion

BOND WOMEN: BIANCA (*Tina Hudson*) - Caribbean-based agent who aids Bond in mission to destroy a spy plane
OCTOPUSSY (*Maud Adams*) - circus impresario, gem smuggler, head of the Octopus cult working with Kamal Kahn, unaware of Kahn's collusion with General Orlov; Bond once confronted her father, who committed suicide rather than face arrest

MAGDA (*Kristina Wayborn*) - associate of Octopussy in both her smuggling and circus ventures

BOND'S ALLIES: JIM FANNING (*Douglas Wilmer*) - art expert working with the British Secret Service
SADRUDDIN (*Albert Moses*) - the British Secret Service's man in Station I, India
VIJAY (*Vijay Armitraj*) - 'special expediter, Universal Exports', Bond's liaison agent in India
PENELOPE SMALLBONE (*Michela Clavell*) - office assistant working with Miss Moneypenny

BOND'S TEAM: M (*Robert Brown - in* Octopussy *through* Licence To Kill) - head of the British Secret Service

BOND'S GADGETS: Reversible jacket and hat; briefcase with false bottom for concealing magnetic mine; horse trailer with fake horse's rear concealing an AcroStar jet; 3-wheeler Honda auto rickshaw; miniature homing device/microphone receiver; watch with an LCD video screen, closed-circuit receiver and radio directional finder; pen filled with metal-cutting hydrochloric acid, bug receiver cap; crocodile submarine; hot-air balloon with closed-circuit TV cameras and receivers in basket

LOCATIONS: Unnamed Cuba-like Caribbean country; London; East and West Berlin; East Germany; West Germany; Moscow; India

Never Say Never Again - 1983

Produced by Jack Schwartzman
Directed by Irving Kershner
Screenplay by Lorenzo Semple, Jr., based on an original story by Kevin McClory, Jack Whittingham & Ian Fleming
James Bond played by Sean Connery

THE VILLAIN: ERNST STAVRO BLOFELD (*Max Von Sydow*) - head of SPECTRE
MAXIMILIAN LARGO (*Klaus Maria Brandauer*) - Hungarian-born billionaire philanthropist, SPECTRE operative Number One, in charge of the hijacking and ransom of the cruise missiles

SUB-VILLAINS: FATIMA BLUSH (*Barbara Carrera*) - seductive SPECTRE agent Number 12 who aids Largo in the hijacking of the cruise missiles
CAPTAIN JACK PETACHI (*Gavan O'Herlihy*) - heroin-addicted US Air Force communications officer stationed in England who has had a corneal implant to match the President of the US and is thus able to authorize the use of real nuclear-tipped cruise missiles in a test rather than dummy warheads, and who is killed by Fatima Blush
LIPPE (*Pat Roach*) - agent working for SPECTRE who tries to kill Bond at Shrublands

VILLAIN'S PLOT: SPECTRE holds the world hostage after stealing a nuclear-armed cruise missile, threatening to destroy oil fields if they are not paid 25% of Western nations' oil expenditures

BOND WOMEN: DOMINO PETACHI (*Kim Basinger*) - sister of Jack Petachi, lover of Largo
PATRICIA (*Prunella Gee*) - physical therapist at Shrublands health clinic
LADY IN THE BAHAMAS (*Valerie Leon*) - beautiful fisherwoman who rescues Bond at sea

BOND'S ALLIES: FELIX LEITER (*Bernie Casey*) - Bond's CIA ally
NIGEL SMALL-FAWCETT (*Rowan Atkinson*) - incompetent British Embassy officer in Nassau who attempts to help 007
NICOLE (*Saskia Cohen Tanugi*) - agent 326 working with Bond in the South of France, killed by Fatima Blush

BOND'S TEAM: M (*Edward Fox*) - head of the British Secret Service who has de-activated the double-0 section, must re-activate at the insistence of the Foreign Secretary
MISS MONEYPENNY (*Pamela Salem*) - M's secretary
Q AKA ALGERNON (*Alec McCowan*) - gadget master of the British Secret Service

BOND'S GADGETS: Rocket-powered motorcycle; pen that fires an exploding dart; laser watch; XT-7B flying platforms

LOCATIONS: London; Shrublands health clinic; various locations in southern England; Nassau, Bahamas; Monte Carlo and the South of France; the Mediterranean; North Africa

A View To A Kill - 1985

Produced by Albert R. Broccoli & Michael G. Wilson
Directed by John Glen
Screenplay by Richard Maibaum & Michael G. Wilson
James Bond played by Roger Moore

THE VILLAIN: MAX ZORIN (*Christopher Walken*) - genius, product of Nazi death camp experiments to create super-intelligent children, fled East Germany in the 1960s, now a leading French industrialist, head of Zorin Industries, a supposed staunch anti-Communist who is in actuality a KGB agent who breaks his ties to the Soviets to pursue his own dream of domination

SUB-VILLAINS: MAY DAY (*Grace Jones*) - Max Zorin's girlfriend, co-conspirator and another steroid-enhanced prodigy of Dr. Carl Mortner
SCARPINE (*Patrick Bauchau*) - head of security for Max Zorin
JENNY FLEX (*Alison Doody*) - beautiful henchwoman working for Zorin
DR. CARL MORTNER (*Willoughby Gray*) - elderly scientist who is actually Hans Glaub,

a pioneer in the development of steroids, who experimented on pregnant women in Nazi death camps in order to produce super-intelligent children, seized by Soviets after the war to help enhance athletes
BOB CONLEY (*Manning Redwood*) - geologist working on Zorin's supposed oil reclamation project in San Francisco Bay, in actuality the brains behind Zorin's plan to create a massive earthquake, formerly chief engineer in a South African gold mine
W. G. HOWE (*Daniel Benzali*) - California director of Oil and Mines, bought, paid for and used by Max Zorin

VILLAIN'S PLOT: Zorin intends to corner the world market on silicon microchips by detonating a huge amount of explosives in a mine, which will trigger a massive double earthquake, flooding Silicon Valley

BOND WOMEN: KIMBERLY JONES (*Mary Stavin*) - British agent who pilots iceberg submarine
STACEY SUTTON (*Tanya Roberts*) - heir to Sutton Oil who lost the company to Zorin in a rigged proxy fight; trained as a geologist, working for the State of California, she is engaged in a legal fight with Zorin over his control of the oil company
POLA IVANOVA (*Fiona Fullerton*) - former ballet dancer, KGB agent trying to gather information on Max Zorin, a past lover of Bond's

BOND'S ALLIES: SIR GODFREY TIBBETT (*Patrick Macnee*) - horse expert working with the British Secret Service
ACHILLE AUBERGINE (*Jean Rougerie*) - French detective looking into the horse racing activities of Max Zorin on behalf of the British government
CHUCK LEE (*David Yip*) - CIA agent working with Bond in San Francisco

BOND'S GADGETS: Microchip tracker; iceberg submarine; bug-detecting device under the head of an electric razor; sunglasses with adjustable polarizing filter lenses; cheque copier; camera concealed in a ring; Sharper Image credit card which opens locked windows; robot surveillance machine ('Snooper')

LOCATIONS: Siberia; London; Paris; Zorin's chateau, France; San Francisco area and Silicon Valley, California

The Living Daylights - 1987
Produced by Albert R. Broccoli & Michael G. Wilson
Directed by John Glen
Screenplay by Richard Maibaum & Michael G. Wilson
James Bond played by Timothy Dalton

THE VILLAIN: GENERAL GEORGI KOSKOV (*Jeroen Krabbe*) - ambitious Soviet mastermind, who, behind the scenes, is plotting to take over the KGB by convincing the British to assassinate General Pushkin
BRAD WHITTAKER (*Joe Don Baker*) - expelled from West Point for cheating, an amoral military-obsessed, American arms merchant in league with General Koskov

SUB-VILLAINS: IMPOSTER DOUBLE-O (*Carl Rigg*) - assassin who infiltrates a training exercise in Gibraltar, killing an SAS soldier and 004, working for Koskov and Whittaker
NECROS (*Andreas Wisniewski*) - cold-blooded killer, formerly in the employ of the Soviets, working with Brad Whittaker and Koskov, possesses a knack for voice impersonations

VILLAIN'S PLOT: Arms merchant Whittaker and rogue Soviet General Koskov collude to re-create Smersh, murder British agents, and force the assassination of General Pushkin in order to secure KGB funds to finance a vast opium-smuggling, arms-trading scheme which will enrich them

BOND WOMEN: LINDA (*Kell Tyler*) - bored woman on a yacht off Gibraltar searching for a real man
KARA MILOVY (*Maryam d'Abo*) - talented Czechoslovakian cellist, lover of General Koskov who aids in faking Koskov's defection to the West, but is betrayed by the Soviet General

BOND'S ALLIES: 004 & 002 (*Frederick Warder & Glyn Baker*) - agents training with 007 in Gibraltar; 004 is killed apparently by a Soviet Smersh agent
SAUNDERS (*Thomas Wheatley*) - officious head of section V, Vienna, for the British secret service
ROSIKA MIKLOS (*Julie T. Wallace*) - operative working with Bond, aiding with Koskov's defection using the Trans-Siberian pipeline
FELIX LEITER (*John Terry*) - Bond's CIA ally
GENERAL LEONID PUSHKIN (*John Rhys-Davies*) - tough and resourceful head of the KGB, falsely accused by Koskov of re-launching SMERSH, the Soviet anti-espionage directorate charged with killing spies
KAMRAN SHAH (*Art Malik*) - Russian-hating, Oxford-educated, *mujaheddin* leader who serves as Deputy Commander of the Eastern District in rebellion against Soviet occupation; also works with opium smugglers, the Snow Leopard Brotherhood
GENERAL ANATOL GOGOL (*Walter Gotell*) - former head of the KGB, now with the Soviet Foreign Service

BOND'S TEAM: MISS MONEYPENNY (*Caroline Bliss - in* The Living Daylights *and* Licence To Kill) - assistant and researcher working for the British secret service, a Barry Manilow fan with glasses and a hopeless crush on 007

BOND'S GADGETS: Pocket binoculars; dinner jacket which transforms into a black sniper's tunic; Walther WA-2000 sniper's rifle with infrared sight; Aston Martin Volante with police-scanner radio, heads up targeting display, bullet-proof glass, laser-cutting device in wheel hubs, front-firing missiles, convertible ice tyres, outrigger skis, rocket booster and self-destruct mechanism; eyeglasses with magnifying binoculars; key-ring finder which emits stun gas when 'Rule Britannia' is whistled, also packed with highly concentrated plastic explosive activated by wolf whistle; keys on ring open 90% of world's locks

LOCATIONS: Gibraltar; Bratislava; Czechoslovakia-Austria border; London and English countryside; Vienna; Tangier; Afghanistan

Licence To Kill - 1989
Produced by Albert R. Broccoli & Michael G. Wilson
Directed by John Glen
Screenplay by Richard Maibaum & Michael G. Wilson
James Bond played by Timothy Dalton

THE VILLAIN: FRANZ SANCHEZ (*Robert Davi*) - Central American drug lord who has political control over the fictional nation of Isthmus and has supposedly killed, bribed or intimidated half the government officials south of the US border

SUB-VILLAINS: DARIO (*Benicio Del Toro*) - former Nicaraguan Contra, expelled for his cruel methods, now a knife-wielding killer working for Sanchez
ED KILLIFER (*Everett McGill*) - corrupt DEA agent who helps Sanchez escape from US custody
MILTON KREST (*Anthony Zerbe*) - owner of Wavekrest, a supposed marine research company; in actuality Krest is a drug smuggler working with Sanchez
PROFESSOR JOE BUTCHER (*Wayne Newton*) - corrupt televangelist broadcasting from Isthmus, preaches cone power and meditation; in fact a conduit of communication between Sanchez and his drug dealers in the US
PRESIDENT HECTOR LOPEZ (*Pedro Armendariz - son of the actor who played Kerim Bey in* From Russia With Love) - puppet leader of Isthmus, under the control of Sanchez
TRUMAN-LODGE (*Anthony Starke*) - young, amoral financial whiz who helps Sanchez apply sophisticated marketing techniques to the cocaine trade
COLONEL HELLER (*Don Stroud*) - head of security for Sanchez
BRAUN (*Guy de Saint Cyr*) - henchman working for Sanchez

VILLAIN'S PLOT: Sanchez is building an Asian/American drug cartel utilizing a unique smuggling operation - cocaine hidden in gasoline tanker trucks delivered to a network of buyers who are signalled through the TV broadcasts of televangelist Professor Joe Butcher

BOND WOMEN: PAM BOUVIER (*Carey Lowell*) - former Army pilot, CIA operative sent by the US Attorney General to get Heller immunity if he turns against Sanchez
LUPE LAMORA (*Talisa Soto*) - former dealer at Sanchez's casino in Isthmus, opportunistic lover of Sanchez, now trapped in an abusive relationship

BOND'S ALLIES: FELIX LEITER (*David Hedison*) - Bond's longtime CIA ally, now working for the US Drug Enforcement Administration, getting married as the story begins; his mutilation by Sanchez inspires Bond to go on a mission of vengeance
SHARKEY (*Frank McRae*) - fisherman friend of Felix's in Key West
DELLA CHURCHILL (*Priscilla Barnes*) - Felix Leiter's bride, killed by Dario and Sanchez's henchmen
HAWKINS (*Grand L. Bush*) - DEA agent working with Leiter
KWANG & LOTI (*Cary-Hiroyuki Tagawa & Diana Lee-Hsu*) - Hong Kong narcotics agents posing as drug dealers to uncover Sanchez's operation

BOND'S GADGETS: Underwater manta ray cloak; Hasselblad camera which can be broken apart and reassembled as a signature gun; cummerbund that holds rappelling gear; toothpaste tube filled with plastic explosive; cigarette pack remote explosive detonator

LOCATIONS: Crab Key, Bahamas; Key West, Florida and environs; London; the Bimini Islands; Isthmus City; Olimpatec Meditation Institute

GoldenEye - 1995
Presented by Albert R. Broccoli
Produced by Michael G. Wilson & Barbara Broccoli
Directed by Martin Campbell
Screenplay by Jeffrey Caine and Bruce Feirstein
Story by Michael France
James Bond played by Pierce Brosnan

THE VILLAIN: ALEC TREVELYAN (*Sean Bean*) - former British secret agent 006, whose anti-Communist Russian parents were betrayed by the British after the Second World War; now head of Janus, a Russian arms trading list

SUB-VILLAINS: XENIA ZARAGEVNA ONATOPP (*Famke Janssen*) - Georgian, former Soviet fighter pilot, psychotic murderess who often kills victims by crushing them with her thighs while making love
BORIS GRISHENKO (*Alan Cumming*) - computer programmer working at Russian Severnaya satellite control centre, the brains behind the technical aspects of Trevelyan's plan
GENERAL ARKADY GRIGOROVICH OUROMOV (*Gottfried John*) - former Soviet Colonel in charge of Arkhangelsk Chemical Warfare facility, now a Russian General in charge of Space Division, in league with Alec Trevelyan; British analysts believe he sees himself as the next 'iron man' of Russia

VILLAIN'S PLOT: Alec Trevelyan intends to gain vengeance for the British betrayal of the Lienz Cossacks 50 years previous by robbing British banks through hacking into their systems moments before using a GoldenEye satellite to fire an electromagnetic pulse over London that will wipe out the banks' records

BOND WOMEN: CAROLINE (*Serena Gordon*) - psychiatrist sent to the south of France to evaluate 007 for MI6
NATALYA FYODOROVNA SIMONOVA (*Izabella Scorupco*) - Russian level two systems programmer working at the Severnaya facility, the only survivor of a murderous attack carried out by Gerenal Ourumov and Xenia Onatopp

BOND'S ALLIES: VALENTIN DMITROVICH ZUKOVSKY (*Robbie Coltrane*) - ex-KGB, Russian crime boss who was shot in the knee by 007, becomes an uneasy ally of Bond's
JACK WADE (*Joe Don Baker - in* GoldenEye *and* Tomorrow Never Dies) - earthy CIA ally of Bond's, gardening enthusiast
DEFENCE MINISTER DIMITRI MISHKIN (*Tcheky Karyo*) - Russian who comes to realize his betrayal by General Ourumov moments before being killed

BOND'S TEAM: M (*Judi Dench - from* GoldenEye *on*) - new head of MI6, steel-nerved bureaucrat known to some as 'the evil queen of numbers', who does not like Bond's methods, but realizes his necessity
MONEYPENNY (*Samantha Bond - from* GoldenEye *on*) - M's assistant, who enjoys a flirtatious relationship with 007
BILL TANNER (*Michael Kitchen - in* GoldenEye *and* The World Is Not Enough) - a senior analyst working for internal operations at MI6

BOND'S GADGETS: Gun which fires piton attached to power-retractable high-tensile wire and emits metal-cutting laser; zoom camera with communications uplink; BMW Z3 with all-points radar and self-destruct system (unused) and stinger missiles behind the headlights (unused); leather belt with 75-foot rappelling cord built into buckle; Omega Seamaster watch which emits a laser and remotely operates magnetic mines; pen which becomes a Class Four grenade

LOCATIONS: Arkangel (Arkhangelsk), Chemical Weapons Facility, USSR; London; Severnaya; St. Petersburg, Russia; Monte Carlo; French Riviera; unnamed Caribbean island; Cuba

Tomorrow Never Dies - 1997
Produced by Michael G. Wilson & Barbara Broccoli
Directed by Roger Spottiswoode
Screenplay by Bruce Feirstein
James Bond played by Pierce Brosnan

THE VILLAIN: ELLIOT CARVER (*Jonathan Pryce*) - Hong Kong-born megalomaniacal head of the Carver Media Group, owner of satellites that are used to launch his worldwide television news network

SUB-VILLAINS: STAMPER (*Gotz Otto*) - *protégé* of Dr. Kaufman, enforcer working for Carver
HENRY GUPTA (*Ricky Jay*) - technical genius behind Carver's ability to manipulate the GPS system
DR. KAUFMAN (*Vincent Schiavelli*) - German professor of forensic medicine sent to kill Bond and Paris Carver
GENERAL CHANG (*Philip Kwok*) - Chinese Army general working in league with Carver to launch hostilities between UK and China

VILLAIN'S PLOT: Carver, working with General Chang, plans to instigate World War III between UK and China, and thus propel General Chang to power and extend the broadcast arm of Carver's media empire into China

BOND WOMEN: PROFESSOR INGA BERGSTROM (*Cecile Thomsen*) - Professor of Danish at Oxford
PARIS CARVER (*Teri Hatcher*) - former lover of Bond's, now married to Elliot Carver
WAI LIN (*Michelle Yeoh*) - agent of China's People's External Security Force

BOND'S ALLIES: ADMIRAL ROEBUCK (*Geoffrey Palmer*) - hawkish, rash Royal Navy official who objects to M and Bond's more cautious methods
JACK WADE (*Joe Don Baker*) - Bond's CIA ally
DR. DAVE GREENWALT (*Colin Stinton*) - USAF expert on Global Positioning System

BOND'S TEAM: CHARLES ROBINSON (*Colin Salmon - in* Tomorrow Never Dies *on*) - Senior Analyst for field operations at MI6

BOND'S GADGETS: Video camera uplink; cigarette lighter grenade; Ericsson cell phone with universal lock-pick in antenna, fingerprint scanner, 20,000 volt electric shock security system, also remotely starts and controls 007's BMW 750 iL with machine guns (unused), roof-firing rockets, GPS tracking system, fingerprint identifier glove box, electrified door handles, bulletproof glass windows and windscreens, armoured body panels, tear gas sprayers, rear nail ejectors, re-inflating tyres, cable-cutting circular saw beneath hood badge; wristwatch detonator

LOCATIONS: The Khyber Pass; London; Oxford; Hamburg, Germany; Okinawa; Vietnam; Halong Bay; South China Sea

The World Is Not Enough - 1999
Produced by Michael G. Wilson & Barbara Broccoli
Directed by Michael Apted
Screenplay by Neal Purvis & Robert Wade and Bruce Feirstein, story by Neal Purvis & Robert Wade
James Bond played by Pierce Brosnan

THE VILLAINS: VICTOR ZOKAS AKA RENARD (*Robert Carlyle*) - global anarchist, terrorist who kidnapped and fell in love with Elektra King, shot in the head by 009;

the bullet, lodged in Renard's brain, is slowly killing him, having shut down his pain receptors, allowing him to push himself harder than any other human
ELEKTRA KING (*Sophie Marceau*) - daughter of Sir Robert King and an Azerbaijani oil heiress, kidnapped by Renard, supposedly escaped after shooting two of her captors in Cyprus, heir to her father's oil fortune, dedicated to completing an important Asian-European oil pipeline

SUB-VILLAINS: MR. LACHAISE (*Patrick Malahide*) - corrupt Swiss banker working in Bilbao, Spain, in league with Renard
CIGAR GIRL (*Maria Grazie Cucinotta*) - beautiful assassin working for Renard
SASHA DAVIDOV (*Ulrich Thomsen*) - Chief of Security for King Industries
BULL/BULLION (*Goldie*) - enforcer for Zukovsky, but secretly working for Renard
GABOR (*John Seru*) - bodyguard for Elektra

VILLAIN'S PLOT: Elektra intends to destroy Istanbul by exploding a nuclear submarine in the Bosphorus, thus forcing the world to rely on Elektra's pipeline

BOND WOMEN: DR. MOLLY WARMFLASH (*Serena Scott Thomas*) - medical officer for MI6
DR. CHRISTMAS JONES (*Denise Richards*) - beautiful physicist working with the International Decommissioning Agency, helping to dismantle excess atomic weapons in the former Soviet Union

BOND'S ALLIES: SIR ROBERT KING (*David Calder*) - read law at Oxford with M, married an Azerbaijani oil heiress, assassinated at MI6 headquarters, father of Elektra King
VALENTIN ZUKOVSKY (*Robbie Coltrane*) - Russian crime boss who first appeared in *GoldenEye*, now owns a casino and caviar factory in Baku, occasionally provides equipment for Elektra, now his nephew is providing her with a nuclear submarine

BOND'S TEAM: R (*John Cleese - promoted to Q in* Die Another Day): the 'young fellow' Q is grooming as his replacement

BOND'S GADGETS: Reading glasses with trigger for 007's Walther P99 pistol to explode with a blinding flash; jet-powered Q boat with afterburner, bulletproof armour-plated hull, submarine function, auto-mapping GPS computer, dry land steering and propulsion, forward-launching torpedoes; ski jacket with concealed inflating protective globe; BMW Z8 with the latest in interception counter-measures, equipped with titanium armour, multi-tasking heads-up display, key fob that drives the car via remote control, outrigger land-to-air guided missiles; X-ray eyeglasses; Visa card lockpick; Omega Seamaster wristwatch with miniature grappling hook and motorized lifting cable

LOCATIONS: Bilbao, Spain; London; Scotland; Baku, Azerbaijan; Kazakhstan; Caspian Sea; Istanbul

Die Another Day - 2002
Produced by Michael G. Wilson & Barbara Broccoli
Directed by Lee Tamahori
Screenplay by Neal Purvis & Robert Wade
James Bond played by Pierce Brosnan

THE VILLAIN: COLONEL TAN-GUN MOON (*Will Yun Lee*) - son of General Moon, educated at Oxford and Harvard, involved with illegal arms smuggling for African conflict diamonds
SIR GUSTAV GRAVES (*Toby Stephens*) - flamboyantly wealthy British *émigré* diamond baron, official bio lists him as an orphan who went from working in the diamond mines of Argentina to controlling a huge diamond mine in Iceland, a champion fencer with a supposed interest in ecological issues, developer of the Icarus space programme

SUB-VILLAINS: ZAO (*Rick Yune*) - North Korean collaborator of Colonel Moon, betrayed by Bond, and subsequently scarred with diamond shrapnel
DR. ALVAREZ (*Simon Andreu*) - leading researcher in gene therapy, runs a clinic where he purportedly helps Cuban leaders extend their life expectancy
MISTER KIL (*Lawrence Makoare*) - security officer working for Graves
VLADIMIR POPOV (*Michael Gorevoy*) - technical genius behind the Icarus satellite

VILLAIN'S PLOT: Gustav Graves plans to use the Icarus satellite weapon to destroy the minefield in the Korean Demilitarized Zone, allowing for the takeover of South Korea and the uniting of Korea, Japan and China into a new, unstoppable superpower

BOND WOMEN: GIACINTA 'JINX' JORDAN (*Halle Berry*) - beautiful African-American NSA agent
MIRANDA FROST (*Rosamund Pike*) - Harvard-educated publicist for Gustav Graves, fencing gold medal winner at the Sydney Olympics, working undercover for MI6

BOND'S ALLIES: GENERAL MOON (*Kenneth Tsang*) - North Korean General with hopes of peaceful relations between North and South Korea, father of Colonel Moon
FALCO (*Michael Madsen*) - NSA agent who believes Bond confessed secrets to North Korean officials under torture
MR. CHANG (*Ho Yi*) - Hong Kong hotel manager actually working for Chinese Intelligence
RAOUL (*Emilio Echevarria*) - Cuban sleeper agent working for MI6 in Havana
VERITY (*Madonna*) - fencing coach at Blades

BOND'S GADGETS: Surfboard with concealed weapons; combat knife with GPS beacon device; watch which emits laser beam cutter; Aston Martin V12 Vanquish gadget car; ultra high frequency single-digit sonic agitator ring; Switchblade personal jet glider

LOCATIONS: Pukch'Ong Coast, North Korea; Korean DMZ; Hong Kong; Havana, Sierra De Los Organos, Isla Organos, Cuba; London; Vatnajokull, Iceland

James Bond: The Filmmakers

Many hundreds of talented actors and filmmakers have contributed to the ongoing success of the 007 films. Presented here are quotes from interviews and published sources with many of the cast and crew. Their recollections provide an inside look into the world of 007 and shed light on the impact of the films, both on their individual careers and on the world at large. All of these creative talents - and many more too numerous to include - have shared in the James Bond legacy.

KEN ADAM (Production Designer, *Dr. No, Goldfinger, Thunderball, You Only Live Twice, Diamonds Are Forever, The Spy Who Loved Me, Moonraker*)
"I think the Bond films were very important, because I was able to use my imagination probably more than on most other films; eventually the sky became the limit. I used to treat them like therapy, you know. I could let myself go, I could explore and do things."

MAUD ADAMS (Andrea Anders in *The Man With the Golden Gun,* Octopussy in *Octopussy*)
"It's great fun, it's a fantasy, and it's really a modern-day fairy tale, in a way, where the men get to identify with a very handsome adventurous person, James Bond, who has all these gorgeous women, and all these fun toys that they can do all kinds of horrendous things with. It's a morality play, always good and evil - in the end, Bond always wins. I also think there is a lot in James Bond movies for women - women like to identify with the heroines, because they are, although usually very beautiful women, also women that are most often in charge of their own lives."

URSULA ANDRESS (Honey Ryder in *Dr. No,* Vesper Lynd in *Casino Royale*)
"*Dr. No* gave me success, it gave me independence. It gave me a lot. [James Bond] is an exciting character. And he has the knowledge and the *savoir faire* and the culture. That's why everybody loved Ian Fleming's books, because you learn so much about everything. It's fun."

MICHAEL APTED (Director, *The World Is Not Enough*)
"I always felt there is no James Bond character, it's whoever is playing it. The great ones are those who have left their fingerprints on it."

VIJAY ARMITRAJ (Vijay in *Octopussy*)
"The funny thing is, when you do a Bond picture, everything else goes out the window. As I often say, I played tennis for 25 years, but it's 'Oh, you were in a Bond film.' It doesn't matter how many audiences you've played in front of and which corner of the earth you've played on, but a Bond film in 25, 30, 50 different languages, you cannot top. Because it is for the masses. Everybody goes out to see a Bond picture. You go to a different level as soon as you do a Bond film - and that takes precedence over everything else."

VIC ARMSTRONG (Stunt performer, *You Only Live Twice, On Her Majesty's Secret Service, Live And Let Die, Never Say Never Again;* stunt co-ordinator, *Tomorrow Never Dies, Die Another Day;* second unit director, *Tomorrow Never Dies, The World Is Not Enough, Die Another Day*)
"I was a stuntman on *You Only Live Twice.* I'd started the year previously on *Arabesque* with Gregory Peck and Sophia Loren, and then in the winter of '66, I had about five weeks on it. It was £65 a week in those days, and the last week we were on a daily rate, £20 a day, which was phenomenal money. Took us right to Christmas Eve. I bought my first car, actually, with the first stunt adjustment I did. I was the first ninja sliding down the ropes, one-handed, firing a machine gun."

DAVID ARNOLD (Composer, *Tomorrow Never Dies, The World Is Not Enough, Die Another Day*)
"I think the reason why I chose to reinterpret the songs the way I did, and also to bring this kind of contemporary technology into the scores, is to try and forge some path forward with the music and with the movies which is going to help bring Bond into the 21st century."

CAROLE ASHBY (Octopussy girl in *Octopussy,* Whistling Girl in *A View To A Kill*)
"I've been taken on by the Bond family. Once you work for them that's what happens. Most of the crew have been there forever and a day - and if they're retiring their kids follow on. When I went back the second time to do *A View To A Kill* it was like going back to school."

CLAUDINE AUGER (Domino in *Thunderball*)
"[A woman] may think she'd like to change her husband for someone like James Bond, but I wonder how long she'd be able to stand the strain. Not for long, I'll guarantee. Even James has a job controlling his nerves. He smokes 60 cigarettes a day."

BARBARA BACH (Anya Amasova in *The Spy Who Loved Me*)
"This is the first really big lucky break I've ever had professionally - it came at a marvellous moment for me. It was a great ego-booster at a time when my life was changing anyway, and I needed a new sense of direction."

JOE DON BAKER (Brad Whittaker in *The Living Daylights;* Jack Wade in *GoldenEye* and *Tomorrow Never Dies*)

"I told Barbara Broccoli they should bring back the bikini girls - you know, these young, luscious girls sitting around this poolside - and she should let me be the casting agent. That's the job I'd really like. I don't know if she's going to listen to me or not. But on the Bond movies, it's pure pleasure, just a great experience."

JOHN BARRY (Composer, *From Russia With Love, Goldfinger, Thunderball, You Only Live Twice, On Her Majesty's Secret Service, Diamonds Are Forever, The Man With The Golden Gun, Moonraker, Octopussy, A View To A Kill, The Living Daylights*)
"I reflect back on that whole period, and only with the happiest of memories. The early days of the Bond movies - the first 15, 20 years, or whatever - they were a lot of fun, they really were. It wasn't taken too seriously; that was the joy of it, and I think that came across on the screen."

SHIRLEY BASSEY (Title song vocalist, *Goldfinger, Diamonds Are Forever, Moonraker*)
"For me, Sean was the best Bond because he was so sexy. He was so right, and he was so cold. Different woman came along and that was okay but he was always on the job. I mean, he never forgot that he was 007."

SEAN BEAN (Alec Trevelyan in *GoldenEye,*
"I like playing the villain, if it's a strong, meaty part... The villain has always been an integral ingredient to the success of the Bond films, and Trevelyan is a good adversary to Bond."

KABIR BEDI (Gobinda in *Octopussy*)
"The Bond saga is special because it makes you immortal; it keeps you alive because these films will always be shown, all over the world, time and again, and will live on forever. It is a feeling of special significance."

STEVEN BERKOFF (General Orlov in *Octopussy*)
"I'd love to be in another Bond film. I miss not being in a Bond film. And I don't know why Barbara hasn't asked me back. I think it's very sad."

HALLE BERRY (Jinx in *Die Another Day*)
"Sometimes, especially women that win Oscars, they get what's called the Oscar curse. They win an Oscar and then sort of fall off into obscurity. So the fact that the next movie out, after I was so lucky to win an Oscar, is a James Bond movie that is bigger than life, that is huge all around the world, is probably the best thing that I could be doing. Being in Bond is a wonderful opportunity for me to be just a woman. And my colour did not precede me in the casting of this project. The fact that I am black isn't why I am in it. I am just able to be a woman and be a formidable opponent and match for Bond."

MARTINE BESWICK (Zora - gypsy girl - in *From Russia With Love,* Paula in *Thunderball*)
"[*From Russia With Love*] put me on the map - if one can be put on the map as being a Bond girl. It really started my career; then I got serious about it and realized I had to go take some training."

DANIELA BIANCHI (Tatiana Romanova in *From Russia With Love*)
"At the time we were just at the beginning. It was the second James Bond film, so there weren't all the expectations there are today. Today James Bond is a legend, and so to work on one of the films is very important. The experience was extraordinary, also because perhaps I didn't realize how much success it would have."

MAURICE BINDER: (Title designer, *Dr. No, Thunderball, You Only Live Twice, On Her Majesty's Secret Service, Diamonds Are Forever, Live And Let Die, The Man With The Golden Gun, The Spy Who Loved Me, Moonraker, For Your Eyes Only, Octopussy, A View To A Kill, The Living Daylights, Licence To Kill*)
"I've never thought of myself or my work as innovative, but others must think so, because my techniques have been copied endlessly in television commercials, title sequences, and in other pictures. My attitude has always been that by having others snapping at my heels I have to keep thinking instead of being allowed to stagnate and become a relic. That's why the Bond films have been around for twenty years."

DON BLACK (Lyricist, *Thunderball, Diamonds Are Forever, The Man With The Golden Gun, Tomorrow Never Dies, The World Is Not Enough*)
"One thing you notice in a Bond picture is that there is a family atmosphere about it. Although it's a big enterprise, costing God knows how many millions, when you're with Barbara and Michael you know it's a family, which is very hard to do."

HONOR BLACKMAN (Pussy Galore in *Goldfinger*)
"The Bond films have survived so long, I think, because he's become everybody's hero, both male and female. There are so many people who were born after two or three, four films had been made, or seven or eight. So there are lots of people who have had Bond in their sights ever since they were born. He does very exciting things. And he has lovely women. Now why wouldn't you be interested?"

CHRIS BLACKWELL (Location scout, *Dr. No*)
"It obviously resonates with people. I'm amazed, because in many ways you would think that it would date because it was such a sort of 60s phenomenon when it first came out. But it hasn't. It's continued all the time."

CAROLINE BLISS (Miss Moneypenny in *The Living Daylights, Licence To Kill*)
"I still don't know why I got the part of Miss Moneypenny. Perhaps it was because I was so relaxed at the audition - but that's only because I thought I didn't stand a chance."

WILLY BOGNER JR. (Ski cameraman, *On Her Majesty's Secret Service*; ski sequence photographer and supervisor, *The Spy Who Loved Me*; ski sequence photographer and director, *For You Eyes Only, A View To A Kill*)
"I think the unique combination of action and humour is what makes Bond Bond. And that typical British sense of humour that I personally love: I think that's a big trademark. As soon as it's too serious, I think you leave that typical Bond recipe."

SAMANTHA BOND (Miss Moneypenny in *GoldenEye, Tomorrow Never Dies, The World Is Not Enough, Die Another Day*)
"I think [Moneypenny] and James are very old friends. They have a very flirtatious relationship, a very witty relationship. And I think a genuine care for one another."

LAMAR BOREN (Underwater cinematography, *Thunderball, You Only Live Twice, The Spy Who Loved Me*)
"Patience is the first prerequisite of underwater filming. On a good day, we'll get two minutes of edited film in the can. On a bad day, when the water is rough or dirty, we might as well stay in dock."

CAROLE BOUQUET (Melina Havelock, *For Your Eyes Only*)
"I'm not a sex symbol, and I'm not frightened of ending up as just another Bond girl."

JAKE BRAKE (Aerial stunts, *The Living Daylights*; parachuter, *GoldenEye*; aerial safety, *Tomorrow Never Dies*)
"I think [the Bond films] are always exciting. There's a lot of action; they try, whenever possible, to do real action, and that makes a difference."

BARBARA BROCCOLI (Executive assistant, *Octopussy*; additional assistant director, *A View To A Kill*; associate producer, *The Living Daylights, Licence To Kill*; producer, *GoldenEye, Tomorrow Never Dies, The World Is Not Enough, Die Another Day*)
"There was a real need for people to be able to go to the movies, to be on somebody else's adventure and just leave their lives for a little while and have some fun. I think [Cubby] felt really extremely honoured to have been able to do that. He felt that James Bond was able to do that for people; James Bond could take people out of their lives, take them to really exotic places and great adventures and meet all kinds of outlandish characters and take that ride."

ALBERT R. 'CUBBY' BROCCOLI (Producer, *Dr. No, From Russia With Love, Goldfinger, You Only Live Twice, On Her Majesty's Secret Service, Diamonds Are Forever, Live And Let Die, The Man With The Golden Gun, The Spy Who Loved Me, Moonraker, For Your Eyes Only, Octopussy, A View To A Kill, The Living Daylights, Licence To Kill*, 'Presented By', *Thunderball*)
"I honestly feel a responsibility toward all the Bond fans out there. I know they look forward to these pictures. And so I'm going to go on delivering them as long as I can. Also, it's a challenge, which I enjoy. We try to make each picture more exciting than the one before, to take Bond somewhere he hasn't already been."

DANA BROCCOLI
"When we were in a strange city anywhere in the world, and if there was a Bond film playing, [Cubby] would go in and sit and listen to the reaction of the audience to find out what they liked, what they didn't like. He had a great respect for the public"

PIERCE BROSNAN (James Bond in *GoldenEye, Tomorrow Never Dies, The World Is Not Enough, Die Another Day*)
"Bond remains a constant. He never changes. He's the one stabilizer within the whole genre. And he's the one who remains somewhat timeless, somewhat trapped within a period of time as well. My task was always trying to find my own reality within it: How do you make it human but still keep the fantasy and mystique of the character?"

ROBERT BROWN (Admiral Hargreaves in *The Spy Who Loved Me*, M in *Octopussy, A View To A Kill, The Living Daylights, Licence To Kill*)
"It's a joy to play M, despite the constant undermining of my authority by 007."

ROBIN BROWNE (Second Unit Cameraman, *On Her Majesty's Secret Service*; optical unit, *The Spy Who Loved Me*; optical effects cameraman, *Moonraker*; aerial team, *For Your Eyes Only*)
"[Cubby Broccoli is] a man who was loved totally in this industry. I've never heard a word said against him."

SYD CAIN (Art director, *Dr. No* (uncredited), *From Russia With Love*; Production designer, *On Her Majesty's Secret Service*; supervising art director, *Live and Let Die*)
"I think the men all want to be Bond, or would like to have been Bond, and the women admire him - he gets away with murder, doesn't he? He's always immaculate. It's a dream, really."

MARTIN CAMPBELL (Director, *GoldenEye*)
"The character of Bond is someone that always struck me that should be very comfortable in his own skin. He is what he is. He doesn't need to defend himself to anybody."

ROBERT CARLYLE (Renard in *The World Is Not Enough*)
"I was sitting in the Bond office at Pinewood, surrounded by all these posters of films I'd been to see with my Dad in the 60s, when I genuinely thought that Sean Connery was the only Scottish actor in the movies. That link between Connery and Bond and the Scottish people is fundamental. Being in a Bond film is like being a part of history."

ADOLFO CELI (Emilio Largo in *Thunderball*)
"I was flying from Hollywood to Madrid, via New York, when I needed something to read. I'd never read a James Bond adventure before, and from the pile available on a New York bookstall, I chose THUNDERBALL. Quite by chance. I very much enjoyed the story, and thought I would like to play this Largo in a film. But it was just a passing thought… Then 20 days later, my agent told me Mr. Saltzman wanted to see me in Paris… Life is so very funny, no? So strange. Destiny is so complicated."

LOIS CHILES (Holly Goodhead in *Moonraker*)
"I think people love the James Bond series because it has women, gadgets, fabulous locations, and a sense of humour. And it always delivers. Fans continue to go to see it because they know that they're gonna get what they want. All those things. The Bond franchise is extraordinary in the way it's survived and adapted to the times. It's the forerunner for all the action adventure movies in the 80s and 90s, but it's kept pace with them. It was the one they all looked to. I heard that Woody Allen used to go see every Bond movie when it came out. What I discovered about being a part of the Bond franchise is how huge it is worldwide. People are obsessed with Bond, and it's a great privilege to be part of it, because it's so beloved by so many people."

TSAI CHIN (Ling in *You Only Live Twice*)
"The first Bond film with Ursula Andress, I'm sure it was a low-budget film. When she came out of the water, I don't think anybody thought it was going to be a big thing. And it became the biggest thing. And still is."

JOHN CLEESE (Q's assistant in *The World Is Not Enough*, Q in *Die Another Day*)
"We should have done a Monty Python Life Of Bond, shouldn't we? [I'm signed for] three more, which sounds wonderful - and it is in its own way - but just to get it in context, what it means is that every three years I do about four days' filming."

ROBBIE COLTRANE (Valentin Zukovsky in *GoldenEye* and *The World Is Not Enough*)
"The first James Bond film came out when I was twelve. Just as the hormones were starting to kick in. Ursula Andress and the Aston Martin. I thought, yes! I know who I want to be now."

SEAN CONNERY (James Bond in *Dr. No, From Russia With Love, Goldfinger, Thunderball, You Only Live Twice, Diamonds Are Forever, Never Say Never Again*)
"Fleming invented Bond after the war when people were hungry for luxury, gourmet touches, exotic settings. And a character jumping in and out of bed all the time - you can see how that would catch on in a place like England… He's tough, ruthless, a compulsive killer, and savage with the women he loves - and leaves. But everybody seems to like the guy. I suppose he represents an outlet for our repressions - whatever they are. I'm not knocking Bond. He's been very good to me… Of course I am not ashamed of the James Bond films. Quality is not to be found only in the Old Vic, and portraying Bond is just as serious as playing Macbeth on stage."

BILL CONTI (Composer, *For Your Eyes Only*)
"[Bond's] music was exciting, large orchestra, and we defined spy music for quite a while. I would do anything for the James Bond people, anything connected with them. It was one of the best musical film experiences of my career."

CHRIS CORBOULD (Special effects, *The Spy Who Loved Me, Moonraker, For Your Eyes Only, A View To A Kill, The Living Daylights*; special effects supervisor second unit, *Licence To Kill*; special effects supervisor, *GoldenEye, Tomorrow Never Dies, The World Is Not Enough, Die Another Day*)
"They're a special effects man's dream. You've got your big explosions, you've got your massive mechanical hydraulic rigs, you've got your teensy-weensy gadgets, and you've got exotic places you're going to. A practical special effects man couldn't ask for a better film to be on. You work in other films, you're heavily involved with CGI, you're heavily involved dependent on lots of other things, whereas on the Bonds you're very much the focus. You know, the stunts and the special effects are the two things which everybody's waiting to see."

SIMON CRANE (Stunts, *A View To A Kill*; Timothy Dalton stunt double, *The Living Daylights, Licence To Kill*, stunt co-ordinator, *GoldenEye, The World Is Not Enough*)
"Most of us have all worked on several Bond films before. And we know how everyone works, we feel at ease with everyone. So you know what is expected of a Bond film, in that we are meant to be setting the pace for other action films to follow. Which is very difficult to do, by the way. You've always got to be pushing things to the limit, but with safety. Barbara and Michael, and obviously all the directors, are very keen, very highly safety-conscious."

SHERYL CROW (Title song vocalist, *Tomorrow Never Dies*)
"I know every James Bond movie. I grew up on them. I saw it as a challenge to take it back musically to the period that I love, the dyed-in-the-wool Bond."

CLIFF CULLEY (Visual effects, *Goldfinger* (uncredited); matte artist, *Dr. No* (uncredited), *From Russia With Love* (uncredited), *Thunderball* (uncredited), *You Only Live Twice* (uncredited), *On Her Majesty's Secret Service* (uncredited), *The Man With The Golden Gun* (uncredited))
"They were great fun to work on. You were all involved, right from day one. You were sent scripts, you were asked for your input, what you thought. It wasn't all cut and dried like all films are. You start off with a sequence, you're going to do it one way, and then somebody has an idea and you change it around."

MARYAM D'ABO (Kara Milovy in *The Living Daylights*)
"I was thrilled. It was like, 'My god, I'm in a Bond movie.' Me, you know. I had a hard time

seeing myself as the Bond phenomenon... James Bond movies have survived so long because you're dealing with the spy world. It's always been intriguing to everybody in the world."

ROALD DAHL (Screenwriter, *You Only Live Twice*)
"The business of making a Bond film is an exciting process. There's no question about that, because they are so technically perfect and inventive. And nearly all the stunts and clever things are done for real. They're not fake, you know. They're dangerous."

TIMOTHY DALTON: (James Bond in *The Living Daylights, Licence To Kill*)
"Bond is a very powerful image known the world over. I once made a documentary on wolves and went to live with some eskimos near the North Pole. When I arrived, they all came dashing out to greet me saying, 'It's James Bond, James Bond!'"

ROBERT DAVI (Franz Sanchez in *Licence To Kill*)
"If you look at the Bond films, you don't get a feeling of anything ancient, you know; there's still a contemporary, classic element to all those films."

ERNEST DAY (Camera operator, *You Only Live Twice*; second unit director, *The Spy Who Loved Me, Moonraker*)
"Ernie Day was a second unit director," said Michael G. Wilson, "on several of our films. He was sort of an old Bond hand, who had the complete confidence of Lewis [Gilbert], and would handle most of the second unit."

JIMMY DEAN (Willard Whyte in *Diamonds Are Forever*)
"All the James Bond movies are entertainment. They're entertaining. They don't have some huge message that bears you down with the weight of the world. It's a fun, noisy, laughing situation."

BENICIO DEL TORO (Dario in *Licence To Kill*)
"If someone would have told me when I was in high school that in about four years, or five years, you'll be playing in a Bond film, I would have never believed them. It was like, almost like a dream come true. I loved the Bond films, I've seen most of them, so it was really like 'Maybe I'm really good...' It was one of the few films that I've had fun from the beginning to the end."

JUDI DENCH (M in *GoldenEye, Tomorrow Never Dies, The World Is Not Enough, Die Another Day*)
"I have always been a huge Sean Connery fan; his films were superb for the 1960s, but Pierce is definitely right for the 1990s. It is much harder now. Bond was part of our 60s culture, whereas we now have to keep on reinventing him for new audiences, with new stories and a modern approach."

KARIN DOR (Helga Brandt in *You Only Live Twice*)
"I can understand that people love to see [the Bond films] because he is a man who always survives, who has charm, who does everything and is always the lucky one who comes out fantastic. This is a good thing nowadays."

SHEENA EASTON (Title song vocalist, *For Your Eyes Only*)
"I remember that my big brothers and sisters used to be really excited to go to the local cinema to see the Bond movies. The thing that I remember most was that they'd always come home and the first thing they'd want to talk about was the opening sequence. I also remember the fact that we were very proud of Sean Connery because he was Scottish. We had a very suave, sophisticated James Bond in Sean. You didn't see a lot of Scottish movie stars back then, so that was a great source of pride for us."

SHIRLEY EATON (Jill Masterson, *Goldfinger*)
"I think the Bond series has lasted so long because they're still escapism films. They haven't got big messages. They're not gory, and they're not explicitly sexy. They're sensual and sexy, but I think there's an innocence and a fun. Let's hope they continue to keep making them. It'll be difficult, probably, because entertainment these days has got very serious, or very ridiculous. They're real entertainment, the Bond films."

BRITT EKLAND (Mary Goodnight, *The Man With The Golden Gun*)
"The one thing it has done is it's given me an image that's - to me, anyway - quite valuable, because I can travel and do things all over the world. Most people will have seen the Bonds, so it enables you to appear in public and be known without having to explain who you are. From that point of view, it's been very useful."

BRUCE FEIRSTEIN (Screenwriter, *GoldenEye, Tomorrow Never Dies, The World Is Not Enough*)
"The question that I get asked all the time as a writer is, who do you write for? And when I wrote *GoldenEye*, before I had ever met Pierce, I wrote *GoldenEye* hearing Connery's voice. And the interesting change is that, on [*Tomorrow Never Dies*], I totally wrote for Pierce. Pierce has become Bond."

VIC FLICK (Guitarist, 'The James Bond Theme', *Dr. No, From Russia With Love, Goldfinger, Thunderball, You Only Live Twice, The Man With The Golden Gun, Licence To Kill*)
"I could have played ['The James Bond Theme'] lots of different ways. But I think the way I played it then, I'm quite happy with it. It's seen me down through the years."

GERT FROBE (Auric Goldfinger in *Goldfinger*)
"I am a big man, and I have a laugh to match my size. The ridiculous thing is that since I played Goldfinger in the James Bond film there are some people who still insist on seeing me as a cold, ruthless villain - a man without laughs."

FIONA FULLERTON (Pola Ivanova in *A View To A Kill*)
"The really great thing about being in a Bond movie when you have children is that you have fantastic parental value. It's like, 'My mum was in a Bond movie.' So [my son] James, although he would never admit this, scores very highly in the classroom because his mummy was in a Bond movie. I'll get his little friends sidling up to me when I pick him up from school, and they say, 'Were you really in a Bond film?' And I say, 'Yes, I was.' 'Hah! Which one?' Every time they're on TV I get other moms and dads coming up to me at the school gate saying, 'Oh, we had to rent your video the other day. We had to rent *A View To A Kill* because little Charlie insisted.' So it's great in a way that children absolutely love them. Even at ten they are absolutely Bond mad. And my son James really can't quite believe that I was in a Bond movie. It's just too good to be true."

EUNICE GAYSON (Sylvia Trench in *Dr. No, From Russia With Love*)
"I loved working with Terence [Young]. He was everything that Bond was - a very elegant man, even on the set. Very well-educated, erudite man. And, oh, he was a gentleman. It was wonderful to just be around him on the set. And he gave Sean that wonderful ease that he had in the part. It came from Terence, which was lovely. I was so upset when he died, because I just felt that a light had gone out of the industry, a very rare light."

LEWIS GILBERT (Director, *You Only Live Twice, The Spy Who Loved Me, Moonraker*)
"Never in the history of films has there been a series like [James Bond]. Because in the old days when you had second features, you might get ten Boston Blackies or something like that, but they were tiny films. When you think of the big films that have been made, there are sequels, but around about number three they give up. For one thing, you can't copy it. There's no way. People try to copy it, but it never works, and it's that combination of humour, romance, wonderful settings; it's unique. I can't see an end to Bond films, because they could just go on forever. I'd like to do the last one in about 50 year's time."

JOHN GLEN (Editor, *On Her Majesty's Secret Service, The Spy Who Loved Me, Moonraker*; director, *For Your Eyes Only, Octopussy, A View To A Kill, The Living Daylights, Licence To Kill*)
"I suppose in a way a Bond film is special to all generations, all ages. We've all grown up with Bond, so it's become a part of our life. It's something that we expect, we know we're going to get an eyeful, get great value, get thrilled. There's a feeling, when the James Bond title comes up, you just settle back in your seat. You know you're in for a feast, don't you? I guess it's just good value."

BRUCE GLOVER (Mr. Wint in *Diamonds Are Forever*)
"The first week we were shooting, we had a scene where we're carrying Sean and we're putting him into the trunk of the car because we're going to bury him alive... I'm holding Sean chest to chest on the edge of this thing, and I'm feeling kind of confident because the role's been going well. I'm looking at Connery, this amazing looking man, and I'm thinking, 'I'll play a little joke'. I'm chest to chest with him,I look at him, I go, 'I think I'm getting emotionally involved.' I thought he would laugh. And he looks, and I could see this pain and this 'Oh no, not this too!' He thought I was serious."

JULIAN GLOVER (Ari Kristatos in *For Your Eyes Only*)
"The nearest I got to being in a Bond film before was testing for Bond himself... The next best thing is to play the naughty."

WALTER GOTELL (Morzeny in *From Russia With Love*; General Gogol in *The Spy Who Loved Me, Moonraker, For Your Eyes Only, Octopussy, A View To A Kill, The Living Daylights*)
"Little did we imagine at that time - perhaps Cubby did, but I don't think anyone else did - that there would be such a history of filmmaking subsequent to [*From Russia With Love*], which also obviously became part of it, because many people still believe that *From Russia With Love* was perhaps the best."

MARTIN GRACE (Stunts, *You Only Live Twice* (uncredited), Roger Moore stunt double, *Live And Let Die, The Man With The Golden Gun, The Spy Who Loved Me, Moonraker, For Your Eyes Only*; stunt team supervisor, *Octopussy*; action sequence arranger, *A View To A Kill*)
" I think every man perhaps feels that he's James Bond. And I think there are a lot of actors who would like to play James Bond. And on the other hand, you've got the girls. You can't have a James Bond without lots of girls, and they always look terribly attractive. I think that mix works very well, and the element of the danger that's involved excites everybody. We all have this feeling of something exciting in our lives, and James Bond does that."

CHARLES GRAY (Dikko Henderson in *You Only Live Twice*, Ernst Stavro Blofeld in *Diamonds Are Forever*)
"There is really nothing to [playing a Bond villain] - just be yourself. Donald Pleasence and Telly Savalas were themselves and so was I. I never found the acting very difficult. It was just a question of turning up on time and hoping to go home on time... I had three pussies. We had to have two stand-ins because the first pussy got awfully cross with me throwing her up in the air. I adored them all but I think they all got rather fed up."

RICHARD 'DICKIE' GRAYDON (Stunts, *From Russia With Love, Goldfinger, Thunderball, On Her Majesty's Secret Service, The Spy Who Loved Me, Moonraker, For Your Eyes Only, Octopussy, A View To A Kill*)
"Working on a Bond film is very much like working within a family. I worked on all the early Bond films, and one builds up a relationship on a Bond film simply because of the sequence of films. You're always pleased to see people that you've met before in

different locations. You can swap stories, reminiscences, and I think that's very important. The family feeling of being on a Bond film is not duplicated on any other film, because no other film has the same sequence of events, one film after another. You cannot help becoming part of a family. And Cubby was very much the father figure."

JOHN GROVER (Assistant editor, *The Spy Who Loved Me*; assembly editor, *Moonraker*; editor, *For Your Eyes Only, The Living Daylights, Licence To Kill*)
"Why have Bond films lasted so long? Because they're good entertainment. You go to the cinema for two hours. You get your eyes bashed and your ears bashed and you come away with a smile on your face. You're not given a political message. You're not upset with too much sex. You're not told what you should be listening to or watching. It's not a message film. It's fun. Going to the cinema is fun. You should be entertained, think it's happening, think it's completely impossible, but come away and love it. Sing the song if it's a good pop song."

ALIZA GUR (Vida - gypsy girl - in *From Russia With Love*)
"If you actually watch *Dr. No* or *From Russia With Love* or even *Goldfinger*, the action is not that much and not that spectacular. Certainly not like what came later. There were no unbelievable tasks or jumps or leaps... It's like a mystery movie. What you suspect will happen is more exciting than what you actually see. And Bond promised so much. We moved from the innocence of the early 60s to the more daring late 60s and Bond fit perfectly into that genre. You have a man who is not rough but elegant, not evil but a lover, and yet everything around him was action. All these gorgeous women were inside the action, and I think that was something totally new and totally captivating. People who watch these pictures now know it, and so they don't expect the super-super-action. They want Bond. And Sean Connery was Bond. We were lucky to be considered pretty and be in those pictures with him. I think that's why *From Russia With Love*, *Dr. No* and *Goldfinger* will always be the highlight of the Bond pictures. And yet they're all great."

GUY HAMILTON (Director, *Goldfinger, Diamonds Are Forever, Live And Let Die, The Man With The Golden Gun*)
"[Cubby] adored Bond, he loved Bond. It was his baby; he protected it, was determined that it would look first-class on the screen, and expected everybody to put their best efforts in... There's a Bondian way of doing things, and you had to pay the entrance fee. Once Cubby felt that you understood Bond, and you understood the Bondian way of doing things, you were accepted and you were family."

MARVIN HAMLISCH (Composer, *The Spy Who Loved Me*)
"You do spend a lot of time and effort on a musical score, and particularly for a Bond film, because you know that a Bond film's going to be scrutinized. You know the soundtrack's going to be listened to by aficionados saying, 'Is it as good or not as good as the last one?' So I would say there's just a little bit more of a consciousness about what you're doing than other films. This one you know there's something riding on it."

JULIUS HARRIS (Tee Hee in *Live And Let Die*)
"[*Live And Let Die*] - it's a godsend, in my opinion. It put us in the same category as the rest of the actors out here. The white actors, that is. And I never looked at it as a blaxploitation film, because I didn't think of it that way. I thought, 'I'm doing a movie.' I am glad to have been part of it... And to be cast in a Bond film, well, it's the highlight of my career."

DAVID HEDISON (Felix Leiter in *Live And Let Die, Licence to Kill*)
"I expect it will be good for a trivia quiz one day – 'Who's the only person to play Felix Leiter twice?'"

LINDY HEMMING (Costume designer, *GoldenEye, Tomorrow Never Dies, The World Is Not Enough, Die Another Day*)
"I always have to say that how [Pierce Brosnan] dresses himself is completely different to how Bond dresses. He said in a television interview that it's like the Batsuit. When he puts on his Brioni, he becomes Bond."

GLORIA HENDRY (Rosie Carver in *Live And Let Die*)
"It's one of the biggest movies I've ever been in in my life. It was awesome. I really had to work hard to settle down from all the excitement and do the work, and doing the work kept me in check. But we were very, very spoiled. Oh! Very spoiled. Extremely spoiled. We had maids. We had dressers, we had people who would make clothes on the spot for us... So, where I'm coming from, it was really awesome."

ALAN HUME (Director of photography, *For Your Eyes Only, Octopussy, A View To A Kill*)
"John Glen took me to Baffin Island to film the stunt where Bond skis off the mountain with a parachute for *The Spy Who Loved Me*. When John got the nod to direct, he brought me along to shoot the films. It was a pleasure to go to work. By the time Saturday was over and Sunday was along, I was looking forward to Monday and going to work because it was such fun. I put a lot of the success of the Bonds on to Mr. Broccoli in his office. He knew how to get things done. He knew how to get help wherever he needed."

PETER HUNT (Editor, *Dr. No, From Russia With Love, Goldfinger*; supervising editor, *Thunderball, You Only Live Twice*; second unit director, *You Only Live Twice*; director, *On Her Majesty's Secret Service*)
"In those early days, editors didn't like cutting on movement. The standard thing was, you mustn't cut on movement because it'll be a jump. Well, that's nonsense. Because nowadays, they don't care what they do. But in those days, they did, and that was the whole thing. Of course, I didn't really care. If it moved the film along, I used my timing and my cutting and cut the film. In those days, they let a track shot go right the way to its end, and however it was shot, that was how it went in the picture. I'm afraid I didn't do that. If it interfered with the pacing of the picture, I cut there in the middle

or wherever it was. I didn't wait for movement to stop me from cutting from one thing to the other, and keeping the timing of the sequences going. And often, it was important for developing the character of the person who was playing in the film. The character of James Bond had to be decisive. He couldn't be ponderous. Well, I suppose he could have been ponderous, but I don't think it would have worked. You had to work within the character again and make him decisive. And you had to make the fights work, so you had to be creative in cutting them together. You couldn't worry about continuity. You couldn't worry about whether things, as they say, 'matched'. It wasn't possible. Well, it wasn't possible in my eyes, let's say."

CLIFTON JAMES (Sheriff Pepper in *Live And Let Die, The Man With The Golden Gun*)
"So many people see it, you know. In one night, more people see you in a James Bond movie that you do than if you ran for a year on Broadway in a play."

FAMKE JANSSEN (Xenia Onatopp in *GoldenEye*)
"[Pierce Brosnan] is exactly what I would have imagined a James Bond person would look like. And I thought he had fun with it. He's funny. He was great to work with, because he's very giving... Our scenes, as you can tell, are very competitive and flirtatious and everything, and we worked on that level constantly throughout the movie."

LYNN-HOLLY JOHNSON (Bibi Dahl in *For Your Eyes Only*)
"This was the first type of movie that was magical. It was luxurious, and it was handsome, and beautiful, so that's what you escape to the movies to go see, right? Today, there's a bit more competition in that area, but still, it's a piece of history. And nothing can take that away. I just hope they continue forever."

GRACE JONES (May Day in *A View To A Kill*)
"They were looking for some real muscular women for the Bond girls, these body-building types, but Mr. Broccoli said they were just too much muscle, really ugly. I had the right amount of muscles and feminine qualities."

LOUIS JOURDAN (Kamal Khan in *Octopussy*)
"The villains in Bond films are always memorable because they are as strong as Bond himself. They have to be an enormous threat to him and he must win in the end by a very small margin. You must always believe that the villain might just be the winner. The threat must be there, the wit must be there, the intelligence must be there... It's in the tradition of Mephistopheles. Never forget the parody. It should be, up to a certain point, the parody of villainy - like James Bond is the parody of the hero."

REMY JULIENNE (Driving stunts co-ordinator, *For Your Eyes Only*; driving stunts arranger, *Octopussy, A View To A Kill, The Living Daylights, Licence To Kill*; car chase stunts, *GoldenEye*)
"The Bond films are exceptional. They know that we are able to do many things but they also know that we have a limit. They are very easy to work with. John Glen is a great director. I know his ways, his talent - he can do anything."

CHARLES 'JERRY' JUROE (Director of publicity, *For Your Eyes Only*; marketing director, *The Living Daylights, Licence To Kill*)
"Looking back over the history of the Bond films over the last four decades since 1962, I've met people who have said, 'Oh, I think no one can ever be better than Sean Connery' or, indeed, my niece was of an age to say, 'Roger Moore is the greatest. There's never been anybody like him' or people I've talked to recently have said, 'My god, Pierce Brosnan is marvellous.' As long as people are born and the human race progresses, there will be new audiences for new James Bonds. I really feel that James Bond is forever."

MICHAEL KAMEN (Composer, *Licence To Kill*)
"I look forward to seeing the next one and the next one and I'm very happy to be a paying customer. I'll be going to Bond movies as long as they're making them. Whether I play them or not."

RICHARD KIEL (Jaws in *The Spy Who Loved Me* and *Moonraker*)
"Turning into a good guy in *Moonraker* kind of changed my acting career. I was playing mostly villains, and after turning into a good guy, a lot of the parts that I've played since then have been more sympathetic characters... I think that the people that grew up with Sean Connery think that he was the best. The ones that grew up with Roger Moore, they think that he was the best. And the ones that are growing up with Pierce Brosnan are going to think that he's the best. As people develop and new ones come along... they're something that can go on forever."

DANIEL KLEINMAN (Title designer, *GoldenEye, Tomorrow Never Dies, The World Is Not Enough, Die Another Day*)
"Bond title sequences are the most famous in the world. If you think of film title sequences, I think the average person would immediately think of James Bond. They're part of the experience of seeing Bond. Part of what you expect to see is a certain type of imagery and a certain type of sequence... I'm actually not particularly interested in being a title sequence director *per se*. I work on the Bond titles because I'm a Bond fan. I love James Bond, grew up with James Bond. I had a James Bond gun when I was a kid. I collected the bubble gum cards. It is the greatest title sequence to do in the world. I think anything else would have to be pretty special not to be an anti-climax after that."

YAPHET KOTTO (Dr. Kananga/Mr. Big in *Live And Let Die*)
"It was kind of bittersweet playing the first black villain in a James Bond film, because while I was making history and while that ground was being broken, I was left out - and the character was left out - of the great publicity junket, because I think United Artists feared

that the role would be criticized by the fact that a black man was playing a villain in a James Bond film. But the film came out, and it opened big and made a lot of money, and it gave me a lot of international attention. It led me to another United Artists film, and another United Artists film, and another United Artists film, so my career was off and running."

JEROEN KRABBE (Georgi Koskov in *The Living Daylights*)
"I wanna come back! I wanna be back in the Bond picture once more. I didn't die, so I *could* come back."

BURT KWOUK (Mr. Ling in *Goldfinger*, SPECTRE 3 in *You Only Live Twice*, Chinese General in *Casino Royale*)
"I'm very proud to have been associated with a lot of the things that I've done, and one of them is the Bond pictures."

MICHAEL LAMONT (Art department, *Goldfinger* (uncredited), *Thunderball* (uncredited); *On Her Majesty's Secret Service* (uncredited), *Diamonds Are Forever* (uncredited), *The Spy Who Loved Me* (uncredited); additional art director, *For Your Eyes Only*, *Octopussy*, *A View To A Kill*, *The Living Daylights*; art director, *Licence To Kill*; art director model unit, *GoldenEye*)
"When we went onto *Goldfinger*, we weren't thinking it was a successful series at that point. It was the third of the James Bond films. When *Thunderball* came out, we all suddenly realized that we were on something a bit special. It was always an honour to get asked back to do another one. And a pleasure to be on one because there was always going to be something exciting to do."

PETER LAMONT (Art department, *Goldfinger* (uncredited), set decorator, *Thunderball* (uncredited), *On Her Majesty's Secret Service*, *Diamonds Are Forever*; co-art director, *Live And Let Die*, *The Man With The Golden Gun*; art director, *The Spy Who Loved Me*; production designer, *For Your Eyes Only*, *Octopussy*, *A View To A Kill*, *The Living Daylights*, *Licence To Kill*, *GoldenEye*, *The World Is Not Enough*, *Die Another Day*)
"A friend of mine called me out of the blue and said would I like to come on to *Goldfinger*? He said, 'It's a James Bond film.' And as it happened at that time, *From Russia With Love* had just come out. I can remember getting in line and going to the cinema; I was absolutely knocked out with the quality of the props that they had, you know, especially that case. And I don't think there will ever, ever be a better fight than the one that Bond had in the railway compartment. So I joined *Goldfinger*."

GEORGE LAZENBY (James Bond in *On Her Majesty's Secret Service*)
"It's hard to top a Bond film. The stigma, or the reality of it all, is there's nothing bigger. There's nothing gone on for so long as Bond. I mean, I thought it was over when I did it, with *Easy Rider* and all that stuff going on, I thought, 'Well, this guy in a suit with short hair's not gonna make it.' And guns were out. Everyone was into love and not war. James Bond lived right through all that and it's still there today. It just goes with the times. People think, 'Hey, what's wrong with a Bond film? Let's go and see a Bond film. It's always entertaining. You get your money's worth.' And, you know, as far as I'm concerned, it'll probably be there long after I'm gone."

SIMON LE BON (of Duran Duran, title song, *A View To A Kill*)
"The way that we approached writing the theme song for *A View To A Kill* is pretty much the same as we actually write any song. In a way it was kind of made simple for us in the fact that we had a title. When you write music the hardest thing is to decide what its going to be about."

BERNARD LEE (M in *Dr. No*, *From Russia With Love*, *Goldfinger*, *Thunderball*, *You Only Live Twice*, *Diamonds Are Forever*, *Live And Let Die*, *The Man With The Golden Gun*, *The Spy Who Loved Me*, *Moonraker*)
"M is the most enduring single 'running' character I've ever played on stage or screen. He's been good to me and I wouldn't want to cross him. He has a built-in survival kit. Screen Bonds may come and go, but M seems to go on forever."

CHRISTOPHER LEE (Francisco Scaramanga in *The Man With The Golden Gun*)
"There was a man called Scaramanga who was at Eton with Ian [Fleming], or so he told me. And he disliked him intensely. Couldn't bear the man. Or the boy, as he was then. And that's why he gave the name to his villain."

GEORGE LEECH (Stunts, *Dr. No* (uncredited), *Goldfinger* (uncredited), *You Only Live Twice* (uncredited), *Diamonds Are Forever* (uncredited), *For Your Eyes Only*, *Octopussy* (uncredited), *Never Say Never Again* (uncredited), *A View To A Kill* (uncredited); stunt co-ordinator, *On Her Majesty's Secret Service*; Lotus Esprit stunt driver, *The Spy Who Loved Me*)
"The character of Bond himself, he's incorruptible, he's a man's man, heterosexual, that's why he's admired. He loves women, and he respects women. He has the virtues, he wears the white hat, he's the hero. He tells the truth, he's an honest, straight individual. People love him because he is the hero. He is King Arthur, he is Prince Valiant, he is Jesus Christ that doesn't turn the other cheek. He hits back... I think the key to the Bond picture's success is superb action, good characters, good writing. And it is the action which has to be realistic, and genuine."

LOTTE LENYA (Rosa Klebb in *From Russia With Love*)
"No bangs, you see. For the first time in my life, people will see my forehead. I have my bangs from my mother. Sometimes I think I was born with bangs... The woman I play is a devoted Communist, absolutely rigid like those frigid sexless types, those spinsters. Bond kills her in the end of course. He has to go on to the next movie."

VALERIE LEON (Hotel receptionist in Sardinia in *The Spy Who Loved Me*, fishing lady in Bahamas in *Never Say Never Again*)
"For *The Spy Who Loved Me*, when I played the part of the receptionist, I had a dress made

for me by Berman's. It was possibly not the sort of dress you would wear as a receptionist in these days. It was a very tight-fitting dress, with a ruffle round the neck, and the cleavage. We mustn't forget the cleavage."

MARGARET LEWARS (Photographer in *Dr. No*)
"One of the reasons the James Bond series is still popular and will continue to be popular is because they are witty, they are sophisticated, they have entered and stuck into the land of make-believe, their sophisticated gadgets, their beautiful surroundings, and there is good triumphing over evil at the end. And I suppose everybody wants to be - every man wants to be a James Bond at heart."

DESMOND LLEWELYN (Q in *From Russia With Love*, *Goldfinger*, *Thunderball*, *You Only Live Twice*, *On Her Majesty's Secret Service*, *Diamonds Are Forever*, *The Man With The Golden Gun*, *The Spy Who Loved Me*, *Moonraker*, *For Your Eyes Only*, *Octopussy*, *A View To A Kill*, *The Living Daylights*, *Licence To Kill*, *GoldenEye*, *Tomorrow Never Dies*, *The World Is Not Enough*)
"You must keep fantasy with Bond, and not only fantasy, but pure relaxation, enjoyment. What you see on the screen is something that you don't have in this world today. You can just sit back and enjoy it... I loved *Licence To Kill* because I had a large part in it, and it was great fun. I mean, I'd never been on vacation much before, doing things, and I loved every moment of it."

JAKE LOMBARD (Aerial stunt double Roger Moore, *Moonraker* (uncredited), *Octopussy* (uncredited); aerial stunt double *The Living Daylights*, *Licence To Kill*)
"I think James Bond films were kind of the first real action adventure films, and they've been the most successful sequels... Everybody's always excited to see what James Bond's doing; he's so cool, and suave, and his pictures are always full of beautiful women - they're always pretty well done, and they seem to still be going strong."

MICHAEL LONSDALE (Hugo Drax in *Moonraker*)
"Some people said, 'How could you do a James Bond?', you know, some intellectuals. But I said, 'Because an actor must be able to do many different things.' And it was great fun. I enjoyed doing it very much."

CAREY LOWELL (Pam Bouvier in *Licence To Kill*)
"Everybody loves Bond. It's a wave that has built up and built up and built up, and the expectations are great... People know what to expect in a Bond film, and they're never disappointed. I think that's why it's been such a successful series of films."

PATRICK MACNEE (Sir Godfrey Tibbett in *A View To A Kill*)
"I don't know how Cubby managed to get this incredible, I mean, probably the best action of any group of films that has ever been made, and at the same time, have this extraordinary, devoted family feeling that everybody who worked with him got. In my opinion, it came from him."

RICHARD MAIBAUM (Screenwriter, *Dr. No*, *From Russia With Love*, *Goldfinger*, *Thunderball*, *On Her Majesty's Secret Service*, *Diamonds Are Forever*, *The Man With The Golden Gun*, *The Spy Who Loved Me*, *For Your Eyes Only*, *Octopussy*, *A View To A Kill*, *The Living Daylights*, *Licence To Kill*)
"All the Bond pictures are brain-busters before they become blockbusters... Writing the villain's caper is the most difficult thing. If you know what he's trying to accomplish - break into Fort Knox and steal all the gold or kill all the people on earth with a nerve gas - you know where the villain has to go to accomplish his ends and what James Bond has to do to foil him. The structure is mythological. It's Theseus and the Minotaur. Bond gets into a maze and he follows the thread, and you must see that you've got the necessary action sequences to bring Bond closer to or push him further away from the Minotaur."

TOM MANKIEWICZ (Screenwriter, *Diamonds Are Forever*, *Live And Let Die*, *The Man With The Golden Gun*)
"I, like everyone else, was a huge Bond fan; I think people forget today what a big event it was when a Bond movie opened. I was just floored at the chance to write one because I was always first in line for a Bond movie. And as a young writer, you thought, 'I can write this. I know the stuff.' And all of a sudden here's someone saying, 'Well, go ahead. We'll give you two weeks to see how good you are.' I thought, 'This is the biggest thing - if it works - that will ever happen to me.' And it certainly was, because of all the things I've done since. To be the writer of the James Bond movies was such an incredible, singular kind of position to be in in those days."

SOPHIE MARCEAU (Elektra King in *The World Is Not Enough*)
"Bond is kind of a fantasy in a real world, and for an actress it's fantastic because everything's classic."

GEORGE MARTIN (Composer, *Live And Let Die*)
"I remember scoring the soundtrack to *Live And Let Die*, the first Bond picture with Roger Moore. In that film they had the very first digital watch, which had a red dial, an LED. It was a great gimmick at the time."

LOIS MAXWELL (Miss Moneypenny in *Dr. No*, *From Russia With Love*, *Goldfinger*, *Thunderball*, *You Only Live Twice*, *On Her Majesty's Secret Service*, *Diamonds Are Forever*, *Live And Let Die*, *The Man With The Golden Gun*, *The Spy Who Loved Me*, *Moonraker*, *For Your Eyes Only*, *Octopussy*, *A View To A Kill*)
"Sean and I and Terence decided on the background of the relationship between James Bond and Miss Moneypenny. That was that when he was a teaboy and she was in the secretarial pool, they had gone off together for a lovely bank holiday weekend to a rose-covered cottage and had fully appreciated each other's qualities. But she realized that if

she allowed herself to fall in love with him, he would probably break her heart - and he knew that if he allowed himself to fall in love with *her*, that he'd never get his double-O. So that was the background of their cozy-ups in the office, that they really adored each other, but on the other hand they were ambitious people. And we also said that when he went off on an assignment and fooled around with a hot blonde or a dreadful brunette or a long-legged brunette or whatever, that he came back and before the next assignment, they probably went off to a rose-covered cottage again."

PAUL McCARTNEY (Title Song, *Live And Let Die*)
"I sort of wrote it, got George [Martin] round to my house, sat down at the piano, worked out an arrangement with him, then he went off and scored it... We worked it up and then went into the studio and did it in just a couple of days. It was quite easy to do and turned out well for the film... [It was a big production] because of Bond. I didn't feel that I could go and do a little acoustic number for a Bond film. What are people going to think, 'Oh, Christ, what is this?'... You're following something, so you've got to keep vaguely within the format."

DEBBIE McWILLIAMS (Casting director, *For Your Eyes Only, A View To A Kill, The Living Daylights, GoldenEye, Tomorrow Never Dies, The World Is Not Enough, Die Another Day*)
"The Bond films have always had huge international appeal. One of the fantastic things for me doing this job is that I have travelled the world. And I'm most like a kind of goodwill ambassador, if you like. Especially if it's a country we're shooting in, I've made an effort to find people locally. Also it gives it much more of a texture and flavour. That's always been the interesting part of the job for me, to be able to cast people who haven't been seen and who aren't familiar. And I think, for the most part, we've been very successful at that."

DEREK MEDDINGS (Special effects, *Live And Let Die*; miniatures, *The Man With The Golden Gun*; special visual effects, *The Spy Who Loved Me*; visual effects supervisor, *Moonraker, For Your Eyes Only*; miniature effects supervisor, *GoldenEye*)
"The thing that was such a success, which actually gave me a footing in the Bond films was that at the end of [*Live And Let Die*], there was the sequence where the poppy fields explode; Guy Hamilton called me over, and he said, 'Could you do this as a miniature, back at the studios?' And I said, 'Yes, I could.' He said, 'And it'll look good?' And I said, 'Yeah, 'course it will. It'll look great.' So we came back to England, and I did the miniatures of this particular poppy field blowing up. Then, the next Bond film I did, they brought more into it, and each Bond film that I've been involved in, they've had more and more miniatures."

MICHAEL MELLINGER (Kisch in *Goldfinger*)
"People always like to have a hero who goes through all sort of vicissitudes but wins in the end. People like to see that. I was a member of the Berlin Ensemble - Bertold Brecht's theatre in Berlin - for some years, and in Brecht's *Galileo*, somebody says to Galileo, 'Unhappy the land that has no heroes', and Galileo replies 'Unhappy the land that has need of heroes.' People still hanker after heroes."

ALEC MILLS (Camera operator, *On Her Majesty's Secret Service, The Spy Who Loved Me, Moonraker, For Your Eyes Only, Octopussy*; cinematographer, *The Living Daylights, Licence to Kill*)
"I never used any diffusion on any of the Bonds that I lit, because it's gotta be clear, it's gotta be clean. I recall Cubby saying to me, 'Alec, we want it to look lovely.' I don't think they were mad about diffusion. Someone did mention this to me; certainly somebody gave me that impression. But I had no doubts about what it was going to be, anyway. It had to be clean. Very clean. Sharp. Otherwise, things get looking soft. And it's not James Bond any longer. You're making it too pretty. James Bond's not pretty."

ROGER MOORE (James Bond in *Live And Let Die, The Man With The Golden Gun, The Spy Who Loved Me, Moonraker, For Your Eyes Only, Octopussy, A View To A Kill*)
"Having played heroes for so many years, I would love to get my teeth into a real baddy role, especially in a Bond film where they are larger than life and have all the best lines."

TED MOORE (Director of photography, *Dr. No, From Russia With Love, Goldfinger, Thunderball, Diamonds Are Forever, Live And Let Die, The Man With The Golden Gun*)
After Ted Moore shot the Warwick Films production *Hell Below Zero*, which was filmed in the Antarctic, Cubby Broccoli remarked that Moore was a true professional who could operate at temperatures of twenty below zero as though he were in Pinewood.

OSWALD MORRIS (Cinematographer, *The Man With The Golden Gun*)
"It's not the photography, I think, that counts. It's the design of them that's the thing that impresses. The photography is just, you're photographing and you're lighting. You're not attempting to put anything into it because it's all there: a) in the story, b) in the performance and c) in the design of the sets. The spectacle and the stunts do it all for you. You just make a very efficient photographic input."

TIMOTHY MOXON (Strangways in *Dr. No*)
"We were sitting there, and Sean Connery was sitting by the pool, and Terence Young said, 'You know, I think this boy's going to make it in spite of his Scots accent.'"

CAROLINE MUNRO (appeared in *Casino Royale* (uncredited); Naomi in *The Spy Who Loved Me*)
"I think it's survived for so long because it has elements of everything. It has adventure, it has glamour, it has tension, it has sex. The writing, the wonderful photography, great scripts, wonderful music scores: you can't lose with that combination."

PETER MURTON (Art director, *Goldfinger, Thunderball*; production designer, *The Man With The Golden Gun*)

"It gives people an excitement of being in places which they wouldn't normally go to. It gives them the idea that Bond is always in danger but seems to get out of it. As a film, I think it's a very exciting medium that they've come up with. Some of them are a bit more exciting than others, but, basically, they have the same trend. Bond always, always, always wins. Like any hero has to. But the moments of torture and danger from start to finish are well-balanced. It's a classic theme, but it's done in a very imaginative new style. *Dr. No* was a prime example which started the whole thing off, and it's been continued all the way through. Bond versus the baddies. What better thing could there be to excite all ages, when you think about it?"

WAYNE NEWTON (Rev. Joe Butcher in *Licence To Kill*)
"We were all raised on the Bond films and it epitomizes what we'd all truly like to believe is out there."

MONTY NORMAN (Composer, *Dr. No*)
"When *Dr. No* came out, I was at the premiere and the reaction was amazing. I mean, the laughs that Sean got were unprecedented, and the whole feeling when he mentions his name, 'Bond, James Bond' and the music begins... Nobody could have realized that it was going to be such an important and successful, not only a film, but you can say a whole industry."

SOON TAIK OH (Lt. Hip in *The Man With The Golden Gun*)
"I got a call one day and my agent asked me if I would like to be in a James Bond picture. Around the 1970s a James Bond picture is a big, big event, so I thought she was joking."

LUCIANA PALUZZI (Fiona Volpe in *Thunderball*)
"My husband says that he fell in love with me when he saw *Thunderball*. He said that he was sitting in the cinema, and I have a scene where I'm riding this motorcycle, and then I come to the lake and you don't know if it's a man or a woman; I take the helmet off, and I shake my hair - and my red hair was much, much longer then - and he said that he looked and he said, 'That's the woman for me.' It took him ten years to find me, though, but that doesn't matter, because we finally met. He always says that that's the reason, for ten years he was saying, 'I've got to find Luciana, and I've got to marry her.' So we did, and we've been married twenty years now."

JOHN PARKINSON (Director of Glidrose Publications Ltd., literary copyright holders to the James Bond stories - 1977-1989; Eon Productions executive - *Licence To Kill* through *Die Another Day*)
"James Bond is not just a literary and film hero, he is a part of our cultural heritage, instantly recognisable to millions of people around the world for style and sang-froid."

TRINA PARKS (Thumper in *Diamonds Are Forever*)
"Sean was the Bond, right? Or what young people say now, the bomb? Or I think it's another word now. You know, I can't keep up with all of them. Tight, Sean was tight... All the men were wonderful, sexy and adventurous, and fantasy-wise you've got everything. Now you've got a lot more action along with that nostalgia type of thing that we had with the love scenes and all, so I think you've got the gamut in the Bond films. And all the gadgets that they used. I think a Bond film cannot ever be uninteresting."

MOLLY PETERS (Patricia Fearing in *Thunderball*)
"Obviously it was a very glamorous thing to be known as a Bond girl. That was very flattering. But people did make mistakes. I went, once, to Windsor Great Park, where Prince Philip and co. were playing polo and they had the Aston Martin car there; Prince Charles and Princess Anne came along - they were very young at the time - and there were lots of people in the crowd. First of all, I met the two young royals and they looked at the car and chatted. But I remember after that someone asked me, 'And what was it like to speak to Prince Charles, Miss Andress?' They thought I was Ursula Andress."

ROSAMUND PIKE (Miranda Frost in *Die Another Day*)
"It's a fantasy, it's challenging and it's desperately exciting. It changes every single day. Before I started filming, I was excited, but I think it gets more exciting as you go on."

JONATHAN PRYCE (Elliott Carver in *Tomorrow Never Dies*)
"I've thoroughly enjoyed being a part of what they call the Bond Family. If you are the villain, you only get one crack at it. Perhaps I should be the first villain to return from cyberspace. With all his communications technology, I'm sure Carver could program his computer revival."

RON QUELCH (Production buyer, *Dr. No* (uncredited), *From Russia With Love* (uncredited), *Goldfinger* (uncredited), *Thunderball* (uncredited), *You Only Live Twice* (uncredited), *Diamonds Are Forever, Octopussy, A View To A Kill, Licence To Kill, GoldenEye, Tomorrow Never Dies*)
"On *Dr. No*, I was working on the Rank payroll at the time. *Dr. No* was just another film. I was employed for two weeks before they went away to Jamaica, and there was a very high level meeting which was held with the director in attendance, Cubby Broccoli, Harry Saltzman, the first assistant, and myself. We discussed at great length the character of Bond, the type of things he would have, including the famous gun-metal cigarette lighter and case... I was relatively inexperienced at the time and I thought, 'Gun-metal cigarette case, how does one go about it?' I thought, 'Oh, yes, I'll be able to find one.' I couldn't find one. It went on and on, we're getting closer and closer to leaving for the location, I was getting a little bit desperate. I phoned Dunhill's in London, and - I'll never forget the man's name - a Mr Dee answered the phone. He said, 'What's the problem?' I said, 'Well, we're doing a Bond film. I'm looking for a gun-metal finish cigarette case and lighter.' And he went very quiet. I said, 'Mr Dee, are you still there?' 'Yes,' he said, 'I'm wondering what star sign you were born under?' So I said, 'Why?' He said, 'Well, I have in front of me on my desk at the moment a gun-

metal cigarette case and lighter.' I said 'Really?' He said, 'Yes, and you can have them for your film.' So I said, 'How come?' And he said, 'Well, one of my clients is an avid reader of Fleming and James Bond stories, and his wife has had these made for his Christmas gift.' I went up that afternoon, presented them to the production, and that was the last thing I had to get before they went to Jamaica."

MICHAEL REED (Cinematographer, *On Her Majesty's Secret Service*)
"At the premiere of *OHMSS*, it was quite an experience. It was the first picture that had been made without Sean Connery. The one thing about the line in it where George Lazenby, after Diana Rigg goes off in the car, turns around to camera and says, 'This didn't happen to the other fella', Peter [Hunt] was bold, in as much as he was saying, 'This is a Bond with another actor in it, and another personality. But I'm going to be bold myself and say that's got to stay in the picture.' It's tongue-in-cheek, but it worked, and got a tremendous applause from the audience. It was a very exciting evening."

DENISE RICHARDS (Dr. Christmas Jones in *The World Is Not Enough*)
"I'd heard so many wonderful things about [Pierce Brosnan] before I got the role, and to work with him, he's really just a class act. He's a gentleman. He's professional. He's charming and sexy too, so I had fun working with him. He was a great guy."

JOHN RICHARDSON (Special effects, *Casino Royale* (uncredited), *Moonraker*; special effects supervisor, *A View To A Kill*, special visual effects, *The Living Daylights*, *Licence To Kill*; miniatures, *Tomorrow Never Dies*, *The World Is Not Enough*)
"There is a lot more to a Bond than the effects. It's got the spectacle, it's got the look, it's got the sets, it's got the costumes, it's got the locations, it's got the girls, but it also has the special effects. And I think they all go arm-in-arm. I mean, they make up the package that makes it a Bond."

DIANA RIGG (Tracy di Vicenzo in *On Her Majesty's Secret Service*)
"It is pure entertainment. I think it melds fantasy and reality very cleverly. The fantasy of this superman who at the same time makes love to this series of women who fall in love with him, and he can be in a dangerous situation, in fact, he is vulnerable at times, is the reality. On the other hand, there's the pure fantasy of the fact that he always gets away scot-free at the end with a lovely girl in his arms."

TANYA ROBERTS (Stacey Sutton in *A View To A Kill*)
"I guess my favourite Bond film is probably *Goldfinger*. I loved Ursula Andress in the first one, but Shirley Eaton, for some reason at that age, I thought she was the most beautiful woman in the world. I also flipped that she was painted in gold. I was very young, and that really impressed me. By the way, just in case you don't know, women go to the Bond movies to see the women. Yeah. Just like men do. They don't go to the Bond movies to see the men, even the lead Bond. I think women are much more caught up with the women, because they're so glamorous and beautiful and the costumes are so off the wall."

IRIS ROSE (Production assistant, *For Your Eyes Only*, *Octopussy*; unit manager, *A View To A Kill*, *The Living Daylights*, *Licence To Kill*, *GoldenEye*, *Tomorrow Never Dies*, *The World Is Not Enough*, *Die Another Day*)
"The Bond films have always been regarded as films everyone wanted to work on, right from the start through to this day. It stems back to the fact that is a family business. I don't think there has ever been a film company that has been a purely family endeavour. The producers took a personal interest in each member of the crew, which made everyone feel special. People appreciate that and they want to come back."

CHARLES RUSSHON (Production liaison, *From Russia With Love*, *Goldfinger*, *Thunderball*, *You Only Live Twice*, *Live And Let Die*)
"He was an ex-Army colonel, I think, who was a great friend of Cubby Broccoli," said Ken Adam. "And he also had some connections at the White House. He used to hear about the latest technology, and then come to us and tell us about it, and try to help us get some of this technology. Like the jet pack in *Thunderball*. That was very Charlie Russhon."

HAROLD SAKATA (Oddjob in *Goldfinger*)
"[Flinging Oddjob's hat], it's not like throwing. It's the whip, the spin, the slicing blade. Like a boomerang that doesn't come back. I worked with a plaster statue of a girl and aimed for the neck. I got so I could topple the head off every time. It made me very conscious of necks. Every time I'd meet a pretty girl, I'd say, 'My, you have an attractive neck '"

HARRY SALTZMAN (Producer, *Dr. No*, *From Russia With Love*, *Goldfinger*, *You Only Live Twice*, *Diamonds Are Forever*, *Live And Let Die*, *The Man With The Golden Gun*; 'Presented By' - *Thunderball*)
"We made the first picture on an $800,000 budget, and we overspent by $40,000. When we had an answer print, there were about eight people there from United Artists, including Arthur Krim, who came to see it. We started the picture at 10 am, and when it was over a few minutes before 12, the lights came up and nobody said anything except a man who was head of the European operation for United Artists. He said, 'The only thing good about the picture is that we can only lose $840,000.' Then they all stood up, and Cubby and I were just shattered."

TELLY SAVALAS (Blofeld in *On Her Majesty's Secret Service*)
"Every villain or every arch-criminal has an ambition, and that ambition has a limited range. With Blofeld, it's the world, and that's what he's shooting for - that is the reason that I find him interesting. He's a cosmopolitan man. He knows his way around. You would imagine that he knows the right wine, and the right girl, and the right time and the right place. And play that as humanely as you can and you get a very interesting villain."

ELAINE SCHREYECK (Continuity, *Diamonds Are Forever*, *Live And Let Die*, *The Man With The Golden Gun*, *Moonraker*, *For Your Eyes Only*)
"Working on a James Bond film was different in the fact that it was a great deal of activity, a lot of stunts and all that sort of thing. But the job is the same, whether you're working on *Love Story* or on *Sleuth* or on a Bond. The great thing about Bonds, of course, is they spend a great deal of money and you can see it on the screen. It's a classy picture - not that the others weren't classy pictures - but you can really see it there."

IZABELLA SCORUPCO (Natalya Simonova in *GoldenEye*)
"I don't think we should ever change Bond. He should still be the same kind of person, the same tough guy, and flirting with everyone. It's just up to the female characters to really be strong and independent."

ANGELA SCOULAR (Buttercup in *Casino Royale*; Ruby Bartlett in *On Her Majesty's Secret Service*)
"Families and friends don't particularly think anything of me being in a Bond movie. People who aren't involved with the profession in any way tend to think it was rather amazing being a Bond girl... I do find it surprising that people still find it interesting to watch. And also, I get an enormous amount of fan mail from people who have watched it and have photographs of it and everything - it's a cult thing, isn't it, being in a Bond movie?"

ERIC SERRA (Composer, *GoldenEye*)
"When I was a kid I was a big fan of James Bond; I wanted to be a secret agent, of course. The whole Bond phenomenon is such a big legend in the movie business that it was amazing suddenly to be involved. Barbara Broccoli, the producer, called me and the first thing that she said was that they loved my work with Luc Besson and they really wanted to update the James Bond image. They wanted me to bring a new sound to James Bond, younger and more modern. It was very exciting to have this responsibility."

JANE SEYMOUR (Solitaire in *Live And Let Die*)
"There is nothing cooler than being able to walk around and have young kids come up to you and say, 'Hey, I saw your movie. It's great.' And you go, 'I wonder what movie that was.' And it wasn't *Dr. Quinn*. Then they say, 'No, *Live And Let Die*'. And you think to yourself, 'God, I'm 48 years old, this is 28 years ago, and they still recognize me.' That's pretty cool. And the fact that they still love it, that this generation loves that movie so it's part of a great legacy, is something I'm very proud of."

ROBERT SHAW (Red Grant in *From Russia With Love*)
"Naturally, I thought [the Bond film] I was in was the best."

BOB SIMMONS (Stunts and Sean Connery stunt double, *Dr. No* (uncredited), *Goldfinger*, *Thunderball*, *You Only Live Twice*, *Diamonds Are Forever*, action sequences arranger, *Goldfinger*; Stunt co-ordinator, *Live And Let Die*; action arranger, *The Spy Who Loved Me*; stunts, *For Your Eyes Only* (uncredited); action sequences arranger, *Octopussy*; stunt team supervisor, *A View To A Kill*)
"The Bond movies have turned out to be today's best action pictures, which is why you end up competing with yourself. We get together with the art department and the special effects departments, and ask, 'Have we done this before? And if we have, how can we do it bigger and better?'"

CARLY SIMON (Title song vocalist, *The Spy Who Loved Me*)
"I always was attracted to spydom, spyhood, spy-whatever, because when I was a child, I was asked what I wanted to be, and my first choice was a spy. It was mainly because of the wardrobe: I wanted to wear a black trenchcoat and walk around with briefcases. And I think I was on to something. I was on to the fact that information is the most coveted of assets. That's probably what I was really seeking. Information.... Gosh, I wish I could do another one. I'd love to do another one."

NANCY SINATRA (Title song vocalist, *You Only Live Twice*)
"I think [*You Only Live Twice*] is the best Bond song. I think I would think that if I hadn't done it. I just think it's the most beautiful of the Bond songs... When I do it on stage, it's like it gives people an uplifting feeling."

MADELINE SMITH (Miss Caruso in *Live And Let Die*)
"Everybody, male, female, boy and girl, loves toys. We never, any of us - I'm the first to admit it - every really, truly grow up. We all still love to play with our toys. The gadgets get bigger and more outrageous, and we all like to run along to see what they can produce next. We like always to see people treading very near the edge. Some of the stunts are just amazing, the best stunts one can see anywhere. And beautiful women for the chaps, and handsome heroes for the ladies. What more do you want?"

PUTTER SMITH (Mr. Kidd in *Diamonds Are Forever*)
"At that time I was an avid reader and constantly read all the Bond books. That was why it was so freaky to me. I had gone to see the movies and *From Russia With Love* was my favourite of the Bond movies. And Sean Connery was my favourite Bond, so this was an incredible experience for me."

STANLEY SOPEL (Associate producer, *Dr. No* (uncredited), *From Russia With Love* (uncredited), *Goldfinger* (uncredited), *Thunderball* (uncredited), *You Only Live Twice* (uncredited), *On Her Majesty's Secret Service*, *Diamonds Are Forever*)
"I like to think that in the early Bonds, the Bonds that I did, we were all talented... I think Warwick Films should have got a royalty on all the Bonds. They provided most of the talent."

TALISA SOTO (Lupe Lamora in *Licence To Kill*)
"The sweet part is my dad is a big Bond fan, so when I got [the role], I was excited for him, because I was going to be part of a series of films that he really enjoyed."

ROGER SPOTTISWOODE (Director, *Tomorrow Never Dies*)
"[Pierce] Brosnan has made my job so much easier. He really understands the character exactly and won't play fast and loose with him, yet he loves trying new things within those pre-set boundaries."

JILL ST. JOHN (Tiffany Case in *Diamonds Are Forever*)
"Who would not want to be in a Bond film? They're so exciting and so interesting, the special effects are so fabulous, and the women are always larger than life. How wonderful to be able to play a character that couldn't possibly exist, and to be able to bring that to life was a lot of fun. Not to mention Sean Connery... And you become a part of the history of Bond. That's very flattering."

JOHN STEARS (Special effects supervisor, *From Russia With Love, Goldfinger, Thunderball, You Only Live Twice* (uncredited); special effects, *On Her Majesty's Secret Service, The Man With The Golden Gun*)
"They were very topical movies at the time. We went far and above what was the norm for effects in those days, and we sort of set the genre for effects. Unfortunately, every car that crashes now gets blown up. But that's neither here nor there. It's odd, though, because there have been a lot of people trying to do spoof Bonds of various types and they've all failed. It's only the Bonds which have kept their vitality."

TOBY STEPHENS (Gustav Graves in *Die Another Day*)
"It's a fantastic opportunity for me. I knew I would never get to play James Bond, so playing the villain was very much second best, but great for me."

RICK SYLVESTER (Asgard ski jump, *The Spy Who Loved Me*; climbing fall stunt, *For Your Eyes Only*)
"The original Bond, *Dr. No*, didn't have any stunts. The plot was through characterization. They evolved into these stunts, and in a way, they've painted themselves into a corner, especially with the opening stunt, because they're in the position where each succeeding film has to top the other ones, and that gets difficult."

LEE TAMAHORI (Director, *Die Another Day*)
"I've been a big fan of the Bond movies most of my life. To me the Bond film is a kind of impregnable fortress of film making. It used to be about girls and gadgets and a good-looking spy and then it changed shape and is now about girls, gadgets, a good-looking spy - and big action. It is a timeless thing and is constantly evolving."

TETSURO TAMBA (Tiger Tanaka in *You Only Live Twice*)
"I think there is no more exciting and sexy foreign actor than Sean Connery."

TOPOL (Columbo in *For Your Eyes Only*)
"The Bond films have lasted as long as they have because of the fun that they bring to the audience. It was made with a feeling of fun, of everybody having fun doing them."

CHRISTOPHER WALKEN (Max Zorin in *A View To A Kill*)
"My 15-year-old nephew will be the same age I was when I first saw *Dr. No* when he sees [*A View To A Kill*]. Being in the movie house, looking down the gun barrel and watching Bond walk into frame - I remember it all very well. I remember Robert Shaw in *From Russia With Love*, trying to strangle James Bond on the train... And now, here I am, trying to kill James Bond myself."

NORMAN WANSTALL (Dubbing editor, *Dr. No, From Russia With Love, Goldfinger, Thunderball, You Only Live Twice, Never Say Never Again*)
"*Dr. No* was a prototype. No one ever had any idea what was going to transpire after *Dr. No* came out. We knew we had something very special, and a lot goes to the credit of Peter Hunt who looked at the rushes and said, 'This is a very special movie. We've got to make it move fast and we've got to make the sound dramatic.'"

KRISTINA WAYBORN (Magda in *Octopussy*)
"It's fantasy personified. It's great for men. Great for women. It transposes us to glamour, and something that most people don't have in their daily life. For me, it was great, because it's part of film history... I'm glad I was part of the Bond legacy."

ANTHONY WAYE (Assistant director, *For Your Eyes Only*; production supervisor, *A View To A Kill, The Living Daylights, Licence To Kill*; associate producer, *GoldenEye*; line producer, *Tomorrow Never Dies, The World Is Not Enough*; executive producer, *Die Another Day*)
"Everyone wants to work on a Bond film, and they'll make sure they're available to do it, and hope they get asked to do it. They all like working for Michael and Barbara, who've kept on that tradition of Cubby, and you know they're very good. They will go on and talk to the crew, and we've always tried to have an open door policy on these films. If anyone's got a moan or a problem they can come to us and they will be treated sympathetically, depending what the problem is. It's great because so often you get on films where the producers never talk to the crew. But on these films the producers are part of the crew, and we all involve the crew in things. If it's very difficult we'll try and have a screening for sequences for the crew to make them feel part of it."

PAUL WESTON (Stunts, *You Only Live Twice* (uncredited), *Live And Let Die* (uncredited), *The Man With The Golden Gun, The Spy Who Loved Me* (uncredited), *Moonraker, For Your Eyes Only* (uncredited); stunt team supervisor and stunt double Roger Moore, *Octopussy*; stunt supervisor, *The Living Daylights*; stunt co-ordinator, *Licence To Kill*)

"I'm sure that the family feeling that you get with a Bond still exists. But in the early days, it was really there. You were working for Cubby. Cubby was the father figure. Any problems you had, you knew you could go to Cubby and say, 'Look, I'm having a problem with this. What do you think?' And he would straighten it out. He was straight down the line, a very honest, sensible producer. He would make a decision, maybe against you, but he would make a decision. That's what you needed. Someone to say yes or no. The feeling of the family was always there, with Michael and Barbara. It was part of the family. And if you were in the family, you felt very comfortable, and enjoyed creating with them their pet, their other son, which was Bond. We all looked after Bond and tried to make him as good as we possibly could."

MICHAEL G. WILSON (Screenwriter, *For Your Eyes Only, Octopussy, A View To A Kill, The Living Daylights, Licence To Kill*; special assistant to producer, *The Spy Who Loved Me*; executive producer, *Moonraker, For Your Eyes Only*; producer, *A View To A Kill, The Living Daylights, Licence To Kill, GoldenEye, Tomorrow Never Dies, The World Is Not Enough, Die Another Day*)
"Cubby was the greatest influence on my life of anyone... Cubby took me right under his wing, and let me get involved in all the elements of the production. We had a partners desk, and we used to sit across from one another. He had it with Irving Allen, the same desk he used for nine years with Irving, and then Harry [Saltzman] worked at it for a while. And then, right after I joined him, he said, 'Oh, come on, sit across from me.' So, even though I was a business affairs type and a lawyer for the company, I was constantly involved in what was going on. I was observing it, and learning from Cubby the whole time. He was so generous that way... I was learning the business from him just like Barbara was learning it from him. I don't know if anyone ever thought, 'Well, he can step into my shoes', because in the film business, you never know how long something's going to go on. James Bond or any series can suddenly go out of fashion. It's just a miracle it goes on and on. We've managed to sort of re-invent it with every decade. And we've just been terribly, terribly lucky."

JOSEPH WISEMAN (Dr. No in *Dr. No*)
"I had no idea what I was letting myself in for. I had no idea it would achieve the success it did. I know nothing about mysteries. I don't take to them. As far as I was concerned, I thought it might be just another Grade-B Charlie Chan mystery."

CHRISTOPHER WOOD (Screenwriter, *The Spy Who Loved Me, Moonraker*)
"My contribution to the Bond legacy - rather a grandiose term - is I think as just a sort of keeper of the flame, one of these guys who run through the street, you know, holding it up and passing it on to the next person. I always have loved Bond movies, and it was an unimagined dream to be involved with them. To have written a couple of them is something that's very important in my life."

ARTHUR WOOSTER (Second unit director and cinematographer, *For Your Eyes Only, A View To A Kill, The Living Daylights, Licence To Kill*; additional unit director and photographer, *GoldenEye, The World Is Not Enough*)
"It was a great excitement, because Bonds have always been a type of film that I've always wanted to do. To have the opportunity of photographing and directing the sort of action they have in Bonds, with the amount of facilities that are thrown at you, is fantastic. It's a great opportunity. I was absolutely delighted to start with a Bond. Terrified, but absolutely delighted. Also, Cubby, in those days, was a tremendous back-up. And Barbara used to come on our second unit a lot. And we would always give Barbara really tough things to do. If we had problems, we'd set Barbara to sort them out. She was a tremendous back-up, and never let you down. Cubby was the same. So working on the Bonds, you do feel part of the family, because you get accepted as a part of the family."

B.J. WORTH (Aerial stunts, *Moonraker* (uncredited), *Octopussy* (uncredited), parachute stunt, *A View To A Kill*, aerial stunts arranger and aerial stunt double Timothy Dalton, *The Living Daylights*; parachute stunt co-ordinator, *Licence To Kill*; parachute co-ordinator, *GoldenEye*; HALO jump co-ordinator, *Tomorrow Never Dies*)
"Working on the Bond films has certainly helped my career in that when people see that, it gives a good amount of credibility to what I can do. And the fact that I've been able to work on seven Bond films, that continuity is important, and probably does help when someone's looking to see if they want you to work with them. Certainly the Bonds have a great reputation, and I'm really glad to be part of that."

MICHELLE YEOH (Wai Lin in *Tomorrow Never Dies*)
"In the old days, the Bond girl was the blonde girl in the swimming pool. We're going into the 21st century and women are not just gorgeous to look at but smart. They're intelligent and just as smart as Bond."

FREDDIE YOUNG (Cinematographer, *You Only Live Twice*)
"Like other James Bond movies, *You Only Live Twice* combined story and action with local colour. In Kyoto we filmed in a traditional garden with sandy paths threading harmoniously between formal fish-ponds, wooden bridges and ornamental rest houses. The gardener found the pressure of a film unit a bit hard to take. Every time we walked on a path, he would follow us, raking over our footprints."

TERENCE YOUNG (Director, *Dr. No, From Russia With Love, Thunderball*)
"We started rather flatly. In *Dr. No*, we didn't have so many gadgets. Fleming himself was a bit shy at first, somewhat arrogant. But he really was a superior sort. At first he was just afraid that we had taken the mickey out of his book. It wasn't true, of course, but *Time* magazine, at the other end of the extreme, thought we were playing the adventure straight, for real. Absolute bunk, naturally. Bond was a send-up from the first."

Index

This index includes references for both real-life people and Bondian characters - other than James Bond himself who appears from cover to cover; all characters are in italics. There are also references for the James Bond movies (*italics*) and novels (IN SMALL CAPS), and for key 007 gadgets, weapons and vehicles. Page numbers in italics refer to pages where the person only appears in a photograph on that page.

Picture Credits

445 middle right (Jacques Lowe), 45 bottom right, 114 top left (Lawrence Schiller), 126 (Jerry Watson), 214 middle, 297 (Jane Bown) - Camera Press London; 14 top, 28 top, middle and bottom, 63 top and middle, 90 bottom left, 107 middle and bottom, 114 top right, 140 both images - Bettman/Corbis; 58 bottom right - Corbis; 260 top - Corbis Sygma; 12 top - Dave G. Houser/Corbis; 10, 14 bottom, 58 middle right, 63 top - Hulton-Deutsch Collection/Corbis; Los Angeles Daily News/Corbis Sygma; 214 top - Wally McNamee/Corbis; 229 top left; 16-17 Bradley Smith/Corbis; 19, 76, 82, 151 top right, 161 top left and top right, 165 bottom, 177 top, 236 top left, 244 middle - Hulton Archive; 264 both images ™ and © New Line Productions, Inc. 2002; 73 bottom, 75 both images, 90 bottom middle left, 93 background, 108 bottom, 135 bottom left, 174 both images, 195 bottom, 198 bottom left, 199 bottom left, 238 background, 239, 247 top right, 264 - Lee Pfeiffer collection; 18 all images - Tony Nourmand/Reel Poster Gallery; 229 (Charlie Cole), 236 top middle (Michael Randou/SIPA), 236 top right (Thierry Bocon-Gibod), 260 middle, 275 top left (SIPA), 275 top right, 284 both images, 296 both images, 299 - Rex Features; 13 - courtesy of Sotheby's, London; 159 bottom right - Thai Airways; 15 bottom, 68 bottom, 69 top left, 79 bottom, 83 all images, 90 bottom right, 91 top left, 177 bottom, 183 top, 190 background, 222 middle, 223, 233, 247 middle right, 270, 281 top right - Dave Worrall collection

All other photographs and illustrations from the Eon archive, the MGM and UA archives, and the John Cork collection.

We would like to thank all the unit and still photographers of Eon, MGM and UA whose dedication to their art has made this book possible. Additional thanks for their help to Matthew Buxham at Hulton Archive, Jonathan Hamston at Corbis, Elizabeth Kerr at Camera Press, Glen Marks at Rex Features, Tony Nourmand at the Reel Poster Gallery, Lee Pfeiffer, Dave Worrall and Grace Worthington at Sotheby's.

Rostrum photography - Phil Cook

Every effort has been made to source and contact copyright holders. If any omissions do occur, the publishers will be happy to give full credit in subsequent reprints and editions.

Authors' Acknowledgements

Material relating to 007 fills several warehouses and archives. We know - we've been through them. Add to this the research materials at public libraries and the vast storehouses in private collections, and you have such a wealth of information that it often becomes difficult to find the kernels of truth under the accumulated layers of misinformation, legend and studio hyperbole. We have diligently attempted to sift out the facts, a job which could not have been accomplished without the help of many others.

Firstly, we wish to thank Dana Broccoli, Michael Wilson, Barbara Broccoli and David Wilson for their enthusiasm and support. Literally everyone at the Eon and Danjaq offices deserves thanks, particularly Michael Tavares, Anne Bennett and Meg Simmonds for their patience and help, and David Pope and Keith Snelgrove for their vision.

We also want to thank Philip Dodd, who has guided us through our first joint book experience with aplomb. Emma Marriott and Gordon Wise of Boxtree/Macmillan proved to be tremendously supportive. David Costa and Sian Rance and the expert designers of Wherefore Art? created this visually arresting tapestry from a mountain of widely disparate materials. Any credit for the creative success of this book must include them.

Our researchers, primarily the talented Robert Rasmussen in Los Angeles and Antonia Watson in London, unearthed many rare gems, as did a host of historians and associates such as Michael VanBlaricum, Richard Ashton, Greg Berman, James Burkart, Ajay Chowdhury, Ed Feider, Peter Janson-Smith, Associate Dean Rick Jewell of the USC School of Cinema-Television, Andrew Lycett, Doug Redenius, and the board members of the Ian Fleming Foundation. We found the answers to many questions only a phone call away thanks to James Bond trivia champ Scott McIsaac and Tom Wendler, whose mind is a steel trap of arcane factoids. We must also pay tribute to the librarians at the Academy of Motion Picture Arts & Sciences Margaret Herrick Library, and transcriber Stephanie Megibben for her tireless work. At MGM we received wonderful assistance from Paige Taylor.

John Cork would like to thank his wife Nicole for her unending patience and his son Jimmy for being a source of unending joy, and Mark and Heather Clubb for providing accommodations in London, while Bruce Scivally would like to thank Azmet Jah, who placed the phone call to Sean Connery that got them admitted to the pre-premiere screening of *Never Say Never Again*.

Finally, we want to thank our family, friends, neighbours and associates who have had to endure many years of our 007 obsessions, and the talented James Bond filmmakers who continue to fuel them.